CW00961754

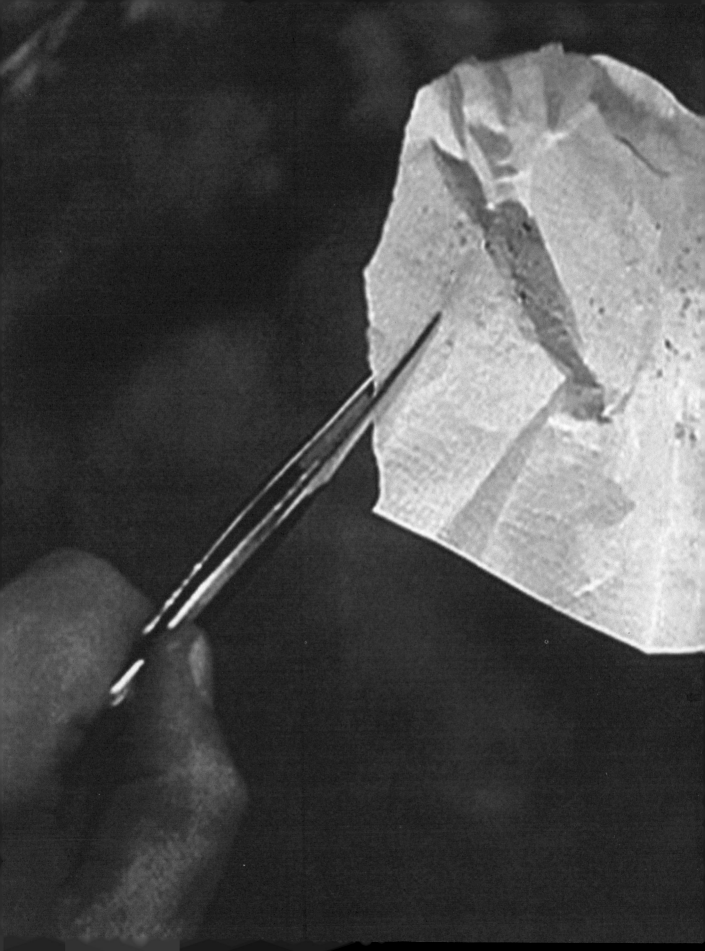

MOVIES OF THE 30ˢ

JÜRGEN MÜLLER (ED.)

MOVIES OF THE 30s

IN COLLABORATION WITH
DEFD AND CINEMA, HAMBURG
DEUTSCHE KINEMATHEK, BERLIN

TASCHEN

HONG KONG KÖLN LONDON LOS ANGELES MADRID PARIS TOKYO

CHAOS AND ILLUSION
Notes on the Movies of the 30s

It's one of the saddest images in cinematic history: a balloon struggling in the wires of a telephone mast. We see that it has a human form, and that its paper arms and legs seem to be trying to clutch the wires. The wind shakes it till it drifts away – the treasured new possession of little Elsie Beckmann, who's just been murdered by a pedophile.

Though we don't see the murder, we do accompany the camera to the scene of the crime. A ball bounces suddenly into the frame and rolls to a halt. A balloon rises and snags itself in the wires. From movement to stasis and randomness: this is as elementary as storytelling gets. The images are all the more compelling for this unbearably dry and laconic presentation. Fritz Lang's objectification of the visual language made cinematic history. Critics have repeatedly stressed that Lang's film marks the transition from Expressionism to the "New Objectivity" of the period to come. He refrains from the explicit, refuses to put a face to the horror of what has happened, and it is precisely because of this that the opening shots have lost nothing of their riveting intensity. Although Lang's style changed over the decades, he always remained true to himself as a formalist.

The bogeyman

M (1931, p. 68) tells the harrowing tale of a child-killer who haunts Berlin. He has already claimed eight victims, and a ninth is now missing. Fear grips the city. Again and again, we see children walking the streets alone; again and again, we're relieved to see a cop, a father, or a mother turn up to ensure the child's safety. Each time, our relief is short-lived; the tension builds and relaxes, before building again, inexorably.

The very first shot captures our attention: a group of children are playing in the backyard of an old tenement building; in the middle, surrounded by the others, stands a girl. She is chanting a children's rhyme about a murderer who chops up his victims and turns them into mincemeat – a reference to Fritz Haarmann, a real-life serial killer who butchered at least 24 young men in the 1920s. The children at play are arranged in one of Lang's typical circular compositions. In this case, the circle signifies a kind of demonic trap, as if the girl at its center were transfixed by some sorcerer's spell. At the end of the film, the cornered killer will himself say: "I cannot escape myself."

The scene is as grotesque as it is macabre; for the very next scene makes it clear that one of the children has failed to come home from school. The monstrous bogeyman of the children's rhyme is a real and terrifying threat. We see the child's worried mother checking the time on the cuckoo clock. We hear how she calls her child's name – "El-siiiie!" – while the camera shows us the table set for dinner, the empty stairwell, and the attic. Lang is not just playing with the expectations his film has aroused; he is also playing with simultaneity – a narrative modus that seems natural and unforced in a modern urban setting. A woman checking the time; parents waiting at the school gates; children heading homeward: these are the kind of things that happen in the same places at the same time every day.

But the Beckmann family's daily routine has just been profoundly disturbed, as Lang reveals in close-ups of the mother's face. She is already beginning to realize that her child will never come home again. Her horror is 'balanced' by the killer's cruelty, and the film seeks the origins of that cruelty in the social structure of the city, which is depicted as a technical organism and a functional, self-sufficient cosmos. This is precisely why the children are in such danger here: they are not yet capable of adapting to this monstrous organism, of finding their place in the belly of the Leviathan. Lang's film makes a political argument in passing by showing how the children of the poor are not picked up from school, and thus made vulnerable to a latent threat. In *M*, we are made constantly aware of the gulf that separates the rich from the poor.

The camera often has a curious life of its own, as if it too were a denizen of the big, bad city. When a crowd forms in the street, the camera searches greedily for the cause of it. When people start fighting, the camera stands watching them, in indecent proximity. It functions less as a guarantor of the narrative than as a symbol of the human hunger to *see*. The camera is excitable, eager for news, and Lang uses it to establish nervousness and agitation as the basic moods of his film. Like the camera, the people are on edge and never far from hysteria and aggression. They are also ruthless interlopers. Right at the beginning, we see one of Frau Beckmann's neighbors carrying a load of washing upstairs. We follow her heavy tread up the common staircase until she stops at the Beckmanns' apartment and rings the bell. The camera remains behind her, at a respectable distance. But as soon as the door opens, the camera moves closer, as if it were a third neighbor joining the women's conversation; and when Elsie's mother turns round to go back in, the camera is there already. The rough presumptuousness with which it enters her apartment underlines the forced intimacy of these urban tenements, in which no one has the privilege of complete privacy.

Man and modernity

"Who is the murderer?" The question runs through the film like a verbal and visual leitmotif. We see it as a giant message on posters in the street, we hear

it in scraps of flustered talk. In one lengthy montage sequence, the film follows a telephone conversation between the police commissioner and the Minister of the Interior, who is demanding to know how the investigation is proceeding. While the policeman reports on the measures taken, we observe his state-of-the-art criminological methods: officers leaf through their files, shift pins on a map of the city, search houses and raid bars. The phone conversation, which sounds like an official police report, serves to link these apparently disconnected images. There is something almost mechanical about the officer's staccato delivery, as if some huge machine had been set in motion to restore public safety. It's an image that suggests the efficiency and superiority of the state's institutions. But Fritz Lang's film is subtler than this. By keeping us in the dark as to the killer's identity even while we follow his every step, Lang builds the suspense. For a long time, the monster remains a shadow, a cipher, a vacuum. We observe how he stands with his back to the window, scribbling; we see his character profiled by means of a handwriting analysis; until, at last, we catch a glimpse of his face in a mirror, grimacing back at us as we watch, fascinated. Peter Lorre plays the child-killer with disturbing intensity – and by revealing his identity to us while the police are still groping in the dark, Lang makes the audience accomplices to his crimes. Though we still don't know the man's name, we've seen his face – and now we follow him as he roams the city. The camera strolls along with him, linking us to the killer and his fate. All the while, Lang is showing us how the city affects our very perceptions, bombarding us with new impressions at every turn. In the city, we can see

without being seen. Seeing is an anonymous act, but also a hidden threat. If a killer had his eye on us, how many of us would notice? Anonymity means safety, and a darkened movie theater is no less anonymous than an urban street.

"Hans Beckert is the killer!" From this moment onwards, we know his name as well his face – and we're still closer to him than the police. As we follow the murderer through Berlin, we can see that he is a driven man. In one particularly impressive scene, Beckert stands gazing into the window of a hardware store, lost in thought. Suddenly, he glimpses a little girl, reflected in a mirror amongst the goods on display; and at once he is possessed by the urge to speak to the child and take her with him. Visibly overwhelmed, his eyes goggling in horror, he sees how her face in the mirror is framed by a display of glittering knives. From one moment to the next, a harmless piece of window-dressing has been charged with symbolic import and a banal storefront has become a terrible invitation to murder.

The killer in us

But *M* is more than a thriller. It is an authentic panorama of the late Weimar period, and Fritz Lang shows us how deep was the crisis Germany underwent in those years. In essence, it was a crisis of meaning brought about by the stresses of modernity. The economic gloom of the 1920s was accompanied by a process of liberalization, and Berlin's nightlife was renowned, or notorious, for its excesses. Many people saw the rise of prostitution and criminality as an unavoidable aspect of big-city life, and many who remembered the bygone *Kaiserreich* felt they had been thrown into a fallen world of rampant immorality. Artists, writers and filmmakers focused on the poverty, anonymity and loneliness associated with urban existence. All of these topics play a major role in Fritz Lang's film.

With loving attention to detail, the director examines the city's criminal milieu, drawing a clear parallel between the police and the gangster syndicate. The criminals feel obliged to join the hunt for the child-killer, but their motives for doing so are far from immaculate. On the contrary: they take action only in order to halt the loss of earnings in their own line of business. What's undeniable is that these denizens of Berlin's demi-monde and underworld are very well organized, and it's the beggars who are sent out to scour the entire city as unobtrusively as possible. Here, too, Lang takes critical note of the state of things in contemporary Germany. Poverty and misery are so ubiquitous that these ragged spies can apparently patrol every street, square and backyard in the city without anyone paying particular attention to their presence. In the end, it is a blind beggar who recognizes the killer, for Hans Beckert has a habit of whistling the same tune every time he finds a new victim.

We can see this as a further allusion to the conditions of modern life. The killer only succeeds in remaining undetected for so long because he can hide behind his anonymity and seeming normality. In the modern world, vis-

ible surfaces no longer provide reliable clues to anyone's true identity. Only the blind can remain undeceived by appearances, so it takes a sightless man to 'see' the culprit.

The urge to keep whistling the same tune is harmless enough in itself; but it's precisely this compulsiveness, this inability to control his own desires or actions, that determines the course of Hans Beckert's life and eventually leads to his undoing. He is caught purely by accident; and then he finds himself, not in a police cell, but in the hands of the city's organized gangsters. The child-killer is arraigned in a bizarre show trial, a kangaroo court. Lang presents it as a farce; because even though the criminals respect the 'form' of the trial, the verdict is never in any doubt. In an unforgettable monolog that is as frightening as it is pitiful, the murderer describes how he fell prey to his own compulsions. Repeatedly, he cries: "I cannot, but I must!" It's a last effort to describe the psychic straitjacket that has held him all his life, but the members of the 'jury' have no sympathy for his alleged helplessness. It's vengeance they want, not justice.

This is not to imply that the police are faultless. Faced with a situation in which everyone is blaming everyone else and the population is in danger of resorting to lynch justice, the cops seem incapable of restoring normality. As a matter of plain fact, it is the crooks who succeed in making the city safe for children again. Thus, Lang dissolves the distinction between those who enforce the law and those who break it. One clear example of this is the boss of the crime syndicate, a fugitive wanted for several

murders, who suddenly turns up in a police uniform and organizes the hunt for the child-killer. If we're relieved to see the culprit caught, our relief is not untainted by cynicism. Whether it's killers or cops who've caught him seems suddenly important, and the film is telling us that not all murders are equal.

Lang's film reads like a sociological argument: large social groupings such as cities cannot be ruled on the basis of moral principles embraced by individuals, but only by means of institutions; yet morality is an individual matter, not an institutional one. In this respect, the film formulates a deep unease with the Enlightenment and its belief that rationality, modernization and the liberation of humanity can go hand-in-hand. Lang shows that reason has its imponderables, that some areas of the psyche are inaccessible to the intellect. It is dangerous to reduce humanity to its capacity for reason. Management cannot replace morality.

Lang's dark and thought-provoking film forces us to recognize that criminality is not the opposite of morality, but simply another form of institutionalization. The underworld is organized just as strictly and just as efficiently as the bureaucratized world of the law-abiding bourgeoisie.

M was one of the earliest significant German sound films. Today, in an era of sophisticated sound design, the film's soundtrack may seem a little meager, for it doesn't even feature any non-diegetic music. Yet this very minimalism lends the film a truly chilling quality: as it lacks any kind of aural 'cushioning,' the brutality shown here is unmediated and comes across nakedly. Rather than being limited by the imperfections of a novel technology, Fritz Lang's handling of the soundtrack is wonderfully creative and efficient.

In fact, he uses sound to liberate the images. The apparently random shots that make up the rapid montage sequences are not merely held together by the soundtrack; Lang crafts that soundtrack to add a new dimension to the film. Even when we don't see the killer, his whistling documents his presence. The effect is peculiarly menacing. Just as the blind beggar had heard Beckert but not seen him, the audience is faced with a threat that is latent and disembodied, but capable of becoming current and brutally physical at any moment.

One of the film's most shocking aspects is that we experience sound and music as something that is within us, capable of being awakened or called forth, as if we ourselves were whistling the melody from Edvard Grieg's "Peer Gynt;" as if we ourselves were the child-killer. In this respect, the director does make some heavy demands of his audience. Again and again, he deploys a subjective camera in order to make us see through the eyes of the killer. Lang is insisting that there is no fixed barrier between the normal and the pathological, and that the spectator, too, is not essentially or necessarily on the 'right' side.

The Cinema of Unease

Although *M* tells the story of a child-killer, its real subject is modernity and the city is its secret protagonist. Berlin is a cipher that represents any modern metropolis, in which none of us can really control what goes on beyond our own four walls. City dwellers routinely perceive public and private space as separate. In such an environment, a man can easily get away with murder, for he doesn't even have to hide. The best hiding-place is the anonymity of an unobtrusive existence, loneliness within the crowd. In *M*, the camera emphasizes this anonymity; for example by drawing closer to a huddled group in the street and looking over their heads at a "Wanted" poster – a classic emblem of anonymity.

The technical manifestations of modernity are ever-present: in this movie, people are constantly making phone calls or poring over streetmaps. Indeed, Lang practically rubs our noses in the abstract nature of modern life, especially when it comes to the police methods of investigation. In an effort to wring some kind of information from even the most harmless-looking objects, the most advanced techniques and technologies are deployed. The more abstract the world, the more abstract are the methods of inquiry. Here, the film also touches on a problem of modernity: although the process of technical improvement demands to be seen as progress, it is hindered by the inevitable and incalculable imperfections of humanity. The limits of prac-

tical reason are manifested precisely in the defective psyche of a single individual who unexpectedly fails to function.

If some archaic force seems to resist the alleged blessings of progress, however, that force doesn't only manifest itself in the sick individual. Lang depicts the city itself as a deeply ambivalent entity that is only superficially ruled by modernity. Besides a head, this beast also has a 'belly:' seedy, smoky, cellar bars populated by sweaty reprobates and raucous whores. Here, fueled by beer, schnapps and cheap food, the underworld exists as it always has done, following its own impulses and satisfying its own desires in blithe indifference to the achievements and strictures of civilization. Lang presents this milieu in all its immediate sensuality; and he does so with great ease and naturalness. We begin to realize how bloodless and abstract is the bureaucratic state, and how limited its ability to penetrate the depths of society.

But the killer is not a part of this underworld milieu; he comes from amongst us. And so the film also acquaints us with the schizophrenia of the average modern citizen, who is well-mannered but mistrustful, and whose politeness can turn into aggression at a moment's notice. A big modern city is the ideal setting for a thriller, not just because anything can happen there, but because it's a place where the familiar can become strange and the commonplace uncanny.

One could pursue a sociological reading of this film almost indefinitely, but that would not do justice to its aesthetic quality. *M* has remained an exceptionally exciting film because it allows us to share the illusion that we are

following the progress of the investigation directly. Repeatedly, we visit the scenes of the crimes in the company of various experts, and this lends the film an almost documentary quality. Nevertheless, Lang complements this restrained, unemotional approach with some particularly poetic images. Thus, he indicates the death of little Elsie by showing us her lost balloon, which the killer had bought for the child in order to gain her trust. The film-maker stimulates the audience's imagination precisely by not depicting the murder itself.

Fritz Lang made his film after a number of serial murderers had shocked Germany. As a man who paid close attention to the world he lived in, he would not have been unaware that the politics and culture of the Weimar period were plagued by sexual repression. One might sum it up as follows: in the 20s and early 30s, repression and liberalization went hand-in-hand as in no other period of German history. One of the most disturbing insights of the Modern age is that 'normality' is anything but normal. In our sexuality, we can become strangers to ourselves, because the "I" that is at work there is not the same "I" that rules our everyday consciousness. We have Sigmund Freud to thank for the knowledge that our sexuality is co-determined by repressed and internalized desires. But what about Hans Beckert? Can a victim be a perpetrator?

Our own unease may have been stilled by the arrest of the child-murderer; but when we leave the movie theater, we'll find it hard to hear the melody from "Peer Gynt" again without seeing the face of Peter Lorre in our

mind's eye, at least for an instant. Lang's dark masterpiece leaves the movie-goer slightly shaken in his everyday existence. In Lang's day, even more than ours, the movies were a medium of distraction, and Hollywood was coming to be practically synonymous with cinema itself. *M* was an exceptional work in this respect, too: it was a forerunner of film noir. And, as we shall see, several years would pass before this 'dark' style of filmmaking would become influential either in Germany or in Lang's new American home.

The age of stars and moguls

The 30s were the decade that made Hollywood the Dream Factory. The Golden Age of the major studios coincided with a period of global economic crisis and political chaos. With unprecedented perfection and astounding efficiency, the U. S. film industry supplied the suffering masses with glamour, romance and adventure – dependable distractions from the grim reality of the Depression years. Never before or since has the silver screen reflected collective yearnings as powerfully as it did then. In the glory days of the studio system, while powerful moguls ruled over an army of stars, Hollywood movies often seemed as far from reality as the fairy tales of the Arabian Nights.

The cinema of the 30s achieved a level of technical perfection that was only marginally improved in the decades that followed. Sound film, introduced at the end of the 20s, soon overcame its teething troubles. By the mid-

30s, Technicolor had arrived; and though still seldom used, it was a huge improvement on all previous color systems. There were also major advances in camera and animation technology. Throughout the studios, highly professional teams were setting new standards in all departments.

Spectacular successes such as *King Kong* (1933, p. 186) and *Gone with the Wind* (1939, p. 470) erased the word "unfilmable" from the studio bosses' vocabulary. Now, anything was imaginable, and realizable on screen – even a giant ape clambering around the pinnacle of the Empire State Building. And while the Dream Factory extended its product palette with a host of extravagant new offerings, it continued to refine its recipes and sustain its output with a torrent of genre films and B-movies.

In the 1930s, Hollywood reached a highpoint in its ability to standardize the production of films, as well as their narrative content and structure. "Movie entertainment" acquired its classical form, which it has retained right up until the present day. Though each of the studios may have cultivated its own image, they were united in adherence to certain basic standards. Every one of these films followed the principle of "invi-sible editing" (or "continuity editing"), in which shots are linked so unob-trusively as to create the impression of a seamless reality. This technique also ensures that the storyline can be followed with a minimum of effort. Meanwhile, "high-key" lighting eased the viewer's optical orientation by illuminating the entire frame in a uniform manner. As a side effect, this created a basic 'mood' that most moviegoers registered as pleasant on the eye.

Top priority was a happy audience. The moguls felt that moviegoers wanted a perfect illusion, right up until the happy ending, so it was important that nobody be perplexed, offended, or disturbed. What the bosses wanted was clear, straightforward storytelling, without shenanigans – and the Production Code gave a further impulse in the same direction. From 1934 onwards, the film industry's moral code regulated (above all) the depiction of sex and violence. Though the consequences were sometimes bizarre, the Dream Factory was reluctant to take any risks. The upshot was a cinema of consensus; and, whenever possible, that meant movies for the entire family.

More than anything else, moviegoers longed to see the stars – and so they did, in precisely the kind of roles the audience wanted them in. Hollywood movies provided an ongoing confirmation of the American Dream – the idea that anyone with enough guts and determination could make it to the top – and the stars were the very embodiment of this alluring promise. In the gloom of contemporary American reality, the stars shone all the more brightly, and so the star system reached its apogee in the 30s. The best and the brightest in the firmament included Greta Garbo, Marlene Dietrich, James Cagney, Jean Harlow, Clark Gable, Joan Crawford, Cary Grant, Errol Flynn, Fred Astaire and Ginger Rogers – and these were just a few of the immortals who emerged in that extraordinary decade.

The triumph of the Dream Factory

In fact, Hollywood looked far from triumphant at the start of the 30s. For an increasing number of people, the mass poverty of the period had made a visit to the movies a luxury. Between 1930 and 1933, the number of moviegoers in the USA shrank by a third. One response on the part of the cinemas was the introduction of the double bill: to lure people into the theatres, the main feature was accompanied by a slightly shorter and cheaper second feature – the B-movie. A further aspect of the crisis was that sound films were not selling well in foreign countries, because dubbing techniques were still in their infancy. These problems brought some of the major studios to the brink of financial ruin, and it was only the support of large banks that saved them. Soon, however, the Roosevelt administration also offered a helping hand, and dubbing then reached a satisfactory standard. By the mid-30s, the studios had not merely saved their skins and gotten their act together; the system was in fact more robust and efficient than ever before.

Hollywood's success story can only be understood when one truly apprehends the enormous concentration of capital and power within the U.S. film industry. Hollywood in the 30s consisted essentially of eight large film production companies; between them, they had the domestic market almost completely under their control. Of these so-called Major Studios, the five biggest – Metro-Goldwyn-Mayer (MGM), Paramount, Warner Bros., RKO and 20th Century Fox – were production *and* distribution companies. More than that: unlike the three smaller Majors, Columbia, Universal and United Artists, they also owned their own chains of movie theatres, including the particularly lucrative premiere palaces in the big American cities.

The eight Majors had also divided up the areas of distribution amongst themselves, and the principle of blind and block bookings ensured that independent cinema operators would show even the studios' less attractive offerings. Thus, the Major Studios could produce movies virtually without risk – and they did so, incessantly. Warner Bros. alone produced around 50 films on average each season. By the mid-30s, the Majors had overcome the slump caused by the Depression. According to the film historian Thomas Schatz, three-quarters of all U.S. films came from the studios of the "big eight," accounting for 95% of the total income from film distribution. De facto, then, the free market for films no longer existed. The American film industry was owned by a handful of corporations; and to a very large extent, they also had the international markets under their control.

Certainly, many countries already had powerful, creative and in some cases long-established film industries – and that includes not only European nations, but also Japan, China and India. But none of these came close to matching Hollywood's trans-national charisma, and the Dream Factory continued to entrench its position as global market leader, mainly with

escapist entertainment. Towards the end of the 30s, an estimated two-thirds of all films distributed were American productions. Despite all the political and cultural upheavals of the last 70 years, the U. S. cinema has managed to maintain this position almost without interruption. And therefore, even today, Hollywood is still the most important propagandist of American ideology.

More stars than in heaven

MGM was generally regarded as Hollywood's swankiest studio. "More Stars than there are in Heaven" was one slogan used by the company, which had more famous actors under contract than any other. At a time when the average moviegoer was feeling the pinch, Louis B. Mayer and his legendary Head of Production Irving Thalberg were all the more convinced that the audience had to be offered something worth paying to see. So the studio deployed an army of stars to combat the prevailing tristesse. *Grand Hotel* (1932, p. 130) is a perfect example of this policy. A gossipy concoction set in a luxury hotel in Berlin, it brings together a Russian ballet diva (Greta Garbo), an elegant jewel-thief (John Barrymore), a brutal industrial magnate (Wallace Beery), his mortally-ill accountant (Lionel Barrymore), and a secretary (Joan Crawford) who is as a pretty as she is pragmatic. Thus, MGM offered moviegoers *five* top stars instead of the usual two.

The directors of such glossy, high-budget productions had very little opportunity to realize their own ideas – nor would their employers have tolerated such independence. At the Major Studios, the art of the cinema was essentially a matter of cool calculation, the result of a standardized process involving a division of labor in a range of specialized departments, all strictly controlled by the studio bosses and their under-managers. The value of a film was equivalent to its box-office returns. The director's task was essentially to ensure that the film's major attractions – the stars – were presented to the audience competently and dependably, and that meant in tried-and-trusted manner. The stars were there to be seen. MGM's approach to lighting was probably the purest expression of the classical Hollywood Style. "High-key" lighting seemed to conjure away the gloomy reality of the Depression years, and it made it easier for the audience to sink into the fiction without any perceptible resistance. Studio bosses wanted moviegoers to give themselves up to the illusion entirely; to be alone with their stars.

It hardly needs stating that the studios' standardized production processes threatened to result in sterile, unoriginal films. Today, indeed, *Grand Hotel* may look a little schematic; and certainly, the period saw no lack of uninspired routine productions that are now justly forgotten. All the more astonishing, then, that a large number of films still have enormous vitality and display a whole range of talents working brilliantly together. Take an MGM production like *Dinner at Eight* (1933), directed by former theater man George Cukor. In many ways, it's clearly aiming to repeat the success

of *Grand Hotel* – for a start, the Barrymore brothers and Wallace Beery are cast in very similar roles. Nonetheless, it's a wonderfully witty and acerbic ensemble film, still a delight to see and hear. It demonstrates that Hollywood's significance was not merely a result of its economic power; it also emerged from a concentration of creative talent that is unique in the history of film.

"I want to be alone"

The star was the center of the Hollywood system; and the most radiant of all stars was undoubtedly Greta Garbo – the "Divine." Like no other actress, she permitted the public the paradoxical experience that is so essential to the phenomenon of the star cult: closeness and distance, identification with the star combined with the knowledge that she is unreachable. Garbo's nimbus extended far beyond the USA. She was a true world star. Yet despite her exceptional position, her career exemplifies perfectly the way in which the studios created their stars' image.

She was born in Sweden and came to Hollywood in the mid-20s. Though she had little experience as an actress, Louis B. Mayer signed her up. The MGM boss recognized her potential, and he used her imperfect English and her unfamiliarity with American ways to build up the image of a silent and mysterious diva. His strategy had the desired result. Within a few years,

MGM had established her image as an aloof, distant, otherworldly creature. So successfully, in fact, that when she appeared in her first sound film *Anna Christie* (1930), the studio could advertise the inevitable as if it were a particular sensation: "Garbo speaks!"

Despite her accent, Garbo had little difficulty negotiating the transition to the talkies, for she was generally cast as a European and her deep, husky voice merely strengthened her exotic aura. She was almost always cast as woman hopelessly yet unconditionally in love. Often, she played an adulteress, doomed by social conventions – and doomed not least because the Production Code demanded it. And it's indicative of Hollywood's self-imposed distance from reality that Garbo embodied these tragic women most convincingly in classics adapted for the screen; many regard George Cukor's *Camille* (1936) as her best film.

MGM's PR department seems to have contributed nearly as much to Garbo's image as the roles she played. The line "I want to be alone" from *Grand Hotel* was used almost as a leitmotif in advertising campaigns for her movies, and the impression that La Garbo never laughed can be easily disproved simply by watching her films. Nonetheless, the illusion of Garbo's impassivity had become so strong that Ernst Lubistch could make ironic use of it in *Ninotchka* (1939, p. 428), when he cast her as an utterly humorless Soviet functionary – only to break that illusion with her famous laughing fit. True to form, the studio advertised the film with the slogan: "Garbo laughs!"

Not all of Garbo's films have aged as well as Lubitsch's splendid comedy. Nonetheless, she has retained her status as screen icon *par excellence*, not least because she exemplified a quality that might be seen as the very measure of star quality in any actor or actress: the ability to turn a close-up into a magic moment. The final shot of Rouben Mamoulian's *Queen Christina* (1933, p. 192) is a perfect example of this ability. It shows Garbo as the Swedish monarch, whose lover has just died. While she stands alone at the prow of her ship and gazes out to sea, the camera slowly approaches her impassive face. It seems frozen in its austere beauty. Not an eyelash moves; only her hair stirs slightly in the wind, emphasizing all the more the rigidity of her mien, which seems to speak of endless loneliness.

"It's hard to be funny if you have to be clean."

Although the history of the studio system is inseparably linked to the standardization of the film production process, the eight Major Studios did attempt to distinguish themselves from each other and to raise their own profiles. They did so by developing more or less pronounced house styles and by specializing in particular genres. MGM, for example, tended to focus on a conservative and mainly female audience, so popular melodramas and harmless family fare made up a substantial part of its program. Paramount, by contrast, cultivated a more 'brilliant' image characterized by frivolity and European sophistication.

"If it's a Paramount picture it's the best show in town." This was one of the studio's advertising slogans, and when their films featured a self-assured sex idol like Mae West, she seemed to confirm its truth in quite spectacular fashion. In contrast to Jean Harlow, for instance, the famous platinum-blonde *Bombshell* (1933), Mae West's sexiness did not signify complete availability. Instead, the former vaudeville star delighted in turning the tables, impressing her own will on the male characters in her movies and frequently making them look ridiculous. In films such as *I'm No Angel* (1933, p. 198), she came out with some of the juiciest *bons mots* in the history of movie quotes. The Golden Age of Mae West ended abruptly in the mid-30s when the Production Code banned any direct representation of sexuality on the screen. Her specific humor was thus effectively buried, and she herself supplied a fitting epitaph: "It's hard to be funny if you have to be clean."

Paramount also produced the six legendary films in which Josef von Sternberg transformed his 'discovery,' Marlene Dietrich, into the classical vamp of the 30s. It was a congenial conjunction of star and director, and quite unique in the history of the studio era. Whether the films were set in foreign lands (*Shanghai Express*, 1932, p. 146), in olden times (*The Scarlet Empress*, 1934) or in present-day America (*Blonde Venus*, 1932, p. 104), they were always suffused with steamy exoticism and an atmosphere of morbid

sensuality. Sternberg achieved these effects mainly through a masterly use of lighting and set design, and he made no secret of the artificiality of his settings. At the center of his extravagant film creations was the mask-like face of Dietrich, who was quite openly androgynous in her cool and ambiguous sex-appeal. In one now-legendary scene in *Morocco* (1930), she caused consternation in a nightclub by turning up in a tuxedo and top hat. Sternberg's films were characterized by this spirit of *libertinage;* so it's no wonder that his career went rapidly downhill when the studio bosses bowed to the ever-increasing demands for greater censorship by imposing a strict Production Code. It goes without saying that the moguls also wished to minimize their own risks. Thus, although the Viennese director's masterpieces were by no means representative of Hollywood's moral standards in the 30s, they do bear witness to a liberal attitude that would soon no longer be possible in that form.

The "Lubitsch cheese"

Sternberg's individual style demonstrates how much freedom Paramount was prepared to grant its directors, at least so long as those directors were successful. Cecil B. DeMille was Hollywood's most gifted showman, and he too was under contract to Paramount. He became famous mainly for directing monumental epics such as *Cleopatra* (1934, p. 220) which offered gigan-

tic sets, huge crowd scenes and no shortage of naked flesh. With *The Sign of the Cross* (1932), DeMille confirmed his reputation as an eccentric with a particular penchant for bathing beauties by filming his leading actress Claudette Colbert immersed in a pool filled with donkeys' milk. From 1934 onwards, DeMille's films were no less opulent than they had been, but the sensual joys of antiquity now gave way to the pioneer spirit. At that time, Westerns became a serial genre, and were looked down on as B-movies. DeMille was one of the few who ventured to make a cowboy movie for a large audience. The result was the impressive *Union Pacific* (1939).

DeMille's bombast can be seen as the opposite of Ernst Lubitsch's timeless lightness and wit. The work of few other directors has carried such an instantly recognizable personal signature. Lubitsch was a Berliner and had worked in Germany, where, like DeMille, he had originally made a name for himself as a director of costume dramas. But after his arrival in the States in 1922, he soon became the king of the erotic comedy, the best of which he made for Paramount. His films have that certain something that made them unmistakable: the famous "Lubitsch touch," an incomparable ability to present delightfully barbed and suggestive dialog in such a way that it never seemed vulgar, but charming and discreet.

Basically, Lubitsch permitted himself to present everything on screen that was forbidden by convention. In his movies, a contented couple is never more than a temporary phenomenon, and in *Design for Living* (1933) he even presented a *ménage à trois* as an alternative. But although his comedies

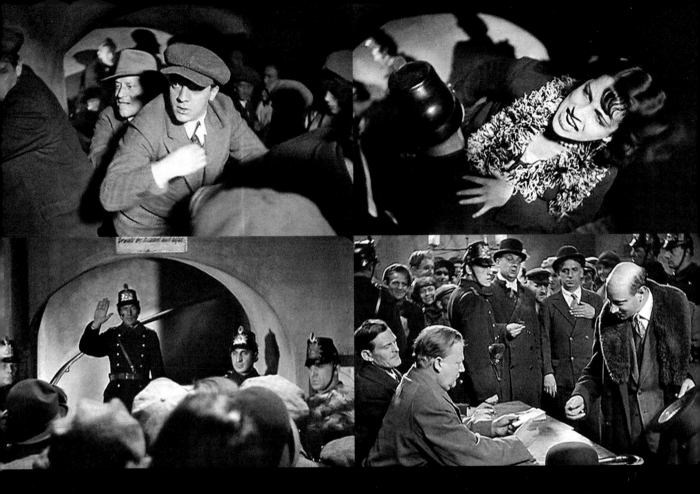

almost always revolve around adultery and seduction, the Production Code never really presented Lubitsch with any major problems. The censors capitulated in the face of his 'indecencies,' for they emerged from an elegant interplay of hints, ellipses and omissions – which inspired François Truffaut to remark that every hole in the "Lubitsch cheese" was a work of genius.

The juiciest scenes in the Lubitsch œuvre always take place behind closed doors, i. e. in the viewer's head. In the operetta film *The Merry Widow* (1934), for instance, Maurice Chevalier plays a dashing officer – a real ladies' man. In one scene, we see him slipping into the Queen's bedchamber just after her spouse has left it. A short time later, the King returns unexpectedly because he has forgotten his saber and the belt that holds it. The audience waits outside the room with bated breath for the inevitable scandalous discovery. But then the door opens again, and the King emerges looking no less complacently content than before. He has the belt in his hand – and only when he attempts to put it on does he realize that it's much too tight for him. The truth begins to dawn on him …

Anything but love

But Lubitsch was also a master of wickedly polished dialog. In a certain sense, his films anticipate the wacky screwball comedies that would become increasingly popular in the second half of the decade. Screwball is a quintessentially American form, in which the eternal battle of the sexes takes the form of sharp and witty verbal duels. In Howard Hawks' *His Girl Friday* (1939, p. 444), a brilliant comedy set in a newspaper milieu, the overlapping dialog is delivered with such extreme speed that it acquires a positively bizarre quality. As this movie demonstrates, the talkies had by now totally overcome the stiff woodenness of the early days and achieved something close to perfection in the staging of dialog. Superb actors such as Cary Grant and Rosalind Russell played a huge part in this, as did the quality of the scripts, which were often the work of successful journalists or Broadway playwrights.

While Hawks' film depicted two dueling journalists in a permanent verbal stand-off, most screwball comedies focused on extremely mismatched couples whose mutual aversion made them paradoxically irresistible to one another. In Frank Capra's *It Happened One Night* (1934, p. 238), a spoiled millionaire's daughter met an impoverished, hard-boiled reporter; in W. S. Van Dyke's *It's a Wonderful World* (1939), a successful authoress confronted a brusque private eye. While the women fought the men's stubborn male idealism (or their simple bad manners), the men struggled to convince these dazzling divas that the simple life was better – and more grittily 'real.'

The Marx Brothers' humor had been decidedly aggressive and truly anarchic. The screwball comedies, by contrast, for all their screwiness, were essentially less threatening to society. Their humor was not really directed at social structures, and the conflicts they depicted were ulti-

mately resolved, often in a bourgeois marriage. Whatever the tensions between the princess and the underdog, they always ended up in each other's arms. Not only did money play no role; much of the time, it even looked like a handicap. Thus, in Howard Hawks' *Bringing Up Baby* (1938, p. 414), Cary Grant played an artless paleontologist trying to complete his life's work: the skeleton of a brontosaurus. In order to do so, he's forced to deal with his patron's utterly chaotic niece (Katharine Hepburn). His task is to help her catch her runaway pet leopard, which can only be pacified by crooning the song: "I can't give you anything but love, Baby." Though this is indeed all he has to offer, the rich girl is happy to accept. By the time Hepburn brings the skeleton crashing down, Cary Grant has capitulated, and the couple are happily united.

Dancing cheek to cheek

It was in another genre, however, that Hollywood took its gleeful escapism to the limit: the musical. The introduction of sound had made the musical possible, and in the 30s, the genre became enormously popular. From the very start, Hollywood attempted to increase the appeal of sound movies by hiring celebrated theatre and vaudeville stars. Their success was so huge that seasoned stage performers were soon seeking their fortune on the silver screen, and this in turn had a big influence on the development of the musical genre.

Although musicals tended to be very expensive undertakings, they soon grew so popular that practically every studio started producing them. The result was a range of different styles and sub-genres. Thus, Republic – one of the smaller "poverty row" studios – brought out a series of well-liked Western Musicals, with singing cowboys such as Gene Autry and Roy Rogers. And naturally, musical numbers could also be included in movies that weren't strictly musicals at all. In the 30s, song and dance routines became standard attractions in almost every cinematic genre.

Nonetheless, two dominant types of musical gradually emerged in the course of the decade. With movies such as Lloyd Bacon's *42nd Street* (1933, p. 170) and Busby Berkeley's *Gold Diggers of 1935* (1935, p. 256), Warner Bros. created the so-called Backstage Musical. Though these showbiz romances were shot in the studio's typically straightforward, no-nonsense style, Busby Berkeley's spectacular choreography was their crowning glory. He arranged massed dancers in strict geometrical shapes and filmed them with a moving camera from a variety of angles including a bird's-eye-view. The final result was an intoxicating montage of almost abstract forms in motion, accompanied on the soundtrack by exuberant choral and orchestral music.

In stark contrast to Berkeley's surreally depersonalized crowd scenes – human petals on a giant flower! – were the virtuoso song-and-dance routines created for RKO Studios by Fred Astaire and Ginger Rogers. In these movies, the musical numbers were perfectly integrated into the romantic-

comedy plot, skillfully expressing the gradual progress of the couple's love relationship. The films of Ginger and Fred were always simple boy-meets-girl tales, in which the happy ending was never in any doubt, though often delayed by some truly hair-raising twists in the plot. The bold playfulness of the storylines corresponded perfectly with the fluent staging, the elegantly stylized upper-class decors, and above all with the incomparable grace and lightness of their dancing, in every style from tap to ballroom. Wonderful compositions by Irving Berlin, Cole Porter and George Gershwin made a major contribution to the huge charm of these movies, and Berlin's "Cheek to Cheek" can be said to embody their joyful, insouciant spirit.

What's striking about the successful Astaire-Rogers movies is how very similar they all are. The plots, casts and even settings of *The Gay Divorcee* (1934) and *Top Hat* (1935, p. 278) are so nearly identical that the two films are almost impossible to tell apart, at least in retrospect. And perhaps the movies of Ginger and Fred provide the clearest example of how the studios deliberately linked certain stars with certain genres. This allowed them to standardize their productions while also controlling the audience's expectations. But they satisfied those expectations too, sometimes unforgettably: at the climax of *The Gay Divorcee*, Astaire and Rogers dance effortlessly past and across the chairs, tables and sofas in their hotel room, as if love had the power to abolish the force of gravity.

Fantastic worlds

Some critics see the rise of the horror film in the early 30s as a reflection of America's unsettled psyche during the Depression years. Whatever the truth of that, it cannot be denied that in this period the horror genre developed a classical repertoire of forms and figures that still serves the cinema today. Certainly, Bela Lugosi's gentleman bloodsucker in Tod Browning's *Dracula* (1931, p. 76) is still the epitome of the Vampire, while Boris Karloff lent the Monster its definitive form in James Whale's *Frankenstein* (1931, p. 86). Both of these legendary horror movies were produced by Universal Studios, and they show just how decisively this decade shaped the iconography of the popular cinema and how much it contributed to the development of a cinematic canon.

The 30s brought us two further milestones of fantastic cinema, each of them located in tropical jungles: *Tarzan the Ape Man* (1932, p. 136), and *King Kong* (1933, p. 186), which set new standards in special effects. Though the former movie was not the first screen adaptation of Edgar Rice Burroughs' novel, Johnny Weissmuller was the ideal embodiment of the jungle hero. This former Olympic swimming champion also invented Tarzan's famous yodeling call. It became so strongly associated with the figure that none of the later adaptations seemed really persuasive without it – even when they were considerably more faithful to the book.

In a series of movies made for MGM in the 30s and 40s, Weissmuller and Maureen O'Sullivan made Tarzan and Jane two of the most popular characters on the screen. The thoroughgoing exoticism of these films shouldn't blind us to the fact that the Tarzan series also underwent a typical process of transformation. While the early movies were sexy, and astonishingly relaxed in their sexiness, the later installments were nothing more than naïve, run-of-the-mill adventure stories for the whole family. Jane's increasingly 'decent' and unrevealing costume illustrates this development as well as her relationship to the athletic 'natural man.' After the 'innocent' sexual curiosity of the first film, Jane is soon attempting to domesticate Tarzan by means of a cozy and comfortable tree house (*Tarzan Escapes*, 1936). The petit-bourgeois idyll is complete when the couple eventually adopt a baby and raise it together (*Tarzan Finds a Son!*, 1939).

Hollywood and the Depression

One genre formed a dark corrective to the high-powered illusionism of 30s Hollywood. Like the musical, the gangster movie clearly needed a soundtrack in order to develop its full potential. The rattling machine-guns, howling sirens and screeching tires in Howard Hawks' *Scarface* (1932, p. 124) leave us in no doubt that acoustic thrills played their part in making the genre so popular. But the introduction of a soundtrack didn't just permit some spectacular auditory effects; it also enabled actors and directors to develop a more naturalistic playing style. This was all the more important as the audience expected realism in this genre if nowhere else. *Scarface* was the most spectacular gangster movie of the decade; but as an independent production financed by the eccentric millionaire Howard Hughes, it was also an anomaly. Otherwise, the genre was firmly in the hands of Warner Bros. No other studio deserved the epithet "film factory" as much as this strictly-managed family firm. Warner Bros. studios were also known as "San Quentin," for they were notorious for keeping their employees on a tight rein, restricting them to certain genres, and submitting them to a punishing production schedule. This included the stars. The movies themselves were also characterized by a feverish tempo and an unusually shady lighting design that gave a heightened feeling of raw realism.

As the "men's studio" among the majors, Warner Bros. specialized in tough genre movies, often with storylines drawn from contemporary newspaper reports. Groundbreaking and influential films like Mervyn LeRoy's *Little Caesar* (1930) and William A. Wellman's *The Public Enemy* (1931, p. 48) had a particular thrill for 30s moviegoers, whose memories of the Prohibition-era gang wars were still fresh. The protagonists of these early classics, Edward G. Robinson and James Cagney, became the dominant stars of the genre – and the studio exploited their tough-guy image in a

thousand variations. Though short and stocky, both of these actors radiated an incredible vitality. Consequently, however threatening the characters they embodied, they always remained fascinating, for they embodied a quint-essentially American idea: anyone can make it big-time, if he's tough and ornery enough.

With much of the United States mired in poverty, the censors soon started worrying about movie gangsters as heroes the audience could identify with. As a result, Hollywood started presenting them in an ever more unheroic light, and the moment of repentance became increasingly important. The studios had in any case always felt obliged to show the death of the gangster, and *crime doesn't pay* was one of Hollywood's iron laws. Nonetheless, though the genre lost its original bite, it retained its socially-critical orientation. Films such as William Wyler's *Dead End: Cradle of Crime* (1937, p. 372) examined the misery and hopelessness of the city slums. The gangsters were frequently "Angels with Dirty Faces," as in the Michael Curtiz 1938 classic of the same name. At the film's unforgettable climax, Cagney's old schoolpal, now a priest, explains to the killer how the slum kids revere him as a fearless hero – and so he goes to his death in the execution chamber weeping and begging for his life. In a last act of disturb-ing bravery, the tough guy demolishes himself as a role model by pretend-ing to be an abject coward.

Gangster movies gave audiences an impression of just how hard life could be in America's great cities. The Depression itself, though, was hinted

at more often than it was examined. Few studio productions confronted the effects of the Wall Street crash directly. The Dream Factory was uncomfort-able with too much unvarnished reality, and the studio bosses were gener-ally unenthusiastic about Roosevelt's New Deal. Of the few films that openly supported the government's policies, most were made outside of the regu-lar studio system. King Vidor's *Our Daily Bread* (1934), for instance, was produced by the director himself. 'Socialist tendencies' were not welcome at MGM, and it was unthinkable that a Major Studio would have produced a film about the successful creation of an agricultural collective. For *Mod-ern Times* (1936, p. 300), as ever, Charles Chaplin had complete financial and artistic control over his own film; but this was an absolute exception at the time.

Yet there were other exceptions: As Columbia's star director, Frank Capra was one of Roosevelt's most important supporters in Hollywood. His films propagated the *ur*-American virtues of solidarity and community spirit, and thus embodied a reminder of the nation's democratic roots. His protagonists were always naive idealists, holy fools struggling bravely in a world filled with cynicism and greed. Therefore, James Stewart was the perfect Capra hero. In *Mr. Smith Goes to Washington* (1939), he plays a kindly and trusting Boy Scout leader who is manipulated into becoming a Senator as the tool of a corrupt industrial magnate. When Smith real-izes what's going on, he rebels – and is slandered and disgraced for his pains. Like all of Capra's protagonists, though, he triumphs miraculously

in the end; before Jefferson Smith can be stripped of his office as a Senator, he grasps the chance of his life and launches into a stirring marathon filibuster in which he appeals to the values that built America. After three days, he collapses, exhausted – and his reluctantly-admiring adversaries admit defeat.

Capra's comedies are thrilling and serious, but their critique is muted. There is something comfortingly fairytale-like in the way they reconcile us to the world. One could also complain that in glorifying the simple man of the people, his films conceal more about reality than they reveal. In any case, it was left to John Ford to draw the clearest picture of the Depression years in his adaptation of John Steinbeck's *The Grapes of Wrath* (1939/40, p. 522). In this Fox production, Henry Fonda plays the son of a farming family from Oklahoma, forced off their land by foreclosure. They pack up what little they possess and set off to make a new life for themselves in California; but all that's waiting for them is slum housing and brutal exploitation. Cameraman Gregg Toland filmed the grotesquely overloaded refugee vehicles, the miserable tent camps and the emaciated people so powerfully that even the documentary filmmaker Pare Lorentz – a vehement critic of Hollywood – was moved to offer rare praise for the "peculiar newsreel quality" of Ford's film.

Robin Hood versus the Nazis

If Hollywood only rarely deigned to notice the Depression, it almost completely ignored the rise of fascism in Europe. In fact, had the studios actually taken a stand against the fascist states in the 30s, they would have been opposing the U. S. government's official policy at the time – and they would also have found no widespread support amongst the American populace, who would have been horrified at the idea of another involvement in a "European" conflict. Nonetheless, Hollywood's lack of interest was not just due to a conviction that anti-Nazi films represented an unnecessary financial risk; it also had to be remembered that Germany was a major market for movies. MGM, Fox and Paramount were still exporting films to the Third Reich while Chaplin was putting the finishing touches to his Hitler satire, *The Great Dictator* (1940, p. 540).

Here too, Warner Bros. were an exception amongst the Major Studios. By 1934, Warner had ceased doing business with Germany; and from the middle of the decade onwards, they were facing down considerable political opposition to produce a series of films with a clear anti-fascist tendency. *Black Legion* (1936/37), for instance, depicted fascist undercurrents in America itself, while *Confessions of a Nazi Spy* (1939) is regarded as the first Hollywood movie to present Nazi Germany as an enemy power. The studio's commitment was also expressed in carefully allegorical films whose inten-

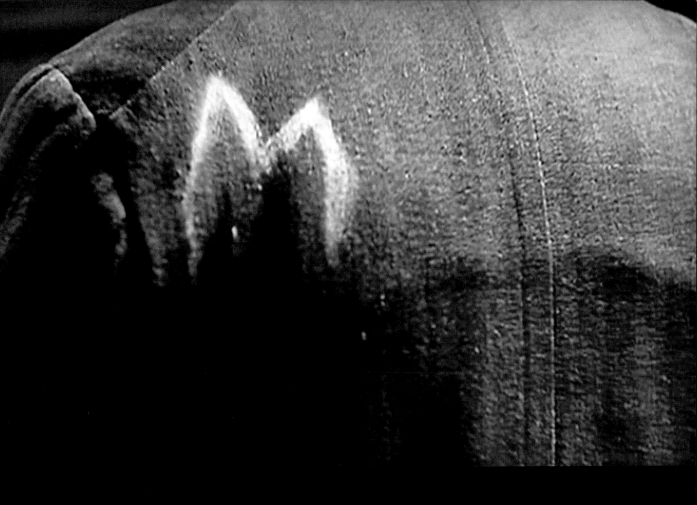

tion is now hard to recognize. Who would guess, for example, that a colorful costume drama like *The Adventures of Robin Hood* (1938, p. 384) was intended as a wake-up call about the threat of fascism?

Robin Hood was one of the first masterpieces to be made in "three-strip Technicolor," which brightened up cinema screens from the middle of the decade onwards. No one who has seen this wonderful movie will forget the young Errol Flynn's luminous green tights, in which he triumphed over the sinister Sheriff of Nottingham. Technicolor was the first technical solution to enable the convincing use of the entire color spectrum. As *Robin Hood* demonstrates, though, more color does not necessarily mean greater realism. In fact, the powerful hues of Technicolor actually led directors to aim for an anti-realistic effect. In a certain sense, this new technological achievement was the crowning glory of the decade's escapism.

The Golden Year

For financial reasons, Technicolor was an attraction that initially remained limited to a few prestigious projects and genres. In the early days, the technology was still quite cumbersome, but it turned out to be particularly suitable for animated films. Walt Disney's was the first studio to make use of the new process, and his full-length animated features *Snow White and the Seven Dwarfs* (1937, p. 258), *Pinocchio* (1940) and *Fantasia* (1940, p. 506).

undoubtedly owed their enormous popularity in large part to their sheer, overwhelming colorfulness. But exotic melodramas also profited from the new color technique, as did expensive Westerns that were designed to stand out from more run-of-the-mill fare. Nonetheless, Technicolor was practically made for spectacular, high-budget epics and musicals. This is demonstrated by two films that are among the most splendidly colorful ever made, both of which played a decisive role in making 1939 the Golden Year of the Dream Factory.

Probably no other single year saw the emergence of so many superb Hollywood films: John Ford's *Stagecoach* (p. 486) was *the* classical Western, and George Marshall's *Destry Rides Again* one of the best parodies of the genre ever made. *Only Angels Have Wings* was the best of Howard Hawks' aeronautical adventures, while Raoul Walsh's *The Roaring Twenties* (p. 440) was another classical gangster movie made for Warner Bros. George Cukor transcended his reputation as a fine director of actresses with *The Women* (p. 434), which featured 135 female speaking parts and not a single male voice. William Wyler's *Wuthering Heights* (p. 450) was a wonderful adaptation of Emily Brontë's dark Romantic novel. The same year saw the premieres of Lubitsch's *Ninotchka* (p. 428), W. S. Van Dyke's *It's a Wonderful World*, and Robert Capra's *Mr. Smith goes to Washington*. All of these were made in black-and-white. But shining above them all, in glorious Technicolor, stood *The Wizard of Oz* (p. 422) and *Gone with the Wind* (p. 470).

Even today, *Gone with the Wind* is regarded as the definitive screen epic. It is hard to think of another film that so convincingly fulfils the movies' promise of glamour and larger-than-life emotions. The film may be dismissed as kitsch, but its breathtaking color photography and its fantastic set design still give a fascinating impression of 1930s Hollywood's vitality, and of its capacity to create beautiful illusions.

Gone with the Wind demonstrated what the Dream Factory was capable of. Yet, curiously enough, it marked the triumph of an independent producer; for the film is seen as, above all, the work of David O. Selznick. He exhibited an almost bizarre perfectionism and went through no less than three directors – which casts an illuminating light on their status in the Hollywood of those years. Selznick's refusal to compromise paid off: *Gone with the Wind* won him eight Oscars, and for years it was recognized as the most successful film ever made. And though Selznick was a maverick amongst the Majors, he embodied like no other the ideals of Hollywood's Golden Age. His credo: "Making artistic pictures that are commercial successes."

Hardly less spectacular than Selznick's epic of the Deep South was the MGM musical, *The Wizard of Oz*, another unusually expensive production. The film is easily seen as an allegory of Hollywood as Dream Factory; for just as little Dorothy (Judy Garland) is transported in her dreams from the black-and-white world of her parents' farm to a Technicolor dreamland "over the rainbow," Americans battered by the Depression were expected to take refuge in the movie palaces. The studios saw it as their task to reconcile the populace with their lot, just as the naive girl from Kansas was solaced by her dream. And so reality was only rarely allowed to intrude into Hollywood's magical realm – but that's a defect that can easily be endured as long as the artificial flowers are as wonderfully colorful as they are in Oz.

King and Country

Britain was one country whose film industry had always been overshadowed by Hollywood. In order to resist the flood of American movies, the government instituted a series of measures that would stamp their mark on the British cinema of the 30s. For one thing, limits were placed on the number of U. S. productions that could be shown in Britain, and this led to a flood of so-called "quota quickies." These were often notoriously poor films, made cheaply and quickly, and they damaged the reputation of the domestic film industry.

At the same time, however, they did provide many home-grown talents with the opportunity to gain experience on the job. Yet this protectionist policy also led to a concentration of power, and the British film industry was soon in the hands of just a few large companies. Nonetheless, popular cinema did exist in Britain, for example in the form of musical comedies that drew on the tradition of the music halls. One big star of this genre was

Gracie Fields, who enjoyed enormous popularity amongst the British working class but remained completely unknown abroad. In the 30s, however, one young British director began a dazzling international career by becoming the leading filmmaker of his native land: Alfred Hitchcock.

In great thrillers such as *The 39 Steps* (1935, p. 266) and *Sabotage* (1936), he was already demonstrating his genius for generating suspense by purely visual means.

Hitchcock often pointed out that he was only interested in politics for its dramaturgy. Yet, from the mid-30s onwards, his spy thrillers give an indication that the shadow of impending war was falling across the British cinema as well as the country as a whole. The thoroughly convincing villain of *The Lady Vanishes* (1938, p. 394) was Dr. Hartz (Paul Lukas), a dubious physician with a harsh accent and a German-sounding name – clearly reflecting the prevailing mood of the times. For all that, Hitchcock's English films can hardly be regarded as works of propaganda. By the time the war broke out, he was already in Hollywood, where he made *Rebecca* (1940, p. 492) for Selznick and quickly became established.

Other big names in the industry showed a greater willingness to serve their King and Country. After the global success of *The Private Life of Henry VIII* (1933, p. 164), producer and director Alexander Korda was regarded as the outstanding personality in the British cinema. A Hungarian by birth, he produced not just historical portraits but also films that glorified the Empire in a manner typical of their time. If *Elephant Boy* (1937) now looks like a relatively harmless exotic adventure, the imperialist arrogance of *Sanders of the River* (1935) and *The Four Feathers* (1939) is barely tolerable. The latter film does demonstrate, however, that Korda's major productions could easily bear comparison to Hollywood's prestige projects in their professionalism and visual perfection.

As an eccentric and a perfectionist, Alexander Korda was also David O. Selznick's equal. His colorful reputation was confirmed by *The Thief of Bagdad* (1940, p. 534). A grand total of six directors are said to have worked on this fairytale epic, including Michael Powell and Korda himself. Made in color, and featuring a host of special animated effects, it is still a visually stunning creation. The London studios were operating under wartime restrictions, and the film was more than they could cope with; so Korda, undeterred, simply had the Oriental sets erected in California's Mojave desert. Though *The Thief of Bagdad* is about as pure a fantasy as one could imagine, contemporary realities still managed to find their way into it. It was surely no accident that the 'baddie' was played by Conrad Veidt, a famous German actor known for his demonic screen presence. In this respect, Korda was ahead of his American counterparts; for after the U. S. joined the war, Veidt went on to have a successful career playing Nazi villains in Hollywood productions.

Poetry and Realism

In the 30s, the French cinema went through a phase of exceptional vitality. Though France was plagued by political and economic instability at the time, this was a decade in which an extraordinary agglomeration of talents found exactly the conditions they needed in order to flourish. Besides the two major companies Pathé and Gaumont, there were also several smaller production companies that offered work to a wide range of creative individuals. Numerous foreign film workers also found a place in France, including many who had been exiled from Germany. This supplied a further fresh impulse to the French film industry. The same can be said about the introduction of sound, which attracted many artists from the world of theater and variété. With their *chansons*, their popular material, and their polished and professional delivery of sophisticated dialog, they played a large part in forming the highly distinctive character of the French cinema.

Even at that time, the cinema was an unusually well-respected art form in France. This was expressed in several ways: in institutions such as the Cinémathèque Française (established in 1936), in a plethora of film clubs, and in a broad range of film-related publications. France's enthusiasm for the cinema can also be seen in the fact that several directors attempted to realize their own ideas far from the Major Studios. Among them was Jean Vigo, who died in 1934 at the age of 29. He only ever made two full-length films,

and they are both poetic masterpieces, created under the most difficult of circumstances: *Zero for Conduct* (*Zéro de conduite*, 1933) and *L'Atalante* (1934, p. 208). Vigo's early death and the astonishing quality of his work made him a role model for every filmmaker who saw the cinema as a medium of personal expression. In a certain sense, then, Vigo was the progenitor of a French cinematic tradition that consciously resists the standards of the commercial film business and insists on its own cultural identity.

If the 30s have now gone down in history as the classical age of the French cinema, this is largely due to the work of the "poetic realists." It was a most unusual 'movement' for its time, and the directors associated with it often had very heterogeneous styles and working methods. What they had in common was their focus on ordinary people, their lives and their fates. René Clair's comedy *Liberty For Us* (*À nous la liberté*, 1931, p. 60) satirized the modern factory workplace and probably inspired Charles Chaplin's *Modern Times* (1936, p. 300). Only with reservations should Clair be included in this context, but the protagonist of the film – a 'gentleman of the road' – was a typical figure in the French cinema of the period: a Laforguian lazybones whose anarchic love of freedom is matched only by his natural sensuality. Such a figure was also embodied, unforgettably, by the incomparable Michel Simon in Jean Renoir's *Boudu Saved from Drowning* (*Boudu sauvé des eaux*, 1932).

Many critics see Jean Renoir as the most important French film-maker of the period. His unmistakable signature, his masterly cinematography

with its enormous depth of field, his mobile camera and extended tracking shots: all this makes his films look like a counter-model to the standardized Hollywood style – as does his preference for amateur actors and his insistence on working on location. Renoir also saw himself as a political artist, and he sympathized with the left-wing Popular Front. In 1936, he worked on a film made for the Communist party, *La Vie est à nous (The People of France)*, but this open gesture of political partisanship remained an exception in his career.

A more typical manifestation of his commitment was the famous anti-war film *The Grand Illusion (La Grande Illusion*, 1937, p. 378), which appealed for human solidarity across barriers of nationality and class. If this film aroused the hatred of fascist regimes, *The Rules of the Game (La Règle du jeu*, 1939, p. 480) provoked the French establishment. A mordantly ironical panorama of hypocrisy and decadence amongst the *haute bourgeoisie*, it presumably came a little too close to the truth: Jean Renoir's film was unceremoniously banned, and it was only rehabilitated as a masterpiece after the war.

The star of the pre-war French cinema was Jean Gabin. He made several films with Renoir, who cast him as a proletarian hero in *The Grand Illusion* and *The Human Beast (La Bête humaine*, 1938). Gabin went on to become the romantic icon of the Popular Front era after his roles as a tight-lipped outsider in Julien Duvivier's gangster film *Pépé le Moko* (1936/37, p. 352) and in Marcel Carné's *Port of Shadows (Quai des brumes*, 1938,

p. 406) and *Daybreak (Le Jour se lève*, 1939). All of these films were masterpieces of poetic realism; and in their existential pessimism, many of them anticipated the American film noir of the 40s.

World War II forced many of the French cinema's major artists into exile. Some, such as Jean Renoir, Julien Duvivier and René Clair, tried their luck in Hollywood. The fact that few of them succeeded in establishing themselves there seems to confirm that there are fundamental differences between the French and American film industries. Darryl F. Zanuck, studio boss of 20th Century Fox, put it in a nutshell: "Renoir has a lot of talent, but he isn't one of us."

State cinema

Europe's dictators – Stalin, Hitler or Mussolini – shared one opinion: that the cinema was of decisive importance to the maintenance and extension of their power. This essential insight, however, had very different effects on the cinematic cultures of their respective spheres of influence.

In the USSR, Stalin's doctrine of Socialist Realism ended the most creative phase of the Soviet cinema. During the 20s, great directors such as Sergei M. Eisenstein and Vsevolod Pudovkin had inspired worldwide acclaim for Russian film. By the 30s, however, the excitingly innovative montage techniques of their revolutionary cinema no longer fitted the mood

of the times. They were regarded as a "formalist" aberration and a dangerous symptom of "individualism."

The Soviet leaders saw traditional narrative forms as a more suitable and dependable means of communicating clear messages. From now on, the cinema was expected to serve only the goal of forming the new Socialist man. Historical dramas attested to the greatness of the nation, adventure films glorified the pioneer spirit, musicals and comedies invoked the joys of collectivist farming, and the cinema was filled with upstanding comrades who contributed to the triumph of Socialism by foiling the plans of traitors and saboteurs. Stalin personally oversaw the operation of this propaganda cinema. It was so tightly controlled that hardly anything outstanding could be made while it lasted. Thus, Sergei M. Eisenstein's patriotic epic *Alexander Nevsky* (*Aleksandr Nevskiy*, 1938, p. 390) is one of the few masterpieces produced during this depressing period.

In Germany, too, the 30s witnessed the end of a great cinematic era. During the age of silent film, the country's film industry had flourished spectacularly. Directors such as Fritz Lang, Friedrich Wilhelm Murnau, George Wilhelm Pabst and Ernst Lubitsch made Germany one of the leading cinematic nations of the world. As the examples of Murnau and Lubitsch demonstrate, however, German filmmakers succumbed to the lure of Hollywood very early on.

When the Nazis seized power in 1933, this led to an enormous exodus of talent, from which – understandably – the German cinema never fully re-covered. Among the emigrants were the directors and writers Fritz Lang, Billy Wilder, Max Ophüls, and Robert and Curt Siodmak; the actors Peter Lorre and Conrad Veidt; the cinematographers Karl Freund and Eugen Schüfftan; the composers Kurt Weill, Hanns Eisler and Erich Wolfgang Korngold; and the legendary Head of Production at UFA Studios, Erich Pommer. They and many others went abroad; and for most of them, the destination was Hollywood.

Before 1933, there had been many promising signs that directors had interesting ideas about how best to exploit the new technology of sound. Lang' thrillers *M* and *The Testament of Dr. Mabuse* (*Das Testament des Dr. Mabuse* 1932/33, p. 160) were made all the more powerfully disturbing by the deployment of noises, music and dialog; and in Sternberg's melodrama *The Blue Angel* (*Der blaue Engel*, 1930), sound made an enormous contribution to the film's atmospheric intensity. *Congress Dances!* (*Der Kongress tanzt*, 1931, p. 38) and *Three Good Friends* (*Die Drei von der Tankstelle*, 1930) were the first noteworthy musicals – a genre that would soon be immensely popular in Germany too. The carefree lightness of these two star-studded UFA productions anticipated the tone of most movies made during the period of Nazi rule.

For, in contrast to the situation in the Soviet Union, the cinema of Nazi Germany did not consist solely of blatant propaganda. Certainly, there was that too, the best-known examples being Leni Riefenstahl's tendentious record of the Nazi party's rallies in Nuremberg, *Triumph of the Will* (*Triumph*

des Willens, 1935) and her two-part documentary, Olympia (Part 1: Festival of the Nations, Part 2: Festival of Beauty [Fest der Völker, Fest der Schönheit], 1936–1938, p. 326). There were also any number of feature films that got the stamp of official approval for their political message. Prime examples include Hans Steinhoff's historical drama The Making of a King (Der alte und der junge König, 1934/35), as well as his tale about a member of the Hitler Youth, Our Flags Lead Us Forward (Hitlerjunge Quex – Ein Film vom Opfergeist der deutschen Jugend, 1933). The latter was one of the few films that actually had the National Socialist 'movement' as its theme. Most of the movies produced in Germany – and in Italy too, by the way – were apparently harmless pieces of light entertainment, quite free of any explicit ideological content. Comedies and musicals simulated a 'lightness of being' that seemed to contrast remarkably with the leaden earnestness of the Nazis' "Blood and Soil" ideology.

The escapist cinema of the Nazi period was explicitly modeled on Hollywood, with its star system and "invisible" editing style. Propaganda Minister Joseph Goebbels controlled the German film industry. Having nationalized UFA Studios, he now planned to develop the place into a powerfully productive Dream Factory that would at least equal the Major Studios of the USA. Technically, and as regards the quality of the acting, UFA came pretty close to achieving these goals, although only a few films fully matched up to what Hollywood could produce. Only rarely was the monopolistic state-run cinema capable of concealing the cynical plan behind its carefully concocted

confections, and the fact that so many great talents had been driven into exile was never overcome.

That Goebbels was well aware of this loss is demonstrated by the case of Reinhold Schünzel, an actor and director he admired. As a so-called "Halbjude" ("half-Jew"), Schünzel was actually forbidden to take up employment, but Goebbels granted him special permission to keep on working in Germany right up until 1937. And indeed, Schünzel's comedies, such as Viktor und Viktoria (Viktor and Viktoria,1933, p. 180) or Amphitryon – Happiness from the Clouds (Amphitryon – Aus den Wolken kommt das Glück, 1935), do have a certain something that's nor-mally sadly lacking in the German cinema of that period: esprit, and a hint of subversion.

A skeptic in Hollywood

If we now take look back at Fritz Lang's M, it is striking how incongruous its pessimism seems in the context of the 30s cinema. In an age of escapism, this dark masterpiece seems like an anomaly. M is still recognizably part of the German Expressionist tradition, which had traced the psychogram of a continent shaken by World War I. In this respect, M marks an ending in German cinema. Yet it can be said with equal justification that Lang's film is ahead of its time. It already expresses a strong unease about the modernity it inhabits, and the same unease can still be felt today. Lang's attitude is

skeptical, indeed cynical. In the face of a world that threatens to sink into chaos, he denies that civilization is progressing inexorably, and rejects progress as an ideology. *M* seems to inform us that man is not free, because he cannot escape the forces that drive him.

When the Nazis seized power, Lang left Germany. After a period in France, he eventually found refuge in the U.S. But even in the Dream Factory, he remained true to his own vision. *You Only Live Once* (1936) and *Fury* (1936, p. 314) were films about hysterical crowds, lynch justice and the thirst for revenge. Lang's disillusioned view of the world made him an outsider in the U.S. cinema of the 30s. He was a stranger to the positive energy of the Hollywood movie, to its optimistic 'American spirit.' Only after the war had cast its shadow on the Dream Factory, bringing an unfamiliar chill along with it, did Lang truly arrive in Hollywood. The film noir of the 40s shows him in his element.

M makes it clear to us that the cinema has always been aware of the issues raised by modernity. By the 40s, many films would evince an unmistakable skepticism about the practicability of Enlightenment ideas; in the movies of the 30s, however, modernity still generally means an unbroken faith in progress. For Hollywood, anything seemed possible, and the result of this can-do attitude was an unprecedented homogenization of the cinematic language. In the illusionist star-cinema of the period, the American Dream found a new home. As the triumphs of the Dream Factory culminated in the Golden Year of 1939, Hollywood movies became ever more popu-

lar. Astonishingly enough, the widespread misery of the Depression years only served to accelerate this mechanism. It would take a world war to put a brake on it. After Pearl Harbor, Hollywood's promises of happiness would begin to seem increasingly absurd, and the studio system would soon be showing the first cracks in its foundations. From then on, the movies would have their doubts.

Jürgen Müller / Jörn Hetebrügge

1931 - USA - 87 MIN. - B & W - TRAGICOMEDY, DRAMA

DIRECTOR CHARLES CHAPLIN (1889–1977)
SCREENPLAY CHARLES CHAPLIN DIRECTOR OF PHOTOGRAPHY ROLAND H. TOTHEROH EDITING WILLARD NICO, CHARLES CHAPLIN
MUSIC CHARLES CHAPLIN, JOSÉ PADILLA PRODUCTION CHARLES CHAPLIN for CHARLES CHAPLIN PRODUCTIONS, UNITED ARTISTS.

STARRING CHARLES CHAPLIN (Charlie, the Tramp), VIRGINIA CHERRILL (A blind girl), HARRY MYERS (An eccentric millionaire), FLORENCE LEE (The blind girl's grandmother), ALLAN GARCIA (The millionaire's butler), HANK MANN (Boxer), HENRY BERGMAN (Mayor / The blind girl's downstairs neighbor), ALBERT AUSTIN (Street sweeper / Eddie Mason, a crook), ROBERT PARRISH (Newsboy), HARRY AYERS (Cop).

"You can see now."

A monument is being unveiled. The Mayor solemnly addresses the assembled dignitaries. Then the veil is drawn, revealing a colossal piece of statuary bearing the title "Peace and Prosperity" … and slumbering amongst the heroic granite figures is the Little Tramp (Charles Chaplin). When he realizes he's been caught napping, he naturally tries to take off, but he's caught once again – this time by the seat of his pants on a stone sword.

Since 1927, the talkies had been forcing silent films out of the theaters, and no other Hollywood star resisted the trend as passionately as Charles Chaplin. He felt it endangered the very basis of his art – mime – and with it, the universality of the cinema. *City Lights*, then, was a gesture of defiance: an essentially silent film made in 1931, it uses the soundtrack solely for music and a few auditory effects. Chaplin's movie is an anachronism, and – as its opening sequence demonstrates – a dazzling argument against the talkies. For the scene with the monument derives its satirical force not only from the comical twist (Charlie's unveiling), but also from the fact that the pompous Mayor's speech is completely incomprehensible. All we hear is a dull metallic droning and quacking – a sideswipe at the sound quality of the early talkies, and a joke at the expense of speechifying politicians.

The unreliability of hearing is further demonstrated when the Tramp meets and falls in love with a blind flower-girl (Virginia Cherrill). Because she hears the door of a limousine bang shut at the very moment of their first encounter, she believes he is a wealthy man. From then on, Charlie does everything he can to uphold this illusion – and to raise the money for an expensive operation that will cure the girl's blindness. At first, it seems that luck is on his side. While searching for a new place to spend the night, he prevents a drunk man from committing suicide. It turns out that this man is a millionaire, and he takes Charlie home with him, where he throws a party in his honor. But when the rich man wakes up next morning, he is amazed and disgusted to find a ragged stranger in his house – and Charlie is back on the street once more.

It's not surprising that left-leaning cinemagoers were pleased by this depiction of a plutocrat who can only show his human face when under the influence of alcohol. Bertolt Brecht had already made use of such a figure in his play "Mister Puntila and His Man Matti." Certainly, *City Lights* marks a new development in Chaplin's work. The British-born comedian had himself grown up in terrible poverty, and his films had always radiated sympathy for the weak and impoverished. When the Depression came, however, Chaplin's social conscience turned into outright social criticism. As the outcast Tramp persists in his efforts to raise the cash for the girl's eye operation, Chaplin is anticipating the situation of his protagonist in *Modern Times*: a penniless individual trapped in the wheels of the capitalist system.

While the blind girl and her grandmother (Florence Lee) are facing eviction from their apartment, Charlie grabs any damn job he can find. Once, he even lands in the boxing ring; the skinny little guy copes surprisingly well against a dumb brute of a bruiser, but here too, he ends up losing. Only when the Tramp meets the millionaire do things once more begin to take a turn for the better: the man is drunk again, and he gives Charlie the money he needs; the girl's operation can go ahead. When Charlie's filthy-rich patron sobers up, however, he has forgotten his good intentions yet again, and Charlie lands in jail as a thief.

Like all of Chaplin's masterpieces, *City Lights* maintains the balance between comedy and pathos, laughter and sympathy. Hardly any other

2

TALKIES

Even during the silent film era, there were some remarkably convincing methods of adding sound to moving images. In general, though, the birth of the talkies is agreed to have taken place on October 6, 1927, with the release of Al Jolson's *The Jazz Singer*. On this day, Jolson spoke the famous words from the big screen at Warner's Theatre in New York: "You ain't heard nothing yet!" There followed a regular "talkies fever," and the movie industry was henceforth encouraged to produce only sound films. *The Jazz Singer* had in fact been merely a 'part-time talkie,' with just a few dialog sequences recorded on a shellac record that played while the film was running. Soon, however, improved systems were available, with sound and image united on a single strip of celluloid. Though the studios and movie theaters had to invest heavily in new equipment, the first film with dialog all the way through was already up and running by 1928: *Lights of New York*, directed by Bryan Foy. By the following year, more than 9 000 cinemas in the U.S. had been fitted out with sound; and by 1930-31, silent films were a thing of the past, at least in the industrialized Western nations. The triumph of the talkies also meant significant aesthetic changes at the visual level. Because the cameras of the early sound era required a bulky soundproof casing to muffle the noise of the machinery, they were extremely large and immobile; as a result, many of these early talkies were pretty uninteresting in visual terms. Nonetheless, the arrival of sound buttressed a realist tendency in the cinema that demanded new ways of acting from the stars. Not a few of them failed to make the transition; John Gilbert was probably the best-known victim. The most vehement opponent of the talkies was Charles Chaplin, though he ultimately survived and prospered in the new era, too.

Chaplin film is so thoroughly sentimental, yet *City Lights* constitutes brilliant proof of the power and truthfulness that can inhere in a purely visual medium. At the same time, this powerful plea for the silent film medium also demonstrates that the faculty of vision must not remain trapped in superficialities. When Charlie is released from prison, he is in visibly poorer shape. He meets the girl once more: following her successful operation, she can now see, and she is the proud owner of a florist's shop. Still waiting for her millionaire, she charitably presents the tramp with a flower and a coin. Only when he touches her hand does the truth dawn on her. In a close-up, we see her pause and consider as the realization takes hold; a counter-shot shows Chaplin's shy, uncertain face. For the first time, we recognize that the Tramp is growing old. UB

"*City Lights* includes one of the funniest sporting events ever filmed, the immortal boxing scene in which Charlie's footwork bedazzles both the referee and his opponent. It also includes a great deal of sentiment, which some of the 1931 critics found excessive. I don't think so. Chaplin goes only so far with sentiment, then makes his getaway with a gag." *Chicago Sun-Times*

1 Smelling is believing: If this blind flower seller (Virginia Cherrill) ever snuggles up to the tramp beside her, she'll discover that he's not the wealthy gent she takes him for.

2 Ring of riches: The tramp needs to knock out the prize fighter, if he intends to pay for his knock-out girlfriend's eye surgery.

3 Friends in need: The tramp saves an eccentric millionaire from taking his own life and then follows him around town to capitalize on his generosity. The film was a favorite with communist sympathizers and inspired Bertolt Brecht to write the play "Mister Puntila and His Man Matti."

4 The blind leading the blind: The tramp nearly loses his balance trying to keep both the flower seller and the liquor-loving millionaire within arm's reach.

CONGRESS DANCES
Der Kongress tanzt

1931 - GERMANY - 97 MIN. - B & W - COMEDY, MUSIC FILM

DIRECTOR ERIK CHARELL (1894–1974)
SCREENPLAY NORBERT FALK, ROBERT LIEBMANN **DIRECTOR OF PHOTOGRAPHY** CARL HOFFMANN **EDITING** VIKTOR GERTLER
MUSIC WERNER RICHARD HEYMANN **PRODUCTION** ERICH POMMER for UFA.

STARRING LILIAN HARVEY (Christel Weinzinger, the Glove Seller), WILLY FRITSCH (Czar Alexander of Russia / The Czar's Doppelgänger), OTTO WALLBURG (Bibikoff, his Adjutant), CONRAD VEIDT (Prince Metternich), CARL-HEINZ SCHROTH (Pepi, his Secretary), LIL DAGOVER (The Countess), ALFRED ABEL (The King of Saxony), EUGEN REX (The Saxon Envoy), ALFRED GERASCH (The French Envoy), ADELE SANDROCK (The Princess), PAUL HÖRBIGER (The Heurigen Singer), JULIUS FALKENSTEIN (The Minister of Finance).

"Once in a lifetime! Never again! Just too beautiful to be true!"

The film's best-known musical number says it loud and clear: you've never seen anything like *this* before. *Congress Dances* is larger than life, and it knows it. This is as good as it never gets, for the film really is too beautiful to be true. What's served up to us is quite fantastically unreal – not just the love story between a poor Viennese glove seller and the Russian Czar, but the film itself and everything that went into it. With the introduction of sound, Germany's biggest film studio, UFA, had seen a chance to contest Hollywood's primacy in Europe. *Congress Dances* was part of this strategy, and was therefore made in three different versions: German, English, and French. The background to the love story is a historical event of pan-European dimensions: the Congress of Vienna, which took place in 1814/15, immediately after the Napoleonic Wars. It was intended to establish the continent's political and territorial boundaries for the remainder of the 19th century.

The mighty ruler traveling incognito amongst the common people has long been a popular motif, from Shakespeare's "Henry V" to Albert Lortzing's comic opera "The Czar and the Carpenter" ("Zar und Zimmerman") to contemporary soaps and *telenovelas*. Another familiar figure is the witty and charming Viennese girl, a kind of German-language answer to the Parisian *mademoiselle*. These archetypal figures are played by Willy Fritsch (as Czar Alexander) and Lilian Harvey (as Christel, the glove seller). The third protagonist is no less important: Prince Metternich, the wily manipulator behind the scenes. As embodied by Conrad Veidt, he is a kind of Doctor Mabuse for the early 1800s. With his bugging devices and his army of spies and letter-inter-

1 Double trouble: Christel (Lilian Harvey) thinks she's about to be kissed by a king, but is actually in for a peck from a pauper. Willy Fritsch stars as both Russian Czar Alexander I and his impersonator Uralsky.

2 Ain't nothin' like the real thing: A man of simple tastes, Alexander shares a glass of wine and a slice of life with a common girl.,

3 Bibikoff knows best: A master of public affairs, the adjutant (Otto Wallburg, left) turns a pair of kings into a winning hand.

4 Squeezing into the role: Trilingual Lilian Harvey was the only major cast member to speak and sing her part in the German, English and French versions of the film.

ceptors, Veidt's Metternich seems like a playful forerunner of the 20th century's totalitarian Big Brothers.

UFA drummed up all the major talents available in Berlin, from the 'dream couple' of the period, Willy Fritsch and Lilian Harvey, to Conrad Veidt and the wonderful comedians Adele Sandrock and Julius Falkenstein. Even the smallest supporting roles in the movie are played by top actors. The sets were designed by Robert Herlth and Walter Röhrig, the music was composed by Werner Richard Heymann, and the cameraman was Carl Hoffman. The highly experienced Hoffman is also credited as co-director, for the movie was in the hands of a film debutante, Erik Charell, who had made a name for himself as the brilliant director of megalomaniac operetta productions. Charell's grandiose revues had filled Max Reinhardt's enormous theater, the Schau spielhaus, and his legendary productions of *Das Weisse Rössl* had been hugely popular in Germany. Sadly, his success was to be short-lived: Charell was Jewish, and UFA dissolved his contract with unseemly haste after the Nazis seized power in the spring of 1933. *Congress Dances* continued to make money for UFA until 1937.

Once in a lifetime … Never again. The famous song doesn't just announce this movie's uniqueness, but also predicts its ultimate failure. Like the romance between Christel and Alexander, UFA's plan to mount a global challenge against Hollywood turned out to be a pipe-dream. *In every summer, there's just one month of May …* the film's bittersweet message is that the illusion of happiness is greatest when it's just beyond our reach.

MH

"This truffle of cinema unfolds its flavors like a heavenly feast for the anonymous millions it is dedicated to." *Lichtbild-Bühne*

MULTIPLE-LANGUAGE VERSIONS

Silent film was an international art and industry, because any movie could be adapted for a foreign audience simply by inserting a different set of captions. Only when sound was introduced at the end of the 20s did the problem of translation rear its ugly head. Besides dubbing and subtitles, another solution was practiced in Europe during the 1930s: multiple-language versions. The same scenes were shot in the same sets in two or more languages, often with a different set of actors. This is how *Congress Dances* was made, in German, French and English. Leading actress Lilian Harvey starred in all three versions, as she spoke all three languages without an accent; but she was partnered by two different Czars: Willy Fritsch for the German edition (*Der Kongress tanzt*, 1931), Henri Garat for the French (*Le Congrès s'amuse*, 1931) and English variants (*Congress Dances*, 1931).

DR. JEKYLL AND MR. HYDE

1931 - USA - 98 MIN. - B & W - HORROR MOVIE, LITERARY ADAPTATION

DIRECTOR ROUBEN MAMOULIAN (1897–1987)
SCREENPLAY SAMUEL HOFFENSTEIN, PERCY HEATH, based on the story *THE STRANGE CASE OF DR. JEKYLL AND MR. HYDE* by ROBERT LOUIS STEVENSON **DIRECTOR OF PHOTOGRAPHY** KARL STRUSS **EDITING** WILLIAM SHEA **MUSIC** HERMAN HAND, JOHANN SEBASTIAN BACH, ROBERT SCHUMANN **PRODUCTION** ROUBEN MAMOULIAN for PARAMOUNT PICTURES.

STARRING FREDRIC MARCH (Doctor Henry L. Jekyll / Mr. Hyde), MIRIAM HOPKINS (Ivy Pearson), ROSE HOBART (Muriel Carew), HOLMES HERBERT (Doctor Lanyon), HALLIWELL HOBBES (General Danvers Carew), EDGAR NORTON (Poole, Jekyll's Butler), TEMPE PIGOTT (Mrs. Hawkins), ARNOLD LUCY (Utterson, Carew's Butler), DOUGLAS WALTON (Blond student), ERIC WILTON (Briggs, Lanyon's Butler).

ACADEMY AWARDS 1932 OSCAR for BEST ACTOR (Fredric March).

"Isn't Hyde a lover after your own heart?"

Ambitious physician Dr. Jekyll (Fredric March) is a man with an obsession. He believes he can restore order to the human soul by using a synthetic substance to separate the two conflicting principles – the Apollonian and the Dionysian. The scientific community takes a skeptical view of his revolutionary research, and his prospective father-in-law, the conservative General Carew (Halliwell Hobbes), feels that Jekyll is too highly-strung for his own good. When Jekyll announces his desire to bring forward the date of his marriage to Muriel (Rose Hobart), the General refuses to give his consent. In his disappointment, Jekyll tests the new synthetic substance on himself. This daring, secret experiment has fatal consequences.

First published in 1886, Robert Louis Stevenson's famous story has inspired innumerable directors, cinematographers and actors. In 1920, John S. Robertson made a full-length silent version starring John Barrymore, and Victor Fleming's 1941 version featured Spencer Tracy in the title role. In both of these adaptations, the 'transformation' of the protagonist was mainly the achievement of the lead actors.

Former theater director Rouben Mamoulian approached the story differently. He wanted to use innovative, visual, cinematic techniques, and the film is filled with surprising visual motifs and exquisite sound experiments. The unusual opening sequence demonstrates Mamoulian's talent, and his feeling for rhythmic narration. The director plays with our expectations by showing us everything through Jekyll's eyes – and immediately, our curiosity is awakened.

Slowly, the camera approaches a mirror in the hall. Sophisticated moviegoers would now expect to see the reflection of a camera appear in the mirror; instead, we see Fredric March as Dr. Jekyll. The trick is simple: instead of a mirror, the set designer had made a hole in the wall, and behind it, he had constructed a mirror image of the hall. March had to synchronize his movement with the camera's, so as to appear in the gap at just the right moment, as if he were his own reflection. This highly effective first appearance prepares us for the split in Jekyll's personality that forms the heart of the story.

"Visual realism is not important. Psychological realism is. If you capture that, the scene will work, no matter what you do." *Rouben Mamoulian*

1. Genius and madness: Man of science, Dr. Jekyll, is so smart it's frightening. Fredric March stars in an unforgettable dual role.

2. Painting the town dead: Dr. Jekyll gets spiffed up for a night out and shows Victorian London what he's really made of.

3. Antidote: Dr. Lanyon (Holmes Herbert) supplies Hyde with a shot of reality and reunites the two faces of insanity – if only temporarily.

4. An animal in the bedroom: Mr. Hyde knocks Ivy's (Miriam Hopkins) socks off and then leaves her down for the count.

5. Waving the white flag: A waiter learns the hard way that some patrons refuse to be ignored.

His transformation into Mr. Hyde is achieved in an almost deliriously inventive piece of filmmaking, a scene achieved without cuts, blends or fade outs. Using only a clever system of filters in front of the lens, as well as some very effective make-up for the actor, Mamoulian creates an astonishingly convincing metamorphosis, as Jekyll swallows the steaming chemical cocktail, grasps his throat and begins to gurgle. Dark shadows form on his distorted face, emerging threateningly from his eyes, his nose and his mouth. Then the camera adopts Jekyll's perspective once more, and begins to turn on its own axis. The camera spins faster until we see nothing but a blur, accompanied by psychedelic sounds and visualized fragments of Jekyll's

ROUBEN MAMOULIAN   Rouben Mamoulian was born in Tbilisi, Georgia, in 1897. His father was an Armenian who served as a colonel in the Russian army. His mother shared her son's enthusiasm for the theater. After studying law in Paris and Moscow, where he made the acquaintance of Stanislavsky, Mamoulian moved to London and made his directing debut aged 25 at the well-known St James Theatre. A job on Broadway finally brought him to America, where he made his breakthrough in 1927: the play he directed, called "Porgy," would later form the basis for Gershwin's opera, "Porgy and Bess." By now, Paramount was interested in this successful stage director. They originally engaged him as a dialog coach, but Mamoulian quickly acquired the technical knowledge required of a film director. Shortly after the invention of the talkies, he was already making film history: his full-length film *Applause* (1929) was notable for its innovative experiments with sound, mobile camera, and surprisingly original narrative strategies. Again and again, Mamoulian astonished the studio bosses with his revolutionary visual ideas and his disregard for cinematic conventions. He used sound, image and editing to create rhythmical narrative units, always preferring a poetic reality to anything resembling naked naturalism. Film works with pictures, theater with words – this was his fundamental belief. With *Love Me Tonight* (1932), he created an early masterpiece of the musical genre. *City Streets* (1931) is said to be the only gangster film Al Capone really liked, and it demonstrates Mamoulian's genius in the deployment of light and shade. His mastery of narrated time is exemplified by the famous sequence in which a slowly burning cigarette creates the perfect alibi for a killer. The final scene of *Queen Christina* (1933) also made movie history: Mamoulian told Greta Garbo to think of nothing, and instead merely to stare into the distance, unmoved. The resulting sequence was so suspenseful that moviegoers were overwhelmed. Rouben Mamoulian died on December 12, 1987.

> **"Fredric March is at the height of his powers in both roles. Although hidden behind ever-increasing layers of makeup, his Hyde is never reduced to a mere movie monster. Instead, his ghastly face always betrays Dr. Jekyll's inner struggles. As Jekyll, March embodies charm and grace as well as a relentless sense of pride, and the curiosity – or rather hybris – of Adam, which led to his expulsion from paradise."**
>
> *Ivan Butler, in: The Horror Film*

6 Poisoned Ivy: After hearing of his love interest's horrific encounter with Hyde, Dr. Jekyll realizes that there's no undoing the damage he's done.

7 Top hat and tails from the crypt: Mr. Hyde's will to survive threatens to crush Dr. Jekyll altogether. Director Rouben Mamoulian presents the alter-ego not as a monster but as a man driven by animal instinct.

memory; then the transformation is complete. Jekyll walks towards the mirror … and, like us, he sets eyes for the first time on the grinning, ape-like face of Mr. Hyde.

Fredric March received an Oscar for his complex, multifaceted performance. His Mr. Hyde is a bestial, evil character, yet wittily played and positively funny at times. Miriam Hopkins is no less impressive as the good-time girl Ivy, whose sex appeal fires up Jekyll in the first place. The Doctor's hubris

tune moments, his friend Dr. Lanyon (Holmes Herbert) puts an end to his existence with a bullet. In the film's final frames, the director demonstrates his gift for the telling image once more: a bubbling cauldron on the fire boils over – a symbol of hell. Mamoulian's version is rightly regarded as the most impressive cinematic adaptation of the novel, not least because Hyde is less a monster than a man: an untamed, anarchistic character, crushed – no less than Jekyll – by the restrictions of the society he lives in.

THE PUBLIC ENEMY

1931 - USA - 84 MIN. - B & W - GANGSTER MOVIE

DIRECTOR WILLIAM A. WELLMAN (1896–1975)
SCREENPLAY HARVEY F. THEW, based on a story by KUBEC GLASMON and JOHN BRIGHT
DIRECTOOOR OF PHOTOGRAPHY DEVEREAUX JENNINGS **EDITING** EDWARD M. MCDERMOTT **MUSIC** DAVID MENDOZA
PRODUCTION DARRYL F. ZANUCK for WARNER BROS.

STARRING JAMES CAGNEY (Tom Powers), EDWARD WOODS (Matt Doyle), JEAN HARLOW (Gwen Allen),
JOAN BLONDELL (Mamie), BERYL MERCER (Ma Powers), MAE CLARKE (Kitty), DONALD COOK (Mike Powers),
LESLIE FENTON (Nails Nathan), ROBERT EMMETT O'CONNOR (Paddy Ryan), MURRAY KINNELL (Putty Nose).

"There's not only beer in that jug. There's beer and blood – blood of men!"

In the early 30s, a slew of gangster films inaugurated an entirely new genre. Besides *The Public Enemy*, these included *Scarface* (1932) and *Little Caesar* (1930). Loud protest ensued, for these movies were accused of glorifying their criminal protagonists. After all, these characters were essentially chasing the same goals as most decent, run-of-the-mill screen heroes; namely, success and happiness. The movie gangster brought the pioneering spirit of the Western frontier to the streets of the big city, taking what he needed and effortlessly achieving radical self-realization.

Yet if we trouble to take a closer look, Hollywood's much-criticized 'hero-worship' of the gangster-figure can also be seen as an early manifestation of a culture as fascinated by death as it is by life. In this ambivalent cosmos, the gangster Tom Powers is both a shining hero and a fallen angel.

He is played by James Cagney, an early icon of the gangster movie. With an unusual sensibility for the interplay between social and individual development, the film traces Powers' criminal career. He begins as a street kid in the Depression years, trying to make his life more bearable by means of petty crime; then he works as a hired gun for various gang bosses; and gradually, he progresses through the ranks to become an indispensable right-hand man. At his apogee, he is an ice-cold, dandyish murderer. The film's disturbing final sequence shows his fall.

The Public Enemy is a kind of fictional biography. Captions are blended in as the years pass, marking selected stages in Tom Powers' development; but they also remind us of the bigger historical picture. We move from the start of the 20th century, when industrialization and economic

> **"James Cagney delivers an impeccable performance as the overgrown street hoodlum, complete with flamboyant gesticulation, demonstrative spitting and an inability to sit still. He is what one might call a ticking timebomb of aggressivity."** *Daniela Sannwald, in: Thomas Koebner (Ed.), Filmklassiker*

re-orientation had brought various weighty problems to the United States, then on to World War I, enthusiastically fought by Tom's brother Mike (Donald Cook), and finally to the Prohibition era, when the demand for illegal alcohol led to modernity's first Golden Age of organized crime. Meanwhile, almost parenthetically, we witness the mother's struggle for her two irreconcilable sons, we note the father's absence, and we see the boys' unstable relationships to the women in their lives – in short, we observe the collapse of the traditional family model. As Tom Powers gradually frees himself from the rules that bind civil society, he repeatedly lands in open-ended situations for which the film offers no simple or premature solutions. Newly awash with money, Tom takes a trip in an expensive limo with his buddy Edward Woods (Matt Doyle), spots the mysterious and attractive Gwen

4

1   Tough guys and platinum blondes: Gwen Allen (Jean Harlow) learns that when you lie down with dogs, you get up with fleas. James Cagney stars as the impulsive Tom Powers.

2   Two-fisted drinker: When Tom needs a refill, he won't take no for an answer.

3   Out of my dreams and into my car: Harlow and Cagney go for a test drive.

4   Target practice: Back alleys are a gangster's boot camp.

JAMES CAGNEY   Born in 1899, James Cagney's earliest experiences of showbiz consisted of vaudeville acts and small parts in the theater. In 1925, he had his first lead roles on Broadway. Cagney's Hollywood career began in 1930 with *Sinner's Holiday,* a film adaptation of the successful stage play "Penny Arcade." His partner in this movie was Joan Blondell, who also appeared in *The Public Enemy* (1931). Cagney's highly-charged performance in the latter film made him a star. From then on, he was acknowledged as the ideal actor for a whole range of gangster movies and social dramas of the Depression era and after, from *G-Men* (1935) to *White Heat* (1949). James Cagney also directed *Short Cut to Hell,* 1957, and he and his brother formed a film production company, Cagney Productions. His lead role in Billy Wilder's Cold War comedy *One, Two, Three* (1961) was his farewell to the movie business. Numerous awards marked the world's recognition of his life's work. In the 80s, he came out of retirement once more, to appear in Miloš Forman's drama *Ragtime* (1981), and in a TV production. James Cagney died in 1986.

> # "Every time I see him work, it looks to me like a bunch of firecrackers going off all at once."

Will Rogers (actor) on James Cagney

Allen (Jean Harlow) on the street, starts an affair with her and ends it with equal abruptness.

From a film-historical perspective, this break with the moral tradition also takes place at the level of cinematic technique, principally in the film's presentation of excessive violence. Examples include the notorious scene in which Tom rams a grapefruit into his girlfriend's face, and the brutal revenge killing of the hoodlum "Putty Nose" (Murray Kinnell). Some of these scenes are now part of the iconography of the gangster genre. Technological progress had enabled small private armies to carry out state-of-the-art murders with machine guns and hand grenades; and for the cinema, this meant new possibilities for the staging of violent crime. Similar considerations apply to this movie's gripping visual language. Numerous close-ups, a rejection of long shots that might ease the claustrophobia, camera-angles that alternate from above to below eye-level, frames that make the characters and tableaux seem like living monuments: *The Public Enemy* is filled with extraordinarily dramatic effects in an ambience of constant uncertainty and threat. And with its shocking finale, this enthralling gangster film reveals its disturbing affinity to the horror genre.

BR

5   Strike and pose: The critics tried to smack some sense into Hollywood by denouncing the gratuitous violence of early 30s gangster pictures.

6   Nookie nookie: Mobsters keep up their energy with an afternoon cookie.

7   Yankee doodle dreamboat: James Cagney was as much a pin-up as he was a public enemy.

"The comedy in the picture, as well as the rough stuff, is in the dialog and by-play with the dames who include, besides Clarke, Joan Blondell and Jean Harlow."

Variety

THE BLUE LIGHT

Das blaue Licht – Eine Berglegende aus den Dolomiten

1931/32 - GERMANY - 72 MIN. - B & W - MOUNTAIN FILM *(BERGFILM)*, DRAMA

DIRECTOR LENI RIEFENSTAHL (1902–2003)
SCREENPLAY BÉLA BALÁZS and LENI RIEFENSTAHL DIRECTOR OF PHOTOGRAPHY HANS SCHNEEBERGER EDITING LENI RIEFENSTAHL
MUSIC GIUSEPPE BECCE PRODUCTION LENI RIEFENSTAHL for L. R. STUDIO-FILM, H. R. SOKAL-FILM.

STARRING LENI RIEFENSTAHL (Junta), MATHIAS WIEMAN (Vigo), MAX HOLSBOER (Innkeeper),
BENI FÜHRER (Tonio, the Innkeeper's Son), FRANZ MALDACEA (Guzzi), MARTHA MAIR (Lucia).

"Junta is a damned witch!"

As the subtitle of Leni Riefenstahl's directing debut *The Blue Light* informs us, this tale of a South Tyrolean nature child is "a mountain legend." Junta, a young woman played by Riefenstahl herself, is the only person who knows the way to the secret crystal grotto of Monte Cristallo. Because of this, the superstitious villagers believe her to be a witch and persecute her cruelly.

The movie is thus immediately established as a kind of fairy-tale. Riefenstahl's aim was to present an alternative to the classic mountain film genre established by the works of Arnold Fanck. Her strapping figure had been a regular feature of Fanck's films (like *The Holy Mountain / Der heilige Berg,* 1925/26) since 1926. These were decidedly melodramatic tales of alpine heroes battling with perilous peaks, yet they were filmed in a straight-forward realistic style. Plot development was usually secondary, for Fanck, a geologist by training, and his skilled cameramen Sepp Allgeier and Hans Schneeberger, had other priorities. Their main aim was to capture the beauty and grandeur of the alpine scenery, as well as its dangers and climatic extremes. Riefenstahl is said to have disdained as aesthetically incongruent

the disparity between 'beautiful' cinematography and 'realistic' themes in Fanck's work. As she put it in her autobiography: "Only when the theme and the imagery express one and the same thing can there be a unity of style, and that's what I was aiming for."

Since Riefenstahl favored 'beautiful' cinematography, she conceived of a fairy-tale infused with elements of German Romanticism, a story that would require a correspondingly stylized visual vocabulary. For semi-civilized Junta, a girl living in a simple mountain hut, the rock crystals she finds do not hold the material value for which they are coveted by the village community. Instead, the girl is fascinated, almost hypnotized, by their beauty. When she makes her way to the grotto she moves safely, yet as if in a trance, whereas the villagers, whose main motivation is egotistical greed, inevitably stumble and plummet to their deaths. Like them, the traveling painter Vigo (Mathias Wieman) is unable to comprehend Junta, although in his case the lack of comprehension is both literal and metaphorical – she speaks nothing but Italian, and his only language is German. Vigo, with his pragmatic mindset

"Riefenstahl pushed Fanck's techniques to their extreme. The film abounds with shots of mountain crags against a backdrop of drifting clouds, shots of Junta silhouetted against the sky, and quiet, pastoral shots."

David B. Hinton, in: The Films of Leni Riefenstahl

1 Rocking role: Leni Riefenstahl unearths a secret of the ages as Junta the mountain climber.

2 Easy in hard places: The mountain air prompts Junta to go after the man of her dreams.

3 Air head: Vigo (Mathias Wieman) doesn't realize that he has lead the avaricious townspeople straight to the crystal grotto.

4

"With the enthusiasm of a documentary filmmaker, Fanck was intent on capturing uncomprisingly pure images of mountains and athletic feats. Magnificently assisted by the camera team on his quest for the best and clearest angles from which to film, his aim was to transport nature's beauty back to the screen. Riefenstahl attempts nothing of the sort for *The Blue Light*. In fact, her goal is to evoke a sense of beauty within the film that can't be found in reality."

Rainer Rother, in: Leni Riefenstahl. Die Verführung des Talents

4   Queen of the hill: Riefenstahl retains her status as a starlet while claiming her birthright as a great European director.

5   Mince meat or shepherd's pie? Junta's young friend Guzzi (Franz Maldacea) fears the worst when Vigo pays a visit to his mountain home.

unwittingly brings about the end of Junta's magic: after secretly following her to the grotto, he reveals the elusive path to the villagers. Although he loves Junta, he believes the crystals to be a danger as so many have died in their pursuit, and he also knows their material value. When Junta finds the grotto looted and all the crystals stolen, she literally loses her grip on the world and falls to her death.

As is to be expected, the aesthetics of the film emphasize the otherworldly aspects of the plot. Riefenstahl and her cameraman Hans Schneeberger, another veteran of the Fanck films, employed artificial fog that creeps slowly over the mountainsides, an unusual soft focus effect to stylize the spray of a waterfall, drastic black-and-white effects created by means of color filters, and a new infra-red film stock that transformed shots taken in daylight into night-time images. The pictorial compositions borrow heavily from Romantic painting. As for Vigo's arrival in Santa Maria with his silent, unapproachable coachman, the coach door that seems to close by itself, and the innkeeper who appears out of nowhere: all this recalls the German horror films of the silent era, particularly F. W. Murnau's *Nosferatu* (*Nosferatu – Eine Symphonie des Grauens*, 1922).

At the same time, *The Blue Light* also continues seamlessly in the tradition of the classic mountain film: shots of steep ridges and precipices, ominous cloud formations, and back-lit figures dramatize the alpine scenery and its archaic inhabitants.

Above all, though, Leni Riefenstahl's directing debut provided her with a choice lead role. In Fanck's films, Riefenstahl had frequently played second fiddle – especially in the many snowstorm and avalanche scenes, which she had grown heartily tired of. Her role in *The Blue Light* gave her ample opportunity to take center stage as an erotic attraction. Although she is dressed in rags for the entirety of the film, the close-up shots of Junta are classic glamour images. In the scene where she offers her hand-picked berries to the villagers in the inn, the cinematography clearly emphasizes that the younger villagers see a desirable woman, whereas the older villagers seem interested only in the large rock crystal dropped from her basket. Riefenstahl's Junta is a mixture of naivety and self-assurance, a strong woman who successfully thwarts Tonio (Beni Führer), the innkeeper's son, when he tries to rape her, and who very assertively chooses Vigo as the man she wants. She captures the painter's attention by throwing a half-eaten apple at his feet when she sees him in the mountains, and later, as if it was the most natural thing in the world, she makes up his sleeping quarters directly beside her own.

Riefenstahl later claimed that Junta was the best role she ever played, although she wasn't aware of it at the time. She may well have been right. Leni Riefenstahl was undoubtedly a strong artist with plenty of self-confidence – and one can't help feeling that she spent the rest of her long life playing a naive, innocent lass pursued by ignorant scoundrels.

LP

THE MOUNTAIN FILM

Mountain tales were being captured on film in the alpine countries as early as World War I, and Ernst Lubitsch was already parodying alpine tourism in his comedy *Meyer from Berlin* in 1918: protagonist Sally Meyer embarks on his alpine excursion with the mandatory lederhosen and mountaineering rope, but he's more interested in *mons veneris* than Mont Blanc and soon finds himself scrambling after women instead of up alpine peaks.

The mountain film didn't become a genre in its own right, however, until the German geologist Dr. Arnold Fanck ventured out in the 1920s to film his dramas of man and mountain directly on location. His films included *Im Kampf mit dem Berge* (1921), *Peak of Fate* (*Der Berg des Schicksals*, 1923/24), *The Holy Mountain* (*Der heilige Berg*, 1925/26), and *White Hell of Pitz Palu* (*Die weiße Hölle vom Piz Palü*, 1929).

Plot was of secondary importance to Fanck, and he treated the mountains themselves like living creatures. A mountain could not only be beautiful and awe-inspiring, but could also stubbornly deny its climbers the ascent, or take terrible revenge on them with dramatic changes in weather or surprise avalanches. The mountain film dramatizes the struggle of man against nature: only *in extremis* is man forced to reveal his moral strength – or fail. Due to the considerable logistical challenges it posed, the mountain film long remained the domain of specialist filmmakers. For many years, the genre was synonymous with the names of Sepp Allgeier and Hans Schneeberger (cameramen), and Luis Trenker and Leni Riefenstahl (actors).

Luis Trenker, a South Tyrolean, proved to be a worthy successor to his mentor Arnold Fanck with films such as *Der Rebell – Die Feuer rufen* (1932), *The Mountain Calls* (*Der Berg ruft*, 1937), and *Barriera a Settentrione* (1950). In these movies, he displayed a greater talent for dramatic storytelling than Fanck, and he often took the lead role himself. Trenker continued to produce mountain films right into the 1960s. Outside the alpine countries, the genre never gained widespread popularity. Edward Dmytryk's *The Mountain* (1956), a drama of two mismatched brothers, was a Hollywood production and a notable exception.

In 1991, Werner Herzog transported the genre into the present with his film *Scream of Stone (Schrei aus Stein)*, based on an idea by Reinhold Messner about two dueling rock climbers and the (fictitious) first ascent of Cerro Torre in Patagonia. The film focuses primarily on the climbers' efforts at self-promotion, million-dollar deals with multimedia corporations, and the TV coverage of the ascent. Although the cinematography of the race to the peak is spectacular, it lacks the magic of the old mountain films – the mountain has been demystified.

"A summary of the story gives no adequate idea of the beauty of the action and the remarkable camera work, especially in connection with the light effects." *The New York Times*

5

LIBERTY FOR US
À nous la liberté

1931 - FRANCE - 104 MIN. / 83 MIN. (SHORTENED VERSION) - B & W - COMEDY

DIRECTOR RENÉ CLAIR (1898–1981)
SCREENPLAY RENÉ CLAIR DIRECTOR OF PHOTOGRAPHY GEORGES PÉRINAL EDITING RENÉ LE HÉNAFF MUSIC GEORGES AURIC
PRODUCTION FRANK CLIFFORD for SOCIÉTÉ DES FILMS SONORES TOBIS.

STARRING HENRI MARCHAND (Émile), RAYMOND CORDY (Louis), ROLLA FRANCE (Jeanne), PAUL OLLIVIER (Jeanne's uncle), JACQUES SHELLY (Paul), ANDRÉ MICHAUD (Foreman), GERMAINE AUSSEY (Maud, Louis' wife), LÉON LORIN (The deaf old man), WILLIAM BURKE (Former prisoner) VINCENT HYSPA (Elderly speaker).

"You remember me?"

Charles Chaplin was so inspired by René Clair's burlesque satire on modern industrial civilization that he borrowed several ideas from the film for his own *Modern Times* (1936). Nazi Propaganda Minister Joseph Goebbels sensed an opportunity to get one over on the popular Jewish comedian, and he instructed the German company Tobis to take legal action against Chaplin for plagiarism; a French subsidiary of Tobis had produced Clair's film. But Goebbels hadn't reckoned with the reaction of René Clair, who happened to be a big admirer of Chaplin. The Frenchman declared that he felt exceptionally honored to have been copied by Chaplin – from whom, after all, the entire cinematic world had learned. The Germans' legal case crumbled.

À nous la liberté was Clair's second sound film, after *Under the Roofs of Paris* (*Sous les toits de Paris*, 1929/30), and both movies were made using Tobis' innovatory sound system. Nonetheless, the co-founder of French *cinéma pur* maintained his skeptical attitude towards the newfangled talkies. He feared for the pure expressivity of the image, gloomily predicting the decline of this still-youthful medium into a mere offshoot of the theater. Therefore, he used dialog only sparingly, though he was happy to let his protagonists sing.

Clair had always felt that the semantic and rhythmical arrangement of images was more essential to the cinematic medium than any words exchanged by the actors. He had already divided the audience with his innovative treatment of the filmic image in the second film he ever made: *Entr'acte* (1924), an experimental short designed to fill an intermission in Francis Picabia's and Erik Satie's ballet "Relâche." Clair loved to play with levels of meaning, and *À nous la liberté* was no exception in his œuvre. On several occasions, off-screen and on-screen sounds are either mischievously played off against each other or else effectively combined. In one scene, we see a

1 And then there's Maud! Actress Germaine Aussey keeps up with the times as Louis' wife – a woman who'll play around with anything that moves.

2 Doing hard time: Director René Clair creates a factory setting more demeaning than prison – complete with cell block warden.

3 Dinner attire: Inmate Louis (Raymond Cordy) may look like a meat and potatoes kind of guy, but he'll soon cultivate a taste for the finer things in life.

"René Clair's view of the world is not so much that of a moralist, as that of a keen satirist whose smile bares bitterness and regret." *Jean Mitry*

RENÉ CLAIR

René Clair was born in Paris on November 11, 1898. His real name was René-Lucien Chomette. His father owned a soap factory, and it was the family's wish that René should take over the running of the business. Instead he became a journalist, then a film critic, and finally a director and writer. In the early 20s, he also appeared as an actor in two films by Louis Feuillade. From an early age, he loved Chaplin and burlesque comedy, but he also maintained lively contact to the Parisian artistic avant-garde. His first film, *Paris qui dort* (1923/24) was a cinematic homage to his native city. His Surrealistic second work, *Entr'acte* (1924) featured appearances by Francis Picabia, Marcel Duchamp, Man Ray and others. The music was composed by Erik Satie, and Clair collaborated with Picabia on the script. The film was a *succès de scandale*, and René Clair was famous overnight. As in *Under the Roofs of Paris* (*Sous les toits de Paris*, 1929/30), Clair was interested in the lives of the common people in the Parisian *quartiers*. His love of the burlesque form is powerfully evident in all the films of this period.

In 1934, the release of *The Last Billionaire* (*Le dernier milliardaire*, 1934) resulted in a scandal, largely kicked up by French fascists. Clair went to London and made *The Ghost Goes West* (1935) for Alexander Korda. When the war broke out, he accepted an invitation from Hollywood and emigrated to the U.S.A. There he made five films, including *The Flame of New Orleans* (1941), starring Marlene Dietrich, and *I Married a Witch* (1942), starring Veronica Lake. After his return to Paris he had another major success with *Silence is Golden / Man About Town* (*Le Silence est d'or*, 1947). Three further films followed, until *The Gates of Paris* (*Porte des Lilas / Il Quartiere dei lillà*, 1957) cemented his reputation as one of the great poets of the French cinema.

The young directors of the Nouvelle Vague took a radically different view of Clair, perhaps in part because he was the first-ever filmmaker to be admitted to the Académie Française. He died on March 15, 1981, leaving an artistic legacy that comprised 30 films and a substantial literary œuvre.

"A fantastic lightness of touch based on absolute mastery of the cinematic medium with its trompe l'œils and associative possibilities: these were the tools of Clair's trade, his world and the playing field of his poetic realism." *Frankfurter Rundschau*

woman singing at an open window; only when the needle sticks in the groove does it become apparent that she's playing a record in her room.

Although the film has a strictly linear narrative structure, the actual plot is less important to the story than the scenic treatment, which incorporates elements of slapstick, burlesque comedy and carnevalesque reversals. The 'story' amounts to an agglomeration of gags and scenic ideas, linked together to form a kind of bizarre fairy tale told at breakneck speed. Yet this fairy tale casts dark shadows on the real world and embodies an earnest critique of modern civilization.

Émile (Henri Marchand) and Louis (Raymond Cordy) are two drunks who've landed in jail, and now they're thinking about escape. Louis succeeds, largely as a result of his friend's unselfishness, while Louis is caught and has

to serve his time. When he's released, the two buddies meet up once again. Louis' former cellmate is now a rich manufacturer of phonographs, and at first he has no desire to see his former pal again; then he remembers the camaraderie of old and invites Èmile to his splendid villa, where the two men happily celebrate their reunion. When a gang tries to blackmail Louis because they know his true identity, he gives away his brand-new, fully-automated factory to the workers and returns to a life on the road with Émile.

There are two metaphors at the heart of this film. Firstly, the image of the prison, reflected in that of the factory; secondly, the conveyor belt, which signifies the unstoppability of progress. Clair thinks both metaphors through carefully, and the film climaxes in a scene where the uniformed and numbered workers take their lunch from the conveyor belt as if they were in a

3

5

4 Line dancing: René Clair depicts all aspects of modern life as mechanized – whether penal, profitable or pleasurable.

5 Rich with experience: When all is said and done, the penniless Émile (Henri Marchand) and Louis discover that freedom and togetherness are what matter most.

6 Private equity: During his brief stint as factory owner, Louis tries to look out for Émile's welfare.

7 A comedy of aesthetics: Despite its farcical nature, Clair's film draws from the era's art, architecture and design to draw a convincing portrait of modernity.

8 Turning tables: In this early talkie, the audiotrack and visual action bounce off each another for maximum comic impact.

21st-century sushi bar. Émile in particular develops into a comic hero. Wherever he appears, chaos ensues. When he tries to hang himself in his cell, he only succeeds in tearing the bars off the window.

Clair's film is an inquiry into the freedom of the individual in a modern, industrialized society. At the end of the film, the ironies of a thoroughly rationalized world culminate in a utopia that is also an extravagant *reductio ad absurdum*. It is not just traditional bourgeois values that are revealed to be hopelessly hypocritical; functional aesthetic tendencies in art and architecture, highly fashionable at the time, are also subtly lampooned. Essentially, René Clair's movie is a bitterly funny attack on everything that characterized the era in which it was made – and that included the talkies.

SR

6

7

"A mere glance at the woman he loves causes him to miss a beat on the job and triggers a full-scale war against an insatiable conveyer belt. When events spiral out of control – causing images, music and more images to collide into one another – René Clair revels in the chaos as if intoxicated. Suddenly, his camera is everywhere all at once, racing through shots, perspectives and flashing details until the viewer is left utterly lightheaded." *die tageszeitung*

M

M – Eine Stadt sucht einen Mörder

1931 - GERMANY - 117 MIN. / 108 MIN. (RESTORED VERSION) - B & W - THRILLER

DIRECTOR FRITZ LANG (1890–1976)
SCREENPLAY THEA VON HARBOU and FRITZ LANG DIRECTOR OF PHOTOGRAPHY FRITZ ARNO WAGNER
EDITING PAUL FALKENBERG PRODUCTION SEYMOUR NEBENZAHL and ERNST WOLFF for NERO FILM AG.

STARRING PETER LORRE (Hans Beckert, the Murderer), ELLEN WIDMANN (Frau Beckmann),
INGE LANDGUT (Elsie Beckmann), OTTO WERNICKE (Inspector Karl Lohmann),
THEODOR LOOS (Inspector Groeber), GUSTAF GRÜNDGENS ("Schränker," the Safe-Cracker),
FRIEDRICH GNASS (Franz, the Burglar), THEO LINGEN (Bauernfänger, the Con Artist),
RUDOLF BLÜMNER (Beckert's Defender), GEORG JOHN (the Blind Balloon Seller).

"This monster does not have the right to exist. He must be removed, stamped out, exterminated. Without mercy!"

The city's going mad. A harmless old man is being dragged to the police station by a couple of rough workers; just round the corner, an angry mob is jumping on a fare dodger who's being escorted off the bus by a policeman. What's going on? For the last eight months, someone has been murdering children, and the police still have no idea who he is or where he's hiding. The tension is palpable: everyone is a suspect, and the killer has just struck again, after luring little Elsie Beckmann (Inge Landgut) into an open field with a colorful balloon. He even sends an open letter to the press, announcing that he's not finished yet ...

Inspector Lohmann (Otto Wernicke) gathers his colleagues for an emergency meeting. One idea is to check every patient who has come out of psychiatric care over the last few years, and investigations soon lead the police officers to Hans Beckert (Peter Lorre). Beckert is an unobtrusive lodger who likes to take walks in the city, on the lookout for little girls who will follow him on the promise of some candy or a toy.

But the police aren't the only ones looking for the killer. An underworld organization known as "The Ring" also has an interest in tracking him down, as the heavy police presence is driving business to the wall. While the cops are dithering about how to proceed, "Schränker" (Gustaf Gründgens), the infamous safe-cracker – "the best man for the job between Berlin and Frisco" – is holding his own crisis session. Soon, all the beggars and drifters in the city are patrolling every corner and alleyway on the lookout for suspicious characters. Beckert eventually betrays himself with a sign of his pathological compulsiveness – he whistles a particular melody whenever his urge to kill surfaces, and a blind balloon seller (Georg John) identifies him thanks to the haunting tune. Branded with a letter "M" chalked on the back of his coat, the

murderer can no longer elude his pursuers. They corner him in the attic of an office building, and drag him back to their headquarters, where these criminals become his judge and jury.

In *Metropolis* (1926), Fritz Lang had already depicted society – specifically urban society – as a system with strict divisions between the upper and lower classes. That film had shown a privileged, wealthy minority pursuing a life of pleasure in the rooftop gardens of gigantic skyscrapers, while an anonymous mass of laborers languished in bleak, subterranean housing compounds. In *M*, a similar social dichotomy is presented in a more realistic, contemporary setting. The city is no longer a futurist construct, but a modern metropolis with all its familiar trappings – tenement houses, factories and industry, dense urban traffic, splendid shopping boulevards, etc.

"It was just a matter of time before someone recognized that there was an undeniably cinematic story to be told in the much-publicized murder trials of names like Haarmann, Großmann or Kürten. What a boon it is that Fritz Lang was the man who braved the waters of this subject matter; for he possessed both the necessary finesse and skill to tackle something this complex." *Filmwelt*

3

4

1 The murderer in the mirror: Beckert (Peter Lorre) is horrified to discover that he is a marked man.

2 Playmates and playthings: No one knows his toys like a pervert.

3 Supreme court: Hans is put on trial by the people in this signature Lang tableau.

4 The hot lights: The roof of this office building seemed like a good hiding place – until somebody tripped the switch.

– but here, too, there is an 'underworld'. Beneath the visible surface of city life lurk criminal organizations; only this time, they happen to share the authorities' interest in capturing a psychopath on the loose. Lang was so inspired by the notion of criminals hunting a murderer in order to curb un-welcome police activity that he lived in constant fear that someone else would beat him to capturing the idea on film. Like *Metropolis*, *M* presents a situation in which the underworld and the 'overworld' are compelled to reach an agreement.

For this disturbing film, Lang chose a visual language that emphasizes the model character of his societal construct. Again and again, the camera shows us full-screen street maps, ground plans, fingerprints, and even samples of the murderer's handwriting. These 'blueprints' provide novel perspectives on the familiar city, and they are examined meticulously for signs of alien life: Where is the killer hiding? What psychotic traits are expressed in his handwriting? Where is the unique twist in his fingerprint? Fritz Lang's choice of the attic as the disturbed murderer's refuge was no accident: even when

5   Wall to wall terror: A murderer at the mercy of the masses.

6   Slayed in the shade: Despite the round-the-clock criminal investigation, Beckert is always one step

ahead of the law. Inge Landgut as little Elsie Beckmann.

7   Name that tune: A blind balloon vendor (Georg John) identifies the killer.

8   Sign language: Baby-faced Peter Lorre adopted some alarming expressions for this star-making role.

"This film has got plenty of everything that normally rattles the censors from a mile off. Here, the murderer reaches into his pocket, sharpens his knife and is the epitome of sadism. The government is mocked and organized crime is cheered on." *Die Weltbühne*

Beckert's murderous compulsion is repressed, it remains as physical and real as the forgotten junk in the loft. In this sense, there is an analogous relationship between the body of the killer and the architecture of the city.

Beckert's 'judges' are the assembled denizens of the underworld, and when they charge him with his crimes, the truth erupts: in a gripping monolog, he tells of the inner voices that compel him to kill. Among the assembled listeners are some who can identify with the confessions of this tortured soul, and Beckert's 'advocate' (Rudolf Blümner) urges the massed vigilantes to acknowledge the killer's insanity and hand him over to the authorities. Led by the safe-cracker, the angry mob shouts down his plea.

Shaken by economic crises and political unrest, the Weimar Republic could appeal to no values that were universally acknowledged. In this moral vacuum, a promise of resolute action and 'a firm hand' presented a tempting alternative to the protean unpredictability of modern city life. The risk inherent in the freedom of anonymity is that an alienated man can kill without being noticed. Seen from this perspective, *M* is an apt portrayal of German sensibilities on the eve of the Nazis' rise to power. When Beckert is saved from lynching by a last-minute police bust and made to face a proper court of law, Lang's preference for the legal enforcement of justice is unmistakable.

EP

PETER LORRE

Born in Hungary in 1904, Ladislav Loewenstein started an apprenticeship as a bank clerk after graduating from high school, but soon dropped out in favor of an acting career. The "Lorre" part of his pseudonym is a wordplay on "Rolle," the German for "role". After a difficult start, he was offered his first theater roles in Vienna and Zurich, and his first, albeit modest appearance on film was in *The Woman Who Disappeared* (*Die Verschwundene Frau*, 1928/29).

Lorre's role as the child murderer Hans Beckert in Fritz Lang's *M* (1931) made him an overnight sensation. Sadly, he was denied a sustained career in German film. Lorre emigrated to the U.S. following periods of exile in Austria, France and Britain, where he played a number of major parts (such as in Alfred Hitchcock's *The Man Who Knew Too Much* in 1934.

In Hollywood, Lorre was predominantly typecast as a psychotic character, a part his diminutive physique, child-like face, and disproportionately large eyes seemed to cut him out for. Mostly playing supporting roles, Lorre brought his unique flair to many movie classics, including *The Maltese Falcon* (1941), *Arsenic and Old Lace* (1942/44), and *Casablanca* (1942). As Agent "Mr. Moto" he even had his own series of B-flicks (1937–1939).

Dissatisfied with the course of his career – Lorre's ambitions lay in serious drama – he returned to Germany in 1949, where he wrote and directed *The Lost One* (*Der Verlorene*, 1950/51), a passionate and critical examination of the Nazi period in which he also played the lead role. The film did not meet with the acclaim Lorre expected, and he returned to the U.S., where he starred in numerous film and television productions until his death in 1964.

8

1931 - USA - 75 MIN. - B & W - HORROR MOVIE

DIRECTOR TOD BROWNING (1882–1962)
SCREENPLAY GARRETT FORT, based on the novel of the same name by BRAM STOKER and the play of the same name by
HAMILTON DEANE and JOHN L. BALDERSTON DIRECTOR OF PHOTOGRAPHY KARL FREUND EDITING MILTON CARRUTH, MAURICE PIVAR
MUSIC PETER ILJITSCH TSCHAIKOWSKI, RICHARD WAGNER, FRANZ SCHUBERT PRODUCTION CARL LAEMMLE JR.,
TOD BROWNING for UNIVERSAL PICTURES.

STARRING BELA LUGOSI (Count Dracula), HELEN CHANDLER (Mina Seward), DAVID MANNERS (John Harker),
EDWARD VAN SLOAN (Prof. Abraham Van Helsing), DWIGHT FRYE (Renfield), HERBERT BUNSTON (Dr. Jack Seward),
FRANCES DADE (Lucy Weston), JOAN STANDING (Briggs), CHARLES K. GERRARD (Martin).

"I never drink ... wine."

When one thinks of the earliest vampire movies, two films immediately come to mind: Friedrich Wilhelm Murnau's *Nosferatu – eine Symphonie des Grauens* from 1922, and of course *Dracula* by Tod Browning, which was cobbled together ten years later in the workshops at Universal. Murnau's silent Expresssionist masterpiece is a 'classic text' that marked the birth of the genre yet produced no real successors (other than Werner Herzog's 1978 remake, *Nosferatu – Phantom der Nacht*). *Dracula*, on the other hand, launched an entire series including films like Lambert Hillyer's *Dracula's Daughter* (1936), in which a lady vampire struts her stuff, and Robert Siodmak's *Son of Dracula* (1943). Artistically, Tod Browning's vampire is a far less ambitious creation than Murnau's, yet he practically created the blueprint for the character of the Gentleman Vampire. In his performance as the Transylvanian aristocrat, Hungarian-born Bela Lugosi combined patrician charm with a diabolical aura. Count Dracula was *sexy*, and the peculiar fascination of the figure was fed by the audience's yearning for the exotic, and by the sexual repression of the times. The act of bloodsucking was a transparent metaphor.

The film portrays the upper-middle-class milieu of 1920s London as progressive and enlightened – in stark contrast to the benighted peasantry in the distant mountains of Romania. Renfield (Dwight Frye), an estate agent, has come to Transylvania to sell a house in London to a certain Count Dracula. When the 'natives' tell him dark tales about vampires, he laughs them off as primitive superstition – and soon suffers the consequences. Turned into a vampire by Dracula, he returns to London as his slave, while the Count moves in to Carfax Abbey, opposite the sanatorium run by Dr. Seward (Herbert Bunston). The cultivated Count is very interested in Seward's daughter Mina (Helen Chandler) and her friend Lucy (Frances Dade). Lucy is his first victim, and from then on she glides through the night as one of the pallid undead. Mina, who is engaged to John Harker, also receive a nocturnal visit from Dracula, but she is not completely 'vampirised.' Physician and scientist Abraham Van Helsing (Edward Van Sloan) is a vampire specialist, and he reveals Dracula's true identity and attempts to protect Mina. Dracula takes Mina with him to Carfax Abbey, where Van Helsing manages to drive a stake through his heart. Mina is saved. The final scene shows her

and her fiancé ascending a flight of stairs, arm in arm, with nothing standing in the way of their marriage.

Universal had bought the rights to Bram Stoker's novel from his widow, Florence. The Victorian sexual morality of the book is carried over into the film adaptation of 1931: the woman's desires are wakened by vampirism, and until these have been eradicated, she is not fit for marriage. Men's fear of emancipated women seems to be very much part of the Dracula myth. As an aristocrat and an Eastern European, the bloodsucking Count is exotic in more ways than one; and as an object of female desire, he also constitutes a threat to bourgeois masculinity, here embodied by Mina's father and fiancé. Van Helsing appears as the savior, and as Dracula's counterpart and nemesis: "Perhaps I am in a position to prove that what was very recently called 'su-

perstition' may today or tomorrow be shown to be scientific truth." Thus, the real battle for the woman takes place between the vampire and the scientist. Although Mina's feelings appear moderate, she too has fallen under Dracula's spell, which has awakened her sexual desires. Admittedly, none of this is actually *shown* in this decidedly wordy film. Only in later films, beginning with the Hammer Horrors of the 50s, was the actual act of vampirism salaciously depicted. Tod Browning's *Dracula* was the very first vampire film of the sound era, and though its horror elements may seem naive or wooden today, they too must have touched a nerve in their time. In the end, traditional values triumph – but the movie's success had at least as much to do with the fact that audiences were as fascinated by illicit desire as were the Count's transported victims. KK

2

3

5

4

1   What a tangled web we weave: Bela Lugosi looks forward to a bite of dinner by candlelight as Tod Browning's *Dracula*.

2   Make a wish: Dracula always has his cake and eats it too.

3   Sweet dreams are made of these: Pine and oak and sycamore trees.

4   Stairwell to hell: John Harker (David Manners) will have to defeat the vampire king if he intends on saving his fiancée's soul.

5   Transylvanian triage: Having determined which of his prey will most benefit from an eternity of twisted immortality, Dracula moves in for the kill.

"Certainly it is Lugosi's performance and the cinematography of Karl Freund that make Tod Browning's film such an influential Hollywood picture." *Chicago Sun-Times*

BELA LUGOSI (1882–1956)

At the grave of Bela Lugosi, who had himself buried in his Dracula costume, Peter Lorre is alleged to have said: "Wouldn't it be better to put a stake through his heart – just to be on the safe side?" History books don't say whether Lugosi ever rose from the grave, yet he has achieved a kind of immortality. His embodiment of Count Dracula as an aristocratic gentleman-vampire made him world-famous, and the role was to haunt him all his life.

He was born in 1882, as Béla Ferenc Dezsö Blaskó, in Lugos/Lugoj, at that time Hungarian and now part of Romania. He later named himself after his home town. As a young theater actor, he spent years treading the boards in various parts of the Austro-Hungarian Empire. After the Empire collapsed, he moved to Berlin, where he appeared in Murnau's *Der Januskopf* (1920), among other films. In 1921, he continued his stage and film career in the U.S., though he spoke little English at first. Six years later, the exotic Hungarian was given the role of his life: as Dracula in the Broadway play of the same name by Hamilton Deane and John L. Balderston. According to the actress Caroll Borland, he was "pure sex" on stage; for the film adaptation directed by Tod Browning (*Dracula*, 1931), however, he was not first choice. It was only the death of his rival for the role, Lon Chaney Sr., that cleared the path for his breathtaking international career. Until his star began to wane in the 1940s, Bela Lugosi had a string of successes, including *White Zombie* (1932) directed by Victor Halperin, and the Edgar Allan Poe adaptation *The Raven* (1935), directed by Lew Landers. In 1931, he had generously allowed his rival Boris Karloff to take over the role of the monster in *Frankenstein*, directed by James Whale; but in *Abbott & Costello Meet Frankenstein* (1948), he played Count Dracula one last time. From then on, he was ever more frequently unemployed, began to drink and developed a morphine addiction. In his penultimate film, Reginald Le Borg's *The Black Sleep* (1956), Lugosi's character was silent, because the actor was no longer capable of remembering his lines. His last appearance before a film camera was a few days' shooting for *Plan 9 from Outer Space* (1956/59), and the scenes featuring Lugosi were actually used. He died on August 16, 1956.

THE THREEPENNY OPERA
Die 3-Groschen-Oper

1931 - GERMANY - 110 MIN. - B & W - MUSIC FILM, DRAMA

DIRECTOR G. W. PABST (1885–1967)
SCREENPLAY LEO LANIA, LADISLAUS VAJDA, BÉLA BALÁZS, based on the stage musical *DIE DREIGROSCHENOPER*
by BERTOLT BRECHT and KURT WEILL (Music) DIRECTOR OF PHOTOGRAPHY FRITZ ARNO WAGNER EDITING HANS OSER
MUSIC KURT WEILL, BERTOLT BRECHT (Lyrics) PRODUCTION SEYMOUR NEBENZAHL, GUS SCHLESINGER, GUIDO BAGIER
for TONBILD-SYNDIKAT AG – TOBIS, WARNER BROS. PICTURES GMBH, NERO-FILM AG.

STARRING RUDOLF FORSTER (Mackie Messer), CAROLA NEHER (Polly Peachum), REINHOLD SCHÜNZEL (Tiger-Brown),
FRITZ RASP (Peachum), VALESKA GERT (Mrs. Peachum), LOTTE LENYA (Jenny), HERMANN THIMIG (Vicar),
ERNST BUSCH (Street Singer), VLADIMIR SOKOLOFF (Smith), PAUL KEMP (Gang Member), HERBERT GRÜNBAUM (Filch),
SYLVIA TORFF (Bordello Madam), GUSTAV PÜTTJER (Gang Member).

"In today's world of law and order, who would be dumb enough to enter a life of crime?"

It's somehow ironic that Bertolt Brecht's *Threepenny Opera* about cops, robbers and the struggle for survival in turn-of-the-century London is his only work that was popular with mainstream audiences. Undeniably, much of the piece's success must be attributed to Kurt Weill's catchy tunes written for the characters Mackie Messer and Jenny Diver, which have been interpreted countless times by recording artists as different as Ute Lemper and Robbie Williams. But the real aim of Brecht's *Lehrstück* – a combination of dime novel, street ballads and a didactic critique of capitalism – was to enlighten the masses about the questionable nature of the dominant economic system.

Brecht apparently began to have misgivings about the play shortly after it premiered to enthusiastic crowds in 1928. By the time the show was picked up for a cinematic adaptation three years later, the author had reworked his denouncement of capitalism along clearer communist lines. When producer Seymour Nebenzahl, co-writer Béla Balázs and director Georg Wilhelm Pabst all surfaced as staunch opponents of his controversial amendments to the script, Brecht unsuccessfully sued the Nero production company for tampering with intellectual property – despite the fact that the film largely adhered to his stage original. As it turned out, however, the finished product did indeed paint a damning and cynical picture of the fraternization among the authorities, the underworld and the economy.

The Threepenny Opera disproves the assumption that early 'talkies' were eternal victims of static staging and labored editing. Here, the camera

1   Penny for your thoughts: After seeing to Mackie   2   Derelicts on parade: London's most destitute   3   Dressed in pearly white: Mackie (Rudolf Forster)
    Messer's arrest, fickle Jenny Diver (Lotte Lenya)   prepare to crash the coronation.   and Polly (Carola Neher) are pronounced man and
    plans his escape.   wife. Hermann Thimig as the vicar (right).

pans, swoops, glides forward and inches at will, shifting gracefully between details and the big picture. Major visual motifs include staircases, ladders and landings. Indeed, the film thoroughly examines the relationship of *high* and *low*, both spatially and metaphorically: gangsters and policemen, upstanding citizens and an army of beggars are all interconnected to the point of being inseparable. Mackie Messer, the character who effortlessly moves between these worlds, is representative of the entanglements among them. Mackie is as friendly with the chief of police (Reinhold Schünzel) as he is with a pack of thieves. He feels just as at home in expensive apartments as he

does loitering by the wharf with a street singer. Actor Rudolf Forster's portrayal of the character reveals him to be a dandy, Casanova and *bon vivant* rolled into one and thus attests to how crime and the good life coalesce in a capitalist society.

Both the film's realistic backdrop of London's docklands district at the turn of century and the naturalistic acting received harsh criticism – even though cast members Ernst Busch, Carola Neher and Lotte Lenya had created their roles during the original stage production at the Theater am Schiffbauerdamm. Brecht's intention was actually to deconstruct the illusionary

5

4   When that shark bites: The street singer's (Ernst
    Busch) macabre tale of scarlet billows and oozin'
    bodies falls on deaf ears.

5   Oh, the line forms on the right: London lowlifes
    climb their way to the top up this film's countless
    ladders, stairs and risers.

**BERTOLT BRECHT
AND THE CINEMA**

Bertolt Brecht rose to fame as one of the most significant German playwrights and poets of the 20th century. Less known are his cinematic endeavors, which amount to more than just the recordings of his stage productions. The 1931 motion picture adaptation of his revolutionary musical, *The Threepenny Opera (Die 3-Groschen-Oper)*, was one of Brecht's first collaborations with the movie industry. Unfortunately, Brecht believed that the film version of his story had been watered down by capitalist production values. An intellectual property lawsuit ensued, with Brecht eventually losing and responding by writing another *Lehrstück* about the trial entitled *The Threepenny Lawsuit (Der Dreigroschenprozess)*. This, in turn, inspired the idea for his next film in support of communism, *Kuhle Wampe oder Wem gehört die Welt?* (1932) (which can be roughly translated as "To Whom Does the World Belong?"). This German-produced piece based its arguments on the effects of unemployment and economic depression in the Weimar Republic.

During his years of exile in the United States, Brecht wrote the screenplay for Fritz Lang's anti-Nazi film *Hangmen Also Die!* (1942/43) about the Heydrich assassination and the massacre at Lidice. Not surprisingly, this production was also plagued by internal strife between writer and director.

6 Three coins in a fountain: Mackie has no qualms about letting other women spice up his relationship with future wife Polly Peachum (left).

7 Johnny on the spot: Mackie meets Jenny Diver (right) while patronizing a troop of working girls.

> "Turn of the century London unfolds as a meticulously constructed wharf district teeming with period costumes. It is a truly historic world yet one that constantly undermines all the things that worked on the Brechtian stage. The realistic performances utterly disqualify the leitmotifs that were designed to expose the artifice of realism." *Frankfurter Zeitung*

mechanisms of bourgeois escapist theater, not to submerge the story in a dreamlike studio atmosphere as this film does. Director Georg Wilhelm Pabst's smooth mise-en-scène was also seen as contributing to the piece's illusionist feel. Nonetheless, Pabst does succeed in creating a world in which a procession of beggars can cross paths with the Queen for one brief, nightmarish moment. It is a world in which Mackie, intoxicated by non-stop media attention from wanted posters and his "Mack the Knife" theme song, twirls like a twinkle-toes from one woman to the next. In the course of the film,

however, we become aware that this is a realm where the women call the shots: Polly Peachum (Carola Neher) goes from being a sweet young thing to running a bank; her mother Mrs. Peachum (Valeska Gert) calls the shots in the beggars' empire; and Jenny Diver (Lotte Lenya), the prostitute responsible for Mackie's arrest, later plays an instrumental role in his escape. And so, in the face of critical onslaught, Pabst did in fact manage to supply Brecht's work with a vision all his own.

MH

FRANKENSTEIN

1931 - USA - 71 MIN. - B & W - HORROR MOVIE

DIRECTOR JAMES WHALE (1889–1957)
SCREENPLAY JOHN L. BALDERSTON, FRANCIS EDWARD FARAGOH, GARRETT FORT, based on the novel
FRANKENSTEIN OR THE MODERN PROMETHEUS by MARY WOLLSTONECRAFT SHELLEY and the play
FRANKENSTEIN: AN ADVENTURE IN THE MACABRE by PEGGY WEBLING **DIRECTOR OF PHOTOGRAPHY** ARTHUR EDESON
EDITING CLARENCE KOLSTER **MUSIC** DAVID BROEKMAN, BERNHARD KAUN **PRODUCTION** CARL LAEMMLE JR. for
UNIVERSAL PICTURES.

STARRING COLIN CLIVE (Doctor Henry Frankenstein), MAE CLARKE (Elizabeth), JOHN BOLES (Victor Moritz),
BORIS KARLOFF (Frankenstein's Monster), EDWARD VAN SLOAN (Doctor Waldman),
FREDERICK KERR (Baron Frankenstein), DWIGHT FRYE (Fritz), MARILYN HARRIS (Maria),
LIONEL BELMORE (Herr Vogel), MICHAEL MARK (Ludwig).

"Look! It's moving!"

Life after death often begins after dark. No-one knows this better than Dr. Henry Frankenstein (Colin Clive) and his hunchbacked servant Fritz (Dwight Frye), who spend the wee small hours either digging up corpses or chopping the limbs off men dangling from the gallows. Yet their looting has a purpose and won't stop until the scientist and his assistant have unearthed a suitable brain. When Fritz finds one preserved in formaldehyde at the local university, the real experiment commences.

The catch however is that Henry's fiancée Elizabeth (Mae Clarke) and his close friend Victor Moritz (John Boles) have voiced their concerns about the twosome's mysterious midnight exploits and sought out some professional advice. As Frankenstein's former mentor Dr. Waldman (Edward Van Sloan) informs them, the dabblings in chemical galvanism and electro-biology can only point to one thing: the creation of new human life by means of reanimation. And so it follows that Elizabeth, Victor, and Waldman arrive back at Henry's laboratory just in time to see a threaded patchwork of appendages

hoisted up on a gigantic apparatus and then shocked into life. It's a miracle and a catastrophe in one; for unbeknownst to Dr. Frankenstein, his creature has been supplied with a criminal mind. Needless to say, a number of innocent people are killed and a great many more left incapacitated before a mob of townsfolk finally back Frankenstein's monster (Boris Karloff) into a windmill and burn him to a crisp ...

The mad scientist, the quintessential monster – complete with bolted neck, rectangular skull, a poorly tailored coat and elevator shoes – and a loyal assistant who could pass for Quasimodo's twin – these vivid images are what most of the countless screen adaptations have in common. Is it any wonder that Frankenstein's monster is one of the silver screen's most readily recognizable creations?

The original novel, *Frankenstein or The Modern Prometheus*, was written by Mary Wollstonecraft Shelley in 1818. As one might gather from the title, Shelley drew from a wide range of narrative styles and myths – including

1   New lease on life: Actor Boris Karloff in the role that jumpstarted his career.

2   On golden pond: It's never too late to discover the beauty of friendship.

3   Keeping a low profile: Tired of standing out, the monster tries to blend in with the scenery.

4   Recycling bin: Today is pickup day.

MAD SCIENTIST

Although he may not have been the first character ever to fit the bill, Henry Frankenstein epitomizes what it means to be a mad scientist. As mainstream Hollywood revels in reminding us, a scientist of this nature is an obsessive compulsive creature, as wicked as he is wacko, partial to wearing lab coats, and generally an adult white male. Deviations from the mold like *Lady Frankenstein* (1971), *Black Frankenstein* (1973) or the mischievous children seen in *Andy Warhol's Frankenstein / Flesh for Frankenstein* (1973) remain the infrequent exception to the rule.

Around 1945, mad scientists became a popular metaphor at the movies for the side effects of progress or what critics might call 'research gone wrong': cooped up in a private universe of chemicals, generators, and who knows what else, he was prone to outbursts of diabolical laughter and playing God if left alone for too long.

By the 60s, however, Hollywood had taken to showing his lighter side. No actor in the business did a better job of accommodating this than comedian Jerry Lewis, who turned the Jekyll and Hyde story on its head in *The Nutty Professor* (1963). Let's just say that mad scientists and dorks have been inseparable ever since.

those of Prometheus, Faust, and Lucifer – to weave her own. But rather than concerning itself with the story's literary origins and inspirations, the movie focuses on its more 'scientific' aspects via anatomic drawings, skull collections, skeletons and organs preserved in formaldehyde. Wielding these artifacts of vintage horror is none other than Dr. Frankenstein himself, an off-his-rocker Einstein who plays God and is punished for his hubris.

It is a character we are all familiar with, though by no means the first of his kind to appear in motion pictures. In fact, to a great extent both the tragic hero and the decaying guard tower he uses to conduct his experiments read like a tribute to the silent era: set pieces with slanted walls evoke images of bygone expressionistic shadow lands, and all the gadgets in Frankenstein's laboratory were taken straight from those created for Rot-

"Imagine the monster with black eyes, heavy eyelids, a square head, huge feet that are covered with matting, long arms protruding from the leeves of a coat, walking like an automaton ..." *The New York Times*

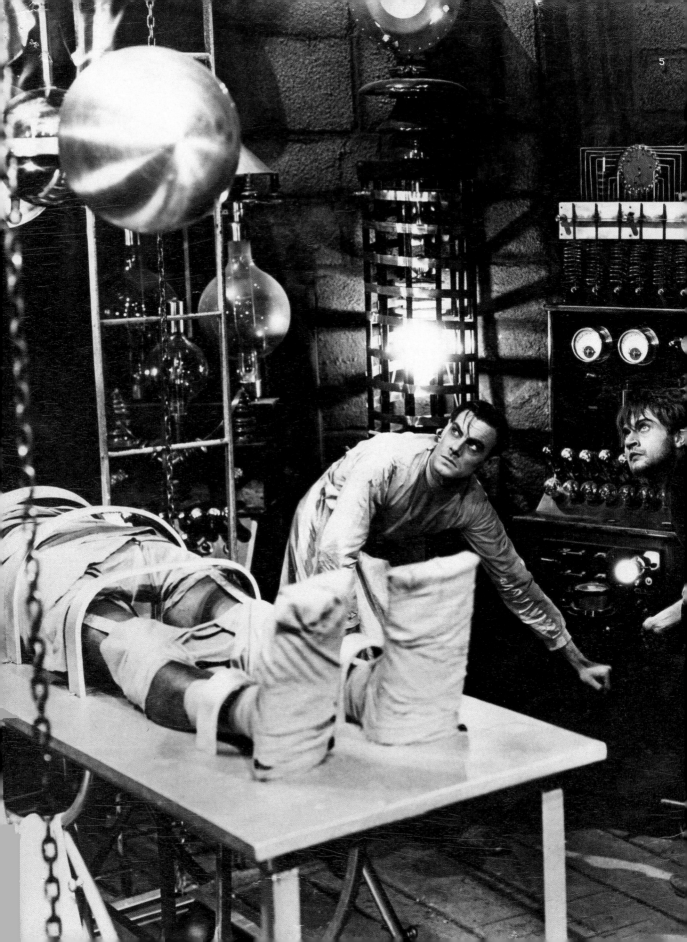

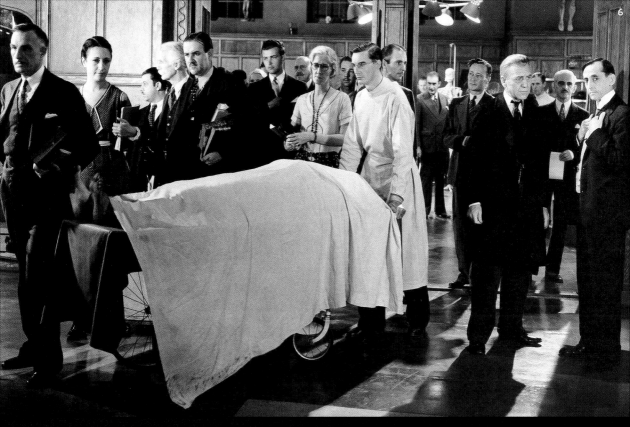

5   It's alive: Dr. Henry Frankenstein (Colin Clive) becomes a daddy.

6   Witch doctor: Henry Frankenstein learns all he needs to know about medicine as a student of Dr. Waldman (Edward Van Sloan).

7   Lights, camera, action: The doctor's groupies arrive in time to witness the scientific breakthrough of the century.

"Feminine fans seem to get some sort of emotional kick out of this sublimation of the bedtime ghost story done with all the literalness of the camera." *Variety*

wang in Fritz Lang's *Metropolis* (1926). As both inventors discover, only diabolical creatures can be begot in such a Satan's bed. Frankenstein climaxes with horror in a poignant and chilling scene lifted from the pages of Shelley's novel when Boris Karloff reveals that the emotions at work in the monster are none other than those that fuel Henry's subconscious.

This connection is a constant reminder of the scientist's own internal conflict: by marrying Elizabeth and upholding the bourgeois conventions his aristocratic father (Frederick Kerr) stands for, Henry would stifle his scientific passion. And so the monster breaks out of captivity, wounding both bride and groom in a fit of rage. Nonetheless, the extent and consequences of this attack are ultimately left up to the audience's imagination.

PLB

BERLIN ALEXANDERPLATZ
Berlin Alexanderplatz

1931 - GERMANY - 88 MIN. - B & W - LITERARY ADAPTATION, DRAMA

DIRECTOR PIEL JUTZI [= PHIL JUTZI] (1896–1946)

SCREENPLAY ALFRED DÖBLIN, HANS WILHELM, KARL HEINZ MARTIN, based on the novel of the same name by ALFRED DÖBLIN DIRECTORS OF PHOTOGRAPHY ERICH GIESE, NIKOLAUS FARKAS EDITING GÉZA POLLATSCHEK MUSIC ALLAN GRAY, ARTUR GUTTMANN PRODUCTION ARNOLD PRESSBURGER for ALLIANZ-TONFILM.

STARRING HEINRICH GEORGE (Franz Biberkopf), MARIA BARD (Cilly), BERNHARD MINETTI (Reinhold), GERHARD BIENERT (Karl), MARGARETE SCHLEGEL (Mieze), PAUL WESTERMEIER (Henschke), ALBERT FLORATH (Pums), HANS DEPPE (Guest at Henschke's), KÄTHE HAACK (Nurse Paula), JULIUS FALKENSTEIN (Thief).

"First rule in life: Don't let the bastards grind you down. Am I right or am I right?"

Construction work on the subway system has torn a deep hole in the heart of Berlin. The city's vast central square, Alexanderplatz, is surrounded with wooden hoardings, and these in turn are covered with advertising posters. Franz Biberkopf (Heinrich George) has taken up position here to sell neckties to passers-by. "A gent takes pride in his elegant appearance, so why shouldn't a working man? Get your neckties here!" This massive bull-like man has spent the last four years in the city's Tegel Prison, serving time for manslaughter. Or rather, womanslaughter, for the victim was his girlfriend. Now he's out; a reformed man, determined to make his way in the world using brains instead of brawn. A smart Berliner with a good loud voice and plenty of chutzpah should have no trouble making a living in his vibrant native city. Hence the neckties.

But life is hard for people like him: once a villain, always a villain. Franz Biberkopf is naive, stubborn, and he likes a drink, and soon he's on the road to ruin before he knows what hit him. His 'buddy' Reinhold (Bernhard Minetti), the boss of a small criminal gang, takes advantage of Franz's innocence and exploits him mercilessly. First Franz forfeits an arm in the course of a heist, then he loses faith in goodness, and finally he waves goodbye to his new girlfriend Mieze (Margarete Schlegel). Eventually, he ends up back on Alexanderplatz, trying to start all over again.

Adaptations of great novels tend to disappoint those who expect a movie to be a mere visual reproduction of the book, as if a literary artwork could be mapped onto another medium, one-to-one. Certainly, the critics of the day complained that Piel Jutzi's film had failed to do justice to Alfred Döblin's complex literary masterpiece, a depiction and analysis of the nature of modern urban existence. As Kurt Pinthus saw it in the evening paper, the *8 Uhr-Abendblatt*, the film had failed to deliver "either an overview or an x-ray image of the streets, classes, people and dwelling-places of Berlin." Instead, the critics saw only the sad story of a poor dumb guy trying and failing to find his feet – and trying again nonetheless. To them, the film's message was embodied in its apparently simple ending: success in life depends neither on luck nor on muscle, but on a good heart. The producer Arnold Pressburger had, however, made the shrewd decision to employ the novelist to write the script. Döblin had been uninterested in silent movies because of their dependence on the purely visual, but he was intrigued by the new possibilities of sound film. Indeed, this movie takes the sounds and languages of

"A pleasant surprise comes halfway through the film when Margarete Schlegel sings along to a hurdy-gurdy in a perky yet grating voice that is all the while warm and loving. It's simply marvelous! It may not have a thing in the world to do with Döblin's glorious novel, but it is very much in tune with its spirit and the way Berlin really is." *Die Welt am Montag*

the city at least as seriously as the images. Scattered impressions of Alexanderplatz – construction workers, a shoeshine man, a war veteran with a wooden leg – are linked on the soundtrack by Biberkopf's raucous sales pitch and the bells of passing streetcars. In the German original, the distinctive Berlin dialect adds depth and color to the working-class milieu with its smoky pubs and dancehalls. And now and again, we hear a song rendered by some buskers on the street, or by Biberkopf himself when a couple of beers have warmed his heart and loosened his inhibitions.

The strapping Heinrich George was an excellent choice for the lead role. His Biberkopf is an active figure, less helplessly subject to the whims of fate than the protagonist of Döblin's novel; for movies, unlike works of literature, do require characters that people can identify with. Döblin and his co-authors also quite consciously gave the film a slightly more optimistic ending, provoking intellectual critics to accuse the production company of pandering to moviegoers' tastes. Even in the early 30s, it seems, the German critical intelligentsia could not approve of a film that took an interest in attracting "the masses."

1   And then there was light: Portly Franz Biberkopf (Heinrich George) discovers magic with Cilly (Maria Bard) while strolling along the streets of Berlin.

2   Peddling to the public: Piel Jutzi, director of *Mutter Krausens Fahrt ins Glück* (Mother Krause's Journey to Happiness, 1929), specialized in the study of working class milieus.

3   Down by love: Biberkopf takes out his aggression on those who care about him most. Margarete Schlegel as Mieze.

3

HEINRICH GEORGE
(1893–1946)

The great Heinrich George once described his acting technique as "controlled trance." There are moments in *Berlin Alexanderplatz* (1931) when this self-induced rapture acquires a positively uncanny quality. Take the sequence at the beginning: fresh out of jail and overwhelmed by the city traffic, he eventually takes refuge in the entrance to a tenement house, stammering, "I don't know my way round here any more!" Then there's the scene when he goes berserk with rage and grief because he wrongly suspects that his girl's been cheating on him … Heinrich George had an enormous physical presence, but there was much more to his acting than that. What made him special was his ability to open up cracks in the armor of his powerful physicality, revealing glimmers of fear, despair and childlike helplessness.

In the years of the Weimar Republic and the Nazi dictatorship that followed, Heinrich George was one of the most highly-acclaimed actors in Germany. Born in Stettin (now Szczecin, Poland) in 1893, he was already working as a stage actor while still in his teens. After WW I, he had engagements at theaters in Dresden and Frankfurt, was cast in productions by Max Reinhardt, and worked for Erwin Piscator at the Volksbühne in Berlin. Movie roles accompanied his ongoing work in the theater. In the 20s alone, he appeared in more than 40 films – for example, as Grot the foreman in Fritz Lang's *Metropolis* (1926).

George was for some time an active supporter of the Communist Party. After Hitler seized power, however, he allowed himself to be exploited by the National Socialists – without ever becoming a Nazi Party member. He was appointed artistic director at the Schiller Theater in Berlin and performed major roles in the most important propaganda films: *Hitler Youth Quex / Our Flags Lead Us Forward* (*Hitlerjunge Quex – Ein Film vom Opfergeist der deutschen Jugend*, 1933), *Jew Süss* (*Jud Süss*, 1940), and *Kolberg* (1943–1945). His greatest success was probably his performance in the title role of *The Stationmaster* (*Der Postmeister*, 1940), a film based on the novella of the same name by Alexander Pushkin. At the end of the war, Heinrich George was interned by Soviet intelligence; and in 1946, he died in Sachsenhausen internment camp as a result of the terrible conditions there. His son Götz – now himself one of the major actors in Germany – worked tirelessly to correct the widespread impression that his father had been a 'Nazi artist.' In 1998, Heinrich George was officially rehabilitated in Russia, and his arrest, as "a creative artist in the service of Fascism," was declared unfounded.

"Replete with beautiful details, inspired ideas and carefully nuanced performances. But ultimately, it is an aimless film. It makes a start in the right direction but stops in its tracks, allowing Biberkopf to sing a few ditties instead." *Berliner Börsen-Courier*

4

4   Making ends meat: Cilly and Franz enter each
    others' hearts via their stomachs. In 1979/80,
    director Rainer Werner Fassbinder also tackled

Döblin's epic novel in a fourteen-part television
miniseries.

5   Arrested development: Ex-con Biberkopf has diffi-
    culty reentering society.

Almost 75 years later, though, attitudes to the film have changed. *Berlin Alexanderplatz* now looks like a fascinating document of its time: firstly, for the way it exemplifies the epochal transition from silence to sound, and secondly, as a record of life in the German capital in the years before the Nazis seized power. However justified some of the criticisms may be, and the film does serve up a few clichés, *Berlin Alexanderplatz* succeeds in giving a strong impression of how people lived in Berlin, what they dreamt of, what they were striving for. And in so doing it also provides a memorable portrait of the city as it was.

At certain moments, the camera departs from the storyline and acquires a curious independence – drifting away from Franz and Mieze, for instance, to take a look out the window while their affectionate banter continues unabated on the soundtrack. What the camera sees is this: a woman on a balcony brushing a jacket; then the façade of the tenement building; and finally the anonymous passers-by and the horse-drawn traffic on the streets. These restrained, unspectacular sequences engender a feeling for the sheer size of the city, and they remind us, ominously, that the story of Franz Biberkopf is the story of one man among millions.   NM

TROUBLE IN PARADISE

1932 - USA - 83 MIN. - B & W - COMEDY

DIRECTOR ERNST LUBITSCH (1892–1947)
SCREENPLAY GROVER JONES, SAMSON RAPHAELSON, based on the play *THE HONEST FINDER* by ALADAR LASZLO
DIRECTOR OF PHOTOGRAPHY VICTOR MILNER MUSIC W. FRANKE HARLING PRODUCTION ERNST LUBITSCH for PARAMOUNT PUBLIX CORPORATION.

STARRING MIRIAM HOPKINS (Lily Vautier), HERBERT MARSHALL (Gaston Monescu a. k. a. La Valle),
KAY FRANCIS (Mariette Colet), CHARLES RUGGLES (The Major), EDWARD EVERETT HORTON (François Filiba),
C. AUBREY SMITH (Adolph Giron), ROBERT GREIG (Jacques), GEORGE HUMBERT (Waiter),
ROLFE SEDAN (Purse Salesman), LUIS ALBERNI (Furious Opera Fan).

"And let me say this with love in my heart: Countess, you are a thief!"

The true test of an on-screen thief is whether or not his crimes can go unspotted by the censors. Gaston Monescu (Herbert Marshall) and Lily Vautier (Miriam Hopkins) are more than up for the challenge. Posing as aristocrats – he as a baron, she as a countess – the pair sit down to a meal under false pretenses at a Venice hotel. After keeping up the charade through the *hors d'œuvres*, they proceed to eat each other alive during the main course. Between bites, Lily suggests that the baron is a pilfering impostor who's pinched the wallet of an unsuspecting hotel guest. "Let me say this with love in my heart," Gaston replies, "Countess, you are a thief!" Clearly, it's a respectable criminal's business to know when a brush against the side is more than just a friendly tickle. And unbeknownst to the viewer, both of these characters have been putting their hands where they oughtn't. Things get even more physical as Gaston shakes Lily by the shoulders until the wallet he had stolen fair and square falls from her dress. Dinner continues with Gaston producing a broach he lifted off of Lily, who offers him his pocket watch back in exchange.

Honor among thieves quickly heats up to intimacy: no sooner has Gaston produced Lily's garter and asked if he might keep it, than she's nestling on her new darling's lap. Cross-fades and loving embraces. Gaston and Lily are officially a couple.

During Ernst Lubitsch's own lifetime, posters for his movies won over audiences by referring to him as "the man with the golden touch." But what exactly was this supposed to mean? According to Billy Wilder, who worked as a writer on the Lubitsch films *Bluebeard's Eighth Wife* (1938) and *Ninotchka* (1939), his idol's genius was essentially an "elegance of spirit," or more specifically, the "utter originality with which he approached any given scene." Wilder maintained that part of the Lubitsch secret lay in his ability to seduce the viewer into believing that they were in on something together: "He'd never provide you with classic equations like 2+2=4, but rather throw you a 1+3 and let you do the math. That was the whole fun of it."

Revealing components of the plot implicitly rather than explicitly was one of the many ways Lubitsch engaged his audience. When Gaston, for ex-

ample, lands a job as personal assistant to dowager Mariette Colet (Kay Francis), heiress to a perfume company worth millions, little must be said for us to realize the obvious: she wants to key into her new employee's heart, whereas he'd satisfy himself with the combination to her safe. Clocks appear in a series of cross-fades, which denote the passage of time as Gaston and Mariette spend their first night together. Isolated words and sounds flutter in from off screen. Although the little that we see of their rendezvous is masked by buckets of champagne and ticking clock-hands, it is still enough to inform us that Gaston has been unfaithful to his Lily.

Throughout the film, *Trouble in Paradise* champions immorality by handling matters of sex and money with cheerful nonchalance. The plot proves entirely incidental, and only at the end do the characters stop to con

"A masterpiece of light comedy, with sparkling dialog, innuendo, great performances and masterly cinematic narrative. For connoisseurs, it can't be faulted, and is the Masterpiece of American sophisticated cinema." *Halliwell's Film Guide*

1 For love or money: Pick-pocket Gaston Monescu (Herbert Marshall) succumbs to the charms of dowager Mme. Colet (Kay Francis).

2 Trillion dollar love triangle: Thief Lily Vautier (Miriam Hopkins, right) refuses to let Mariette Colet steal away with lover Gaston.

3 Takes one to know one: Gaston lambastes the director of Mariette's company (C. Aubrey Smith) for embezzling, but doesn't whisper a word of his own double dealings.

4   Out of his league: The Major (Charles Ruggles) thinks he's scoring big with Colet. In truth, however, she's just being a good sport.

5   A dirty dish: Unaware of what she's really up against, Mariette Colet feeds out of secretary Lily Vautier's hand.

sider which woman is better suited for Gaston. What's essential here isn't the outcome, but rather how a line is said or a given situation plays out.

Watching a sophisticated comedy of this caliber is a delight. The snappy dialog and a supporting ensemble that nearly steals the show – Edward Everett Horton and Charles Ruggles on-going battle for Mme. Colet's hand come to mind – are topped up with Lubitsch's meticulous attention to detail. What would amount to an ordinary establishing shot of Venice in the hands of many directors becomes a springboard for Lubitsch's black humor. He swims

in it like a fish, picking up on its currents to find a creative means of tying up loose ends within the script. It follows that in Lubitsch's Venice there's more to the magical canals, gondolas and singing gondoliers than meets the eye. And, indeed, we can practically smell the romance with our very first peek as a garbage man empties the contents of a trashcan into a gondola and then paddles off downstream to the tune of "O sole mio."

LP

HERBERT MARSHALL (1090–1966)   Herbert Marshall is most revered for his performance as a suave European in Ernst Lubitsch's *Trouble in Paradise* (1932). The role itself is a variation on many others he brought to the screen in his works of comedy and melodrama. Indeed, Marshall felt most at home playing a distinguished gentleman with impeccable manners – accentuated with a tuxedo and the Queen's English.
As one might expect, Marshall's life as a thespian first began on the British stage in 1911. Several years later, he took a break from acting to serve his country in World War I and lost a leg during battle. Yet this handicap didn't prevent him from later dazzling both the London and New York theater scenes. On screen, however, his parts were usually staged to ensure he could remain stationary.
Marshall was one of the many stage actors who broke into film shortly after the advent of sound. His silver-screen debut came in 1927 with *Mumsie* (directed by British filmmaker Herbert Wilcox), in which he played a colonel. By 1929, Marshall was employed in Hollywood, appearing in writer W. Somerset Maugham's production of *The Letter* (directed by Jean de Limur) about the unfaithful wife of a British plantation owner in Malaysia. Marshall quickly became a Maugham favorite and went on to appear in a 1940 remake of the *The Letter* directed by William Wyler, Albert Lewin's *The Moon and Sixpence* (a fictionalized account of the life of the painter Paul Gauguin) and Edmund Goulding's *The Razor's Edge* (1946).
The 30s and 40s are generally regarded as Marshall's golden age, for this period of his career saw collaborations with master directors like Alfred Hitchcock, Josef von Sternberg, Ernst Lubitsch and William Wyler. His astonishing success in Hollywood prompted him to give up the stage altogether and permanently relocate to Southern California. As the years advanced, leading roles became few and far between. Nonetheless, he continued to be in demand as a supporting actor, even after the collapse of the studio system in the 50s.
Herbert Marshall died of a heart attack on January 22, 1966.

BLONDE VENUS

1932 - USA - 93 MIN. - B & W - DRAMA

DIRECTOR JOSEF VON STERNBERG (1894–1969)
SCREENPLAY JULES FURTHMAN, S. K. LAUREN DIRECTOR OF PHOTOGRAPHY BERT GLENNON MUSIC OSCAR POTOKER, RALPH RAINGER (Music), SAM COSLOW (Lyrics) ("Hot Voodoo") PRODUCTION JOSEF VON STERNBERG for PARAMOUNT PICTURES.

STARRING MARLENE DIETRICH (Helen Faraday, Helen Jones), HERBERT MARSHALL (Edward 'Ned' Faraday), CARY GRANT (Nick Townsend), DICKIE MOORE (Johnny Faraday), GENE MORGAN (Ben Smith), ROBERT EMMETT O'CONNOR (Dan O'Connor), RITA LA ROY (Taxi Belle Hooper), MORGAN WALLACE (Doctor Pierce), SIDNEY TOLER (Detective Wilson), FERDINAND SCHUMANN-HEINK (Henry).

"She has too much class for this joint."

A troupe of African warriorettes jiggle to intoxicating jungle rhythms on a cabaret stage with spears and shields in hand. A squatting gorilla appears from nowhere. With unexpected grace it removes its right paw like a glove, revealing an unmistakably female, human hand. Then it's off with the left paw. And finally the head. Out from under surfaces a white woman with a blonde afro, who sings incantations of "Hot Voodoo." More than sizzling, it was the entrance of a career for actress Marlene Dietrich as well as perhaps the wackiest idea for a musical number director Josef von Sternberg ever had.

In *Blonde Venus*, there is beauty in the beast, and a beast lurking in every beauty. It's a dichotomy that the picture's star, Marlene Dietrich, revels in exploring. As Helen, she takes the stage as a night-club singer, only to then take up as a kept woman, nearly end up as a fallen woman, and finally advance to super-stardom. The one role she maintains throughout the film is also the one that was entirely new to her professional repertoire – namely, that of loving mother.

The story begins in Germany, where the still single Helen captures the eye of American chemistry student Ned Faraday (Herbert Marshall). One jump cut later, the happy couple are in New York raising their six-year-old son Johnny (Dickie Moore). Ned, however, becomes poisoned with radium and needs to undergo expensive treatment if he expects to have any chance of being cured. Wife Helen returns to night-club work in an attempt to raise the money and becomes popular as the Blonde Venus. But when "Hot Voodoo" doesn't bring in the money quickly enough, she allows herself to become the mistress of millionaire Nick Townsend (Cary Grant). Ned wises up to her infi-

delity on the road to recovery, and makes his wrath felt. Unable to appease her outraged husband, Helen grabs son Johnny and lives on the run in the Deep South. But the authorities soon catch up with her, and she has no choice except to return Johnny to his father and start over from square one *sans* husband and child. Once again Helen's name lights up the marquees, this time around the world. Then, at long last, she truly becomes the woman who has it all as an unanticipated turn of events reunites her with her family.

Critics and viewers concur that *Blonde Venus* reads like a tear-jerker gone awry, for the structure is episodic and the happy ending contrived. Cary Grant, in one of his early leading roles, is little more a pretty boy in a suit. It's understandable why von Sternberg was quick to write off the film altogether.

The undeniably problematic production was the product of the unhappy marriage between Paramount and its two stars. Under contract to produce another picture, the creative duo wanted to keep up its end of the bargain by cranking out a quick and painless piece. However, the pressures of the studio escalated to such a point that Dietrich only just managed to prevent von Sternberg from being replaced towards the end of the shoot.

Ironically, one could argue that this fifth von Sternberg-Dietrich collaboration also served as an anthology of all their previous work. After all, when else did the blonde from Berlin ever have the opportunity to play a medley of her most celebrated roles and intertwine her screen and real-life selves while she was at it? Back when von Sternberg 'discovered' her for the cinema, Dietrich was in fact working as a cabaret singer. And the *Blonde Venus* scenes in which agents and variety-show producers fawn over her

"What does a man know about mother-love?"

Film quote: Helen (Marlene Dietrich)

read like a fictionalization of the way the director shaped his ingenue into a big-screen icon. Furthermore, the real Dietrich was as partial to taking her then eight-year-old child with her on location shoots as the character she played. However – according to daughter Maria Rivas' autobiographical account of growing up on and off the road with Marlene – the pleasure was mommy's alone.

And yet the scenes of Helen and her little boy are those that by and large breathe depth into this highly sentimental piece. The entire time she does her

best to keep two lovers at bay, it's clear that her son is the only man who'll ever possess her heart. Ned and Nick invariably misinterpret her actions and take her for a conniving hussy. For while her beaus may be right in thinking that Helen wears many masks, the movie suggests that her roles as mother, wife and glamorous adulteress are all components of a bigger picture her peers are incapable of seeing. Indeed, only an actress like Marlene Dietrich, who viewed all the parts she ever played as acts of purely aesthetic expression, could so effectively communicate the complexity of womanhood.

1   A wolf in cheap clothing: Actually it's the remains of Marlene Dietrich's gorilla costume – and boy did it ever drive audiences bananas!

2   Iron grip? While Helen (Marlene Dietrich) can't keep a handle on her duties as wife, mother and night club singer, the actress playing her never misses a beat.

3   Masked bandits: Helen and little Johnny (Dickie Moore) disguise themselves to stay together.

"The film is certainly a mess at one level ... but it remains enough of a visual triumph to earn its place in the series of Dietrich movies. Dietrich is here not only married but also a mother, forced into a career as a nightclub singer to pay for her husband's medical fees, and then lured into an affair with playboy Grant. Her misadventures ... are a bizarre mixture of fairytale and social-realist drama, snapping into sharpest focus when she performs the legendary 'Hot Voodoo' number while emerging from a gorilla-skin." *Time Out Film Guide*

4   The cradle will rock: Johnny becomes the ball in
     Ned and Helen's game of keep away.

5   You've got to hand it to her: No one can work a
     stage like the sultry Helen.

6   The lady is a tramp: What night-club singer could
     say no to an adoring fan as handsome as this one?
     Cary Grant as Helen's wealthy lover, Nick Townsend.

"A work of genius: the director waves his magic wand over the
trappings of melodrama and conjures up an overwhelmingly tragic
tale of sacrifice and duty. The staging, transfigured by the sublime
photography of the great Bert Glennon, casts a crystal light on
what is at times a sordid drama." *Les lettres françaises*

In opposition to the actress' means of storytelling is von Sternberg's highly visual artistic genius. The effort he put into creating exquisite decor for *Blonde Venus* was astounding even by his standards: stage sets built to look like palm tree jungles, decrepit Southern homes rocked by the Depression, not to mention the people who seem to vanish against them. Then, of course, there were Marlene Dietrich's sensational song and dance numbers, which her Pygmalion, von Sternberg, lighted to perfection like never before. In the film's final theatrical sequence, the actress is seen clad in matching white top hat and tails as she blows kisses to chorus girls and appears to be as much a man as either of her two co-stars. All else aside, Marlene's magic with costumes would have won her a place in cinematic history.

PB

MARLENE DIETRICH (1901–1992)

No other star of the 20th century, not even the utterly alluring Garbo, had an aura that spelled perfection like Marlene Dietrich. It was her immaculate appearance, mysterious and yet so undeniably human, that made her a true glamor girl. Her overall impact arguably left a more indelible mark on culture than it did film history. She inspired women to wear slacks, and her high-profile romances with Jean Gabin, three of the Kennedys and several women made her a true pioneer of the sexual revolution. She voiced in-vogue, anti-fascist opinions, which earned her political glory as well as the hatred of her fellow Germans. Marlene Dietrich – the mere mention of either her first or surname is enough to evoke the image of an unforgettable star. The woman herself was born into an affluent Berlin family. Her father died when she was very young, and she wasn't much older when she made up her mind to become an actress. It was at Max Reinhardt's Theater Seminar that she received her formal training. Still, her face was made for the screen – not the stage. And after establishing herself in silents thanks to numerous supporting roles, she finally landed her first lead with *The Woman One Longs For* (*Die Frau, nach der man sich sehnt*, 1929).

However, she was officially 'discovered' by Josef von Sternberg a year later, when he cast her as the chunky nightclub singer Lola Lola in his screen adaptation of Heinrich Mann's *The Blue Angel* (*Der blaue Engel*, 1930). It marked the beginning of a prosperous collaboration between the master and his "Geschöpf" – German for 'creation' – as he dubbed her in a letter. *The Blue Angel's* success prompted both director and actress to pack their bags for Hollywood, where they collaborated on six films including *Morocco* (1930), *Blonde Venus* (1932), *Shanghai Express* (1932) and *The Devil Is a Woman* (1935). Unfortunately, the artistic slumps they experienced en route together ended up taking a toll on their friendship.

Not that Marlene's career suffered. Quite the contrary. The next few pictures she shot, such as *The Garden of Allah* (1936) and *Kismet* (1944), solidified and contoured her star. In *A Foreign Affair* (1948) and *Witness for the Prosecution* (1957), director Billy Wilder used her public image to make ironic reference to cinematic history – and contributed to launching Dietrich's brief stint as a character actress in the process. But only in a few other pictures, the most noteworthy being *Judgement at Nuremberg* (1961), did she get the chance to strut her stuff in this arena.

Over the years, she began to dedicate more time to her aspirations as a concert performer. As someone who started off by singing in film, the choice marked a return to her roots. In fact, her most famous number "Ich bin von Kopf bis Fuß auf Liebe eingestellt" ("Falling in Love Again" in its English version) stemmed from *The Blue Angel* and remained her most famous piece to her dying day. Until her passing in Paris in 1992, Marlene Dietrich spent her final years totally removed from the public eye. In accordance with her personal wishes, she was laid to rest in Berlin.

FREAKS

1932 - USA - 64 MIN. - B & W - HORROR FILM, LITERARY ADAPTATION

DIRECTOR TOD BROWNING (1882–1962)
SCREENPLAY WILLIS GOLDBECK, LEON GORDON, EDGAR ALLAN WOOLF, AL BOASBERG, based on the short story *SPURS* by TOD ROBBINS DIRECTOR OF PHOTOGRAPHY MERRITT B. GERSTAD EDITING BASIL WRANGELL PRODUCTION TOD BROWNING for MGM.

STARRING OLGA BACLANOVA (Cleopatra), WALLACE FORD (Phroso), LEILA HYAMS (Venus), HARRY EARLES (Hans), DAISY EARLES (Frieda), ROSCOE ATES (Roscoe), HENRY VICTOR (Hercules), DAISY HILTON (Siamese Twin), VIOLET HILTON (Siamese Twin), FRANCES O'CONNOR (Armless Girl), JOSEPHINE JOSEPH (Half-Woman, Half-Man).

"Offend one and you offend them all."

Politically correct viewers be warned! The horrors of the traveling circus are about to come alive as a group of malformed entertainers put themselves on show to earn an honest buck. Moviegoers too shocked to turn away had better hold on to their hats – for *Freaks* ends with an image so frightening it burns indelibly into the mind.

The story is simple as a fairy tale. Hans (Harry Earles) is a dwarf in love with a stunning high-wire acrobat named Cleopatra (Olga Baclanova). Billed as the 'Peacock of the Air,' this queen of the trapeze makes eyes at the little guy, much to the chagrin of his fellow Lilliputian and fiancée, Frieda (Daisy Earles). One thing leads to another and soon jealousy prompts Frieda to have a word with her rival. Only, when she does, the tiny woman makes the mistake of informing Cleopatra that Hans is heir to a massive fortune. Every bit as evil as she is beautiful, Cleo works out a scheme with her strongman lover

Hercules (Henry Victor) to marry Hans and then poison him on their wedding night. The 'freaks', however, quickly wise up to her and devise a counterattack to give these 'normal folk' a taste of their own medicine.

While *Freaks* does indeed expose how side-shows exploit handicapped performers, that isn't the point of the film. Instead, Tod Browning points the camera at Siamese twins, hermaphrodites and pinheads because of their unique ability to entertain viewers while simultaneously creeping them out with acts like the torso man's cigarette lighting trick – performed using only his lips and teeth.

Despite the simplicity and predictability of the plot, Browning creates suspense with artistic precision. At the start of the film, the 'Peacock of the Air' is introduced by the master of ceremonies as "the most amazing, most astounding living monstrosity of all time;" but only at the end of the picture do we

glimpse her disfigurement. The framing story therefore puts the act of watching movies on a par with peering into a curiosities cabinet. Tod Browning, who had worked in a circus as a contortionist and clown in his youth, believed that a voyeuristic audience was as essential to freak shows as it was to film.

Even so the picture itself is substantially more complex than it may first appear. What starts out as a harsh examination of malformation subtly is made bearable by the film's element of black humor. For example, a stuttering circus member leaves the viewer in stitches by courting one of the Siamese twins (Daisy and Violet Hilton) to the dismay of the other. Another amusing encounter comes when the Half-Man Half-Woman (Josephine Joseph) flashes the strongman a toothy grin, and Phroso the clown (Wallace Ford) tells him, "I think she likes you, but he don't." And when little Hans is

"*Freaks* is filled with poignancy; it offers a premonition of eugenics, as well as a provocative comparison with the alienated condition of women and the freakish nature of all showbiz celebrity. It is a work of genius." *The Guardian*

1   Give me your tired, your poor: The freaks look to each
    other for support and find a loving soul to lean on.

2   Love in a pinch: Cleopatra (Olga Baclanova) lowers
    her standards for a bit of hard cash. Harry Earles
    as Hans, the acrobat's pint-sized Romeo.

3   Fallen star: The former peacock of the air has to
    live off her looks after a freak accident leaves her
    permanently grounded.

4   Sex is her strong suit: But off stage, colleagues
    Hercules (Henry Victor, left) and Phroso (Wallace
    Ford) accept the gender-bending performer
    (Josephine Joseph) as one of the guys.

seen leaving Cleo's trailer, the performers nudge one another and remark that the trapeze star must have gone on a diet.

Beyond looking to humor for mere entertainment, Browning has the wisecracking Phroso demonstrate its powers as 'the great equalizer'. By laughing at the unwanted attention that 'abnormalities' tend to attract, the clown is one of the few members of the circus who succeeds in meeting the freaks on equal footing. Conversely, the other 'normal' circus performers only succeed in revealing their personal shortcomings every time they make fun of the outcasts. Such is the case when Cleopatra marries Hans and belittles the wedding party's gesture to accept her as "one of their own." This is the moment when she is confronted by her evil nature and made to see that a warped soul is a disfigurement all its own.

The scene implicitly shows us how the hostile outside world has forced these outcasts to form ties with each other. The resulting close-knit community, founded in humanity and solidarity, provides a welcome contrast to a 'normal' world dominated by the vanity and malevolence. For, as Tod Browning teaches us in this extraordinary piece of cinema, it is the freaks' handicaps that shield them from the vanity of placing themselves above other people, and ultimately make them better people.

SH

TOD BROWNING (1882–1962)

Born with a silver spoon in his mouth, Tod Browning said goodbye the good life at age sixteen to join the circus. It was there that he made the acquaintance of director D. W. Griffith and decided to pursue a career in film. *Intolerance* (1916) gave Browning the chance to assist Griffith and try his hand at screen acting. A year later he was directing silent movies of his own. Known as the Edgar Allen Poe of the cinema, Browning had an obsession with all things macabre and spooky, which always found a way into his art. For earlier works like MGM's *The Unholy Three* (1925), *London After Midnight* (1927) and *West of Zanzibar* (1928), the director teamed up with 'man of a thousand faces' Lon Chaney to conjure up the dark side. This prosperous collaboration, which lasted ten pictures, came to an abrupt end when Chaney unexpectedly died during the pre-production stages of *Dracula* (1931). Browning chose the Hungarian Bela Lugosi, who had played the vampire on stage, to replace his favorite actor, and the rest – as they say – is history. Still, *Dracula*, was not to be the director's sole masterpiece: *Freaks* (1932), a film very much inspired by Browning's years at the circus, is every bit as poignant as his adaptation of Bram Stoker's tale. *Mark of the Vampire* (1935), *The Devil-Doll* (1936) and swan-song *Miracles for Sale* (1939) were the last three pictures completed in the Hollywood career of this erstwhile circus clown and leading pioneer of the thriller and horror genres.

I AM A FUGITIVE FROM A CHAIN GANG

1932 - USA - 93 MIN. - B & W - PRISON FILM

DIRECTOR MERVYN LEROY (1900–1987)
SCREENPLAY HOWARD J. GREEN, BROWN HOLMES, based on the autobiography *I AM A FUGITIVE FROM A GEORGIA CHAIN GANG!* by ROBERT E. BURNS DIRECTOR OF PHOTOGRAPHY SOL POLITO EDITING WILLIAM HOLMES MUSIC BERNHARD KAUN, LEO F. FORBSTEIN PRODUCTION HAL B. WALLIS for WARNER BROS., THE VITAPHONE CORPORATION.

STARRING PAUL MUNI (James Allen), GLENDA FARRELL (Marie Woods), HELEN VINSON (Helen), NOEL FRANCIS (Linda), EDWARD ELLIS (Bomber Wells), PRESTON FOSTER (Pete), BERTON CHURCHILL (Judge), LOUISE CARTER (James' Mother), HALE HAMILTON (Rev. Robert Clinton Allen), SALLY BLANE (Alice).

"How do you live?"
"I steal."

I Am a Fugitive from a Chain Gang is the mother of all prison movies, from *The Defiant Ones* (1958) to *The Shawshank Redemption* (1994). All the essential elements are already there: the prisoners' camaraderie, the brutality of the guards, the escape. Director Mervyn LeRoy threw them all into the pot, and what comes out is a movie with a clear message. More than just a bitter indictment of prison conditions in the Deep South, LeRoy's film shows how the entire system of criminal justice turns innocent men into delinquents. Clear political statements like that were a rarity at the time, but if there was one major studio where such things could be said, it was Warner Bros. Here we

have a rare case: a story with a (belated) happy ending, but a less-than-happy ending for Hollywood itself. After all, this was the age of the Great Depression.

Though the film is set in the 20s – a boom time for the U. S. economy – the Depression already casts its long shadow. Returning from WWI, James Allen (Paul Muni) wants to do something with his life. He sets off on a kind of odyssey across the U. S. and takes up a number of jobs, none of which work out for him. He's as little responsible for these failures as he is for the crime that lands him a ten-year sentence and a place in the chain gang. But James Allen escapes from the brutal gang, adopts a new name and heads north

1　Gunning for trouble: Cinematic original Paul Muni lights up the screen as fly-by-night felon James Allen.

2　Underground railroad: The wrongly convicted Allen makes a break for it, only to find equally grueling conditions on the outside.

where he succeeds in building the new life he's always dreamed of. As a construction engineer working on bridges, he's now a valued member of society; but once again, he's betrayed, and despite the protests of his friends and the media, he's sent back to the chain gang in Georgia. Though he's promised a pardon, it's never granted – because of the "slanderous" campaign from the Yankee north. Eventually, James Allen succeeds in escaping once again. His famous last words come from the abysmal depths of a black screen: "I steal."

The film was shaped by the brilliant Paul Muni, a Stanislavsky Method Actor before his time. His James Allen has the quiet pathos of a man deprived of his rights. He is the epitome of integrity – but also of naiveté: as a pseudonym, he chooses the name "Allen James"! It's not exactly a surprise when he's ground down by the mills of the justice system: Muni's James Allen is a forerunner of Harrison Ford's Dr. Kimble in The Fugitive (1993).

Allen's first escape, through the swamps, formed the template for a host of prison films that followed. Like the cameraman, the runaway jailbird uses hollow reed as a snorkel. But although these scenes are enthralling, LeRoy tells his story soberly and economically, without using music as a crutch and with no gratuitous visual shocks. When the prisoners are whipped, the torture takes place off-screen: we only hear their screams. A sick man staggers through the frame in the background: in the scene that follows, we see him carried to the grave in his coffin. The strongest image is the chain that binds the prisoners' legs in the daytime, and that binds them together at night. In a dialectical montage worthy of Eisenstein, we see the prison camp's horses chained together in the same way.

A shot like this makes it clear that LeRoy is anything but an impartial observer, despite his use of a dispassionate documentary style reminiscent of the German *Neue Sachlichkeit*. For long periods, *I Am a Fugitive from a*

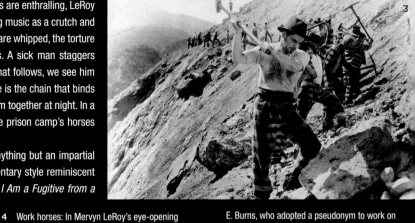

3 Chip away at the system: Allen is determined to serve his community in whatever capacity he can, but whether his story will reform criminal justice remains to be seen.

4 Work horses: In Mervyn LeRoy's eye-opening motion picture, prisoners are treated like animals. The film is based on the autobiography of Robert

E. Burns, who adopted a pseudonym to work on the screenplay.

"*I Am a Fugitive from a Chain Gang* is a movie with guts ... When the sad fade-out eventuates as the broken fugitive shuffles off into the night, it's a shocker for the average fan." *Variety*

5   Perfect little woman or parole officer in disguise? James finds married life with Marie (Glenda Farrell) about as pleasurable as his stint behind bars.

6   Wouldn't pull your chain: LeRoy's movie about the U.S. criminal justice system is one of the most uncompromising films of the decade.

Chain Gang is a social drama, in which the brave war vet has to sell his medal, deal with prostitutes and shady characters, and endure blackmail, then betrayal, from a woman he loves. Although James Allen is unfailingly decent and honest, he never gets an even break – and his fate is just one among many. But LeRoy's almost slavish insistence on factual accuracy turns his 'neutral' stocktaking into pure agitprop. Every wage payout is documented with an insert; on a blackboard, the prison guards record the numbers of black and white prisoners; lead articles in newspapers vehemently discuss Allen's case; and when the man gets married, all we actually see is the marriage certificate. Bertolt Brecht's film work for the Communist Party employed very similar methods.

In the State of Georgia, the message was received and understood, and the film was banned as a result. Having started out as a petty criminal, scriptwriter Robert Elliot Burns had once suffered the same fate as James Allen. Years later, however, his remaining prison sentence was waived and the notorious chain gangs were abolished throughout the southern States. Sometimes a movie founds more than a new genre.

PB

MERVYN LEROY (1900–1987)

Mervyn LeRoy was a director with the professional ethics of a producer. Once he was convinced of the quality of a script, he was happy to work in any genre. In the course of a successful career spanning almost four decades, he made comedies, dramas, romances and musicals.

He began his life in showbiz at the age of twelve, appearing in vaudeville as a "singing newsboy" and Chaplin imitator. His family were impoverished after losing everything they had in the San Francisco earthquake of 1906. Luckily, LeRoy's cousin was the film producer Jesse Lasky, and with his letter of recommendation, LeRoy gained access to Lasky's Famous Players studio, where he worked his way up from the costume department via various small roles to the position of gag-writer. From 1927 onwards, he worked as a director, making his breakthrough in 1930 with *Little Caesar*. This tough-as-nails gangster thriller established a new genre and made a Hollywood star of the lead actor, Edward G. Robinson. The unvarnished realism and the sheer success of this film paved the way for *I Am a Fugitive from a Chain Gang* (1932). In this period, LeRoy made several films that cemented his reputation as a director with an interest in 'social' themes.

The change came with his move to MGM, where LeRoy began by producing *The Wizard of Oz* (1939). The film's initial lack of success – it later became a classic, of course – persuaded him to return to directing. The biopic *Madame Curie* (1943) was as big a box-office hit as *Quo Vadis?* (1951), and the latter – a three-hour epic starring Peter Ustinov as the pyromaniac Roman emperor – is certainly LeRoy's best-known work. His later works, mainly comedies and war films, were popular with moviegoers but otherwise fairly forgettable. He also advised John Wayne when "The Duke" was making *The Green Berets* (1968), a film that attempted to justify the Vietnam war. Mervyn LeRoy was universally respected, and he received the prestigious Irving Thalberg Award in 1976. The Oscar eluded him all his life.

6

I WAS BORN, BUT
Umarete wa mita keredo

932 - JAPAN - 91 MIN. - B & W - DRAMA, COMEDY

DIRECTOR YASUJIRÔ OZU (1903–1963)
SCREENPLAY AKIRA FUSHIMI, GEIBEI IBUSHIYA, based on an idea by JAMES MAKI a. k. a. YASUJIRÔ OZU
DIRECTOR OF PHOTOGRAPHY HIDEO SHIGEHARA **EDITING** HIDEO SHIGEHARA **PRODUCTION** SHOCHIKU FILMS LTD.

STARRING TATSUO SAITO (Father, Yoshi), HIDEO SUGAWARA (Older Son, Ryoichi), TOKKAN-KOZOU as TOMIO AOKI (Younger Son, Keiji), MITSUKO YOSHIKAWA (Yoshi's Wife, Eiko), TAKESHI SAKAMOTO (Executive, Iwasaki), TERUYO HAYAMI (Iwasaki's Wife), SEIICHI KATO (The Iwasakis' Son, Taro), SHOICHI KOFUJITA (Delivery Boy, Shinko), ZENTARO IIJIMA (Playmate, Kamekichi), SHÔTARÔ FUJIMATSU (Playmate).

"Father, you weakling!"

Yasujirô Ozu originally wanted to shoot a light-hearted picture about kids. He ended up with something rather different: *I Was Born, But (Umarete wa mita keredo)* was a rather dark look at the lives of adults. This bittersweet comedy remains the best-known of the director's silent pictures. Like the majority of other Ozu works, the movie can be categorized as a *Shomingeki*, a Japanese film genre that chronicled the everyday lives of lower-middle class families. To create the look he wanted, Ozu drew from both Japanese and Western influences: in addition to the filmmaker's preferred camera perspective, with shots angled from the point of view of someone seated on the ground (a setup that can be interpreted in a number of ways), *I Was Born, But* incorporates American scene-editing techniques and references to René Clair's social comedies.

The film follows the lives of the Yoshis, a family who have recently moved to the outskirts of Tokyo. The change of address has an unexpected effect on the way the two Yoshi sons, ten-year-old Ryoichi (Hideo Sugawara) and eight-year-old Keiji (Tomio Aoki), regard their father. For now that Mr. Yoshi (Tatsuo Saito), an office clerk, lives next door to his employer, Ryoichi and Keiji suddenly see their father in a disturbing new light, bowing and scraping to the boss.

I Was Born, But (Umarete wa mita keredo) is a cinematic investigation of the separate social orders governing the lives of children and grownups. In the adult world, hierarchies are based on the social class one happens to belong to and seem virtually impermeable. Just how haphazard the makeup of these classes can be is attested to by Mr. Yoshi and his boss Mr. Iwasaki (Takeshi Sakamoto), who are in different social strata despite their both being relatively foolish men of weak moral fiber.

The flip side of this is the children's hierarchical structure, which allows for rapid social mobility depending on how strong or sly a person is. In their new neighborhood, Ryoichi and Keiji encounter a gang of kids containing boys of all ages and social classes. The group includes everyone from Taro (Seiichi Kato), Iwasaki's son, to the poorest kid around. The leader of the pack is the tallest and strongest of the bunch, something he makes clear to Ryoichi and Keiji by using brute force to claim Keiji's ring puzzle for himself. During the attack, Keiji's roll falls to the ground, and Ozu uses this masterfully to show the children's hierarchy in action. The smallest member of the gang quickly snatches it up, only to have it grabbed out of his hand by the next biggest member, with the same thing happening again and again until the leader ends up keeping it.

From then on, the panic-stricken Ryoichi and Keiji go out of their way to avoid the rowdy bunch, even if it means cutting school. But before long the two boys discover that they are significantly cleverer than the gang leader, who lacks the brain power to solve the ring puzzle he stole. And so they decide to hire an even bigger kid, Shinko the delivery boy (Shoichi Kofujita), to beat him up. Ryoichi and Keiji get their first bitter taste of adulthood when Shinko refuses to do the same thing to Taro on the grounds that the boy's father is a much better customer than Mr. Yoshi. Nonetheless, the two brothers still manage to assume command of the gang and instate a new policy once they do: whenever the Yoshis give the signal, all the other kids – including Taro – have to drop to the ground before them.

With such a triumph under their belts, Ryoichi and Keiji are appalled when they see an Iwasaki home movie that shows their father making an ass

of himself. All this time, they have considered their father to be the best dad on the planet and now they are forced to sit back and watch how he behaves like a chimp at the behest of his boss. The spectacle results in an explosive confrontation between Mr. Yoshi and his sons that starts off with boys accusing him of being a weakling and a coward. When they refuse to let their father explain himself, Mr. Yoshi is left with no choice but to spank the pigheaded Ryoichi. The boy, however, strikes back. And soon father and son are engaged in a heated fist fight – a sight that must have sent shockwaves through the conservative Japanese public.

Although the film ends on a note of melancholy resignation that became commonplace in Ozu's later work, the director introduces a lighthearted episode to get the family back on track. This takes the form of a short-lived

1   Bowing down to authority: Young Ryoichi (Hideo Sugawara) learns the hard way to respect who's boss. Tatsuo Saito as Mr. Yoshi.

2   Of rice and men: The two Yoshi sons demonstrate self-reliance by refusing to eat – until dinner time.

3   The sincerest form of flattery: Keiji (Tomio Aoki, right) tries to imitate his older brother's every move.

4   Tender as a mother's heart: Mrs. Yoshi (Mitsuko Yoshikawa) emerges as the family's rock of support after all is said and done.

5   The brat pack: He may be the boss's son at home, but it doesn't score him extra points on the playground. Seiichi Kato (center) as Taro.

"In this film Ozu brought together in almost perfect form the various elements which made up his style, his personal way of looking at the world." *Donald Ritchie, in: Ozu: His Life and Films*

THE SHOCHIKU COMPANY   Yasujirô Ozu worked at Shochiku Films from 1924 until his death in 1963, starting off as a camera assistant and then advancing to the director's chair. Shochiku is considered to be the oldest existing movie studio in Japan and celebrated its 110th anniversary in 2005. Originally, however, twin brothers Matsujiro Shirai and Takejiro Otani founded the business as a production company for Kabuki Theater, an industry that Shochiku monopolizes to this day. Only in 1920 did the studio truly start to make films.

Shortly after entering the world of cinema, Shochiku carved a niche for itself with the sort of contemporary social dramas Ozu would become famous for, and established itself as one of Japan's three biggest movie studios. Filmmakers like Ozu used their work at Shochiku to explore the relationship between Japan's younger and older generations as well as how changing values affected the culture.

Beyond producing the films of masters like Ozu, Kurosawa, Mizoguchi, Kinoshita, Oshima and Imamura, Shochiku is also responsible for turning out the longest and most successful film series of all time: created by writer director Yôji Yamada, the 48-picture Tora-san series ran from 1969 to 1995 and starred Kiyoshi Atsumi as its unlikely protagonist. The Tora-san movies were officially retired when Atsumi died in 1996.

Beyond its obvious contributions to film history, Shochiku is known for upholding cinematic tradition: not only does the studio have an extensive archive of classic films, but it also maintains a good number of salaried personnel – an all but antiquated studio system practice. Still, today's Shochiku Co. Ltd. is just as interested in cornering future markets and has branched out to include an animation department, a large chain of movie houses and a studio theme park.

hunger strike the boys go on after their father tells them that he has to stay in Mr. Iwasaki's good graces in order to put food on the table. Kids, however, will be kids, and the boys silently throw in the towel at the mouthwatering sight of rice balls. As hunger triumphs over Ryoichi and Keiji's idealism, they recognize the reality of the situation their father is in and understand what their parents mean about life being full of woes. When Mr. Yoshi and his sons run into Mr. Iwasaki on their way to work and school, the boys encourage their father to greet his boss as he always has. While Ozu was all too happy to have children unmask and question the social order of the adult world in *I Was Born, But*, he had no intention of changing it.

5

SCARFACE

1932 - USA - 93 MIN. - B & W - GANGSTER MOVIE, LITERARY ADAPTATION

DIRECTOR HOWARD HAWKS (1896–1977)
SCREENPLAY BEN HECHT, SETON I. MILLER, JOHN LEE MAHIN, W. R. BURNETT, FRED PALSEY, based on the
novel of the same name by ARMITAGE TRAIL DIRECTORS OF PHOTOGRAPHY LEE GARMES, L. WILLIAM O'CONNELL
EDITING EDWARD CURTISS MUSIC ADOLPH TANDLER, GUS ARNHEIM PRODUCTION HOWARD HUGHES for
THE CADDO COMPANY.

STARRING PAUL MUNI (Tony "Scarface" Camonte), ANN DVORAK (Cesca Camonte), GEORGE RAFT (Guino Rinaldo),
KAREN MORLEY (Poppy), BORIS KARLOFF (Gaffney), OSGOOD PERKINS (Johnny Lovo),
C. HENRY GORDON (Inspector Ben Guarino), VINCE BARNETT (Angelo), PURNELL PRATT (Mr. Garston),
INEZ PALANGE (Mrs. Camonte).

"There's only one law – do it first, do it yourself, and keep doing it."

As their predecessors had done before them in the closing credits to William A. Wellman's *The Public Enemy* (1931), the producers of *Scarface* felt obliged to make it clear that they weren't glorifying violence. Anticipating complaints and calls for censorship, they added a title card condemning "gang rule in America." This was, of course, a result of the historical circumstances governing film production in Hollywood in the 20s and 30s, and it also points towards the tension between real violence and its depiction in the media. The film takes its inspiration from the real-life career of legendary Mafia boss Al Capone.

But however the facts may be communicated in fictional form, Howard Hawks' carefully and resourcefully directed film has no need to insist on its good intentions. Film historians now see *Scarface* as a prototype for the entire gangster-film genre. Its pioneering iconography and narrative economy are the result of a clever combination of several elements: a fast narrative tempo, thrilling action scenes, aggressive humor, psychological precision, the physical presence of the leading actor Paul Muni, and the fascinating immorality of Tony "Scarface" Camonte, the character he plays. Yes, this is a violent and sweatily physical movie, but it's also an

1 Punctuation marks: Gangster Tony 'Scarface' Camonte (Paul Muni) knows how to make a statement.

2 Shoot to kill: Scarface's sister Cesca (Ann Dvorak) speaks his language.

3 Security inspection: Criminals check each other's weapons at the door.

Illuminating piece of filmmaking that refuses to prettify the world it examines.

Chicago in the Prohibition era: the end of a wild party. A shadow approaches, revolver in hand. We hear a whistled tune we'll come to recognize as the murderer's signature. He says the words "Hello, Louis," two shots ring out, and a gang boss is dead. It's hard to imagine a film about organized crime beginning in a more laconic fashion. Tony Camonte is a man on the make, a future Prince of the Underworld. Having struck once

he'll strike again and again, with increasing brutality. Cold-blooded, devious and cruel, he clears his way to the top with tommy-guns and hand grenades until he's finally made it to the upper echelons of criminal High Society. This macabre cinematic orgy of violence climaxes in the slaughter of Camonte's rival gang bosses in a warehouse. It's a scene that recalls the real-life St. Valentine's Day Massacre, and what makes it so disturbing is that we see nothing directly: just the collapsing shadows of the victims as the bullets crash into the wall behind them.

PAUL MUNI Paul Muni was born in 1895 in the town of Lemberg, which was then part of the Austro-Hungarian empire. His parents were theater people, and he gained his first stage experience as a child. In 1918, after the family had moved to the U.S., Paul Muni joined the Yiddish Art Theater in New York. In 1936, he made his Broadway debut in "We Americans." Three years later, he signed his first Hollywood contract with 20th Century Fox. His very first film performance, in *The Valiant* (1929), brought him an Oscar nomination, and this was soon followed by another, for *I Am a Fugitive from a Chain Gang* (1932). With Warner Brothers, Muni enjoyed great success with a string of film biographies, including *The Life of Emile Zola* (1937), *The Story of Louis Pasteur* (1935) and *Juarez* (1939).

Following a difference of opinion about the roles he should play, Muni left Warner early and returned to the theater. He was universally regarded as a highly conscientious actor who chose his roles with care and discretion, but deteriorating health and the threat of blindness made acting increasingly difficult, and he was eventually forced to give it up. Paul Muni died in 1967.

4   The powers that be: And not one of them is present here.

5   Nothing a tailor can't mend: Still if Scarface doesn't watch his step, he might just get sent to the cleaners.

6   Untouchable: As someone who can talk the talk and walk the walk, Scarface think he's above the law.

4

This is one side of Tony Camonte, the side the public is most curious about – the gangster as media star. Director Howard Hawks was certainly aware of the media's shared responsibility for public attitudes to organized crime, and of how the sensationalist press gave men like Camonte the publicity that made them thrillingly scary antiheroes. But Hawks also shows us the brutal private life of Tony Camonte. Any guy who approaches his sister Cesca (Ann Dvorak) gets beaten senseless, and he insists on the authority of a patriarch within his own family. His self-confidence is almost grotesquely inflated. When the police arrest him on suspicion of having murdered Big Louis, he's vainly and arrogantly certain they can't touch him for it. Camonte also knows how to use his autocratic yet sexually charged presence to get his way: it might have been another twenty years before the term became common currency, but he is the very embodiment of cool. The only blemish on his glossy surface is the cross-shaped scar on his face, an outward manifestation of a deep disturbance within. As his power increases, Tony Camonte completely fails to notice how his breathtaking criminal career is bound to end in an ignominious death. Brought low by a policeman's bullet, he lies outstretched beneath a neon sign that tells the lie he's lived by: "The World Is Yours." Comment would be superfluous.

BR

"*Scarface* contains more cruelty than any of its gangster picture predecessors, but there's a squarer for every killing."

Variety

GRAND HOTEL

1932 - USA - 112 MIN. - B & W - DRAMA

DIRECTOR EDMUND GOULDING (1891–1959)
SCREENPLAY WILLIAM A. DRAKE, based on the novel *MENSCHEN IM HOTEL* by VICKI BAUM
DIRECTOR OF PHOTOGRAPHY WILLIAM H. DANIELS EDITING BLANCHE SEWELL MUSIC WILLIAM AXT, CHARLES MAXWELL
PRODUCTION PAUL BERN, IRVING THALBERG for MGM.

STARRING GRETA GARBO (Grusinskaya), JOHN BARRYMORE (Baron Felix von Geigern),
LIONEL BARRYMORE (Otto Kringelein), JOAN CRAWFORD (Flaemmchen), WALLACE BEERY (Preysing),
LEWIS STONE (Dr. Otternschlag), JEAN HERSHOLT (Senf), RAFAELA OTTIANO (Suzette),
PURNELL PRATT (Zinnowitz), FERDINAND GOTTSCHALK (Pimenov).

ACADEMY AWARDS 1932 OSCAR for BEST PICTURE.

"Grand Hotel ... always the same. People come, people go. Nothing ever happens."

Dr. Otternschlag (Lewis Stone) couldn't be more wrong. Berlin's "Grand Hotel" is a veritable hotbed of action for the rich, famous and utterly decadent. Beyond all the wining, dining, loafing, flirting and other usual goings-on, the hotel has seen its share of suffering and passion, highlife and death. Of course, in this world of closed doors, ephemeral intrigues are even harder to keep track of than the names of the hotel's current occupants.

Good-natured hotel thief Baron Felix von Geigern (John Barrymore) falls head over heels for suicidal ballerina Grusinskaya (Greta Garbo) and is thus rendered incapable of robbing her. Terminally-ill bookkeeper Otto Kringelein (Lionel Barrymore) has checked into the hotel so that he can live out the rest of his days amidst high society – and is so rejuvenated by the experience that he ends up checking out a new man. Not so for Kringelein's former boss, General Director Preysing (Wallace Beery), who suffers his per-

sonal and professional downfall in these interiors. Nonetheless, Preysing's trusty stenographer, Flaemmchen (Joan Crawford), maintains her movie-star ambitions and is brazen and sassy enough to realize them – provided she plays her three beaus right.

Dr. Otternschlag, of course, misses it all. Too busy spending his time checking for messages at the front desk, he'd rather believe that "over a hundred doors lead to a single hallway, and nobody has a clue what their neighbors are up to." Poor Dr. Otternschlag, if only he'd open his eyes.

Made in 1932, *Grand Hotel* is actually a retrospective look at an era in upheaval. With the Roaring Twenties a thing of past, both in Hollywood and Berlin, MGM mastermind producer Irving Thalberg decided that a star-studded work of nostalgia was just the thing to fill the studio's coffers. With great industry names like Greta Garbo, brothers John and Lionel Barry-

1 Please hold my calls: Grusinskaya (Greta Garbo) tries to have a moment alone in her hotel room.

2 Insanity at the vanity: Though just 26, actress Greta Garbo considered herself too old for the world of ballet – a complex she shared with her character.

3 Put your money where your mouth is: Joan Crawford shows Preysing (Wallace Beery) (still standing) what happens to poor slobs who overstep their boundaries.

more, Wallace Beery and Joan Crawford headlining the production, the *Grand Hotel* premiere was dubbed the society event of the year, and the picture enjoyed overnight success. The film's basic framework, which became the prototype for the still popular ensemble film, was Thalberg's brilliant ploy to lure Depression Era audiences back to the cinema. If viewers were reluctant to spend their hard-earned wages on a picture with just one star, the producer was prepared to give them a handful. MGM, which had already secured the film rights to the novel by Vienna-born Vicki Baum, was

certain that *Grand Hotel* had all the ingredients of a hit, especially in view of the studio's recent success with the Broadway version of the piece.

Grand Hotel's ambience is one of melancholy draped in glamor, bidding a teasing farewell to a decade of decadence. Characters are afflicted by financial disarray or the certainty, like Garbo's Russian ballerina, that their best days are behind them. And yet, as the Baron proves (John Barrymore briefly exits his smoke cloud with the utmost finesse), they would willingly try their luck anew at the baccarat table to balance their gambling

"Garbo gives the role of the dancer something of artificiality, risking a trace of acting swagger, sometimes stagey, but for that reason probably giving it a touch of theatrical vigor that the fans will like. Her clothes are ravishing in the well-known Garbo style, and tricky camera treatment sets her off shrewdly for a romantically compelling performance." *Variety*

debts, should the old fail-safes give out on them. As far as games of chance go, only the endearing Kringelein will come out a winner. In the role of the submissive clerk, Lionel Barrymore emerges as the champion of the common man, while providing the male audience with someone it can identify with. In this respect, Flaemmchen is very much his female counterpart: she is willing to do whatever it takes to rise above her station – even if it means entering into an affair with her boss, the repugnant Preysing.

Well aware that Joan Crawford's role would launch her to the ranks of a fully-fledged sex symbol, Greta Garbo took precautionary measures. To counterbalance Joan Crawford's appeal, the Swedish sphinx insisted that several scenes be re-shot to ensure that the two female leads would never appear in the same frame or upstage one another. Garbo must have known what she was doing. For despite her confinement to the plot's periphery, she delivers a whimsical performance that makes its presence felt even when the actress is off-screen. Indeed, as the ballerina who feels deeply unappreciated by her fans, it's almost as if Garbo is playing her own public image – especially when she utters those immortal words, "I *want* to be alone." The tabloids forever relished the line as a reference to her shielded personal life, and it quickly became a source of parody. Yet it wasn't so much that the actress longed for absolute solitude as reports suggested, but rather that she was unwilling to become a plaything of the press.

4 A lucrative affair: The debonair John Barrymore sends sparks flying opposite a young Joan Crawford and secures her a place in the Hollywood heavens.

5 A long line of stars: Brothers John and Lionel Barrymore (here as Otto Kringelein) were born into a family of celebrated thespians.

6 Reich and wrong: Kansas native Wallace Beery sports a German accent as Preysing and is removed from the hotel by the authorities.

To this day, *Grand Hotel* remains the only film to win the Oscar for Best Picture and not be nominated in any other category. Seldom has the Academy made such an accurate and telling decision. Edmund Goulding's direction is solid, but apart from the total absence of exterior shots, by no means noteworthy. The script seems somewhat contrived and the acting borderline artificial. However, the sheer magic of so many stars coming together on screen leaves no vacancy in terms of entertainment, making for a picture that is undoubtedly one of the decade's best. That very grandeur is what couldn't be replicated in either the U.S. or German/French remakes (1945 and 1959 respectively).   PB

LIONEL AND JOHN BARRYMORE

The Barrymore acting dynasty left an indelible mark on the American stage and screen, its most revered members being Lionel and his younger brother John. The sons of actors Maurice Barrymore and Georgiana Drew appeared on screen together in a total of five films, including 1932 titles like *Grand Hotel*, *Arsène Lupin* and *Rasputin and the Empress*, which also starred their sister, Ethel Barrymore. Indeed, their legacy thrives to this day via John's son John Drew Barrymore and granddaughter Drew Barrymore.

Good looks and a quick wit enabled John Barrymore to advance to one of the most popular actors of the 20s. Between the curtains calls of a brilliant Shakespearean stage career, Barrymore began making motion pictures. Notable performances of the silent screen include his work in *Dr. Jekyll and Mr. Hyde* (1920), the title roles in *Sherlock Holmes* (1922), *Beau Brummel* (1924) and *Don Juan* (1926), as well as an unforgettable Captain Ahab Ceeley in *The Sea Beast* (1930). With the rise of the talkies, he played opposite female leads like an up-and-coming Katharine Hepburn in *A Bill of Divorcement* (1932) and Jean Harlow in *Dinner at Eight* (1933). Nonetheless, this most illustrious of all Barrymores was also the first to expire: a life of alcoholism first lowered his star to B status then caused his demise at 60.

Much to the dismay of their parents, the Barrymore brothers originally had their hearts set on pursuing arts other than acting; and throughout his life, Lionel would continue to think of himself primarily as a composer and writer. It didn't seem to matter that his stage career took off even before his brother's, and that he was personally discovered for the screen by cinematic pioneer D. W. Griffith. Not even his continued popularity during the 20s or an Oscar win for his work in *A Free Soul* (1931), could totally convince him of the fact that acting was his calling.

Nonetheless, it seemed that his star was destined to burn ever brighter with age: with the slender man of his youth a distant memory, a full-figured Lionel began portraying imposing patriarchs in films like Frank Capra's *It's a Wonderful Life* (1946) and King Vidor's *Duel in the Sun* (1946). Although arthritis had left the actor permanently wheelchair-bound by 1938, both of these roles were tailored to allow for him to perform while seated. Lionel Barrymore suffered a fatal heart attack in 1954.

TARZAN THE APE MAN

1932 - USA - 99 MIN. - B & W - ADVENTURE MOVIE

DIRECTOR W. S. VAN DYKE (1889–1943)
SCREENPLAY CYRIL HUME, IVOR NOVELLO, based on the novel *TARZAN OF THE APES* by EDGAR RICE BURROUGHS
DIRECTORS OF PHOTOGRAPHY CLYDE DE VINNA, HAROLD ROSSON EDITING TOM HELD, BEN LEWIS MUSIC GEORGE RICHELAVIE
PRODUCTION BERNARD H. HYMAN, IRVING THALBERG for MGM.

STARRING JOHNNY WEISSMULLER (Tarzan), MAUREEN O'SULLIVAN (Jane Parker), NEIL HAMILTON (Harry Holt),
C. AUBREY SMITH (James Parker), DORIS LLOYD (Mrs. Cutten), FORRESTER HARVEY (Beamish),
IVORY WILLIAMS (Riano).

"Jane. Tarzan. Jane. Tarzan. Jane. Tarzan. Jane. Tarzan. Jane. Tarzan. Jane ..." Oh, please stop!"

Tarzan was the 20th century's first serial star as well as a multimedia phenomenon beyond compare. Books, movies, comics and merchandising that included everything from collectable trading cards to T-shirts testify to the early popularity of the man in the loin cloth. Tarzan first appeared in 1912 as a recurring character in a pulp-fiction adventure serial written by Edgar Rice Burroughs. Hollywood immediately recognized the fictitious he-man's cinematic potential and, in 1918, various men began to swing across the screen as King of the Jungle. Among them, only former competitive swimmer Johnny Weissmuller proved to have any staying power. MGM introduced him as the new 'face' of Tarzan in a 1932 production simply entitled *Tarzan the Ape Man*. It was to be the first of twelve pictures in which the muscle-bound Weissmuller impressed audiences in the role.

Needless to say, any acting ability Weissmuller might have possessed paled in comparison to the gold medals he'd picked up at the Olympics. His Tarzan shone through brute strength and baby-smooth skin, both of which could instantly spice up any performance. Furthermore, Weissmuller's unpolished amateur charm proved better suited to the role than the tricks of the trade offered by the professionals that had preceded him. For *Tarzan the Ape Man* was not only the first talkie in the series, but also the story of an uncivilized man who learns to speak. While those famous words "Me, Tarzan – you, Jane" are noticeably absent from the dialog, Weissmuller communicates their primitive impact through the very essence of his being. His Tarzan was not meant to be a fallen British aristocrat, as Burroughs had written him, but a specimen of pure red-blooded masculinity – a breed apart from modern man.

No one knew this better than the worldly Jane (Maureen O'Sullivan), who turned Hollywood's masculine gaze on its head as desire filled her eyes, an impulse to which the female audience responded: longing to be held in Tarzan's meaty arms, to be tossed around and protected by him, while taming him a little. Male viewers, conversely, liked to imagine themselves slipping into the role as Johnny. But as the Janes of this world discovered, they were all too tame to live up to the fantasy.

Needless to say, when Jane sets off for darkest Africa with her father, James Parker (C. Aubrey Smith), and his assistant, Harry (Neil Hamilton), it's not love she's after. Instead, the purpose of the exhibition is to locate a legendary elephant cemetery, containing an unlimited supply of ivory. Predictably, Harry – Jane's would-be suitor – is the ape man's rival, but he doesn't stand a chance. For even if Jane's upbringing prevents her from ever discarding her western fig leaves, it's the idyllic lifestyle with Tarzan *à la* Adam and Eve that she opts for in the end.

While there's no denying the implicit sensuality of Tarzan's tale, other aspects of the story prevent younger fans from picking up on it. From Tarzan's battles with lions and crocodiles to the trademark call of the wild he uses to summon help from friends, elephants and hippos alike, director W. S. Van Dyke made sure that plenty of excitement was in store for kids. To this day, the debate continues among viewers of all ages as to whether Weissmuller's jungle yodel was his own creation or really a mixture of human and

> # "A jungle and stunt picture, done in deluxe style and carrying large draw possibilities from the following of the Burroughs books series." *Variety*

animal sounds. Whatever the case, with Tarzan either swinging from vine to vine or swimming freestyle upstream, action was never lacking. Yes, MGM did its best to deliver a colorful assortment of jungle eye candy. And the mix certainly would have been incomplete without a fair share of politically incorrect pygmies and other indigenous peoples, often resembling the cast of a minstrel show.

As an actual trip to Africa was considered too costly for the first Weissmuller flick, heaps of unused jungle footage shot for Van Dyke's African adventure *Trader Horn* (1931) were used to create an imperfect illusion. Be that as it may, *Tarzan the Ape Man's* phenomenal success meant that this factor was no longer a matter of debate. Indeed, MGM began planning big things for its new hero. To many film buffs, *Tarzan and His Mate* (1934) would be the

1 Where the wild things are: Swimmer Johnny Weissmuller and co-star Maureen O'Sullivan find love atop a tree in *Tarzan the Apeman*.

2 Janie get your gun: A woman of the world takes a crash course in safari survival.

3 Rosemary's mama: MGM ingénue Maureen O'Sullivan played peek-a-boo in six Tarzan pictures before leaving the jungle for director John Farrow and the perils of motherhood. Johnny Weissmuller, however, braved the wild without her in six further adventures at RKO.

4 Positively primeval: What better way to get close to Jane than by telling tall tales of the jungle's many dangers?

"It is a cleverly photographed film and, although some adults may doubt that Mr. Weissmuller kills two lions and a leopard with a knife after a prolonged struggle, there is good enough camera trickery for lads and lassies and mayhap a few parents to believe that Johnny Weissmuller took his life in his hands when he agreed to act in this jungle feature."

The New York Times

His tombstone reads: Johnny Peter Weissmuller, Tarzan: 1904–1984. Who can blame Weissmuller for wanting to be remembered as the "King of the Jungle" and not as Hollywood's first male pin-up? Many fans recognize his undying commitment to the character and readily credit him with having come up with Tarzan's trademark primal scream. Some even say it was inspired by the legend's own ancestors, who spent their weekends yodeling in the mountains. Throughout his life, Weissmuller took great pains to hide the fact that he emigrated from the former Austro-Hungarian Empire, where Romania is today. Claiming to be American-born, Weissmuller claimed five gold medals for the U.S. as an Olympic swimmer. In addition, he set 67 world records and won 52 national championships. When MGM was looking for a new Tarzan, Weissmuller was the studio's top pick; all Louis Mayer needed to do to get him to sign on was to buy out the remainder of his contract as a swimwear model.

As MGM's primordial stud, Weissmuller swung from the vines of a whooping twelve features. In the series' initial installment, *Tarzan the Ape Man* (1932), he lost his heart to Jane, a role Maureen O'Sullivan would continue to play for the first six pictures. *Tarzan and His Mate* (1934) had him combating cannibals and gorillas, whereas profit-hungry game hunters served as equally worthy villains in *Tarzan Escapes* (1936). *Tarzan's New York Adventure* (1942) catapulted him into modern civilization and *Tarzan Triumphs* (1942) brought him face-to-face with the Nazis in a fight to maintain control of the jungle. But by the time *Tarzan and the Mermaids* (1948) came along Weissmuller was all washed up, and Lex Barker was hired to replace him for MGM's next Tarzan movie. *Jungle Jim* (1955) brought Weissmuller to television audiences in what was publicized as a brand new role – even though he'd already played the character for the big screen on thirteen separate occasions.

By the end of the 50s little was left of the fortune Weissmuller had amassed in the course of his Hollywood career, and he became a regular on the talk-show circuit. With none of his six marriages ending happily, the final years of his life were spent in a home for impoverished actors, where he is said to have often startled the neighbors by howling like Tarzan in the middle of the night. By this time, Weissmuller was suffering the effects of mental illness. He died in Acapulco.

series' crowning achievement – if not the best Tarzan movie of all time; but later episodes were also packed with entertainment for the young and young at heart. Arguably, the downfall of Tarzan and Co. came when the Production Code went into effect: steamy costumes were toned down; Tarzan and Jane 'adopted' a son; and beloved chimp sidekick, Cheeta, gradually took on an all-too-central role. To top it all, Johnny Weissmuller cultivated himself a set of love handles that the people at wardrobe couldn't cover. Yet for what it was worth, his tongue-tied, somewhat oafish, but altogether well-meaning Tarzan is still the one audiences love best. Perhaps the greatest irony is that despite being a pacifist and friend of the environment, Tarzan became the prototype modern action heroes like Clint Eastwood, Arnold Schwarzenegger and Sylvester Stallone built their careers on. But just how Tarzan ever got to the jungle remains the great mystery of the Weissmuller movies.

PB

5   Mr. Hunky and his monkey: Although Jane isn't sure what to make of Cheeta at first, the two of them become fast friends. In later episodes, the monkey serves as the celibate couple's surrogate child.

6   Nudie cuties: One of the steamier displays of savage love.

THE VAMPIRE

Vampyr – Der Traum des Allan Gray / Vampyr ou l'étrange aventure de David Gray

1932 - GERMANY / FRANCE - 74 MIN. - B & W - HORROR MOVIE

DIRECTOR CARL THEODOR DREYER (1889–1968)
SCREENPLAY CHRISTEN JUL, CARL THEODOR DREYER, based on the novella *CARMILLA* by JOSEPH SHERIDAN LE FANU
DIRECTORS OF PHOTOGRAPHY RUDOLPH MATÉ, LOUIS NÉE **EDITING** PAUL FALKENBERG, TONKA TALDY **MUSIC** WOLFGANG ZELLER
PRODUCTION CARL THEODOR DREYER, NICOLAS DE GUNZBERG for TOBIS-FILMKUNST GMBH.

STARRING JULIAN WEST [= NICOLAS DE GUNZBERG] (Allan Gray), MAURICE SCHUTZ (Lord of the Manor),
RENA MANDEL (Gisèle, the younger daughter), SYBILLE SCHMITZ (Léone, the elder daughter),
JAN HIERONIMKO (Doctor Marc), HENRIETTE GÉRARD (Marguerite Chopin), ALBERT BRAS (Old Servant),
N. BABANINI (His Wife), JANE MORA (Nurse).

"In the land of the shadows."

Vampyr relates the strange adventures of Allan Gray (Julian West = Nicolas de Gunzberg), a young man with psychic abilities. The film opens with his arrival at an abandoned inn in the French village of Courtempierre. In the middle of the night, he receives an unexpected call from an old man (Maurice Schutz) who declares that his daughter must not die, and entrusts him with a sealed package that is only to be opened after his death. As Gray discovers the following day, this nocturnal apparition was the owner of a nearby castle –, who has just been ambushed and shot dead. The young man also finds out that one of the nobleman's daughters, Léone (Sybille Schmitz) is dying of an unknown disease. In the sealed package, he finds an ancient chronicle whose contents help him understand what is going on. Marguerite Chopin (Henriette Gérard) was an old woman who had been buried in the village graveyard in unhallowed ground; now she's a vampire who needs the blood of children and young people in order to prolong her own life. Chopin has already placed several people under her ghastly spell, transforming them into

representatives of the undead, and she has a devoted lackey in the physician Doctor Marc (Jan Hieronimko). But Allan Gray falls in love with the second daughter, Gisèle (Rena Mandel), and agrees to give blood for Léone. Together with a servant (Albert Bras), he sneaks out to the vampire's grave, opens her coffin and pierces her heart with an iron stake. The power of the monster is extinguished, Léone is on the way back to health, and the physician pays for his wicked deeds with his life.

Vampyr was made in France as a silent film, and some sound was later added in Berlin. There has still been no satisfactory restoration of the movie, which makes it quite a challenge to follow the complex plot. The story is based on Joseph Sheridan Le Fanu's *Carmilla*, published in 1872 as part of the collection *In a Glass Darkly*. What makes the film so memorable is its evocative pictorial language. The flickering, shadowy cosmos of *Vampyr* recalls the dream worlds of Surrealist film experiments. Dreyer filmed on location, but the settings acquire an eerie quality thanks to the sparing use of

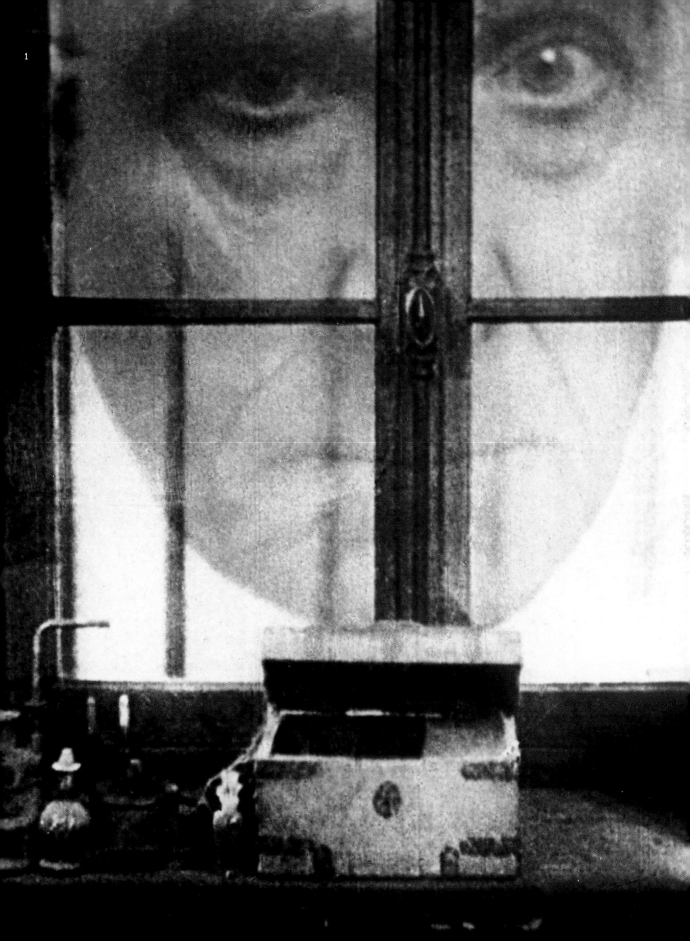

1   Window pains: The mysterious things Allan Gray
    (Julian West) sees take place in a world beyond
    his reach.

2   Me and my shadow: Expressionistic silhouettes and
    use of light are reminiscent of Friedrich Wilhelm

Murnau's silent picture *Nosferatu* (*Nosferatu –
Eine Symphonie des Grauens*, 1922).

3   For whom the bell tolls: Grim reapers and other
    omens of death creep out of every the corner.

4   Clipped feathers: Evil has ensnared Gisèle (Rena
    Mandel) in its talons and left her with no means
    of taking flight.

5   A little something to lift his spirits: Recently
    deceased, Allan Gray sees himself as he is –
    or rather was – for the very first time.

"The film contains scenes that are so eerily atmospheric, impressively eloquent in their depiction of human emotion, and such a tribute to the magic of motion pictures that one can only express the utmost gratitude when making reference to the film." *Berliner Tageblatt*

sound effects, an extremely mobile camera and the subtle treatment of light. Dream and reality merge and mingle unpredictably, and these delicate alterations of tone, which are sometimes barely perceptible, slowly but surely evoke an atmosphere of unfathomable menace. A river, a ferry, a tolling bell and a man with a scythe recall the iconography of death, and an engraving on the wall of Gray's room at the inn appears to anticipate the events that follow: when the protagonist examines the picture in the guttering light of a candle, we see the outline of a deathbed containing a skeleton in an attitude of mourning. We're left with the possibility that Allan Gray merely *dreams* the film after viewing this fragmented and bizarrely suggestive image; but, if so,

his dream is a nightmare from which there is no awakening, and at any given point in the movie, it is almost impossible to decide which level of reality we find ourselves on. In due course, the adventurer actually leaves his body, to wander as his own ghostly doppelgänger in the kingdom of the dead: helplessly, Gray witnesses the burial of his still-living body, with the camera adopting the position of the figure in the coffin. Ultimately, however, the film takes the elements of the engraving and orders them anew: death does not triumph over the living; instead, it is the vampire Marguerite Chopin whose flesh crumbles to dust. She's gone for good; but everyone else seems to linger forever in the mysterious shadow-world of the cinema.   PLB

CARL THEODOR DREYER   The Danish director Carl Theodor Dreyer was born in Copenhagen on 3 February, 1889. In 1912, after a brief period as a journalist, he went to work for the Danish film industry, at that time one of the most powerful in Europe. Dreyer wrote screenplays and made his debut as a director in 1919–1921 with *Præsidenten* (1918/19). The next film he directed was *Leaves from Satan's Book* (*Blade af Satans Bog*, 1919–1921). Borrowing from D. W. Griffith's classic *Intolerance* (1916), it consists of four episodes concerning the temptations of evil. In 1923, he spent some time in Berlin, where he made *Michael* (1923/24), a film about a painter's homosexual relationship. Dreyer became famous in 1928 with *The Passion of Joan of Arc* (*La Passion de Jeanne d'Arc*); his powerfully expressive close-up images of the actress Maria Falconetti and her astonishing performance gave the film a permanent place in cinematic history. *The Vampire* (*Vampyr – Der Traum des Allan Gray / Vampyr ou l'étrange aventure de David Gray*, 1932), however, was a box-office flop and prevented Dreyer from realizing any further film projects for years. Eventually, in 1943, during the Nazi occupation of Denmark, he made *Day of Anger* (*Vredens dag*), another study of the lure of evil. After making several documentaries for the Danish government, he directed (*Ordet*, 1954) and *Gertrud* (1964), two films that built on and developed his typically ascetic visual language. Carl Theodor Dreyer died in Copenhagen on 20 March, 1968.

4

5

SHANGHAI EXPRESS

1932 - USA - 80 MIN. - B & W - MELODRAMA

DIRECTOR JOSEF VON STERNBERG (1894–1969)
SCREENPLAY JULES FURTHMAN, based on a story by HARRY HERVEY DIRECTOR OF PHOTOGRAPHY LEE GARMES
MUSIC W. FRANKE HARLING PRODUCTION ADOLPH ZUKOR for PARAMOUNT PICTURES.

STARRING MARLENE DIETRICH (Shanghai Lily / Madeleine), CLIVE BROOK (Captain Donald Harvey),
ANNA MAY WONG (Hui Fei), WARNER OLAND (Henry Chang), EUGENE PALLETTE (Sam Salt),
LAWRENCE GRANT (Mr. Carmichael), LOUISE CLOSSER HALE (Mrs. Haggerty),
GUSTAV VON SEYFFERTITZ (Eric Baum), EMILE CHAUTARD (Major Lenard), CLAUDE KING (Mr. Albright).

ACADEMY AWARDS 1932 OSCAR for BEST CINEMATOGRAPHY (Lee Garmes).

"It took more than one man to change my name to Shanghai Lily."

"Original stories aren't what put filmmaker Josef von Sternberg on the map. Instead, he had a way of taking ordinary melodrama and transforming it through direction." So said Spanish auteur Luis Buñuel of von Sternberg in his autobiography, having observed his artistic methods firsthand in the early 30s. Buñuel's succinct analysis of the Viennese-born director certainly applies to *Shanghai Express*. The film culminates in an against-all-odds romance – after a group of Chinese rebels take over a train containing an assorted mix of passengers – but it's actually classic melodrama.

The story is simple. British officer and physician Donald Harvey (Clive Brook) and his former flame Madeleine (a.k.a. the notorious Shanghai Lily, played by Marlene Dietrich) cross paths for the first time in five years on board a locomotive headed from Peking to Shanghai. Although it's immediately apparent that they still feel affection for one another, Harvey still bears the scars of their separation and has lost all faith in his love, who has led the life of a kept woman with many bedfellows. The knots of melodrama tighten swiftly when Henry Chang (Warner Oland), the leader of the rebels, agrees to release Harvey unscathed provided that he can become Lily's new keeper. Thank heavens for the genre's beloved *deus ex machina*: not only does Hui Fei (Anna May Wong) kill the despot in cold blood to avenge her own rape, but the theologian Mr. Carmichael (Lawrence Grant) vouches for Lily's honorable

2

"But the subject of the film is Dietrich's face, on which it plays an endless series of variations: veiled, shadowed, wreathed with smoke, nestling in furs or feathers, framed in patterns of black and white. Even more than in Sternberg's previous films, the action is claustrophobically confined, thus concentrating yet further the emotional charge of the mise-en-scène." *Philip Kemp, in: John Wakeman, World Film Directors*

conduct while held captive and deems her soul cleansed. A happy ending is clearly on the cards.

Although the variety pack of entertaining travelers succeed in juicing up what would otherwise be a pretty flat story, that's not what makes *Shanghai Express* classic cinema. It is manifestly Sternberg's extravagant depiction of an imagined China and the deification of his leading lady that take center stage as Dietrich coolly beguiles and nonchalantly teases her way through exotic Asia. For his stunning backdrop, von Sternberg used everything Paramount's set decoration and costume departments had at their disposal, and they certainly ran wild. A master cameraman himself, Sternberg was the only filmmaker of the era who was also a member of the American Society of Cinematographers (an association that can be joined by invitation only). As the man behind the lighting and set construction for a series of her glamour shots, he was considered an undisputed genius when it came to showing Dietrich at her best.

Shanghai Express was the fourth of Sternberg's seven collaborations with his prize discovery Marlene Dietrich, who followed him to Hollywood shortly after they shot *The Blue Angel* (*Der blaue Engel*, 1930). As with all their other pictures, Dietrich's character in the Chinese adventure drew from the actress's trademark poses and gestures made famous by Svengali Joe's still photography. Here, his camera recreates all the allure as Marlene lasciviously smokes, runs her fingers through her hair and provocatively sports army caps. The picture's official cameraman, Lee Garmes, carried off the Oscar for Best Cinematography, and his contribution is not to be underestimated.

1 Full steam ahead: A hot romance awaits former lovers Captain Donald Harvey (Clive Brook) and Madeleine (Marlene Dietrich) – the woman who commands his heart.

2 Use your noggin: Madeleine a. k. a Shanghai Lily puts her honor and her life on the line for Captain Harvey's freedom.

3 Chinese checkers: Hui Fei (Anna May Wong) and rebel leader Henry Chang (Warner Oland) keep tabs on potential enemies – including each other.

4 Ambush on the Orient Express: With this many bloodthirsty rebels on board, you don't need to be Agatha Christie to figure out whodunit.

5 Bullet train: Von Sternberg travels from California to China in record time by relocating Peking to San Bernardino.

"Mr. Sternberg keeps his camera continually darting hither and thither, but never without lending the eye time to rest upon a scene, which gives his story a chance to progress." *The New York Times*

6 Sweet and sour sex pistols: Madeleine and Hui Fei are known for being as naughty as they are nice.

7 Three little pigs: They're only friendly to those who don't squeal.

8 Risky business: If a life of espionage doesn't kill her, cancer will.

Von Sternberg's talent was not limited to scenes with the legendary Dietrich. His superb orchestration of shadow and light is on stunning display in the scene where the rebels swarm over the train as it pulls into a station at night while agitated soldiers are enveloped in a smokescreen of steam. The hustle-bustle of the introductory sequence at the Peking's main train station (actually filmed in San Bernardino, California) is just as impressive: hundreds of extras rush every which way as the tracking shot glides alongside the moving train, while dissolved and superimposed images of count-er-running motions combine to create a maelstrom impression of compressed urban chaos.

Dialog scenes, in contrast, are as tranquil as can be. Dietrich and Brook speak slowly, exaggerate their delivery, and allow for dramatic pauses long enough to accommodate the text inserts of the silent-movie era. While many critics sight this as an obvious shortcoming, it actually complements von Sternberg's overall concept of artificiality, the product of an imagination at its all-time high. LP

ANNA MAY WONG (1905–1961)

When it came to on-screen Asians, most early moviegoers preferred powdery white actors to the real thing. Los Angeles native Anna May Wong (born Wong Liu Tsong) was the exception to the rule. She premiered in *The Red Lantern* (1919) at the age of 14 and developed into Hollywood's great – and for decades sole – Asian star. A regular glamor girl, Wong was cast as the female lead in the industry's second ever two-color Technicolor picture, Chester M. Franklin's *The Toll of the Sea* (1922). For her next major role, she appeared opposite Douglas Fairbanks and won the attention of both press and audience alike as a sadistic Mongolian slave in Raoul Walsh's *The Thief of Bagdad* (1924).

Yet in spite of her astounding breakthroughs and popularity, racial prejudice limited Wong's career. Never did she get the guy – as ethnic mixing was unthinkable – and seldom did things end happily for her character. In the tradition of the countless incarnations of *Madame Butterfly* Wong portrayed for the cinema, more often than not a tragic death was the inevitable end for the parts she played.

Fluent in French and German and hoping to be cast in more interesting roles, the actress headed for Europe in 1928: she found work in England, went on to shoot pictures with German directors like Richard Eichberg and E. A. Dupont, and had a theater engagement in Vienna by 1930. Despite all this, Wong is believed to have suffered the pitfalls of her exoticism even more in Europe than she did in the United States. She won critical and public acclaim for her performance in *Shanghai Express* (1932) but had little prospect of landing more prominent roles in the future. For the next decade, Wong's career would consist of supporting roles in B-pictures, and by the 40s, it was mainly theater-based. Nonetheless, she did have a short-lived series while television was still in its infancy. A few years after being diagnosed with heart disease, Anna May Wong died in her sleep of a cardiac arrest. She was 56 years old.

"Von Sternberg, the director, has made this effort interesting through a definite command of the lens. As for plot structure and dialog, *Shanghai Express* runs much too close to old meller and serial themes to command real attention. Hence, the finished product is an example of what can be done with the personality and photographic face Miss Dietrich possesses, and ways to circumvent a trashy story." *Variety*

LIEBELEI

1932/33 - GERMANY - 87 MIN. - B & W - DRAMA, LITERARY ADAPTATION

DIRECTOR MAX OPHÜLS (1902–1957)
SCREENPLAY MAX OPHÜLS, CURT ALEXANDER, HANS WILHELM, based on the play of the same name by
ARTHUR SCHNITZLER DIRECTOR OF PHOTOGRAPHY FRANZ PLANER EDITING FRIEDEL BUCKOW MUSIC THEO MACKEBEN
PRODUCTION CHRISTOPH MÜLLENEISEN for ELITE TONFILM-PRODUCTION GMBH.

STARRING WOLFGANG LIEBENEINER (Second Lieutenant Fritz Lobheimer), MAGDA SCHNEIDER (Christine Weyring),
WILLY EICHBERGER (Lieutenant Theo Kaiser), LUISE ULLRICH (Mizzi Schlager), GUSTAF GRÜNDGENS (Baron von Eggersdorf),
OLGA TSCHECHOWA (Baroness von Eggersdorf), PAUL HÖRBIGER (Old Weyring), PAUL OTTO (Major von Eggersdorf),
WERNER FINCK (Binder, the Musician), EKKEHARD ARENDT (Lieutenant von Lensky).

"Any shot that isn't fired in self-defense is murder!"

Liebelei was the fourth and final film made by Max Ophüls in Germany. Barely three weeks after the premiere, the 30-year-old director went into exile in Paris: as a Jew and an intellectual, he had no future in Hitler's Germany, where his dwindling work prospects were the least of his worries.

It was a quiet departure, and one he hadn't chosen. As he headed for Bahnhof Zoo, the Station in the heart of Berlin, Ophüls passed the Atrium cinema, where the name of his best movie to date was up in lights. With Liebelei, he had found his style. The film already displays all the essential characteristics of an artist who would reach perfection in his maturity: the play with levels of representation; the weird fluctuation between the theatrical and the real; the use of music to heighten the effect of a scene; and last but not least, the creation of cleverly planned sequences coupled with elaborate tracking shots through opulent film sets – these are the elements of Max Ophüls' unmistakable style.

If the producers had gotten their way, the film would have been a cheesily romantic tale of Old Vienna. Ophüls had something very different in mind: he had little interest in an authentic Viennese setting, but wanted to transport Arthur Schnitzler's turn-of-the-century drama to the present day. For years, he had had his own poetic vision of the film's total look. In the leading roles, he cast young, dynamic actors with loads of self-confidence. Only the supporting roles were played by popular and experienced stars, such as Gustaf Gründgens, Paul Hörbiger and Olga Tschechowa. This unorthodox casting proved to be a very smart move. Ophüls' direction lends enormous intensity and emotional power to the story of young Second Lieutenant Fritz Lobheimer (Wolfgang Liebeneiner) and the virtuous musician's daughter Christine Weyring (Magda Schneider)

The two meet by accident during a performance of Mozart's "Abduction from the Seraglio." At first, they seem to have no interest in one another; but

"This drama's carefully constructed sequence of events is a perfect example of epic cinema. The picture also demonstrates just how little the talkie has actually changed the cinematic medium as a whole."

Deutsche Filmzeitung

then, on a night walk through the snow-covered city of Vienna, they suddenly become aware of their feelings. Ophüls directs this episode as a rhythmic sequence of sensual images, underscored with a string composition that combines light and shade. Tiny, apparently insignificant gestures reveal the emotional turmoil of the two young lovers: Fritz has a headache, so Christine holds his military cap while pressing a cold handkerchief to his forehead; and by the time they part, the cap has been wholly forgotten.

Their love grows quickly before being wrecked by convention; by an outdated social system in which true human feelings are subordinated to a military code of honor. Before he met Christina, Fritz had had a brief affair with the Baroness von Eggersdorf (Olga Tschechowa). Although it's now over, the Baroness's husband (Gustaf Gründgens) suddenly finds out. Furious, he challenges Fritz to a duel. It is a vain and murderous act of revenge, dressed up as a desire for justice. Fritz's best friend, Lieutenant Theo Kaiser (Willy Eichberger) desperately tries to stop the duel by pleading with his regiment's commanding officer, who is too stupid and narrow-minded to get the point. When Fritz tries to persuade him that the duel is senseless, the old officer is merely confused: "What, does the young fellow wish to *evade* the challenge?"

1   Crystal ball: Christine Weyring (Magda Schneider) sees herself falling in love but cannot predict the crash that follows.

2   Nutcracker sweethearts: Max Ophüls' fresh cast of actors. From left – Willy Eichberger as Lieutenant Theo Kaiser, Luise Ullrich as Mizzi Schlager, Magda Schneider as Christine Weyring, and Wolfgang Liebeneiner as Lieutenant Fritz Lobheimer.

3

3 Noises off: An evening gathering ends on a sour note when news of death arrives on the doorstep.

4 Flirting with disaster: All Mizzi wanted was a night cap, but ended up turning the military hierarchy on its head.

The duel scene exemplifies Ophüls' ability to tell more by showing less. As in the opening sequence in the theater, he trusts entirely in the audience's imagination to make manifest things that could barely be shown adequately with conventional techniques. In the theater, it's the German Kaiser's arrival in his box. By skilfully changing camera perspectives in the auditorium, Ophüls makes us aware of the Kaiser's presence without ever showing us that he's there. The same thing happens at the duel. The duelists' coaches drive up and then disappear into the snow-covered forest. The camera pans round to Lieutenant Theo Kaiser and his girlfriend Mizzi (Luise Ullrich), who are watching events from a distance. "Just 30 seconds more," says Theo nervously. It's been agreed that each man may fire his gun three times, and the Baron has first shot … The crack of gunfire cuts through the silence. Mizzi and Theo recoil in shock. Time stretches endlessly. The couple waits for the next shot; but it never comes. And when Christina hears that Fritz is dead, she chooses to die herself.

SF

GUSTAF GRÜNDGENS Born in Düsseldorf in 1899, Gustaf Gründgens was an actor, director and theater manager. Though he worked mainly in the theater, his film performances were hardly less impressive. In Max Ophüls' *Liebelei*, where he had the thankless task of playing a cuckolded Baron, Gründgens works wonders with his eyes alone, firing off icy, unfeeling glances like bullets. A performer of masterly precision, Gustaf Gründgens studied acting with Louise Dumont in Düsseldorf before moving to Berlin, where he worked with the great German director Max Reinhardt.

From 1926–1929, he was married to Erika Mann, daughter of the novelist Thomas Mann. Her brother Klaus Mann later wrote a novel ("Mephisto", 1933) that painted an unflattering portrait of the talented and ambitious actor. Gründgens took legal action to ensure that no further edition of the book was printed. Only in 1981 was the novel published in Germany again; in the same year, Istvan Szabó produced a memorable film adaptation, starring Klaus Maria Brandauer as the Gründgens character (*Mephisto*, 1981).

On stage, Gründgens was principally admired for his classical roles, from Shakespeare's Hamlet to Goethe's Mephistopheles. After the war, he was artistic director at the theater in Düsseldorf, and from 1955 onwards he ran the Deutsches Schauspielhaus in Hamburg. Not only did he stage "Faust" repeatedly, and play the demonic tempter himself; in 1960, he even made a film adaptation of it, together with Peter Gorski.

In the cinema, he had other successes in Fritz Lang's *M* (*M – Eine Stadt sucht einen Mörder*, 1931), in *Pygmalion* (Erich Engel, 1935), in the two Hans Steinhoff films, *Tanz auf dem Vulkan* (1938) and *Ohm Krüger* (1941), and in Helmut Käutner's *A Glass of Water* (*Das Glas Wasser*, 1960). Of the nine movies he directed himself, the most memorable are his adaptation of Fontane's novel "Effi Briest", *The False Step* (*Der Schritt vom Weg*, 1939) and a musical *galanterie* starring Heinz Rühmann and Theo Lingen: *The Grand Duke's Finances* (*Die Finanzen des Grossherzogs*, 1934). Gustaf Gründgens died in Manila in 1963.

THE TESTAMENT OF DR. MABUSE
Das Testament des Dr. Mabuse

1932/33 - GERMANY - 122 MIN. - B & W - THRILLER, LITERARY ADAPTATION

DIRECTOR FRITZ LANG (1890–1976)
SCREENPLAY THEA VON HARBOU, based on the novel *DR. MABUSES LETZTES SPIEL* by NORBERT JACQUES
DIRECTORS OF PHOTOGRAPHY FRITZ ARNO WAGNER, KARL VASH EDITING CONRAD VON MOLO, LOTHAR WOLFF
MUSIC HANS ERDMANN, WALTER SIEBER PRODUCTION SEYMOUR NEBENZAHL for NERO-FILM AG.

STARRING OTTO WERNICKE (Inspector Lohmann), RUDOLF KLEIN-ROGGE (Doctor Mabuse),
OSCAR BEREGI (Professor Baum), THEODOR LOOS (Doctor Kramm), GUSTAV DIESSL (Kent),
WERA LIESSEM (Lilli), KARL MEIXNER (Hofmeister), CAMILLA SPIRA (Jewelen-Anna),
THEO LINGEN (Karetzky), RUDOLF SCHÜNDLER (Hardy).

"For the ultimate purpose of crime is to establish the unlimited dominion of crime."

Waking nightmares: a weirdly harsh voice behind an ominous curtain in an unknown room … a mysterious force that dictates the actions of a criminal gang … a demented driver speeding through the night. If you didn't know better, you could take it for a David Lynch movie, which would of course be putting the cart before the horse. When we watch Fritz Lang's Mabuse films today, it soon becomes clear just how much the contemporary cinema has profited from his creativity. Lang added a whole new dimension to the representation of subjective experience on the screen. A contemporary master of the artfully manipulated sound track such as David Lynch doesn't merely borrow freely from Fritz Lang's artistic and thematic vocabulary; he builds on a tradition actually founded by Lang. This is impressively demonstrated by the opening sequence of *The Testament of Dr. Mabuse*.

We are in the production hall of a printing plant, and the entire room seems to be vibrating. Invisible machines are beating out a repetitive pound-

ing rhythm that drowns out everything else – an 'industrial' soundtrack *avant la lettre*. A frightened man armed with a pistol is hiding behind a large wooden crate. Two other men enter the building, walk up to the crate and extract some freshly printed counterfeit bills. They notice the intruder but ignore him. The poor man doesn't realize that his fate is already sealed; outside, a group of thugs are lying in wait with a petrol-filled drum. A flash of lightning and an ear-splitting crash of thunder: Fritz Lang's transition from silent to sound film is an audiovisual masterstroke and a lesson in cinematic exposition.

This stunning prolog is followed by a crime story that's no less gripping for being unusually complex. In contrast to the earlier Mabuse films (*Dr. Mabuse, the King of Crime – Part 1: The Gambler* and *Part 2: Inferno*, 1921/22), the mad criminal mastermind Dr. Mabuse is now pitted against a worthy opponent – the burly Inspector Lohmann (Otto Wernicke). Nonetheless, with the patient, rational process of police investigation facing off

against hypnotism and telepathy, it's still very far from a fair fight. Though locked away in a mental asylum, the mad genius manages to invade the mind of his physician, Professor Baum (Oscar Beregi), and to use him as his medium to convey instructions to an underground terrorist organization. Meanwhile, the inspector struggles to thwart Mabuse's henchmen, using only his wits, his fists and his guns.

Lang's aesthetic strategy includes the repeated use of sound and imagery that is intentionally 'subjectivized' and psychologically charged. His means include a pronounced emphasis on diagonal lines in the composition of the shots, dramatic high and low-angle camera perspectives, extreme facial close-ups, and a style of acting that is unequivocally theatrical. The

evident throughout. This elaborate play of audiovisual ciphers helps to create a sinister cosmos in which straightforward actions can be so radically stylized that they acquire an odd significance. Take the scene in which Professor Baum's friend Dr. Kramm (Theodor Loos) is shot dead in broad daylight while stuck in a traffic jam. To the accompaniment of a cacophonous car horn concerto, the camera documents the killing from a peculiarly choreographed bird's-eye perspective. The vertical view simply shows us how one of the vehicles remains immobile once the traffic starts moving again. The film's chilling atmosphere is also perfectly exemplified by the closing scene, in which the new Dr. Mabuse eludes the long arm of the law by escaping into the lap of psychiatric care.

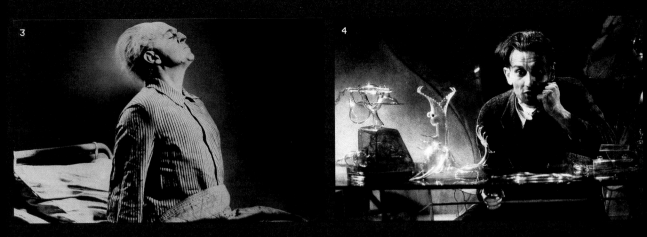

"This sequel to the silent picture and the novel, which both had enormous successes more than 12 years earlier, certainly shows the influence of American mystery pictures." *Variety*

FRITZ ARNO WAGNER (1889–1958)

German-born cameraman Wagner learned his trade in the French film production company of the Pathé Brothers, which he joined during his studies at the Academy of Arts in Paris. His interest in cinematography initially took him to New York, where he worked as a cameraman on newsreel productions. In 1914, he returned to Germany, where he joined the army one year later. After 1918, he worked for the Berlin production company Union PAGU and later for the feature film production unit of Germany's Decla-Bioscop. In Berlin, Fritz Arno Wagner soon became one of the most important cameramen in Germany during the silent-film era. Besides Fritz Lang, he worked with numerous other directors, including Friedrich Wilhelm Murnau, Georg Wilhelm Pabst and Robert Wiene. He was responsible for the cinematography in several landmark films of the time, from *Between Two Worlds* (*Der müde Tod*, 1921) to *Burning Soil* (*Der brennende Acker*, 1922) and *Westfront 1918* (1930). Wagner preferred realistic lighting design and seamless camera motion, but his work also displays traits of Expressionism. He used stark black-and-white contrasts and deep shadows to invoke feelings of tension and claustrophobia. Fritz Arno Wagner died in 1958 after falling from a camera car while working on a film.

1   Bed bugs: Criminal mastermind Dr. Mabuse (Rudolf Klein-Rogge) is itching to make his escape from the mental ward.

2   The handwriting is on the wall: While all clues seem to point to Mabuse, Commissioner Lohmann (Otto Wernicke) still lacks the evidence to solve the string of crimes.

3   Exercising his power: Mabuse harnesses his energy from an inexhaustible source – evil.

4   Bequeathment and bereavement: Trying to break Dr. Mabuse's will could drive a person mad.

5   Getting frisky: In a desperate attempt to crack the case, the cops round up as many shifty characters as they can.

6   Doctor's orders: The crime ring waits to receive instructions from Mabuse.

THE PRIVATE LIFE OF HENRY VIII

1933 - GREAT BRITAIN - 96 MIN. - B & W - HISTORICAL DRAMA

DIRECTOR ALEXANDER KORDA (1893–1956)

SCREENPLAY LAJOS BIRÓ, ARTHUR WIMPERIS DIRECTOR OF PHOTOGRAPHY GEORGES PÉRINAL EDITING STEPHEN HARRISON
MUSIC KURT SCHRÖDER PRODUCTION ALEXANDER KORDA, LUDOVICO TOEPLITZ for LONDON FILM PRODUCTIONS.

STARRING CHARLES LAUGHTON (King Henry VIII), MERLE OBERON (Anne Boleyn), WENDY BARRIE (Jane Seymour), ELSA LANCHESTER (Anne of Cleves), BINNIE BARNES (Katherine Howard), EVERLEY GREGG (Katherine Parr), ROBERT DONAT (Thomas Culpeper), FRANKLIN DYALL (Thomas Cromwell), LADY TREE (Henry's midwife), GIBB MCLAUGHLIN (French executioner), SAM LIVESEY (English executioner).

ACADEMY AWARDS 1933 OSCAR for BEST ACTOR (Charles Laughton).

"Six wives, and the best of them's the worst."

Much to the annoyance of historians, the life and work of Henry VIII are constantly reduced to his neurotic dealings with women. The worst offender of them all may well have been Alexander Korda, with his cheerfully bawdy screen biography, *The Private Life of Henry VIII* – a film that ushered in a new era in British cinema. It provides a keyhole view of the most famous English king, massively embodied by the great Charles Laughton in one of his finest roles. He's supported by five female co-stars, though by none of them for very long.

In the year 1536, Henry marries his third wife, the none-too-clever Jane Seymour (Wendy Barrie). Days previously, her predecessor Anne Boleyn (Merle Oberon) had been decapitated in the Tower. Jane bears Henry a son, but dies after giving birth. Henry takes his time before getting hitched again; the numerous ladies at court offer him enough distraction. For reasons of state, however, he can't stay unmarried for long, and so it comes to pass that

he becomes betrothed to German countess Anna von Kleve (Elsa Lanchester). Henry enters the bedchamber with a sigh: "The things I've done for England!" After this marriage is annulled, he takes the court lady Katherine Howard (Binnie Barnes) for his fifth wife. She too has her head chopped off when it turns out that she's an adulteress (the same accusation had been leveled at Anne Boleyn, with less justification and more calculation). Henry spends his last years under the command of his sixth wife, Katherine Parr (Everley Gregg) – and he mutters in frustration: "Six wives, and the best of them's the worst."

There's little indication in the film that politics was ever committed at Henry's court. A caption at the start of the film informs us that Henry's first wife, Katharine of Aragon, was "respectable and therefore of no interest." The fact is, in order to create the legal conditions that would allow him to end a marriage of 24 years, he had to take the small step of establishing the

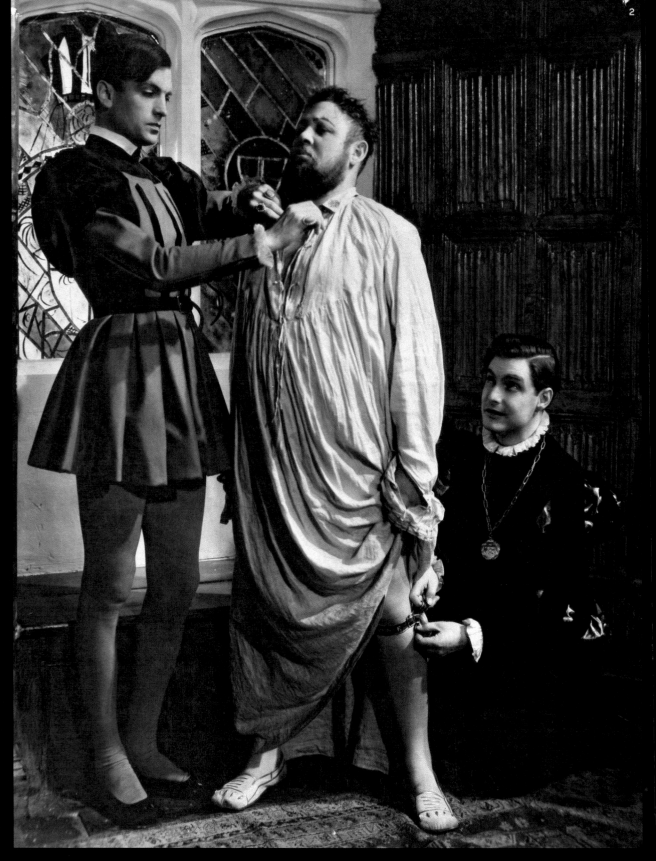

Church of England. But the other women in Henry's life are of no greater interest to Alexander Korda. The only one of them that leaves a lasting impression is the clever Anne of Cleves, played by Laughton's wife, Elsa Lanchester. Like Ernst Lubitsch before him, Korda is more interested in what the man (and woman) in the street have to say. Even in the opening scenes, the chatter of maids, executioners and spectators at the chopping-block conjures up the image of a popular king whose peccadilloes were cheerfully pardoned by the common folk.

The 'real' Henry enters the scene through a door that frames him as if he were his own portrait. Charles Laughton seems indistinguishable from the man in Holbein's famous painting. Yet this noble apparition is immediately demystified: Laughton, the Renaissance Man, boozes, belches, blubbers and bellows his way through the role, and the spectacle is an unmitigated delight. His Henry is a man of flesh and blood who suffers like a dog at his failure to produce a male heir. He can demand terrified deference whenever he will; when he laughs, and he likes to laugh, the world laughs with him, neces-

1   Fit for a king: Holbein's portrait of England's favorite churchgoer comes to life in *The Private Life of Henry VIII*, starring Charles Laughton in the title role.

2   Eye on the unmentionable(s): In this behind-the-scenes look at history, Henry often gets caught with his pants down.

3   When the cat's away, the monarch will play: Anne Boleyn and Jane Seymour (Wendy Barrie) are in a neck-to-neck race for Henry's affections.

3

4   Six-course meal: Henry works up an appetite for his fifth wife Katherine Howard (Binnie Barnes) while watching her sing for her supper.

5   All work and no play: Henry won't rest until he has given England a royal successor.

Henry VIII: Ah, what am I, what am I going to do with you!
Anne of Cleves: Chop my head?
Henry VIII: Probably ...
Anne of Cleves: I would consent to a divorce.
Henry VIII: You are a very reasonable woman.

Film quote: King Henry VIII (Charles Laughton) and Anne of Cleves (Elsa Lanchester)

> "Mr. Laughton may be guilty of caricaturing the role, but occasionally truths shine in the midst of the hilarity. He gives an admirable idea of Henry's vanity and also of his impetuousness, his sense of humor, his courage, and fear. There is Laughton's amusing twist of his mouth and nose when he outwits, as Henry thinks, other persons in his entourage. This Henry is seldom able to conceal his actual thoughts. If he admires a woman, not only she knows, but everybody else." *The New York Times*

sarily. But he cannot succeed in hiding his feelings, and so he roars them out – as in the famous banquet scene, in which Henry, with his mouth full to overflowing, laments the "tactlessness" of those who are urging him to marry again.

The budget of £60,000 meant that *The Private Life of Henry VIII* was not an expensive movie. There is something decidedly theatrical about this royal farce, and its best qualities are undoubtedly Laughton's masterly performance, the witty screenplay, and the exquisite designs by Korda's brother Vincent. It was, however, a hugely important movie for the British film industry.

The historical theme and the artistic quality of the film brought the cinematic medium the respect it had always lacked in skeptical England. Even more importantly, Korda's movie was a big success in the States. Until then, British films had struggled to compete with Hollywood products, even in the domestic market; now, the British cinema was suddenly an international contender. Alexander Korda used the enormous profits to set up his Denham Studios, and Charles Laughton won an Academy Award as Best Actor for the role. He was the first Brit ever to do so, and it marked his ascension to true international stardom.   PB

ALEXANDER KORDA (1893–1956)

The director and – for a while – extremely powerful producer Alexander Korda is best known for his large-scale adventure movies and episodic film biographies. He was no less important to the British cinema than Alfred Hitchcock.

Korda was born in Hungary and began his working life as a journalist. He was a member of that small but extremely productive Hungarian film community that also produced Michael Curtiz. After directing numerous films in his native country, Korda worked in Vienna and Berlin and suffered a disastrous interlude in Hollywood before finally arriving in Britain in 1932. *The Private Life of Henry VIII* (1933) marked a huge breakthrough for British cinema and for Korda's own career. He set up Denham Studios, and his company London Film Productions reached a distribution agreement with United Artists.

With *The Private Life of Don Juan* (1934) and *Rembrandt* (1936) – another showcase for Charles Laughton's unique talent – Korda carried on using his successful formula. As a producer, he created the conditions for such opulent colonial epics as *Elephant Boy* (1937), *The Four Feathers* (1939) and the fairytale classic *The Thief of Baghdad* (1940). Most of these films were directed by his brother, Zoltan Korda, and it's often been complained that they are decidedly imperialist in their tone and attitude. The films directed by Alexander Korda himself are very different. Intelligent and occasionally cynical, *The Private Life of Henry VIII* and *Rembrandt* are clearly the work of a less conventional observer of human behavior. Korda's success was also due to his photographic memory, his fluency in half a dozen languages, and his eloquent conversation, which was described as "hypnotic."

He made stars of Leslie Howard, Robert Donat, Vivien Leigh and Merle Oberon, who became his second wife. But his films were expensive, and in 1938 he had to give up Denham Studios. Five years later, he merged London Film Productions with the British section of MGM – a decision he later regretted and reversed. In 1949, Alexander Korda made film history once more with a legendary co-production: *The Third Man* (1949). He died in 1956, shortly before London Film Productions closed down for good.

42ND STREET

1933 - USA - 89 MIN. - B & W - MUSICAL

DIRECTOR LLOYD BACON (1890–1955)
SCREENPLAY RIAN JAMES, JAMES SEYMOUR, based on the novel of the same name by BRADFORD ROPES
DIRECTOR OF PHOTOGRAPHY SOL POLITO EDITING THOMAS PRATT, FRANK WARE MUSIC HARRY WARREN (Songs)
and AL DUBIN (Lyrics) PRODUCTION DARRYL F. ZANUCK for WARNER BROS.

STARRING WARNER BAXTER (Julian Marsh), BEBE DANIELS (Dorothy Brock), GEORGE BRENT (Pat Denning),
RUBY KEELER (Peggy Sawyer), GUY KIBBEE (Abner Dillon), UNA MERKEL (Lorraine Fleming),
GINGER ROGERS (Ann Lowell), NED SPARKS (Thomas Barry), DICK POWELL (Billy Lawler),
ALLEN JENKINS (Mac Elroy), GEORGE E. STONE (Andy Lee).

"You're going out there a youngster, but you've got to come back a star!"

Had there been no Black Tuesday in 1929 and no Great Depression thereafter, *42nd Street* would have never been written. Building its story on the economic crisis weighing upon the era, the picture begins with Broadway star director Julian Marsh (Warner Baxter), a man the stock market crash has left in the red. Although Marsh's health is failing fast, he refuses to throw in the towel on his career without a penny to show for it. "Pretty Lady" is to be the director's swan song and all involved are desperate for a hit: the company's chorus girls need a show that will ensure them a steady meal ticket, whereas the producers are pushing for a vehicle that'll make stage diva Dorothy Brock (Bebe Daniels) shine like never before. For, as everyone knows, Broadway only has one 'pretty lady' as far the production's primary financial backer, Abner Dillon (Guy Kibbee), is concerned. Little does he suspect that his dibs on Brock's heart are by no means exclusive …

42nd Street is an in-depth look at what goes into putting up a show. Beginning at square one, the film slides into auditions, where chorus hopeful Peggy Sawyer (Ruby Keeler) shines despite a mean case of butterflies. Once the production is cast, we shadow the group through back-breaking rehearsals and opening preview jitters. At this point, it seems that disaster has officially befallen the show when its star unexpectedly waxes hysterical. In front of the entire company, she ends her relationships with the production's wealthy sponsor, divulges that she's having an affair with someone else, and – on top of all that – breaks her foot. Despite the humiliation, Dillon continues to see things from an economic point of view – and demands that a suitable replacement be found for Dorothy. All eyes now turn to Peggy, the rookie everyone is counting on to save the show. She learns the blocking in no time

flat and is a bona fide star by the time the opening-night curtain falls. Of course, the fairy tale doesn't end there: Peggy goes on to win the heart of the show's male lead, Billy (Dick Powell), and Mr. Moneybags gets the wounds of his broken heart dressed by a revue girl named Lorraine (Una Merkel), who suddenly seems to have a big future ahead of her …

In the spirit of its plot, *42nd Street's* off-screen story was also a tale of debuts. Broadway star Ruby Keeler had never appeared before the big-screen camera and was thus a Peggy Sawyer in her own right. 42nd Street gave Keeler the chance to blow audiences away with her song and dance stylings, while establishing her and co-star Dick Powell (in the role of Billy) as an unstoppable dream couple of Warner musicals fame. The movie was also magic for Ginger Rogers, who delivers a pre-Astaire, breakout performance as Peggy's friend 'Anytime Annie.' This character and her equally sassy counterpart Lorraine introduce viewers to a type of shrewd-minded but good-natured showgirl, who always keeps her eyes peeled for a big spender. Known as *Gold Diggers*, this breed of woman dominated the big-screen musical in a four-picture series – made in 1933, 1935, 1936 and 1938 – that was a favorite of the decade.

Just as significant, if not more so, was the impact Busby Berkeley's revolutionary choreography had on *42nd Street* and the cinema as a whole. As the director of musical sequences, Berkeley created three production numbers for the final third of Lloyd Bacon's film that outshone all the others. Loosely integrated into the backstage goings-on, these song and dance sequences have a life of their own that refuses to adhere to the logic of the physical world. Rather than witnessing the company 'practicing on stage'

1 The city so nice, they named it twice: Manhattan's skyscrapers shake, rattle and roll at the sight of new dance sensation Peggy Sawyer, played by Ruby Keeler in her first starring role.

2 Start spreading the news: Billy Lawler (Dick Powell) finds out why New York is the city that never sleeps.

BUSBY BERKELEY Shortly after the U.S. troops landed in France in 1917, a young soldier named Busby Berkeley (1895–1976) got his first shot at choreography by staging the victory marches. As someone who was raised in a family of traveling actors, show business was in the young man's blood. Back on American soil, he began to establish a career for himself as a Broadway actor and choreographer. At the behest of producer Samuel Goldwyn, Berkeley went to Hollywood in 1930 and built up a career as a so-called 'director of musical sequences.' It was the year when Goldwyn Studios began priding itself on the Berkeley touch, which had turned pictures like *Whoopee!* (1930) into smash hits. Nonetheless, it was to be the production numbers he created for Warner musicals like *42nd Street* (directed by Lloyd Bacon, 1933) that would later be credited as bearing his official seal. In the same season, Berkeley continued to astonish audiences with his work in Mervyn LeRoy's *Gold Diggers of 1933* (1933) and Lloyd Bacon's *Footlight Parade* (1933). Two years later, *Gold Diggers of 1935* gave him his first opportunity to take full responsibility for direction, with his choreography for its "Lullaby of Broadway" sequence bringing him the first of three Oscar nominations. Movie musical sensation *Babes in Arms* (1939), starring Judy Garland, revitalized Berkeley's career and he continued to reap Hollywood laurels for the next decade. 1949's *Take Me Out to the Ball Game* marked the last time he would direct a picture on his own. From then on, his contributions would solely on dance. The great film innovator Busby Berkeley died in Palm Springs in 1976.

> ## "In and of themselves, Berkeley's dances constitute a theory of art, a neo-Romantic explanation of the origins of dance and song."
>
> *Rick Altman, in: The American Film Musical*

or 'rehearsing in the wings,' we are transported to an imaginary cinematic space without physical constraints – one where snappy tunes and tapping chorus girls meet an autonomous camera and montage.

Close-ups of chorus girls play up the element of seductive eroticism, which increasingly acquires the abstraction of a pattern as the camera turns its attention from the ladies to the troop as a whole. Such is the case in "Young and Healthy," as the individual dancers virtually disappear after joining together in a synchronized kick-line. It's a trend toward total ornamentation that also pops up in segments with highly extravagant and compartmentalized decor, like "Shuffle Off to Buffalo" – staged in sleeper cars – as well

in the piece's specialty number and title song "42nd Street," featuring dancing skyscrapers. And yet nowhere is the tendency to abstract geometric shapes clearer than in the famous Berkeley top shot, where a group of girls filmed from overhead melts into various kaleidoscopic formations, focusing not on the bodies of the individual dancers but their impact as a whole. It was unlike anything that moviegoers had ever seen before.

It comes as no surprise that *42nd Street* became a blueprint for the many backstage musicals that followed. Berkeley's three production numbers or variations thereof were responsible for the success of these pictures and continued to shape this branch of the genre for years to come.   JS

3 Come and treat my broken feet: One star's injury is another's big break.

4 Thank heaven for little girls: Young Hollywood starlets light up a Broadway chorus line.

From left – Una Merkel as Lorraine, Ruby Keeler as Peggy and Ginger Rogers as Ann.

DUCK SOUP

1933 - USA - 68 MIN. - B & W - COMEDY

DIRECTOR LEO MCCAREY (1898–1969)
SCREENPLAY BERT KALMAR, HARRY RUBY, ARTHUR SHEEKMAN, NAT PERRIN
DIRECTOR OF PHOTOGRAPHY HENRY SHARP EDITING LEROY STONE MUSIC HARRY RUBY, BERT KALMAR
PRODUCTION HERMAN J. MANKIEWICZ for PARAMOUNT PICTURES.

STARRING GROUCHO MARX (Rufus T. Firefly), HARPO MARX (Pinky), CHICO MARX (Chicolini),
ZEPPO MARX (Lieutenant Bob Roland), MARGARET DUMONT (Gloria Teasdale), RAQUEL TORRES (Vera Marcal),
LOUIS CALHERN (Ambassador Trentino of Sylvania), EDMUND BREESE (Zander), CHARLES MIDDLETON (Prosecutor),
EDGAR KENNEDY (Lemonade Vendor).

"You wanna be a public nuisance?"
"Sure, how much does the job pay?"

This brief exchange between the newly inaugurated President of Freedonia, Rufus T. Firefly (Groucho Marx), and the agent Chicolini (Chico Marx), who is disguised as a peanut vendor, encapsulates the Marx Brothers' mission perfectly: *Duck Soup* is an all-out attack on the pathetic illusion that the world is rationally ordered and that decent, law-abiding citizens can have any influence at all on the way things are run.

The tiny state of Freedonia is just like its inhabitants: free, but broke. The only person with a few million at her disposal is banker's widow Mrs. Teasdale (the indomitable Margaret Dumont, in one of her best roles), but she's only prepared to invest in the bankrupt economy if Firefly agrees to take over the running of the country toot sweet. For some unfathomable reason, this brawny lady on the verge of a nervous breakdown has fallen for Rufus, a shady cigar addict with a painted-on mustache who misses no opportunity to wisecrack at her at everyone else's expense. But in order to ruin an entire country, even a chaos machine like President Firefly needs some reliable support. The dialog with Chicolini continues: "Have you got a license?" – "No,

1 Working out the menu: Dictator of Freedonia Rufus T. Firefly (Groucho Marx) considers what sort of mayhem to serve up next.

2 Life's a breeze: Until Chicolini (Chico Marx) and Pinky (Harpo Marx) show up and it spirals into a tornado.

3 Soda jerk: Pinky teaches the guy at the refreshment stand a thing or two about seltzer.

4 Lose something? When the Marx Brothers are on the case, things are prone to turn up in the oddest of places. Just be sure you're not bending over when they do.

5 Knock knock jokes: Wealthy widow Gloria Teasdale (Margaret Dumont) and Rufus T. Firefly fool around after hours.

but my dog's got a million." – "How about a job in the mint?" – "No, I no like a mint. What other flavor you got?" The whole bizarre "job-interview" takes less than a minute, and the Marx Brothers sustain this breakneck tempo for the remaining sixty-seven.

Champion lunatic in this festival of madness is Chicolini's companion Pinky (Harpo Marx), a man who's remarkably noisy for someone who can't speak. Armed with a car horn and a pair of scissors, he even manages to pack the other Marx Brothers into his endlessly capacious pockets, from which he's also capable of conjuring a blowtorch (lit, of course). Anyone rash enough to approach this jovial one-man army is soon missing several items of apparel along with his sanity and equanimity. Instead of shaking hands with you, he's more than likely to offer you his foot. "You're pulling

"The last man nearly ruined this place, he didn't know what to do with it. If you think this country's bad off now, just wait till I get through with it."

Film quote: National Anthem of Freedonia

5

6 Army fatigue: After making Duck Soup, Zeppo (second from the left) backed out of the troop's screen antics. His role as the fourth Marx brother, often spotlighted him as the voice of reason and a ladies' man. In real life, however, jokester Zeppo was anything but suave.

7 Surefire comedy: When it comes to knocking 'em dead, these guys never miss their Marx.

my leg" indeed. The Marx Brothers' anarchy is their response to the pomposity of the powerful, a principled objection to communicating with windbags, a stubborn refusal to take anyone or anything seriously. From their point of view, an actual war is just the continuation of everyday lunacy by other means.

The battle between the Peanut Vendors and the Lemonade Vendors is one of the funniest film sequences ever made, and it demonstrates that there can be no winner in such a conflict – unless it's the person who can rise above the tedium of reality by laughing out loud at it. What's comforting is the knowledge that, ultimately, all parties involved will end up looking equally dumb.

And the dialog is glorious: "If you're found, you're lost." – "You're crazy. How can I be lost if I'm found?" In 1933, at the peak of the Depression, many people were grateful for an hour's liberation through the forces of surrealism. Nonetheless, the Marx Brothers' last film for Paramount was a financial flop, and a short time later, MGM president Irving Thalberg ordered Groucho & Co. to cut down on the gags and work on their plotlines.

His advice was taken to heart. Many "Marxists" regard the first MGM movie, *A Night at the Opera* (1935) as their very best work. But for those who prefer Groucho, Harpo, Chico and Zeppo as unbridled Lords of Misrule, *Duck Soup* remains the pinnacle of the Marx Brothers' achievement.

SH

WAR SATIRES Most films in a military setting give an idealized picture of the army, and they aim, more often than not, to sanctify the business of soldiering. By contrast, movies that satirize war almost inevitably take a very dim view of the military. The Marx Brothers' *Duck Soup* (1933) depicted war as rooted in the vanity and arrogance of politicians. In one of the most famous war satires, *Dr. Strangelove or: How I Learned to Stop Worrying and Love the Bomb* (1963), Stanley Kubrick showed war as the work of an unholy and uncontrollable alliance between mad scientists and unscrupulous military leaders. The grunts on the ground have also been subjected to withering satire, as in Richard Lester's *How I Won the War* (1967), which starred John Lennon. The personal failures of individuals reveal the essential absurdity of war, for inhuman circumstances are hardly likely to bring out the best in human beings; on the contrary.

As one might expect, war satires tend to proliferate during periods of actual war: generally, though, they deal with safely historical conflicts rather than directly addressing the current slaughter. Good examples of this phenomenon are two satirical movies produced during the Vietnam War years: Robert Altman's *M*A*S*H* (1969), which is set in an army field hospital during the Korean conflict, and Mike Nichols' *Catch-22* (1970), which examines the dubious deployment of Allied troops in Italy during WWII.

7

VIKTOR AND VIKTORIA
Viktor und Viktoria

933 - GERMANY - 100 MIN. - B & W - COMEDY, MUSICAL

DIRECTOR REINHOLD SCHÜNZEL (1888–1954)
SCREENPLAY REINHOLD SCHÜNZEL **DIRECTOR OF PHOTOGRAPHY** KONSTANTIN IRMEN-TSCHET
EDITING ARNFRIED HEYNE **MUSIC** FRANZ DOELLE **PRODUCTION** ALFRED ZEISLER, EDUARD KUBAT for UFA.

STARRING RENATE MÜLLER (Susanne Lohr), HERMANN THIMIG (Viktor Hempel),
ADOLF WOHLBRÜCK [= ANTON WALBROOK] (Robert), HILDE HILDEBRAND (Ellinor), FRITZ ODEMAR (Douglas),
FRIEDEL PISETTA (Lilian), ARIBERT WÄSCHER (Francesco Alberto Punkertin), RAFFLES BILL (Variety Artiste),
TRUDE LEHMANN (Guard), ILSE GRAMHOLZ (Dancer).

"That's a man?"
"Of course!"

You have to read the closing titles of Blake Edwards' *Victor/Victoria* (1982) right to the end before you discover that this popular cross-dressing comedy and Julie Andrews vehicle was based on a German movie made in 1933. Who would have guessed it? For even in Germany, Reinhold Schünzel's *Viktor und Viktoria* – the biggest box-office hit in the first year of Hitler's dictatorship – had been almost totally forgotten by the 1980s. It was made during a period of transition, just after the Nazis had seized power, but before they had subjected the film industry to the policy of *Gleichschaltung* that ensured conformity with the party line. After the war, the film and its director were forgotten by most Germans, like so much else from that period. Yet this 'apolitical' and thoroughly likable film operetta is well worth rediscovering. In a tale of a woman who pretends to be a man pretending to a woman, the anti-authoritarian spirit of the Weimar Republic breathes one glorious last breath.

It all begins when failed actor and drag-show artiste Viktor Hempel (Hermann Thimig) meets singer Susanne Lohr (Renate Müller). He has a cold, he's unemployed, and so she becomes 'Viktor', taking over his role as a female impersonator in a small cabaret. At the end of the number, she has to whisk the wig from her head to reveal her 'true' male identity; and as a singer, she's a hell of a lot more convincing than Viktor. Susanne ('Viktoria') goes on to make a successful international career accompanied by the real Viktor but, unfortunately, she's expected to keep up the pretense offstage . . .

This becomes a problem when she encounters a particularly grateful public in London. Sir Douglas (Fritz Odemar), his lady love Ellinor (Hilde Hildebrand) and man-about-town Robert (Adolf Wohlbrück, a.k.a. Anton Walbrook) are enchanted by the young fellow with the impeccable manners. But not for nothing is Robert known as London's most eligible bachelor, and Viktoria promptly falls in love with him. By the time she finally confesses and clears the way for a happy ending, he's put her through an embarrassing test of her manliness.

Like Robert, most moviegoers will have difficulty seeing anything other than a lady under that carefully parted hair. But for one thing, the gender is less important here than the personality behind it; and for another, what we have before us is a 'talky operetta.' Back then, this early form of the musical

2

"Admirers of well-mounted musical comedy carrying the proper amount of romance, embodying several tuneful songs and presented by an excellent cast are likely to fall in love with *Viktor and Viktoria* ... The audience is not let in on the happy ending until the charming Renate, disguised as Viktor, the impersonator of Viktoria, and Herr Thimig, the real man in woman's clothing (on the stage), have got into and out of all kinds of more or less embarrassing and merry pickles." *The New York Times*

3

1 Suited for stardom: Susanne Lohr (Renate Müller) hits the big time as a woman pretending to be a man pretending to be a woman.

2 Clothes make the man: Female impersonator Viktor Hempel (Hermann Thimig) teaches a woman to beat him at his own game.

3 Our victor Victoria: Even backstage, no one suspects Susanne of being a she.

"People are going to fall at your feet when they see you as a man."

Film quote: Viktor Hempel (Hermann Thimig)

film was highly popular in Germany, and it was a good way to escape from the hard reality of everyday life. "I want a career," sings Susanne, right at the start of the film; and her dopey friend Hempel takes charge of the closing number as a tempestuous Spanish lady. Franz Doelle's score is beautifully complemented by Bruno Balz's wittily rhyming lyrics and Reinhold Schünzel's sparkling dialog. In lines like "Ich muss Whisky trinken und Hosen tragen und dummen Frauen was Liebes sagen" ("I've got to drink whisky, wear trousers and talk to stupid women about love"), the language of Goethe meets the age of Tin Pan Alley.

The gender-bending is less explicit than in Edwards' remake, more relaxed and more subtly done. Moviegoers with their eyes and ears open will spot a host of gay references -when Viktoria is subjected to Robert's curious gaze, for instance, or when she's lured onto the bed by Ellinor. Though often sorely tested in such situations, she always copes manfully. For the sake of

Robert, she has to drink whisky, take part in fist-fights and make eyes at pretty girls. The gorgeous Renate Müller sails through these scenes with a coquellish yet tomboyish charm that bowled over German audiences of the Weimar years. Sadly, in 1937, aged only 31, she died under mysterious circumstances under Gestapo observation.

Reinhold Schünzel, who was classified as "half-Jew," fled to the U.S. in the same year. Today, it's clear why Blake Edwards was so fascinated by *Viktor and Viktoria* that his remake preserved not only the plot but entire scenes from the original movie. It's also tragically clear that Germany and the world lost a highly talented director in Schünzel. *Viktor and Viktoria* is a treat of a movie, wonderfully staged and wittily edited: a synchronized ballet of two barbers recalls the shaving scene in Chaplin's *The Great Dictator* (1940) – with the important difference that Charlie had a shavable face.

PB

183

4 Balls to the wall: The real Viktor Hempel is cruci-
fied by the critics when his portrayal of Hamlet
proves to be a comedy of errors.

5 What a handsome couple: Susanne falls head
over heels in love with the dapper Robert (Anton

Walbrook) but fears he will leave her for what
she's lacking.

"The most successful musical comedy of this season's German products and by far the best ... Reinhold Schünzel leaves no laugh possibilities unused and supplies a long footage of laughter with lots of novel ideas and hardly any empty spaces." *Variety*

REINHOLD SCHÜNZEL
(1886–1954)

In Germany between the wars, Reinhold Schünzel was well-established as a director, screenwriter and producer of light but highly sophisticated musicals and romantic comedies. He was even an actor, and a magnet at the box office in that capacity. Nowadays, only a handful of fans have even heard his name.

Born in Hamburg, he acted in the theater before making his first film in 1916, abandoning his career as an accountant to do so. He was usually cast as a con man, a villain or a pimp. In *Anders als die Anderen* (1918/19), he appeared alongside Conrad Veidt as a crook who blackmails a homosexual. He started working as a director in 1918, and his filmed tales of Berlin life were often compared to those of his colleague Ernst Lubitsch. In 1919, he had a role in Lubitsch's *Madame Dubarry*. Schünzel was most successful, however as a UFA director during the period following the National Socialist takeover in 1933. In Nazi parlance, he was a "half-Jew," yet he received work permits for the gender-bending comedy *Viktor and Viktoria* (1933) and for the music film *Amphitryon – Aus den Wolken kommt das Glück* (1935). The latter film formed the pinnacle of his career – but with its Greek gods on their Olympus, it was also interpretable as a parody of Leni Riefenstahl's *Triumph of the Will*. Schünzel's next two films, described as "typically Jewish concoctions" by Nazi Propaganda Minister Joseph Goebbels, were subjected to massive cuts. Before the premiere of *Land der Liebe* (1937), Reinhold Schünzel had fled to the U.S.A.

In exile, he was unable to escape his past. The American Jewish Congress and the Anti-Nazi League accused Schünzel of working for the Nazis for four years. He made three films for MGM and was never employed as a director again, and worked as an actor instead. Fritz Lang cast him in *Hangmen Also Die!* (1942/43), as did Alfred Hitchcock in *Notorious* (1946): he played a Nazi in both films. When the war ended, Reinhold Schünzel tried without success to pick up his career in Germany. He died in Munich of heart failure in 1954.

KING KONG

1933 - USA - 100 MIN. - B & W - AVENTURE MOVIE, HORROR MOVIE

DIRECTORS MERIAN C. COOPER (1893–1973), ERNEST B. SCHOEDSACK (1893–1979)
SCREENPLAY MERIAN C. COOPER, EDGAR WALLACE, JAMES ASHMORE CREELMAN, RUTH ROSE
DIRECTORS OF PHOTOGRAPHY EDWARD LINDEN, J. O. TAYLOR, VERNON L. WALKER, KENNETH PEACH EDITING TED CHEESMAN
MUSIC MAX STEINER PRODUCTION MERIAN C. COOPER, ERNEST B. SCHOEDSACK for RKO.

STARRING FAY WRAY (Ann Darrow), ROBERT ARMSTRONG (Carl Denham), BRUCE CABOT (John 'Jack' Driscoll),
FRANK REICHER (Captain Englehorn), SAM HARDY (Charles Weston), NOBLE JOHNSON (Native Chief),
STEVE CLEMENTE (Witch King), JAMES FLAVIN (Shipmate Briggs), VICTOR WONG (Charlie), LYNTON BRENT (Reporter).

"Beauty killed the Beast."

King Kong reflects the artistic techniques established by its documentary filmmaker protagonist, Carl Denham (Robert Armstrong), as elements of scientific expedition meet the sensationalism of cinematic horror. It all starts when Denham embarks on the search for an actress willing to play vulnerable in his upcoming wildlife movie. A victim of the Great Depression, Ann Darrow (Fay Wray) is desperate enough to take on any job if it means getting out of New York. Six weeks later, she and an entire film team lay anchor on an East Indian island, where a skull-shaped mountain is the only thing more imposing than insurmountable cliffs. Those cliffs form a huge wall dividing the terrain, with humans inhabiting the one half and an untamable beast occupying the other. This creature is, of course, none other than the leg-endary King Kong, a forty-foot gorilla that can only be appeased with human female sacrifices. Needless to say, a love-struck Kong wants Ann from the moment he sees her, and the young woman is powerless to resist his advances.

In the rescue mission that follows, a spectacular prehistoric rain forest unfolds beyond the divisive wall. Dinosaurs claim a good portion of the ship's crew before Ann's love interest Jack Driscoll (Bruce Cabot) finally manages to free his dream girl from captivity. Carl Denham uses gas explosives to knock out King Kong and ship him back to the urban jungle of New York City.

On Broadway, billboards advertise the colossal ape as the wonder of the century. Then, at his stage debut, press photographers flashbulb him into a

"Imagine a 50-foot beast with a girl in one paw climbing up the outside of the Empire State Building .... clutching at airplanes, the pilots of which are pouring bullets from machine guns into the monster's body." *The New York Times*

1 Hanging by a thread: Not to worry, King Kong hasn't let Ann Darrow (Fay Wray) down yet.

2 Battle royal: King Kong knocks down opponent after opponent to save the woman he loves.

3 Scream queen: Robert Armstrong can't calm Fay Wray's nerves for the life of him.

frenzy and he breaks free of his chains. Kong's next move is to reclaim Ann. This accomplished, he seeks seclusion at the top of the Empire State Building. Only the National Guard has its own interpretation of his actions and sends in an airborne unit to shoot him down.

King Kong tickets sold like hot cakes. The movie's many prehistoric animals appealed to an audience that had been won over by a silent era classic entitled *The Lost World* (1924/25, directed by Harry O. Hoyt). Indisputably, evolutionary theory was a popular topic in 30s cinema. One could argue that bottle blond Fay Wray a. k. a. Ann was the nexus between the 'big

black beast' from the virgin forest and the superior 'civilized world' as presented by the film.

King Kong's main theme is views of other forms of society: Carl Denham comes across as a typically arrogant colonialist when he attempts to film the secret ritual of the island's inhabitants; conversely, the people he spies on look like something out of a spoof on voodoo tribal worship. It follows that heavy makeup, grass skirts, shell necklaces and coconut bras are all the rage with these peculiarly black natives. India, it seems, looked a whole lot like Africa back in the 30s, with Hollywood's confusion of the two

4   Dinner at ape: Tonight's entrée is sacrificial lamb.   5   New Yorkers won't allow King Kong to play with dolls.   6   Air show: The U.S. military disposes of Kong and reclaims its title as king of the skies.

STOP MOTION PHOTOGRAPHY

Used to animate three-dimensional models and machines, stop motion is one of the oldest techniques in cinematic trick photography. As early as 1910, Ladislas Starevich (1882–1965) was employing it in Russia and France to make entire movies. The principle was simple: stationary figures were placed on a set before a painted backdrop, where they were photographed and then minutely repositioned for the following shot. While the Starevich pieces demonstrate a degree of seamless perfection that would rarely be topped let alone matched by any other filmmaker, *King Kong* (1933) is considered to have made the most significant breakthrough in stop motion photography. Credited with this accomplishment is Willis O'Brien and his team of painters, miniaturists, and technicians.

Stop motion would continue to improve in the decades to come. In particular, Ray Harryhausen's special effects for films like *Jason and the Argonauts* (1963) were hailed by industry experts and audiences alike. Even recent movies like *Wallace & Gromit: A Grand Day Out* (1988/89) and *The Nightmare Before Christmas* (1993) were filmed according to the principles of the age-old technique. Movies like *Toy Story* (1995) then brought the stop-motion look into the digital age.

"Kong is bigger than all the world's movies combined."

Film quote: Carl Denham (Robert Armstrong)

at its most striking in the scenes of King Kong's slave-trade inspired journey from his homeland to America, followed by the caged scenes, which are reminiscent of old New York freak shows and living village exhibits. There are no two ways about it: *King Kong* equates dark skin with savagery and worse. Its representation of the U.S.A., on the other hand, is of a rational society rooted in order and progress. The overgrown baboon's fate is thus already sealed as he climbs to the then newly completed Empire State Building (1931); for the modern machinery of war must reign supreme in this piece of colonial propaganda. There is, however, more to the story than meets the eye. Having worked as ethnographic filmmakers in the 20s, direc-

tors Merian C. Cooper and Ernest B. Schoedsack were quick to show how even a documentary examination of far-off worlds can be prone to the artificiality of media hype. The Denham character proves this by having his actress practice her big scene while still on board the ship. As the scene suggests, real documentary films did in fact rely on paid actors, or ape costumes if necessary, to make other cultures and wild animals behave according to viewer expectations. As with any other cinematic genre, much of what appears so strange on screen is nothing more than a construct of the filmmaker's mind.

PLB

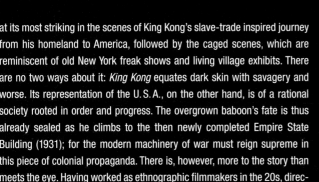

6

QUEEN CHRISTINA

1933 - USA - 97 MIN. - B & W - MELODRAMA

DIRECTOR ROUBEN MAMOULIAN (1897–1987)
SCREENPLAY H. M. HARWOOD, S. N. BEHRMAN, based on a story by SALKA VIERTEL and MARGARET P. LEVINO
DIRECTOR OF PHOTOGRAPHY WILLIAM H. DANIELS EDITING BLANCHE SEWELL MUSIC HERBERT STOTHART PRODUCTION WALTER WANGER
for MGM.

STARRING GRETA GARBO (Queen Christina), JOHN GILBERT (Don Antonio de la Prada), IAN KEITH (Count Magnus),
LEWIS STONE (Oxenstierna), REGINALD OWEN (Prince Charles), ELIZABETH YOUNG (Countess Ebba 'Belle' Sparre),
C. AUBREY SMITH (Aage), GEORGES RENAVENT (Chanut, French Ambassador), DAVID TORRENCE (Archbishop),
GUSTAV VON SEYFFERTITZ (General).

"Must we live for the dead?"
"For the great dead, yes, Your Majesty."

A milky light pours into a dark corridor from above. Midfield stands a woman with a candelabra – a vision of radiance draped in white. Erect, tall and solitary, the image could almost be one of a statue as we behold Queen Christina of Sweden (Greta Garbo) in her moment of darkest desperation.

The story begins halfway through the Thirty Years' War (1618–1648), shortly after Wallenstein has claimed the life of King Gustav Adolf in 1632 and daughter Christina assumes the throne. The young woman makes it her mission as sovereign to return Sweden to a state of peace, and promote the arts and sciences. Personal happiness, however, is not on the agenda. Unable to pursue her dreams, she makes do with the pleasant distraction of horseback rides in the snow-covered forest. Having learned from her father to think like a boy, sport is Christina's great outlet for satisfaction. It is out on her own on one of these excursions that she meets Spanish ambassador Don Antonio (John Gilbert), who is en route to the royal court and mistakes her for a man. Rather than correcting the error, she accompanies him to a local inn for a bit of food, drink and conversation about Spain, poets, painters and the like. The hours fly by and, as night falls, the travelers opt to take lodging at their

presentation location. The problem is that a lack of vacancies would mean that the two 'men' would have to share. As there's no other choice, the inevitable takes its course. Christina reveals herself to be a woman, and the sparks begin to fly.

Several days later, and a perplexed Antonio arrives at the royal court in Stockholm only to discover that the girl from the inn is none other than the Queen herself. However, given Sweden's political position and Christina's obligation to her bloodline, a long and lasting love is not to be: the young monarch's hand was promised long ago to Prince Charles (Reginald Owen), a hero of the Thirty Years' War and her biological cousin. Director Rouben Mamoulian (*Silk Stockings*, 1957) and leading actress Greta Garbo succeed magnificently in bringing one of history's most fascinating figures to the screen. Curiosity is Christina's guiding light; warmth and openness her tools of diplomacy. She appreciates the simple things in life, champions the arts and sciences, and yet has a statuesque quality of aloofness. In essence, Christina is a modern woman surrounded by archaic men all but trapped in the Dark Ages. Rather than sharing her interests, these aristocrats fight for religion and

"Christina is one of the best written, strongest female characters in cinema history – a leader who steadfastly refuses to crumble under the unmitigated pressures from her powerful male advisers and relies on her distinctly female brain, heart and instincts to rule well." *Danny Peary, in: Guide for the Film Fanatic*

honor, celebrate warriors and disdain poets. Her common subjects prove no better: allowed to voice their views at the royal court, they too back the war efforts – only unlike their lords, their battle cries will cost them their lives.

The battles lines are clear: on the one side, an impassioned lady liberty; on the other, men blinded by heroism and convention. Christina is thus expected to marry in the interest of politics, and the struggle associated with this brand of dilemma is much of what makes the story intriguing. But even this element is eclipsed by the picture's real lifeblood, which is Garbo's fervent and unbeatable performance.

MGM studios did everything in its power to ensure that *Queen Christina* would be a hit. The role was written specially for Greta Garbo, and William H. Daniels, the cinematographer who shot the majority of her films, was entrusted with the visuals. And Daniels delivered the goods, creating breathtaking compositions that made the actress herself look like a work of art. In addition to all this, MGM signed on Garbo's off-screen flame, actor John Gilbert, to play the Spanish Antonio and managed to hook itself a fair amount of free tabloid publicity in the process. While there's no getting around the fact the picture was designed to be a star vehicle, it has stood the test of time and

1 Wild oats: Disguised as a stable boy, Queen Christina (Greta Garbo) discovers life's simple pleasures with Don Antonio (John Gilbert).

2 A woman's work is never done: Sweden's Queen Christina is poised for battle.

3 Book smart: Her Highness is versed in the arts and sciences but not in the ways of the world.

3

continues to delight film buffs. Part of the treat is that the story itself deviates relatively little from the actual historical facts. As purported by the plot, the real Christina (1626–1689) was not only raised by her father Gustav Adolf to think like a boy but did in fact foster the arts. Likewise, she was just six when her royal parent lost his life in the Thirty Years' War and she became his successor. Aged 18, she had assumed her full responsibilities as a monarch and abdicated from the throne ten years later to avoid marrying her cousin 'Charles,' actually Karl Gustav. The love affair with the Spanish ambassador, however, was pure invention. Entirely absent from the movie are the more unflattering aspects of the real-life Christina, who led a very expensive lifestyle and drove Sweden to the brink of ruin – behavior that was anything but fitting for a sovereign of Hollywood.   HJK

"The parallel between Garbo's legendary refusal to blend into the Hollywood scene and the queen's refusal to abide by the rules prescribed by her royal role was embedded early in the construction of the film."
Marcia Landy, Amy Villarejo, in: Queen Christina: BFI Film Classics

4 Her Majesty's Secret Service: Don Antonio is sur-
   prised to discover that he's been aiding and a-bed-
   ding the Queen of Sweden.

5 It's not the alcohol talking: For Christina stepping
   into a man's shoes is all in a day's work.

6 The envelope please: Chancellor Oxenstierna
   (Lewis Stone, center) entrusts Don Antonio with
   a message for the King of Spain.

"Garbo was the most instinctual film actress ever: *Queen Christina* is her showcase." *Evening Standard*

**GRETA GARBO
(1905–1990)**

Enigmatic, ethereal, forever foreign, and elusive – no one embodied this set of characteristics like actress Greta Garbo. Hungarian film critic Béla Balázs called her "a sad, suffering beauty, whose gestures seem to suggest an utter repulsion toward the tainted world she was made to live in." Others continue to be blown away by the stoicism and boyish yet statuesque physique that spelled sexual ambivalence in *Queen Christina* (1933). Perhaps no other screen legend was as successful at shielding her personal life from the public eye or delineating the terms of her public and private images as she was. In one of the contracts she signed with MGM, the studio even prohibited her from granting interviews, having recognized that secrecy was the essence of her star appeal.

The woman born Greta Lovisa Gustafsson spent her formative years in Stockholm, Sweden, where she would later attend the Royal Dramatic Theatre. Director Mauritz Stiller, who saw her perform at the school, was the driving force in launching her career. He gave her the name Garbo, Swedish for 'goblin' and Spanish for grace, cast her in her first leading role with *The Story of Gosta Berling* (*Gösta Berlings Saga*, 1924), and then took her with him to Hollywood. Ten silent pictures later, including titles like *Wild Orchids* (1929), and Garbo was an international superstar.

When talkies came along, Garbo had no difficulty making the transition. Her smoky, rough voice infused roles like seductive spy *Mata Hari* (1931) with mystery and *Grand Hotel's* (1932) aging ballerina Grusinskaya with bitter tragedy. In Ernst Lubitsch's *Ninotchka* (1939), Garbo added comedy to her repertoire as a love-struck Russian spy. With the slogan, "Garbo laughs!" *Ninotchka* delivered what world audiences had believed impossible. After George Cukor's *Two-Faced Woman* (1941), Garbo withdrew entirely from the public eye. The 50 years of solitude that followed only added to her myth and mystery.

I'M NO ANGEL

933 - USA - 87 MIN. - B & W - COMEDY

DIRECTOR WESLEY RUGGLES (1889–1972)
SCREENPLAY MAE WEST DIRECTOR OF PHOTOGRAPHY LEO TOVER EDITING OTHO LOVERING MUSIC HARVEY BROOKS (Songs)
GLADYS DUBOIS (Lyrics) PRODUCTION WILLIAM LEBARON for PARAMOUNT PICTURES.

STARRING MAE WEST (Tira), CARY GRANT (Jack Clayton), GREGORY RATOFF (Benny Pinkowitz),
EDWARD ARNOLD (Big Bill Barton), KENT TAYLOR (Kirk Lawrence), RALF HAROLDE (Slick),
DOROTHY PETERSON (Thelma), GERTRUDE MICHAEL (Alicia Hatton), GERTRUDE HOWARD (Beulah),
LIBBY TAYLOR (Libby).

"When I'm good, I'm very good. But when I'm bad, I'm better."

Just who was Mae West? A blonde bombshell? An actress? A woman with a capital W? She was all these things, but she was never bigger or better than the character she plays in *I'm No Angel*. Mae West is Tira – a hootchie-kootchie dancer and lion tamer who can make men jump through hoops of fire. She starts off sleeping with the best of them in circus tents and wiggles her way up to the suites of ritzy New York hotels. As if is this weren't impressive enough, she asserts her independence every step of the way and even fights for it in court.

While striking, the parallels to the behind-the-scenes West are hardly surprising. Let's not forget that she'd penned the script herself, and filled it with classic lines that read like snippets from a diary. Whether it's "when I'm good, I'm very good, but when I'm bad, I'm better," or "it's not the men in your life that counts, it's the life in your men," West always let her experience do the talking. And if her "come up and see me sometime" is to be any indication, Mae's life was full of scandalous ones to say the least. Image was everything for Mae West, who could well be considered an auteur in her own right.

I'm No Angel has all the vital ingredients of the actress' winning formula: double-entendres, a chorus of muscle men, dumb-as-they-come gigolos with "guns in their pockets," outrageous costumes designed to accentuate her hour-glass figure, a little song, a little dance and that signature Mae West strut. She knew how to play with the big boys, and her over-the-top body language contains a distinctly masculine brand of self-confidence that almost seems to parody the way men think women move.

Beyond her standard shtick, *I'm No Angel* offers that little something extra only Tira's circus act could provide: she really does stick her head into a lion's mouth and gets herself noticed by high society while she's at it. In no time, she's schmoozing with millionaire Kirk Lawrence (Kent Taylor) and giving his fiancée the kiss-off. Moments later she gets his cousin, Jack Clayton (Cary Grant), to propose to her and then, when she fears he'll renege, serves him a court order to make sure he'll stick to his word. Unfortunately, she's the one who's put through the wringer when giving testimony. Suddenly, Tira's moral conduct becomes the subject of scrutiny and she's forced to explain herself (not that she minds all that much, given that her sexual experience usually turn men on). With artistic flair, she cross-examines the witnesses brought in to testify against her and disqualifies every one, flooring the judge and jurors in the process. Mae West's secret? She shamelessly uses her charm to get whatever she wants, and shows America how sexy forty can look. Indeed, the men she encounters can't seem to get enough of her an

"It is a rapid-fire entertainment, with shameless but thoroughly contagious humor, and one in which Tira is always the mistress of the situation, whether it be in the cage with wild beasts, in her boudoir with admirers or in a court of law." *The New York Times*

gawk at her as if she were missing everything from the waist down – not that the comparison applies in her case.

No one would deny that the plot of this base, borderline crude film is a bit straightforward, but certain elements of the picture are teeming with subtext. Tira/West gets on well with other women (probably while they don't present any sort of threat to her). Wealthy ladies admire her; many don't register what's really behind advice like "take all you can get and give as little as possible." But when it comes down to it, Tira's true friends are the black maids in her employment (including Libby Taylor, who really was a servant in West's employ). These are her only confidantes when it comes to men and their sad flaws. For an era marked by segregation and racial stereotypes in film, such cross-cultural interaction was highly unusual. It also pointed to West's love of black culture and entertainment. It's even been suggested

that West's nonchalant delivery was a tribute to the black women she surrounded herself with throughout her lifetime.

Despite being such a pioneer herself, Mae West's characters almost always found conventional love with Mr. Right, a role filled here by Cary Grant. Not a year prior, West had helped turn her co-star into an overnight sensation with *She Done Him Wrong* (1932/33), a picture that saved Paramount from bankruptcy and created uproar among the defenders of propriety. Needless to say, West's uncurbed irreverence in *I'm No Angel* didn't do much to satisfy those with moral misgivings regarding the cinematic content of the day. In fact, many people in the industry believed that it was the clincher in the Hay's Office decision to instate the Production Code. If so, it was a necessary evil.

1   Blonde and beyond: Mae West struts her stuff as the most risqué hootchie-kootchie dancer in Hollywood history.

2   I tawt I taw a puddy tat: Tira (Mae West) poses for a picture with one of her tamer co-stars.

3   A wicked witch named West: Titillating Tira strong-arms the strong man and anyone else who tries to stand in her way.

MAE WEST (1893–1980)

Scandal was her constant companion and taboo-breaking her goal. The woman dubbed America's 'Statue of Libido' was also one of the most handsomely paid stars of 1930s Hollywood. Mae West did more to promote sexual liberation than any of her rivals like Jean Harlow or Marlene Dietrich. At the same time, she also did more to conserve the established norms: for 'self-respecting' America fought back against dirt and smut depicted on screen with a weapon known as the Production Code, a reaction West's pictures and inordinate popularity were commonly thought to be largely responsible for. West's flagrant display of her genetic advantages, sultry glamour and insouciant attitude towards sex were a thorn in the side of prudish moviegoers. The actress' self-coined, racy one-liners propounded her notoriety both in and out of the public eye. To this day, West is still quoted for originals like "is that a gun in your pocket, or are you just glad to see me?" and "a hard man is good to find."

It comes as no surprise that young Mae West was destined for show business while still in the crib. A Brooklyn native, she was born in the dog-days of August to a prizefighter of Irish Catholic descent and a Jewish Bavarian actress. She made her stage debut at the age of five and left school while just thirteen. Billed as 'Baby Vamp', she sang and danced in small time musical revues, variety acts and Broadway shows. In 1926, she went on to become the subject of major scandal while starring in her self-penned Broadway play "Sex" and was thrown in jail for ten days for her "public displays of obscenity." Her play on homosexuality, "Drag" (1927), never made it to Broadway.

West was nearly forty by the time she made her Hollywood debut as a supporting player in *Night After Night* (1932). The movies that followed, *She Done Him Wrong* (1932/33) and *I'm No Angel* (1933) – both with Cary Grant – were wildly successful. It was, however, at this point in her career that the censors began wielding their power in Hollywood. Serving as her own screenwriter to the bitter end, West responded to the backlash by reworking her trademark straight talk into innuendo for later scripts like *Belle of the Nineties* (1934), *Go West Young Man* (1936) and *Every Day's a Holiday* (1937). While these pictures continued to draw crowds at the box office, their humor fell short of her previous work. Further West credits of the day include a brilliant Western spoof entitled *My Little Chickadee* (1940), in which she starred in opposite the equally impressive Hollywood original W. C. Fields.

Unfortunately, the censors' damage to West's career was long lasting. Following a long absence from the public eye – a fate the actress shared with W. C. Fields – she was rediscovered in the 60s, emerging as a trash icon and honorary mother of the gay movement. West shot the last two of her total of twelve films while in her so-called golden years. Critics consider *Myra Breckinridge* (1970) to be one of the worst films ever made, but its cult status is undeniable. *Sextette* (1978), a washed-out, rock-star-studded screen adaptation of "Sex," gave new meaning to the word flop. She believed herself to be the quintessence of sex appeal to her dying day and heaps of fan-mail made it hard to argue with her. Mae West exited Hollywood for good on November 22, 1980.

ECSTASY
Extase/ Ekstase / Symphonie der Liebe

1932/33 - CZECHOSLOVAKIA / AUSTRIA - 83 MIN. - B & W - DRAMA

DIRECTOR GUSTAV MACHATÝ (1901–1963)
SCREENPLAY GUSTAV MACHATÝ, FRANTIŠEK HORKÝ, based on a story by VITEZSLAV NEZVAL
DIRECTORS OF PHOTOGRAPHY JAN STALLICH, HANS ANDROSCHIN EDITING ANTONÍN ZELENKA MUSIC GIUSEPPE BECCE
PRODUCTION GUSTAV MACHATÝ, MORIZ GRUNHUT, FRANTIŠEK HORKÝ for ELEKTRA-FILM.

STARRING HEDY KIESLER [= HEDY LAMARR] (Eva), ARIBERT MOG (Adam), PIERRE NAY (Adam in the French version),
ZVONIMIR ROGOZ (Emil), ZVONIMIR ROGOZ (Emil in the French version), LEOPOLD KRAMER (Eva's father),
ANDRÉ NOX (Eva's father in the French version), KAREL MÀCHA-KUCA (Lawyer in the Czech version),
JIRINA STEIMAROVÁ (Secretary in the Czech version), JAN SVITÁK (Dancer in the Café), EDUARD SLÉGL (Farmhand),
ANTONIN KIBOBÝ (Farmhand).

"What happened?"
"Nothing, Papa."

Ever since its premiere in January 1933, *Ecstasy* has been one of the most talked-about movies of that decade. The Czech director Gustav Machatý confronted his contemporaries with a film that was as remarkable in form as in content. Yet today, *Ecstasy* is rarely shown in cinemas, and is remembered mainly for the scandal it aroused. For the first time, the legend goes, a commercially-distributed mainstream film included images of a naked woman. As film historians can confirm, this is not strictly true; but the scenes in question must have had an enormous effect on audiences at the time. Here was the 17-year-old actress Hedy Kiesler swimming naked in a lake, and then pursuing her horse when it wanders away with her clothes.

Machatý and his cameraman Jan Stallich actually filmed these scenes with tremendous discretion, and reflections in the water ensure that we don't actually see very much bare skin at all. In any case, most film critics had little to say about the 'scandal', preferring instead to discuss *Ecstasy* as a work of cinematic art. In its visual language – its montage sequences and its erotic and nature symbolism, for instance – *Ecstasy* was considerably closer to the silent era than to sound, which had already triumphed worldwide years previously. Machatý's film used dialog only very sparingly, and this provoked lively discussions. Was it a step backwards? Or was it in fact showing a new way forward for sound film? It wasn't just the nakedness of the female star

that worried the censors. It was above all the 'immoral' nature of the plot that bothered them: Young Eva (Hedy Kiesler) is newly wed, yet she wants to leave her much older husband Emil (Zvonimir Rogoz) because he refuses to consummate their marriage. Eva takes a lover, a virile engineer called Adam (Aribert Mog), with whom she experiences sexual fulfillment. During their night of love, the ecstasy of the title is clearly visible on her face. When Emil realizes what's going on, he takes his own life – and Eva leaves her Adam. An epilogue shows Eva with a baby; or at least it does in the German and Czech-language versions of the film.

Nature won't be stopped. Seen today, Machatý's treatment of this theme is still a highly impressive piece of filmmaking: there's the sun-soaked impressionistic landscape where Eva goes riding and bathes in the lake; the clear sexual symbolism (a mare attracted by a stallion, a bee alighting on a flower); Eva's growing excitement in the evening, which corresponds with a sultry before-the-storm feeling and increasingly rapid editing; and finally, the act of love that releases all her feelings.

To the censors, all this was unacceptable, for a whole range of reasons: extra-marital orgasms, illegitimate children and suicide were matters that politicians and clerics were in no hurry to see propagated. As a result, moviegoers in different countries saw some very different versions of

1   Catch her in the raw: Adam (Aribert Mog) tries to return a horse gone astray and stumbles upon Lady Godiva. Hedy Kiesler stars as Eva.

2   The agony and the ecstasy: Married to a man who doesn't know she's alive, Eva can either dream of sexual fulfillment or look for it elsewhere.

3   Happy hour: Adam and Eva drink to their future together. But their dreams are shattered when Eva's husband commits suicide.

Ecstasy. The orgasm scene, in particular, was often heavily cut, and the U.S.A. was one of the countries that removed it entirely. There were also frequent additions in the form of inserts or off-screen voices, assuring viewers that Eva and Emil were already legally separated before Eva had even met her engineer.

It was 1940 before *Ecstasy* was permitted to run in the U.S., and even then, the film was so badly cut up and jumbled that moviegoers believed Eva had met Adam *before* her marriage to Emil. It also included an insert of Eva's diary, which informed us that she and Adam had married in secret before

their night of love. This version of the film can hardly have made much sense, and it's not surprising that it was a flop amongst both moviegoers and critics in the States – even though Hedy Kiesler had by then become the famous Hollywood star, Hedy Lamarr.

In Germany too, where the Nazis had seized power in January 1933, the film was originally banned. In 1935, however, after certain cuts had been made, it was released for a short period under the title *Symphonie der Liebe*. Apparently, the film was being interpreted as an embodiment of Germany's "new spirit." One magazine provided a plot summary, which emphasized that the film concluded with images of "noble motherhood." The many versions of *Ecstasy* feature many different endings, partly because it was shot in three language versions: Czech, German and English. The Czech version ends with a montage sequence reminiscent of the Russian avant-garde cinema: after a celebration of the joys of collective work, we see Adam watching a child playing with a hammer; then, an associative montage makes the transition back to Eva and her newborn baby. All the while, a voice on the soundtrack is reciting a poem, a kind of hymn to labor. The original German version presumably had the montage sequence without this poem. In the French version, the entire passage is missing, and the film ends with the previous scene, in which Eva leaves the sleeping Adam at the railway station, which has normally been interpreted as a tragic ending, while the conclusion with the aforementioned montage is seen as more open and ambiguous. As if all this weren't confusing enough, the German post-war version of 1950 concocted a happy ending for the film: the montage sequence includes a shot that shows a couple holding hands and reflected in the waters of a lake: a perfect bourgeois idyll.

Gustav Machatý, an astute businessman, clearly wasn't bothered by all this. He gave his blessing to every version, no matter how much it had suffered from cuts demanded by the censors. Perhaps he also realized that *Ecstasy* is a film that's interpretable in very many ways. That Eva leaves a selfish husband who doesn't care for her, and confidently takes a lover – this can be seen as the story of an emancipation. That the film gives Eva the attributes of Nature, while Adam represents work – this has occasionally been called anti-emancipatory. And what is Eva really striving for,

3

"With its highly emotional theme, exquisitely interpreted, largely in pantomime, by Hedy Kiesler, and beautifully photographed in typical European 'art' manner, the picture presents what is quite the acme, to date, of symbolic artistry." *The Washington Post*

HEDY LAMARR For around 15 years, Hedy Lamarr was one of the top glamour stars in the Dream Factory. She was stunningly beautiful and much photographed, and her six marriages, numerous court cases and various minor scandals kept the gossips columnists happily and gainfully employed. When one tries to recall one of her big box-office hits, however, not much comes to mind. Maybe the movie that launched her Hollywood career: John Cromwell's *Algiers* (1938), a remake of Julien Duvivier's classic French thriller *Pépé le Moko* (1936/37); or Cecil B. DeMille's Biblical epic *Samson and Delilah* (1949), made as her career was gradually going into decline.

Her real name was Hedwig Eva Maria Kiesler, and she was born in Vienna in 1914 (or 1913, sources vary). She attended Max Reinhardt's acting school in Berlin before playing the female lead in Gustav Machatý's *Ecstasy* (*Extase*, 1932/33). The publicity aroused by her 'scandalous' nude scenes brought her to Hollywood a few years later. In 1938, no one in the U. S. was allowed to see the film, but everyone had most certainly heard about it. If the actress Hedy Lamarr is now so little remembered, it may also be due to the fact that her first Hollywood employers, MGM, gave her a new name but no clear image. In adventure movies, melodramas, comedies and musicals, she played the exotic temptress, the sophisticated lady, or the girl next door; yet she was never to enjoy a really major success. At the end of the 40s, she began to produce her own films; but here too, Hedy Lamarr was far from lucky, and she eventually lost a lot of money. From 1951 onwards, she appeared only sporadically on the screen. She played an ageing Hollywood star in Harry Keller's melodrama *The Female Animal* (1957) and made her last film appearance in *Instant Karma* (1990). Hedy Lamarr died in 2000.

4 Where there's smoke: Director Gustav Machatý depicts Eva's fiery romance with evocative symbols.

5 Side-tracked: Eva leaves Adam and catches the first train out of Eden.

6 Peek of perfection: Hedy Kiesler kissed Europe goodbye and redesigned herself as Hollywood glamor girl Hedy Lamarr.

"The utter lyricism of Machatý's staging owes much to the sparing use of sound, the impressive visual symbolism and exquisite photography. However, whatever shock value the film once had has been lost to the ages." *Kölner Stadt-Anzeiger*

anyway? Sexual joy? Or the joy of motherhood, as the Nazis would have preferred?

The American writer Henry Miller was probably the most famous interpreter of the film. To him, *Ecstasy* stood in the tradition of D. H. Lawrence's novel *Lady Chatterley's Lover* (1928), and he saw the characters as embodiments of a principle: the lovers represent the life-force battling blindly to assert itself, while the pedantic, impotent husband by contrast is a personification of death, or society, as it is. From this perspective, *Ecstasy* is the utopian vision of a future freed from social constraints – a goal that has yet to be reached.

LF

L'ATALANTE

L'Atalante

1934 - FRANCE - 89 MIN. - B & W - DRAMA

DIRECTOR JEAN VIGO (1905–1934)
SCREENPLAY JEAN GUINÉE, ALBERT RIÉRA, JEAN VIGO   DIRECTOR OF PHOTOGRAPHY BORIS KAUFMAN   EDITING LOUIS CHAVANCE
MUSIC MAURICE JAUBERT   PRODUCTION JACQUES-LOUIS NOUNEZ for G. F. F. A. – GAUMONT-FRANCO FILM-AUBERT.

STARRING MICHEL SIMON (Père Jules), DITA PARLO (Juliette), JEAN DASTÉ (Jean), GILLES MARGARITIS (Salesman),
LOUIS LEFEBVRE (Cabin Boy), MAURICE GILLES (Supervisor), RAPHAËL DILIGENT (Raspoutine),
FANNY CLAR (Juliette's Mother), CHARLES GOLDBLATT (Thief).

"You'll see someday when you really try!"

Jean Vigo was not destined to witness the immense admiration elicited by *L'Atalante*, his only full-length feature film. Weakened by an exceptionally arduous filming schedule, he died of tuberculosis shortly after the unsuccessful premiere of his masterpiece. To add insult to injury, his distributors had butchered the film on the cutting floor with little regard for Vigo's artistry. Tragic and melodramatic as the circumstances of its making may seem, *L'Atalante* has nevertheless come to be regarded as one of the most beautiful and poetic films ever made. The melancholy love story between Jean (Jean Dasté) and Juliette (Dita Parlo) is narrated with the lightness of a floating feather, yet loaded to the brim with magnificent imagery. Set on a river barge traveling down a canal, this simple romance unfolds with an expressive force that has yet to be matched.

The trip is no honeymoon for the newly-weds, although it may seem so at first. Juliette, still in her wedding dress, is unsure of her footing on the deck of "L'Atalante." The barge is the be-all-and-end-all of Jean's world, and it has just become Juliette's new home. Like most lovers, she finds it difficult to come to terms with her partner's mundane day-to-day routines. His wardrobe, for example, is full of clothes that are washed exactly once a year. The couple's social life is limited to an eccentric sailor named Père Jules (Michel Simon), a stubborn cabin boy, and half a dozen cats. To Jean, the barge signifies the freedom to travel without bounds; to Juliette, it only offers joyless toil and confinement. When they take berth in Paris and a charming street artist invites Juliette to a dance, the girl sneaks off the barge. Jean is incensed with rage and jealousy and departs without her.

There follows one of the many touching cinematic moments that have made *L'Atalante* the milestone film it is. In his desperation, Jean remembers something Juliette once said - "Under water you will recognize the one you

"There is an intense lyrical romanticism in *L'Atalante*, a fervour and a candid eroticism which coexists with a profound gentleness towards the young newly-weds. Nothing else is exactly like *L'Atalante*, but F. W. Murnau's *Sunrise* has obvious similarities and in its relationship with Vigo's earlier works, *L'Atalante* is comparable to *Fires Were Started* by England's Humphrey Jennings. Vigo is the visionary and experimentalist who brought his boldly inventive film-making language to a tale of glorious, luminous simplicity."

The Guardian

love." When his young wife first said this to him, he had seen nothing in the water. Now, he jumps into the canal, and in the waters he sees the face of his Juliette. Images such as this one, created with a simple film overlay, gain their power not from some enigmatic complexity but from sheer lyrical clarity. How many men acknowledge their love only when it's too late? Another highpoint is the famed split-screen love-making scene, spread over two distant beds with the lovers fervently caressing their bodies in an all-

consuming passion. In scenes like these, *L'Atalante's* significance as a boundary-breaking work becomes especially apparent: Jean Vigo marries the surrealism of a Luis Buñuel with the poetic realism of a Jean Renoir. *L'Atalante* also represents a bridge between silent and sound film; at many of the film's decisive moments, the enticingly tender music of Maurice Jaubert does half the work. The actors take care of the rest with their astonishingly charismatic and sensual presence. Dita Parlo, the film's lead

1   Sleeping potion: Gilles Margaritis (pictured) plays a dream peddler who'd rather not wake up to reality.

2   Papa bear: Certain that father knows best, Jules (Michel Simon) reunites the film's star-crossed lovers.

3   The unfathomable depths: A venerable seaman discovers a mermaid in the galleys of his vessel. Dita Parlo as Juliette.

4   Love's labors lost: Juliette admits to feeling adrift without Jean to anchor her.

5   Abandon ship: Juliette makes waves back on land after hitting a dry spell with Jean.

actress, is so powerfully erotic that Madonna paid tribute by having her initials engraved on a gold tooth.

But there is a third actor who practically seizes the film, and who most purely embodies its spirit of wild abandon. Vigo's techniques were revolutionary, but Michel Simon's performance as Jules is sheer anarchism. Jules is a boisterous seaman who maintains his high spirits by dancing like a demon and wrestling with himself. At first, the tattooed giant appears to be a sexual threat: the unexpected presence of a young woman on the boat is too much for him to keep his cool. As the two become more familiar with each other, however, this filthy monster of a man – he smokes through his bellybutton! – turns into a reflection of Juliette's self. She loves her husband dearly, but she also craves the freedom represented by Jules. He has traversed the oceans of the world, collected a wealth of souvenirs (which he proudly presents to Juliette in his tiny cabin), and – more importantly – jettisoned all the gender stereotypes she dreads. The oddball sailor happens to be an expert at the sewing machine, and even models one of Juliette's dresses for her. In the end, it is Jules who brings Juliette back to Jean. The glamour of Paris was a beautiful illusion: the naive country girl was robbed of her meager possessions there and she soon found herself longing for the man she had left.

It is precisely the contrast between this rather conventional love story and Vigo's visionary rendition thereof that makes *L'Atalante* such a com-

5

> **"The film is a masterpiece, not because of the tragic story of its maker or its awkward genesis, but because, as Truffaut has said, in filming prosaic words and acts, Vigo effortlessly achieved poetry."** *The Guardian*

6 The shirt off his back: Jean would give anything to be with Juliette.

7 On cloud nine: One of the many moments when Jean Vigo's film makes a poetic statement without saying a word. Jean Dasté as Jean.

pelling film. Vigo's production company Gaumont supplied the storyline, but unfortunately the film Vigo delivered did not meet with the producers' approval. The revisions undertaken in post-production were severe; the film was shortened from 89 to 67 minutes and Maurice Jaubert's music was dropped altogether. It was replaced by the next-best crowd pleaser, which just so happened to be a thematically related chanson – "Le chaland qui passe," or "The Passing Barge." The song title was also used as the new title of the movie. A restored version, approximating Vigo's original intentions as closely as possible, has only been available since 1990. That even the mutilated version managed to enthrall audiences the world over is ample testimony to the film's miraculous quality.

PB

JEAN VIGO (1905–1934)

With less than three hours of celluloid to his name when he died at the age of 29, Jean Vigo had a greater impact on the course of cinematic history than many a lesser director with an entire life's work. The idolization of Vigo as a romantic martyr by later generations was also rooted in the directors early biography. Vigo's childhood was marred by disease and the early death of his father: Miguel Almereyda, a militant anarchist, was allegedly strangled to death in prison. The son, who wholeheartedly shared the father's political convictions, had to spend the remainder of his youth under a false name and was moved from one boarding school to the next. Using a second-hand Debrie camera, he shot his first short film in 1930, *À propos de Nice*. It was a sardonic record of the luxurious lifestyle led on the French Riviera. Following his biographical documentary of swimmer Jean Taris (*Jean Taris, Swimming Champion / Taris, roi de l'eau*, 1931), Vigo made an important acquaintance: independent producer Jacques-Louis Nounez was to produce his next films. By this stage, Vigo had already secured Russian cameraman Boris Kaufman, brother of the widely admired avant-garde film maker Dziga Vertov.

The result of this collaboration was the 44-minute feature *Zero for Conduct* (*Zéro de conduite*, 1933), in which Vigo dealt with his bitter experiences at school. The film was a poetic rebellion against the educational system and defied formal logic on all levels – just as the students shown in the film do, in response to their teachers' disciplinary attempts. The film was banned until 1945; the proponents of the Nouvelle Vague movement, François Truffaut in particular, elevated it to iconic status. Jean Vigo, greatly liked by his colleagues for his warmth and humor, was never to see the fruits of his fame. The filming of *L'Atalante* (1934), his only full-length feature, was a grueling winter marathon which proved to be too much for the director's already failing health.

Numerous filmmakers since have cited *L'Atalante* as a decisive influence on their own works, and its rich, poetic imagery has frequently inspired comparisons to F. W. Murnau's *Sunrise – A Song of Two Humans* (*Sonnenaufgang – Ein Lied von zwei Menschen*, 1927). References to *L'Atalante* are to be found in many modern classics, including Bernardo Bertolucci's *Last Tango in Paris* (*Ultimo tango a Parigi / Le dernier Tango à Paris*, 1972).

DAVID COPPERFIELD

1934 - USA - 130 MIN. - B & W - DRAMA, LITERARY ADAPTATION

DIRECTOR GEORGE CUKOR (1899–1983)
SCREENPLAY HUGH WALPOLE, HOWARD ESTABROOK, based on the novel of the same name by CHARLES DICKENS
DIRECTOR OF PHOTOGRAPHY OLIVER T. MARSH EDITING ROBERT KERN MUSIC HERBERT STOTHART PRODUCTION DAVID O. SELZNICK
for MGM.

STARRING FREDDIE BARTHOLOMEW (David Copperfield as a child), FRANK LAWTON (David Copperfield as a man),
EDNA MAY OLIVER (Aunt Betsy Trotwood), ELIZABETH ALLAN (Mrs. Clara Copperfield), JESSIE RALPH (Nurse Peggotty),
LIONEL BARRYMORE (Dan Peggotty), W. C. FIELDS (Mr. Micawber), BASIL RATHBONE (Mr. Murdstone),
VIOLET KEMBLE COOPER (Jane Murdstone), LENNOX PAWLE (Mr. Dick), LEWIS STONE (Mr. Wickfield),
ROLAND YOUNG (Uriah Heep), MAUREEN O'SULLIVAN (Dora), MADGE EVANS (Agnes Wickfield),
ELSA LANCHASTER (Clickett).

"Generally speaking I don't like boys. How do you do, boy?"

The sheer length of Dickens' novels makes them a little unwieldy for the film industry. Nonetheless, during the hundred years of cinema history, most of his better-known works have been adapted for the screen a dozen times. In the mid-30s, Hollywood took its obligations to literature particularly seriously. Following an unspectacular *Oliver Twist* (1933), Paramount came up with *Scrooge* (1935), based on Dickens' much-loved tale, "A Christmas Carol." In the same year, David O. Selznick launched two separate prestigious projects for MGM: *David Copperfield* and *A Tale of Two Cities* (1935). The former made the studio a net profit of two million dollars, which enabled Selznick to make *Gone with the Wind* (1939).

The hard life of David Copperfield (Freddie Bartholomew) begins with his birth to a widowed mother (Elizabeth Allan) in London. So that the boy will not grow up without a father, she marries the grim, unfeeling Mr. Murdstone (Basil Rathbone). David is sent to work in a factory, where he finds his first good friend, the talkative Mr. Micawber (W. C. Fields). Sadly, Micawber winds up in debtors' prison. David is then robbed in the street, and walks 72 miles to

Dover, where he takes refuge with his Aunt Betsy (Edna May Oliver). He enters into an apprenticeship with the cheerful advocate Mr. Wickfield (Lewis Stone) and his "very 'umble" employee, the hypocritical clerk Uriah Heep (Roland Young). David grows up (and is now played by Frank Lawton), becomes a writer, and makes a terrible mistake when he marries the immature Dora (Maureen O'Sullivan). Yet all's well that ends well: Uriah Heep's machinations are exposed, Dora dies tragically and David weds Agnes Wickfield (Madge Evans), the faithful girl he'd known since his early youth.

Moviegoers lapped up stories like this during the Depression years. Selznick himself had a very personal connection to the book: his father, a Russian immigrant, had learned English by reading it – and had read it to his son for nights on end. Charles Dickens always described David Copperfield as his "favorite child," and the story reworks many elements from his own life. Dickens' novel is a bitter arraignment of Victorian childrearing and education, inhuman factory work and the varieties of human viciousness – all of it described from a child's point of view. It is a protocol of a loveless era, in

"The classic story of David's triumphs and sorrows, and of the amazing people who were his friends and enemies, has been made into a gorgeous photoplay which encompasses the rich and kindly humanity of the original so brilliantly that it becomes a screen masterpiece in its own right."

The New York Times

1   Raising cane: Mr. Micawber (W. C. Fields) teaches David (Freddie Bartholomew) how to stand tall.

2   Wet nurse: The touching relationship between David and sweet Mrs. Peggotty (Jessie Ralph) could bring anyone to tears.

3   Don't let the fine binding fool you: W. C. Fields stays true to his Hollywood reputation and dazzles audiences as an ash-can existentialist.

4   Earn your keep: David's guardian Mr. Murdstone (Basil Rathbone) teaches the boy to value a hard day's work.

5   Every man for himself: The wily Uriah Heep (Roland Young) lets his adversaries wear each other out before making his move.

which Good ultimately prevails; a tale of innocence and experience. Director George Cukor managed to translate this sprawling narrative into an episodic film structure without betraying the original, but it's the actors who really make this the definitive movie version of a much-loved book.

Dickens himself would have been delighted by the angelic Freddie Bartholomew as the young David. Then there's Edna May Oliver near-slap-

stick performance as the feisty Aunt Betsy, who would have preferred to have a girl, yet defends her boy when the chips are down; there's the eccentric lodger Mr. Dick (Lennox Pawle); and there's Roland Young as Uriah Heep, whose name is still a byword for slimy obsequiousness. The main course in this feast of acting talent is W. C. Fields as Mr. Micawber, a lapsed aristocrat in eternal flight from his creditors, lending each sententious

6 Beggars can't be choosers: Sworn enemy of children everywhere, W. C. Fields goes the extra mile
   for this Dickens adaptation.

7 Classics confusion: Apparently, no one told Lionel
   Barrymore that he was signed to play Dan Peggotty
   and not Captain Ahab.

"Being himself pretty generally a spiritual descendant of Mr. Micawber, W. C. Fields manages with the greatest of ease to become one with his illustrious predecessor according to the directions laid down in the text of Dickens and the drawing of Phiz."

The New York Times

remark the weight of a Declaration of Independence: "When the stomach is empty, the spirits are low!" Charles Laughton had been the first choice for the role, but he struggled with the outrageous comedy of the character and eventually recommended Fields for the role instead. Hollywood's legendary drinker barely needed to act the role: he was Micawber, to the very fingertips.

George Cukor was famed for his work with actors, and the unforgettable characters in this film develop a life of their own that carries the picture over any gaps in the plotline. In addition, David Selznick had taken infinite pains to ensure that 19th-century England was reconstructed as accurately as possible in the MGM studios. It was not only the leading actor who was imported specially for the production, but real British sand from a real British beach. His efforts were rewarded by a major success at the box office. Within a few years, however, Hollywood was leaving it to the limeys to interpret one of their greatest novelists.

FREDDIE BARTHOLOMEW (1924–1992)

For a while, Freddie Bartholomew was a one of the biggest child stars in Hollywood. An angelic, curly-haired boy with dimpled cheeks, Bartholomew was born in Dublin, rejected by his parents and brought up by his Aunt Cissy. She introduced him to show business at an early age; and after some acting lessons and a few small-scale British film productions, she brought him to Hollywood, where David O. Selznick was searching feverishly for someone to play the lead in *David Copperfield* (1934). It's said that Freddie Bartholomew introduced himself to the producer with the words: "I am David Copperfield, Sir" – and that the producer promptly replied: "Right you are." When the film came out, the boy was famous overnight. He was the best-paid child star after Shirley Temple.

Freddie Bartholomew went on moving audiences to tears in his next film, *Anna Karenina* (1935), where he played the son of a mother played by Greta Garbo. In *Little Lord Fauntleroy* (1936), he even softened the heart of his embittered grandfather. *Captains Courageous* (1937) featured him as a spoiled upper-class brat who's shown the ropes and toughened up by a rough-diamond fisherman played by Spencer Tracy. But after *Kidnapped* (1938) and *Swiss Family Robinson* (1940), his career took the sad downturn typical of so many child stars. He was no longer in demand. Following a struggle for custody between his Aunt Cissy and his parents (who had turned up again, for reasons not hard to discern), he lost the millions he had earned. In later years, Bartholomew earned his living as the moderator of a TV program showing old films, as a producer of soap operas, and as an employee of an advertising agency. He did not like it when people asked him about his past. Freddie Bartholomew died in Florida in 1992, at the age of 67.

CLEOPATRA

1934 - USA - 100 MIN. - B & W - ANCIENT EPIC, DRAMA

DIRECTOR CECIL B. DEMILLE (1881–1959)
SCREENPLAY WALDEMAR YOUNG, VINCENT LAWRENCE, BARTLETT CORMACK **DIRECTOR OF PHOTOGRAPHY** VICTOR MILNER
EDITING ANNE BAUCHENS **MUSIC** RUDOLPH G. KOPP **PRODUCTION** CECIL B. DEMILLE for PARAMOUNT PICTURES.

STARRING CLAUDETTE COLBERT (Cleopatra), WARREN WILLIAM (Julius Caesar), HENRY WILCOXON (Mark Antony),
IAN KEITH (Octavian), ARTHUR HOHL (Brutus), JOSEPH SCHILDKRAUT (King Herod), GERTRUDE MICHAEL (Calpurnia),
LEONARD MUDIE (Pothinos), C. AUBREY SMITH (Enobarbus), IRVING PICHEL (Apollodorus).

ACADEMY AWARDS 1934 OSCAR for BEST CINEMATOGRAPHY (Victor Milner).

"Together we could conquer the world."
"Nice of you to include me."

The screen world's image of Cleopatra will be forever caked in Elizabeth Taylor's mile-long mascara. If nothing else, the 44-million-dollar production, which nearly drove 20th Century Fox into the ground circa 1963, succeeded in doing that. But as all film buffs know, Cecil B. DeMille's 1934 contribution to Egypt's most told story is the superior adaptation. As this gaudy spectacular makes clear, its creators spared no expense in draping the queen of queens in decadence. Only a true Puritan like DeMille, who would later deliver *The Ten Commandments* (1956) to Mount Hollywood, was capable of conjuring up such an orgy of scantily clad bodies, lascivious dances and overbearing decor. The greatest attraction of this cinematic Sodom and Gomorrah was, of course, the Jewel of the Nile herself, played by the legendary Claudette Colbert. And what a show she gave. Banking on more costume changes than a Versace opening in Milan, the star pulled out seven veils and all the stops to seduce her audience with tricks her mundane successor didn't dare attempt.

It's hard to imagine Taylor ever allowing herself to be rolled out in a carpet and landing at Caesar's feet as Colbert did. Yet with this 'giving' of herself,

Cleopatra launches the series of historic and intriguing events, which differ in their various celluloid incarnations no more than the pyramids do to the eye.

The year is 48 B.C., and Cleopatra faces a revolt in her kingdom of Egypt as she seeks the allegiance of Julius Caesar (Warren William) to safeguard the independence of her realm. When Caesar, whom she has led astray, is murdered, she transfers her affections to Mark Antony (Henry Wilcoxon), whose days on earth are clearly numbered. When Caesar's successor Octavian (Ian Keith) flexes his military muscle, the lovers Cleopatra and Mark Antony opt for suicide.

As always, DeMille finds ways of turning world history into pure circus. This penchant finds its most glorious expression in the scene where Mark Antony is first lured aboard Cleopatra's barge – no less stately than a floating palace – and welcomed by a troupe of oriental dancers. Undulations abound and continue to do so until the stoic field soldier finally concedes to crack a smile. Mermaids then free themselves from reams of fishing net and present him with pearl offerings, which a smiling Cleopatra tosses to the floor. "The golden streams of Egypt never run dry!" she protests. By the time

"**Photographically the picture is superb. Here DeMille is on firm ground and he makes ornate and eye-filling pictures of Roman life and Egyptian licentiousness impartially.**" *Variety*

the tigress slaves come in to turn some tricks with the lion tamer, Mark Antony's fate is sealed: he has fallen head over heels for the Queen of Egypt, a woman intent on drawing him over to her side – both in bed and in the political arena.

Claudette Colbert milks the scene for all it's worth. Curious, coquette, buddy-buddy, and a regular tease – her Cleopatra knows exactly what men of modest intellect desire. And this picture is full of them. For all the embarrassment caused by the miscast Shakespearean actors clad as Romans – a staple ingredient of ancient epics – Colbert's performance is modern, astute and absolutely original. At times it even seems as if she were poking fun at both the film itself and DeMille's sublime interpretation of the tale. Rather than playing a classic beauty in a chorus of maids, Colbert gives her character the same sort of comic edge that made her later roles so popular. Adorned with a solid-gold asp tiara, this working girl of the 30s puts her body on the line as she interprets what love of country meant back in the days before Christ.

Yet if this *Cleopatra* seems too 20th century to be true, DeMille is the man to blame. As a man who specialized in comedic social criticism rather than period pieces, his bombastic interiors are more akin to "Roaring Twenties" night clubs than Egyptian mausoleums. The flipside of this is that the actors seem less out of place than those who starred in the 1960s remake, and with a clever use of full shots and close-ups, DeMille reels in the historic figures and succeeds in making them more accessible.

Although the mass-scale sequences like Cleopatra's arrival in Rome and the Battle of Actium may not compare to those of the later movie – not to mention Liz Taylor's sphinx-mobile – the 30s version still trumped everything that had previously graced the screen. The fact that the earlier edition also required significantly less than four hours to arrive at its tragic ending, when Colbert dramatically thrusts the poisonous snake to her breast, is also a major point in its favor.

1 Hijinks atop the sphinx: Comedienne Claudette Colbert reinterprets history as Ancient Egypt's most captivating queen.

2 Chaise sera sera: After showing Caesar who rules the bedroom, Cleopatra lays down the law with Marc Antony (Henry Wilcoxon).

3 Love is a battlefield: Marc Antony fights public opinion by allying with Cleopatra and doing her bidding instead of Rome's.

4 Orator and gladiator: All the rhetoric in the world can't do Marc Antony any good now that Octavian's army has defeated him at Actium.

5 Straight from the horse's mouth: It took approximately 8000 extras plus crew for Actium to rise and fall again. The undertaking was as monumental for Hollywood as it had been for Rome.

"Don't you think I know you're my enemy – you and your hungry Rome?"

Film quote: Cleopatra (Claudette Colbert)

"With its magnificent backgrounds, each episode affords much interest. There are the three men plotting the murder of Caesar in the Roman baths, and later Mr. DeMille gives an even more expansive view of the baths, a feature seldom neglected by the director in any of his productions."

The New York Times

6 Asp me no questions: There's simply no telling how Cleo got all those Art Deco party favors for her provincial palace.

7 Ptolemy about it: Cecil B. DeMille puts on a parade that makes those 5th Avenue to-dos look like amateur affairs.

CLAUDETTE COLBERT (1903–1996)

The hungry-eyed Claudette Colbert embodied a blend of French savoir-faire and American ease that made her one of the most revered not to mention handsomely paid actresses of the 30s. At the age of three, the girl born Lily Claudette Chauchoin in Paris in 1903 (or 1911, sources vary) assimilated to life in New York when her father moved the family across the Atlantic. Like so many of her contemporaries, Claudette was the toast of Broadway prior to arriving in Hollywood. Her first screen appearance came with the Frank Capra film *For the Love of Mike* (1927), a production that didn't go as swimmingly as planned. Seven years later, Colbert was officially born a star after modernizing ancient history in Cecil B. DeMille's *The Sign of the Cross* (1932) and *Cleopatra* (1934). The same year audiences bowed to her as Egypt's queen, Colbert revealed an uncanny knack for comedy in Frank Capra's sleeper hit *It Happened One Night* (1934). Despite her condemning the picture as "the worst film (she) ever made," her acting in it was kooky enough to be deemed Oscar worthy – a one-time-only career distinction.

Off-screen, she was a diva beyond compare, who allegedly forbade directors to film the 'unflattering' right side of her face. But quirks and a fiery temperament weren't enough to scare off Hollywood's greatest filmmakers. And rightly so as Claudette created one masterful character after another in pictures like Ernst Lubitsch's *Bluebeard's Eighth Wife* (1938), W. S. Van Dyke's *It's a Wonderful World* (1939) – opposite James Stewart – and John Ford's Western *Drums Along the Mohawk* (1939). Later, as her star began to fade in Hollywood, the screen legend made a splash in the waters of European cinema and kept afloat on the Broadway stage and in television. Claudette Colbert died on Barbados in 1996.

THE PRODIGAL SON

Der verlorene Sohn

1934 - GERMANY - 80 MIN. - B & W - DRAMA

DIRECTOR LUIS TRENKER (1892–1990)
SCREENPLAY LUIS TRENKER, REINHART STEINBICKER, ARNOLD ULITZ, based on the novel of the same name by
LUIS TRENKER DIRECTORS OF PHOTOGRAPHY ALBERT BENITZ, REIMAR KUNTZE EDITING WALDEMAR GAEDE, ANDREW MARTON
MUSIC GIUSEPPE BECCE PRODUCTION FRED LYSSA for DEUTSCHE UNIVERSAL-FILM AG.

STARRING LUIS TRENKER (Tonio Feuersinger), MARIA ANDERGAST (Barbl Gudauner), BERTL SCHULTES (Barbl's Father),
MARIAN MARSH (Lilian Williams), FRANZ W. SCHRÖDER-SCHROM (Aston Williams), JIMMIE FOX (Tonio's American Friend),
PAUL HENCKELS (Schoolteacher), EDUARD KÖCK (Tonio's Father), MELANIE HORESCHOVSKY (Rosina),
EMMERICH ALBERT (Woodcutter).

"If you never leave, you can never come home."

By rights, Tonio (Luis Trenker) should be a very happy man: Barbl (Maria Andergast), the girl he loves, loves him back in spades; his buddies and colleagues, woodcutters like himself, respect and value him (what's the odd punch-up amongst friends?), and life in their little Tyrolean village is pleasant, prosperous and peaceful. Here, the people work hard and play hard – religion, tradition and ancient custom govern their entire lives. But Tonio longs for a kind of freedom that this place just can't offer him. For some time now he's been visiting the village schoolteacher (Paul Henckels) in the evenings, taking geography lessons and dreaming of the big wide world. Africa … Canada … New York!

Tonio wins a skiing race, and when he collects his prize, he meets the American millionaire Aston Williams (Franz W. Schröder-Schrom), who has stopped off here in the course of a round-the-world tour with his daughter Lilian (Marian Marsh). Mr. Williams is very impressed by the sun mask worn in the village each year during the midwinter *Rauhnachtsfest*; and as the mask is not for sale, he orders a copy, to be made by Tonio's father (Eduard Köck) for a large fee. Lilian makes a big play for Tonio and talks him into taking a dangerous trip into the mountains; there, they are caught by an avalanche, and a member of their climbing party is killed. Tonio sees this as his cue to leave the village. He will seek his fortune in the world's biggest city: New York.

The immigrant in the metropolis is wide-eyed with wonder. He gazes at the peaks of the massive buildings, and when he's made the ascent, he stands on the viewing platform and peers into the dark concrete canyons below. In its sheer scale and stoniness, this man-made landscape reminds him of home – but it can't be a home to him. He visits the Williams residence, where he's quickly sent packing: the family is out of town. Soon, he can't pay the rent, and odd jobs on construction sites barely bridge the gap. A short time later, he's one of the nameless thousands who press their noses to the storefront windows, sleeping on park benches or in tenement stairwells and stealing scraps of bread from market stalls. Finally, Tonio resolves to go home. By chance, though, he does run into Williams one more time; but when Tonio sees the sun mask replica at the millionaire's stylish home, he remembers his promise to be back in the valley for this year's *Rauhnachtsfest*.

In the very first images of the opening titles, Luis Trenker presents the two poles of his narrative: on the one hand, the majestic crags of the Dolomites; on the other, the cruel skyscrapers of the urban jungle. The resemblance between these two worlds is only superficial; in their essence, they could hardly be more different. Life in the mountains is based on family ties and takes place in harmony with nature, while life in the city has become

"Just once, I'd like to look out at the great wide world and see a ship and a big city. Living in a city must be a million times more thrilling than things are here. When you live in the mountains long enough, you start to feel like a fox in a trap." *Film quote: Tonio (Luis Trenker)*

1   I want to be a part of it: Unable to find a vacancy in the big city, Tonio Feuersinger (Luis Trenker) seeks refuge in a cardboard box.

2   Sun worshippers: Somehow the weather seemed cheerier back in Tonio's home town.

3   No handouts: Tonio joins the million other New Yorkers who are desperate for work.

4   Homeward bound: Luxury liners take wide-eyed travelers to Europe each and every day. If only Tonio could afford to go with them …

5   Children of the wind: The people of Tonio's village are all united by a common history and sense of community. Still, it's easy to get swept up in the promise of a better life.

6   Candy is dandy, but liquor is quicker: Lilian Williams (Marian Marsh) is ready to forget her inhibitions and climb every mountain with Tonio.

a radically individualized struggle for survival. Certainly, solidarity can be found there, but it's a rare and fleeting phenomenon amongst a mass of people damned to anonymity.

Working without a definitive script, Trenker and his camera team created this tendentious portrait of city life on location in New York City. The result has often been praised as a precursor of Italian Neorealism. Indeed,

Trenker filmed many scenes with a hidden camera, so that he could record passers-by without their knowing it, and the film presents an unvarnished view of the United States during the Depression years: extended tracking shots show us blocks of run-down houses, long lines of people at the soup kitchens, and homeless men and women on the city's sidewalks. Yet we should also remember that Trenker could call on his own German film tradi-

"**... initially a typically romantic Bavarian mountain film, switching dramatically to a mind-section shot in New York and offering some of the most startling photographic imagery of the Bowery in the Depression ...**" *William K. Everson, in: Cinefest 6*

7

7 Man without a country: Crisp, on-location cine-matography and actor Luis Trenker's subtle facial expressions paint a moving portrait of immigration.

8 The old switcheroo: It's just a matter of time before Lilian whisks ski champion Tonio away from Barbl

Gudauner (Maria Andergast, left) and runs a slalom of her own with him.

tion of close attention to urban realities: its exemplars include *Berlin: Symphony of a Great City* (*Berlin – Die Sinfonie der Grossstadt*, 1927, directed by Walther Ruttmann), *People on Sunday* (*Menschen am Sonntag*, 1929, directed by Robert Siodmak, Edgar G. Ulmer and Rochus Gliese with a screenplay by Billy Wilder) and Phil Jutzi's *Berlin Alexanderplatz* (1931).

For Trenker, these realist antecedents formed a starting-point for his own free narrative style. Its elements include major temporal leaps in the plotline, as well as passages of English dialog left untranslated and without subtitles. The movie's aesthetic highpoints are passages in which Trenker leaves the storyline aside and takes time to construct some thrilling mon-

tages: felled trees, cleared of their branches and careering down the hill into the valley below; a hair-raising ski race on the snow-covered mountain slopes; a dizzying sequence showing men at work on half-completed sky-scrapers; and the climactic *Rauhnachtsfest* in the Tyrolean mountain village. In these episodes, the images are condensed into an almost abstract maelstrom of lines and movements. For all its surface folksiness and the respect it pays to tradition, Trenker's film is fascinating in its formal adventurousness. *The Prodigal Son* marshals all the expressive resources of the cinematic avant-garde.

EP

LUIS TRENKER (1892–1990)

Luis Trenker was born in 1892 in the Grödnertal in South Tyrol. Originally, he studied to become an architect. It was while working on the side as a mountain guide and ski instructor that he first became involved in the movies. The famous "filmmaker of the mountains" Dr. Arnold Fanck employed Trenker as an advisor before casting him as an actor in his production *Mountain of Destiny* a. k. a. *Peak of Fate* (*Der Berg des Schicksals*, 1923/24). Further roles in Fanck's films ensued, while Trenker continued to write novels and screenplays. In 1931 he made his debut as a director with *Mountains on Fire* (*Berge in Flammen*). In this tale of a village occupied by enemy troops, Trenker found his main theme – a deep skepticism about 'outsiders' coupled with a passionate down-to-earthness.

His next film, *The Rebel* (*Der Rebell – Die Feuer rufen*, 1932), told the story of a Tyrolean freedom fighter struggling heroically against Napoleon's army. Though it attracted the attention of the Nazis, Trenker could never submit totally to their artistic or ideological precepts. He went on to make films that were both successful at the box office and visually stunning, including *The Emperor of California* (*Der Kaiser von Kalifornien*, 1936), *The Mountain Calls* (*Der Berg ruft*, 1937) and *The Fiery Devil* (*Der Feuerteufel*, 1940). By 1940, however, it had become increasingly difficult for him to work in Germany; indeed, he was practically forbidden to make films. In 1942, Trenker emigrated to Italy. After the war, he concentrated mainly on nature documentaries, but he also collaborated with Pier Paolo Pasolini on a drama about an escaped prisoner: *Il prigioniero della montagna / Flucht in die Dolomiten* (1955). Luis Trenker died in the South Tyrolean town of Bolzano in 1990.

THE THIN MAN

1934 - USA - 93 MIN. - B & W - DETECTIVE CAPER, LITERARY ADAPTATION

DIRECTOR W. S. VAN DYKE (1889–1943)
SCREENPLAY ALBERT HACKETT, FRANCES GOODRICH, based on the novel of the same name by DASHIELL HAMMETT
DIRECTOR OF PHOTOGRAPHY JAMES WONG HOWE EDITING ROBERT KERN MUSIC WILLIAM AXT PRODUCTION HUNT STROMBERG for COSMOPOLITAN FILMS, MGM.

STARRING WILLIAM POWELL (Nick Charles), MYRNA LOY (Nora Charles), MAUREEN O'SULLIVAN (Dorothy Wynant), NAT PENDLETON (Lieutenant John Guild), MINNA GOMBELL (Mimi), PORTER HALL (Herbert MacCaulay), CESAR ROMERO (Chris), HAROLD HUBER (Arthur Nunheim), NATALIE MOORHEAD (Julia Wolf), EDWARD ELLIS (Clyde Wynant).

"The important thing is the rhythm. Always have rhythm in your shaking. Now a Manhattan you always shake to fox-trot time, a Bronx to two-step time, a dry Martini you always shake to waltz time."

Seldom has a filmmaker paid homage to a novelist as stylishly as Woodbridge Strong Van Dyke did to the man who penned *The Thin Man*: the director simply has the opening credits play over a hard-cover copy of Dashiell Hammett's bestseller featuring a dust-jacket photo of the writer. As this sort of practice is hardly commonplace, cinematic sleuths seated in the audience are left to wonder whether the shot is a hidden clue or a red herring. After all, it could hardly be coincidence that Hammett is not only the first 'thin man' viewers see, but that his portrait also dissolves into the silhouette that will be associated with the title character for the rest of the movie.

The story opens on former private investigator Nick Charles (William Powell) and his wealthy, socialite wife Nora (Myrna Loy) as they enjoy a vacation in New York City. The news of inventor Clyde Wynant's (Edward Ellis) mysterious disappearance and the sudden death of his secretary (Natalie Moorhead) put a damper on the trip, and before long Nora urges her husband to come out of retirement. Nick would rather not get involved, but inexplicable events pull him deeper into the case and leave him with no other choice. The situation takes an unexpected turn when a dinner party brings all the potential suspects together, and Nick gets his chance to unmask the killer.

Although the premise has the makings of a classic detective story, nonstop one-liners give it the veneer of a screwball comedy. Here, wry exchanges between husband and wife make crime-fighting and voicing of disapproval seem more like fun and games:

Nora: How many drinks have you had?
Nick: This will make six Martinis.
Nora: Well alright. Waiter, would you bring me five more Martinis …

While Hollywood may have been no stranger to either happy marriages or jealousy and intrigue, there was something unique about Nick and Nora: for the first time on screen, the audience saw a husband and wife share an inseparable life together. To quote legendary comedy director George Cukor, "There had always been romantic pairings, but Powell and Loy were fresh and original. They were the first to breathe life into comedies of marriage. They got

"A strange mixture of excitement, quips and hard-boiled sentiment ... full of the special touches that can come from nowhere but the studio, that really make the feet a movie walks on."

Otis Ferguson, in: The New Republic

the tone just right, having hit on a winning combination of exaggeration and understatement that was rounded off by grace, charm and a carefree air."

In fact, it was not out of character for either of them to embrace Christmas with childlike enthusiasm: Nora would rather sweat than take off her new mink coat inside the apartment; and Nick, from his vantage point on the couch, wouldn't dream of changing out of his robe and pajamas until he had popped all the balloons hanging from the Christmas tree with his toy pistol.

For the most part, however, Powell plays the smooth man about town to Loy's modern, self-assured woman. The Nora character, incidentally, was modeled on screenwriter Lillian Hellman, Dashiell Hammett's real-life significant other. While the studio was less than enthusiastic about casting the aging Powell or the virtually unknown Loy in the leading roles, W. S. Van Dyke had worked with the actors that same year on *Manhattan Melodrama* (1934) and was certain they would fit the bill. Limited to a 230,000 dollar budget, 'One Take Woody' Van Dyke shot the entire picture in under three weeks. To

general astonishment, the film that was conceived as a B-mystery-comedy raked in more than two million dollars in ticket sales and turned Powell and Loy into a Hollywood dream team overnight.

Throughout the entire *The Thin Man* series, elegant attire and lavish hotel décor define the look of the films, with the initial picture's parlor-room feel owing much to James Wong Howe's subtle use of light. Indeed, the cinematographer was known throughout Hollywood as 'Low Key Howe' – a moniker that spoke to his predilection for recreating soft, natural light on screen. Howe took great pains to make viewers believe that the light source originated from within the action they were watching on screen. For instance, to underline the sense of danger that Van Dyke breathed into the opening sequence, Howe made a large searchlight cast mysterious shadows onto a back wall.

The fact that the film's comedy of marriage aspects don't take away from the suspense can be attributed to Albert Hackett and Frances Goodrich's

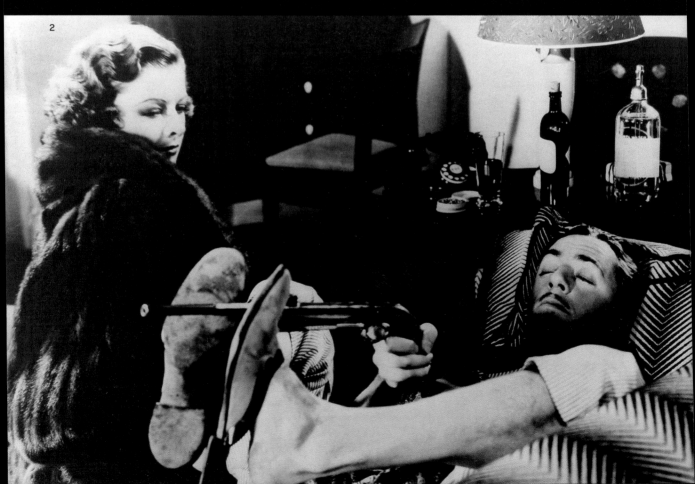

1 Look but don't touch: Alcohol's grip on Nick Charles (William Powell) may be strong, but his wife's is stronger. Myrna Loy as the sobering Nora Charles.

2 Kids at Christmas: Furtive Nora doesn't mind watching Nick play hunter with his toys, as long as he doesn't confuse her with the quarry.

3 Of hounds and hangovers: After a night of serious drinking, Nora and Fido both wake up with pounding headaches.

masterful screenplay, which eliminates the underlying sexual tension and innuendo that mark Dashiell Hammett's novel. In the opening scene, when Wynant bids his future son-in-law to show his daughter that "there is such a thing as a happy marriage," Hackett and Goodrich let us know what they have set out to prove: Nick and Nora's marital bliss is far stronger than the ties that bind underworld thugs and murder victims. Using champagne bubbles to penetrate class differences, the detectives lead a fairytale existence that could persuade even the most hardened of criminals to soften.

What Van Dyke couldn't have imagined at the time he made the film is that the Hammett photo in the credit sequence would create such an uproar among fans determined to unmask the thin man's real identity. By the picture's sixth and final installment, many moviegoers believed Nick Charles and actor William Powell to be the mysterious man without a face. In truth, the story's title was simply intended to refer to missing scientist Clyde Wynant.

OK

WILLIAM POWELL (1892–1984)

Actress Myrna Loy once said that she "never enjoyed work more" than when she worked with William Powell. According to Loy, Powell "was a brilliant actor, a delightful companion, a great friend, and above all, a true gentleman." Indeed, this final attribute was what he was famous for both on and off the screen. It didn't matter whether the actor was flashing a friendly smile or playing a mobster, he was always debonair. A native of Pittsburgh, Powell learned to act at the American Academy of Dramatic Arts in New York City. He went on to perform on a vast number of stages before becoming a Broadway fixture in 1917. The transition to celluloid came in 1922, when he performed opposite John Barrymore in *Sherlock Holmes*. After residing in Italy for a short while, Powell returned to his homeland and went under contract with Paramount Pictures, where he was soon typecast as the villain. Acting in a total of 34 silent movies, Powell gave his most memorable non-speaking performance as a Russian stage director gone Hollywood filmmaker opposite Emil Jannings in Josef von Sternberg's *The Last Command* (1927/28). When the advent of sound took the cinema by storm, Powell's roots as a stage actor afforded him an easy transition to talkies, where he quickly made a name for himself in the Philo Vance detective series.
In 1931, Powell left Paramount for Warner Bros., only to jump over to MGM three years later. Although studio boss Louis B. Mayer and many others were convinced that the aging star was all washed up, filmmaker W. S. Van Dyke Mayer was not. The director cast the actor as protagonist Nick Charles in *The Thin Man* series (1934–1947), re-launching Powell's career and enabling him to shed his bad-guy screen image once and for all. Hit after hit followed including *The Great Ziegfeld* (1936), *My Man Godfrey* (1936), *How to Marry a Millionaire* (1953) and *Life with Father* (1947). William Powell, one of the most revered and well-known character actors in the business, died of a cardiac arrest in 1984.

IT HAPPENED ONE NIGHT

1934 - USA - 105 MIN. - B & W - COMEDY

DIRECTOR FRANK CAPRA (1897–1991)
SCREENPLAY ROBERT RISKIN, based on the story *NIGHT BUS* by SAMUEL HOPKINS ADAMS **DIRECTOR OF PHOTOGRAPHY** JOSEPH WALKER
EDITING GENE HAVLICK **MUSIC** LOUIS SILVERS **PRODUCTION** FRANK CAPRA, HARRY COHN for COLUMBIA PICTURES CORPORATION.

STARRING CLARK GABLE (Peter Warne), CLAUDETTE COLBERT (Ellie Andrews), WALTER CONNOLLY (Alexander Andrews),
JAMESON THOMAS (King Westley), ROSCOE KARNS (Oscar Shapeley), CHARLES C. WILSON (Joe Gordon),
ALAN HALE (Danker), ARTHUR HOYT (Zeke, The Motel Proprietor), BLANCHE FRIDERICI (Zeke's Wife),
WARD BOND (Bus Driver #1).

ACADEMY AWARDS 1934 OSCARS for BEST PICTURE, BEST DIRECTOR (Frank Capra), BEST ACTOR (Clark Gable),
BEST ACTRESS (Claudette Colbert), and BEST ADAPTED SCREENPLAY (Robert Riskin).

"Your ego is absolutely colossal." "Yeah, yeah, not bad, how's yours?"

It happened one Oscar night. During one of the first ever Academy Award ceremonies, an unassuming picture from an insignificant studio did the impossible and garnered a trophy for each of the categories in which it was nominated: best picture, best director, best adapted screenplay, best actor and best actress – all five top honors – went to *It Happened One Night*. When the movie was first released, few theaters had bothered to run it. But word of mouth led to this sleeper comedy winning over the hearts of American audiences, and it gradually worked its way up to smash-hit status.

In hindsight, it seems only logical that its cut-and-dried plot would hit a nerve with viewers of the Depression Era. This was a picture that put a new spin on finding out 'how the other half lives' by having devil-may-care heiress Ellie Andrews (Claudette Colbert) become a woman of modest means and love every minute of it. The headstrong young lady has run away from her father who is hell-bent on annulling her unconsummated marriage to a worthless, stuffed-shirt playboy. On the bus to New York, Ellie crosses paths with out-of-work journalist Peter Warne (Clark Gable). Although each finds the other morally repugnant, the newspaperman knows a front-page story when he sees one and the young bride snags an opportunity to throw off a pair of detectives hot on her trail. Disguised as newlyweds for the convenience of travel, Peter and Ellie stage a full-blown lover's quarrel that has more

than just theatrical consequences. For somewhere down the line, the street-smart Peter manages to have a lasting impact on Miss Ellie and change the way she sees the world. As if lifted from the pages of a fairy tale, the film ends with the make-believe couple becoming a real one.

Without question, *It Happened One Night* is Capra's Cinderella. His feature film gives the audience an amazing glimpse of the 'secret dreams' of the idle classes, as one of its members rids herself of the burden of money to become truly alive. To expose Colbert's character to all she's been missing, Capra has her take a road trip clear across grassroots America. Her modes of transportation are a cumbersome Greyhound Bus and a good old fashioned Model T. No fancy accommodation here, just a couple of no-frills roach motels and a blanket of stars. With Peter at her side, Ellie learns what it means to scrimp and save for a meal while indulging in all that free love has to offer. Still, it is not moral doctrines, but rather the outstanding performances and the filmmaker's ingenious direction that makes this movie what it is. Unbeknownst to Capra, he had given birth to the first screwball comedy without even trying.

The show really gets rolling with the "Walls of Jericho" scene in which Peter drapes a sheet over a clothesline to divide the cabin bedroom he shares with Ellie. In the time of the newly established Production Code, this was a

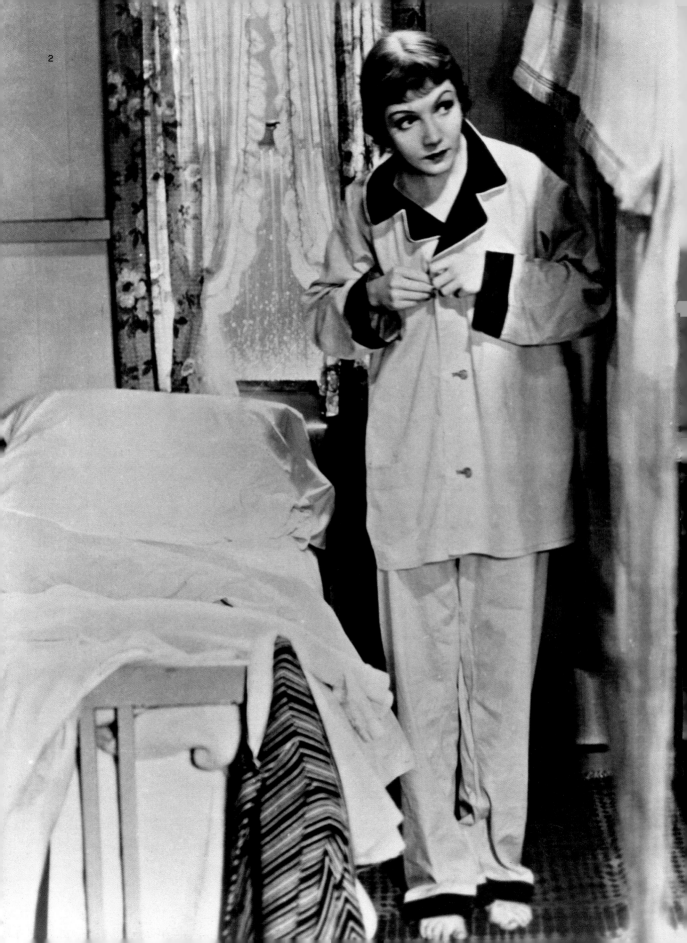

1 Two thumbs up: Street-smart Peter Warne (Clark Gable) and sheltered heiress Ellie Andrews (Claudette Colbert) prove that opposites attract in this Frank Capra classic.

2 The pajama game: The impromptu wall of Jericho had better come a tumbling down if Hollywood intends to keep things interesting.

3 Unscheduled stop: Seeing an opportunity to escape her father's investigators, Ellie makes a spectacle of herself aboard a Greyhound bus.

4 When it's bad, I'm better: Claudette Colbert considered this skid row studio production to be the worst film she ever made. All the more reason why she was stunned to receive an Oscar for her performance in it.

5 Roaming reporter: A journalist does a brief stint as a fly-by-night Romeo to land an exclusive interview with the beauty beside him.

"**The cinema equals Hollywood equals the great American comedy equals Frank Capra equals** *It Happened One Night.* **A closeup isn't just a closeup – it's an individual! Every two-shot – a couple! A medium long-shot of a group reads as a scene of community! A little intercutting between extreme closeups and group closeups is all that is needed for an outsider to be accepted by a group. Talk about an American approach to filmmaking.**" *Enno Patalas, in: Süddeutsche Zeitung*

way to spark sexual chemistry while appeasing the censors. Indeed, their courtship is kept clean as can be thanks to the subtlety of suggestion, which is at its raciest when Peter teaches Ellie how to dunk donuts and initiates her in the art of hitchhiking. Moments like these seem to chronicle Gable's development as a silver-screen 'shrew tamer', a role that would peak five years later with the actor's portrayal of Rhett Butler in *Gone with the Wind* (1939). Nonetheless, Claudette Colbert's knack for taking the wind out of his sails is every bit as impressive as his efforts to show her the ropes. When, for

example, Gable can't stop a car by sticking out his thumb, Colbert gets the job done by flashing a stocking top instead.

Seldom was a film cobbled together with such minimal resources as successful as this. Capra showed unusual flair in using the "Walls of Jericho" to illustrate Ellie Andrews' sexual trepidation, and Gable knew how to transform a simple undressing scene into a crowd pleaser that spawned a no-undershirt fashion trend and had Fruit of the Loom up in arms. The fast-paced action can be attributed to a whirlwind shoot, which was shortened to four weeks after Colbert demanded that her salary be doubled. Indeed, both the actress and her co-star wanted to have as little as possible to do with the project. Columbia, after all, was one of the so-called skid row studios, and Gable considered an engagement at Harry Cohn's production company akin to a period of Siberian exile. MGM boss Louis B. Mayer, who loaned the star out for the movie, tried to make the project worth his while by securing the actor a most handsome salary. After *It Happened One Night*, the Depression Era was a thing of the past for Columbia. It was to be forty years until *One Flew Over the Cuckoo's Nest* (1975) matched the film's record of winning all the top Oscar honors and another sixteen until *The Silence of the Lambs* (1991) did it again.

PB

HARRY COHN (1891–1958)

Tough-as-nails producer Harry Cohn held on to his authority as Columbia Picture's boss until his death in 1958. In fact, there was a saying in Hollywood that anyone who could get him to budge on any issue had what it took to make it in the movies. A New York native, Cohn founded C. B. C. Productions in 1920 with his brother Jack and mogul Joe Brandt, later expanding operations to Hollywood in 1924. Jack continued to run things in their home-town, while Harry took over the West Coast end of business – a wise decision considering that two brothers were always at each others' throats. For years, Columbia was branded by the industry as a skid row studio. Rita Hayworth was among the few true stars who called the production company her home. Still, it was *The Batman* (1943) movie serial and the countless *Three Stooges* (1930–1964) flicks that helped the studio keep its head above water throughout the Great Depression. The studio's real renaissance came shortly thereafter when Cohn's winning instincts prompted him to sign on young director Frank Capra. Indeed, the filmmaker reeled in five major Oscars and critical acclaim for Columbia with *It Happened One Night* (1934). Two years later, *Mr. Deeds Goes to Town* (1936) won Capra another Oscar and further prestige for the studio.
Stars like Rita Hayworth, Jack Lemmon and Kim Novak were cultivated under King Cohn's guidance. Howard Hawks and Cary Grant landed the studio another major hit with *His Girl Friday* (1939). In the 40s, Columbia made celebrated film noir pieces including *Gilda* (1946) and *The Lady from Shanghai* (1947). Then, in the 50s, Cohn opened his doors to both television productions and independent directors like Fred Zinnemann, Elia Kazan and David Lean. This resulted in Oscars all around for films like *From Here to Eternity* (1953), *On the Waterfront* (1954) and *The Bridge on the River Kwai* (1957). Harry Cohn, a man who could be as giving as he was rigid, enjoyed one of the most lavish burials in Hollywood history.

1934 - USA - 115 MIN. - B & W - WESTERN, LITERARY ADAPTATION

DIRECTOR JACK CONWAY (1887–1952)
SCREENPLAY BEN HECHT, based on the novel *VIVA VILLA! A RECOVERY OF THE REAL PANCHO VILLA, PEON, BANDIT, SOLDIER, PATRIOT* by EDGECUMB PINCHON and O. B. STADE DIRECTORS OF PHOTOGRAPHY CHARLES G. CLARKE, JAMES WONG HOWE
EDITING ROBERT KERN MUSIC HERBERT STOTHART PRODUCTION DAVID O. SELZNICK for MGM.

STARRING WALLACE BEERY (Pancho Villa), LEO CARRILLO (Sierra), HENRY B. WALTHALL (Francisco Madero),
FAY WRAY (Teresa), DONALD COOK (Don Felipe de Castillo), STUART ERWIN (Johnny Sykes),
JOSEPH SCHILDKRAUT (General Pascal), KATHERINE DEMILLE (Rosita Morales), GEORGE E. STONE (Emilio Chavito),
PHILLIP COOPER (Pancho Villa as a child).

ACADEMY AWARDS 1934 OSCAR for BEST ASSISTANT DIRECTOR (John Waters).

"You can't win a revolution on love alone. You gotta have hate, too."

Mexico, circa 1911. Rebel bandito Pancho Villa (Wallace Beery) is the hero of the country's oppressed people. As a child he was forced to watch as lackeys of the Díaz regime whipped his peasant father to death. Now, he takes his revenge by pillaging rich landowners. With his intellectual partner in crime Francisco Madero (Henry B. Walthall) at his side, Villa learns to harness his hate and assumes leadership of a revolutionary army that overthrows the despotic Díaz in record time. As president of the new government, Madero plans to implement the promised land reform, but is assassinated by the minions of the turncoat General Pascal (Joseph Schildkraut) before he gets the chance. Villa then successfully starts – and wins – a second revolution, but his triumph is short-lived; a few years later he is shot dead on the street in broad daylight. But the fame and glory of his deeds lives on, and becomes the stuff of history books and cinematic legend, although Hollywood doesn't always get its facts right, as *Viva Villa!* and countless other fictionalizations of his story reveal.

Pancho Villa, one of Mexican history's flashiest figures, was both a dangerous outlaw and champion of the people. Here, however, it's hard to distinguish the man from the actor who plays him. In a touching performance, Hollywood original Wallace Beery portrays Villa as an overgrown child who hasn't quite yet grown into the size of his sombrero or the ammunition belt that hangs over his belly. His Villa may be a killer, cheerfully disposing of both wealthy landowners and those wounded in battle, but, if he is, we never actually get to see any of it. Furthermore, his little bearded mentor, Madero, need but say the word and this illiterate renegade is suddenly a man of mercy. Off the job, he is a real ladies' man, who 'weds' a different woman every time the sun sets. His machismo charms peasant girls as easily as it does Spanish aristocrats like Teresa (Fay Wray). But when death comes knocking on Teresa's door, her brother, Don Felipe (Donald Cook) won't rest until Villa's head is his.

WALLACE BEERY
(1885–1949)

Wallace Beery was convinced that he had his sour puss of a face to thank for his success in Hollywood. It was a hard point to argue. His acting range was limited, his presence somewhat sluggish, and his taste for alcohol – like many of his fellow actors – a bit too cultivated. Still, audiences liked Wallace Beery just as he was. A native of Kansas, Beery transitioned from the circus to motion pictures in 1913 and played an oafish Swedish servant in the series *Sweedie* (1914–1916).

After ripping his servant's uniform to shreds once and for all, Beery landed acting jobs at Keystone and Universal. A brief and stormy marriage to silent screen legend Gloria Swanson also counts among his earlier claims to fame. Often typecast as a villain, Berry was up to no good in adventure movies like *The Last of the Mohicans* (1920), *The Four Horsemen of the Apocalypse* (1921), *Robin Hood* (1922) and *The Lost World* (1924/25). That all changed when infallible MGM producer Irving Thalberg welcomed the actor into his line-up of stars and jumpstarted his career. Before long, Beery was keeping movie houses packed with *The Big House* (1930) and had an Oscar credit to his name for his portrayal of an aging boxer in *The Champ* (1931). He also managed to revamp his image with several comedic performances.

As attested to by his appearances in the big MGM ensemble films like *Grand Hotel* (1932) and *Dinner at Eight* (1933), these were the years when Beery was among the top ten stars in Hollywood. Later notable successes would follow, including memorable performances as Long John Silver in *Treasure Island* (1934) and as the title role in the Mexican Revolution Western *Viva Villa!* (1934). After that, Beery managed to maintain his popularity with several comedies opposite Marie Dressler and Marjorie Main, but the decline and fall of his career proved inevitable. In 1949, the actor died in Beverly Hills at the age of 64.

1 Three caballeros: Francisco 'Pancho' (Wallace Beery) Villa and his two compadres wet their whistles in the name of revolution.

2 Eat like a horse and drink like a fish: Just be sure to make out like a bandit or at least die like a man.

3 Caveat emptor: When shopping at a bordello, what you see isn't always what you get.

In real life, Francisco 'Pancho' Villa was killed by the same government that later erected monuments in his honor. His baffling 'attack' on the U.S.A. is also altogether ignored in this adaptation of his story. Yet despite these discrepancies, *Viva Villa!* is more than just another enjoyable piece of film-making, and is a dazzling account of revolution thanks to the script delivered by the legendary Ben Hecht, which reveals just how such myths are made. His Villa is smart enough to win the sympathies of American newspaperman Johnny Sykes (Stuart Erwin), a man who writes of the freedom fighter's heroic deeds for a gringo public and carefully avoids any mention of his

brutality. Not only that, but when Sykes prematurely reports of a city's occu-pation, Villa turns yellow journalism into hard news. The climax of their col-laboration comes during the revolutionary's moving death scene as his American friend thinks up an epitaph fit for a hero. Decades later, Villa's plans to get Hollywood to eat out of his hand became the main focus of the film *And Starring Pancho Villa as Himself* (2003), with Antonio Banderas in the title role.

Howard Hawks might have delivered a more layered piece had this 1930s production remained under his direction. The picture's desert shoot

highly unusual for the day, was strenuous to say the least. According to later reports, Hawks and his crew survived on a diet of brandy and oranges. Besides dealing with a barrage of David O. Selznick memos from the Hollywood end of things, Hawks found that the Mexican government was anything but positively disposed towards his depiction of their favorite son. The dispute reached a head when, perched up on a rooftop in a drunken stupor, actor Lee Tracy 'rained' on a military parade on the day commemorating the revolution. When Hawks refused to fire Tracy, Selznick fired Hawks and replaced him with Jack Conway. Tracy's role, in turn, was filled by Stuart Erwin. Having never felt quite at home in the confines of MGM's machinery, Hawks shed no tears over this adieu. More unfortunate still was the fact that approximately

6,000 yards of exposed celluloid, amounting to nearly all of the original director's work on the project, went up in flames in a plane crash. As a result, it is unclear to this day just which segments of the film Hawk was responsible for. He himself claimed to have created the rousing crowd sequences at the start of the picture, often compared with those from Sergei M. Eisenstein's *Que Viva Mexico!* (1930–1932/79). Equally spectacular, however, is Conway's vision of the revolution that has wild, gun-slinging Mexicans in umbrella-like sombreros ignite hand grenades with the tips of their cigars. And, after a good day's work, they sing themselves to sleep after with a few bars of "La Cucaracha" – a song forever associated with the great and glorious Pancho Villa.

"An uncredited Howard Hawks directed some of the material in this rumbustious traversal of the Mexican revolutionary leader's rise and fall, with Beery leading from the front as future president Pancho, part moral crusader, part crazy bandito. The big MGM production typically plays fast and loose with the facts so it's as much an action spectacular as a genuine historical chronicle, but there's much good humor and a terrifically hammy death scene where one unfortunate villain is coated in honey and left under the sun for the ants."

Time Out Film Guide

4   Spare the rod and spoil the scene: Be that as it may, Jack Conway's film wipes all traces of blood and gore from Villa's vita.

5   Holy Moses! Villa is named Mexico's greatest revolutionary, only to be kept out of its capital. Talk about a Pyrrhic victory.

6   Call in the cavalry: Equal opportunity employer Pancho Villa gives every man a chance to fight for Mexico's freedom. The crowd scenes were shot by the film's original director, Howard Hawks.

7   No last requests? It doesn't seem fair for a guy to get executed without as much as a final cigarette. Then again, maybe this isn't the end after all.

ANNA KARENINA

1935 - USA - 95 MIN. - B & W - DRAMA, LITERARY ADAPTATION

DIRECTOR CLARENCE BROWN (1890–1987)
SCREENPLAY CLEMENCE DANE, S. N. BEHRMAN, SALKA VIERTEL, based on the novel of the same name by LEO N. TOLSTOY
DIRECTOR OF PHOTOGRAPHY WILLIAM H. DANIELS EDITING ROBERT KERN MUSIC HERBERT STOTHART PRODUCTION DAVID O. SELZNICK for MGM.

STARRING GRETA GARBO (Anna Karenina), FREDRIC MARCH (Count Alexei Vronsky), BASIL RATHBONE (Karenin), FREDDIE BARTHOLOMEW (Sergei), REGINALD OWEN (Stiva), MAUREEN O'SULLIVAN (Kitty), GYLES ISHAM (Levin), MAY ROBSON (Countess Vronsky), PHOEBE FOSTER (Dolly), JOAN MARSH (Lili).

"This can't go on. I have a husband and a child. This must end."

Before she appears on the screen, we seen nothing but smoke; the train from St. Petersburg has just arrived in the station. When the face of Greta Garbo finally swims into view, Count Vronsky falls in love at first sight. The movie-going public was equally smitten. Garbo was a box-office magnet, in silent films and talkies ("Garbo speaks!"), as Tolstoy's tragic heroine or as the Queen of Sweden (*Queen Christina*, 1933). For Anna Karenina, Vronsky's passion has fatal consequences: as a result of their affair, she loses her husband and – far worse – her beloved son. In the end, she will throw herself in front of the same train, as it carries her lover away from her.

Anna Karenina – a panorama of life in Czarist Russia – was one of her most popular films, and it is certainly the best adaptation of a novel so dense, rich and subtle that it strongly resists translation into cinematic form. Clarence Brown, Garbo's director in seven films, focuses on the love story between Anna and Vronsky. Their relationship fails because her husband Karenin (Basil Rathbone), a cold-hearted diplomat, resists it so bitterly and refuses to countenance a divorce. Karenin is someone who is entirely at one with the principles that govern his time and place: a man must uphold his reputation at all costs, a son's welfare always comes first, and marriage is indissoluble. In violating these principles, Anna seals her own fate. As she tries to make a life with Vronsky, she is subjected to the worst that wagging tongues can do; and when she longs to embrace her son, she has to sneak into a house that has barred its doors to her. The woman of the early scenes,

Right and Vronsky: The wedded Anna Karenina (Greta Garbo) engages a game of Russian roulette by taking a lover. Fredric March as the dashing officer who wins her heart.	**2** Everything and nothing: All the comforts of home can't compensate for Anna's loveless marriage.	**3** An uncharoned affair: If Anna's brother Stiva (Reginald Owen) doesn't get on the ball, his sister is liable to fall from grace.

whose noble beauty had lit up the world, is eventually reduced to a gaunt outcast.

The splendid settings include a marvelous ball scene, in which various characters' fates are woven together, but this shouldn't distract us from the essential: *Anna Karenina* is Garbo's film, and she loses herself entirely in the role. This isn't acting so much as being. Her performance is almost expressionless: mostly, her eyes are cast downwards, as if she were aware of the doom hanging over her. From her very first encounter with Vronsky to the

last moments before her suicide, Anna – like the audience – is aware of her heroic but tragic destiny. What makes Garbo mysterious is her ability to suggest passion while showing no emotion whatsoever, and to communicate this passion so that the audience immediately and intuitively understands it.

It may be doubted whether Frederic March, as Vronsky, earned this adulation. March didn't want the role, and it shows. For this reason, Anna's love for the dashing officer seems far less plausible than the hatred she bears for her husband. Basil Rathbone makes the best of his thankless task, although

"Miss Garbo, the first lady of the screen, sins, suffers and perishes illustriously in the new, ably produced and comparatively mature version of the Tolstoy classic ... The photoplay is a dignified and effective drama which becomes significant because of that tragic, lonely and glamorous blend which is the Garbo personality." *The New York Times*

4   Looking the other way: Anna's husband Karenin (Basil Rathbone) is too absorbed in his own pastimes to take a healthy interest in those of his wife.

5   Glove story: Vronsky never oversteps his bounds in public. In real life, however, Garbo was aware that co-star Fredric March was notorious for seducing his leading ladies and ate garlic to stave off his advances.

7

6   Father's little fibs: Wanting to spare his son Sergei
    (Freddie Bartholomew) the truth about Anna's
    ways, Karenin tells the boy that she is dead.

7   Coach and first class: MGM pulled out all the stops
    to recreate czarist Russia. Karenin is the crown
    jewel of aristocratic hypocrisy.

his Karenin is unquestionably more English than Russian – that quilted dressing gown would eventually become a familiar sight in his Sherlock Holmes films. In a purely delightful supporting role, the wonderful Maureen O'Sullivan, already Tarzan's Jane at the time, plays Anna's youthful niece, Kitty. Her love for Tolstoy's alter ego Levin (Gyles Isham) is central to the novel, but marginal to the film, and sadly much of their story is lost to the exigencies of a 95-minute script.

But this was nothing in comparison to an earlier, silent film in which Greta Garbo had already played Anna Karenina. It wasn't called *Love* (1927;

directed by Edmund Goulding) for nothing: the movie was distributed with two different closing reels, and the American public was treated to a version of Tolstoy's tragedy that provided a happy ending. Understandably, Garbo (who, by the way, was never married herself) didn't want to leave it at that, and it was largely due to her persistence that David O. Selznick finally abandoned his stubborn opposition to the idea of a proper adaptation. He had been reluctant to waste his star in costume dramas … but who could say no to Garbo for long?

PB

BASIL RATHBONE
(1892–1967)

He was the cinematic embodiment of Sherlock Holmes, playing Conan Doyle's austere gentleman detective in a grand total of 14 films. With his lean figure and his long nose, Rathbone also bore a remarkable resemblance to the familiar book illustrations. The movies still have a large army of fans. Born in South Africa, Rathbone had other roles in his repertoire. In his early British films, he made a name for himself playing a series of romantic or treacherous lovers. When he moved to Hollywood, he often found himself cast in eccentric supporting roles in prestigious costume dramas. Thus, he appeared alongside Greta Garbo in *Anna Karenina* (1935) and with Marlene Dietrich in *The Garden of Allah* (1936). As a brilliant baddie, he was particularly successful in cloak-and-dagger movies, where he could make good use of one of his greatest passions: Basil Rathbone was an outstanding fencer. He played the villain to Errol Flynn's hero in *Captain Blood* (1935) and *The Adventures of Robin Hood* (1938), and in both films he had great difficulty not injuring Flynn, who was a far less gifted swordsman. Nonetheless, the scripts insisted that he lose, even in his famous dagger duel with Tyrone Power in *The Mark of Zorro* (1940).
When offered the chance to play Sherlock Holmes in *The Hound of the Baskervilles* (1939), Rathbone saw it as a welcome opportunity to escape typecasting. Wrong! The film was so popular that it spawned countless sequels, including *The Adventures of Sherlock Holmes* (1939), and Rathbone was cursed with another image he couldn't shake. After a long pause and a successful self-parody in *The Court Jester* (1955), Basil Rathbone saw his career peter out in a string of horror films.

GOLD DIGGERS OF 1935

1935 - USA - 98 MIN. - B & W - MUSICAL

DIRECTOR BUSBY BERKELEY (1895–1976)

SCREENPLAY MANUEL SEFF, PETER MILNE, ROBERT LORD DIRECTOR OF PHOTOGRAPHY GEORGE BARNES EDITING GEORGE AMY
MUSIC HARRY WARREN (Music) and AL DUBIN (Lyrics) PRODUCTION ROBERT LORD for FIRST NATIONAL PICTURES INC.,
WARNER BROS.

STARRING DICK POWELL (Dick Curtis), ADOLPHE MENJOU (Nicolai Nicoleff), GLORIA STUART (Amy Prentiss),
ALICE BRADY (Matilda Prentiss), HUGH HERBERT (T. Mosley Thorpe III), GLENDA FARRELL (Betty Hawes),
FRANK MCHUGH (Humbolt Prentiss), JOSEPH CAWTHORN (August Schultz), GRANT MITCHELL (Louis Lampson),
DOROTHY DARE (Arline Davis), WINI SHAW (Winny).

ACADEMY AWARDS 1935 OSCAR for BEST ORIGINAL SONG ("Lullaby of Broadway"; Music: Harry Warren; Lyrics: Al Dubin).

"Listen to the lullaby of old Broadway!"

While the majority of Hollywood's backstage musicals are set in the wings of a theater, *Gold Diggers of 1935* alters the formula by moving the action to another of celluloid's beloved retreats – the grand hotel. Within its Art-Deco interiors, the Wentworth Plaza's employees do their best to land tips, big or small. Multimillionaire widow Matilda Prentiss (Alice Brady) is a regular hotel guest known for being a tightwad who'll have none of it. Things get more complicated however when the dowager has wedding plans for her daughter Ann (Gloria Stuart) that require the assistance and discretion of the staff. For unbeknownst to the young woman, Mother Prentiss has found her a perfect mate and intends to make sure that sparks go flying between them. Dick Curtis (Dick Powell), the charming front-desk attendant, has been chosen to see to it that Ann keeps out of mischief while cajoling her dud of a Romeo into showing a little interest. You don't have to be a rocket scientist to figure out that Ann and Dick are the ones who end up falling in love, considering that actor Dick Powell always got the girl in these light-hearted Warner Brothers' musicals. The mere fact that this time it's Gloria Stuart and not regular partner Ruby Keeler who is paired opposite him doesn't disrupt the formula in the least.

Despite the change of venue, *Gold Diggers of 1935* does its best to parallel the backstage musical mold. En lieu of a Broadway producer, Mrs. Prentiss fronts the necessary cash to stage a little charity event that quickly becomes a backbreaking undertaking complete with a hearty helping of backstage shtick. Actor Adolphe Menjou gives a laugh-a-minute performance as the no-budget director with an ego the size of the Empire State Building.

And Busby Berkeley outdoes himself dreaming up two specialty numbers chock-full of his trademark razzle-dazzle.

Gold Diggers of 1935 marked the first time Berkeley oversaw the direction of an entire film and not just its musical numbers. While the acting may have been neglected under his command – as was the consensus of the film critics – the production numbers in *Gold Diggers of 1935* emerged as more important than ever before. Equally apparent is that Berkeley's free reign as director enabled him to integrate song and dance more fully into the general story. For example, the film begins with the hotel staff making final preparations before opening up for the season as gardeners, maids, bellboys and desk clerks – going about their business in rhythmically choreographed sequences. On another occasion, the action simply dissolves into the song-and-dance number "I'm Goin' Shoppin' With You." Likewise, the first bars of "The Words Are in My Heart" are introduced mid-scene as Dick professes his love to Ann.

Yet despite these instances of ingenuity, it is still the charity event performed in the final third of the movie that contains the two truly spectacular film-within-a-film musical sequences. The first of these is a more developed version of "The Words Are in My Heart" infused with all the magic Berkeley is known for. Here, the larger-than-life geometric structure is made up of uniformly costumed girls and a series of white pianos. The initial arrangement then melts into infinite kaleidoscopic patterns by means of ever-changing spatial positions, lighting and camera direction, reverse-action and bounce shot trick photography. The *pièce de resistance*, however, is a Berkeley number entitled "Lullaby of Broadway." Here, Wini Shaw, who apart from this

> ## "It is a striking blend of music, choreography and highly skilled camera work, and reveals Mr. Berkeley in one of his happiest moods."
>
> *The New York Times*

1 Good as gold: The personnel of the Wentworth Plaza shine on stage after making up the beds.

2 Lulla Blondes of Broadways: The enthusiasm of chorus girls Nina, Pinta and Santa Maria raises hotel sales threefold.

3 Will that be all ma'am? Lovelorn Amy Prentiss (Gloria Stuart) puts in a personal request with front-desk attendant Dick Curtis (Dick Powell).

sequence only has a throw-away role as a cigarette girl, gives a star-making and critically acclaimed performance. Serving as the bookends for the number, Wini's face starts off as a little white dot against a black background and slowly increases in size until it fills the entire screen; later, as the song dies down, this shot is run in reverse, reeling the sequence back to reality. Still, the heart-note of the piece is a fast-and-furious tap-dance that allows us a view of the action from every conceivable angle – including from below a glass floor. As if this weren't enough, the number also chronicles how a woman comes back from a night on the town, watches as New York awakes,

and then returns to the "Club Casino" in the evening. The corresponding visual montage reads like a homage to the avant-garde city-symphony silent films from the 20s, and makes particular allusion to Dziga Vertov's waking city from *Living Russia, or The Man with a Camera* (*Chelovek s kino-appa-ratom*, 1929). It goes without saying that the musical was the only genre in Classic Hollywood whose freedom to deviate from the confines of plot allowed it to embrace such extravagantly stylized experiments. Grabbing the opportunity by the horns, Berkeley used it to earn himself an Oscar nomination for the movie's two specialty numbers.   JS

4   Tap dancers and one-armed bandits: An unmistakable winning sound clatters through the "Club Casino" dreamscape.

DICK POWELL (RICHARD EWING POWELL)

Arkansas native Dick Powell (1904–1963) started off in show business singing with his own band before going on to perform with Charlie Davis' Orchestra. After years of success as a vocalist, he added stage comedy to his repertoire and became a highly regarded radio show actor. The multi-talented Powell made his way to Hollywood just as the first movie musicals were becoming popular. Playing the male lead in director Lloyd Bacon's *42nd Street* (1933), this baby-faced tenor became a favorite of the Warner musicals. He was a regular feature in the productions of legendary choreographer Busby Berkeley, and went on to become one of the genre's greatest draws at the side of on-screen sweetheart Ruby Keeler.

Following more than a decade of smash-hit song-and-dance pictures, the actor revamped his image to suit film noir and began taking on darker parts like that of Philip Marlowe in Edward Dmytryk's *Murder, My Sweet* (1944) and the title role of Robert Rossen's *Johnny O'Clock* (1946). Although he continued to appear on the silver screen until 1954, with later credits including Vincente Minnelli's *The Bad and the Beautiful* (1952), Powell had ventured into other aspects of show business by 1950. From then on, he was mainly active as a director and producer of films for cinema and television. In the twilight years of his career, Powell performed in numerous television series and hosted *The Dick Powell Show* (1961–1963) for the small screen. He was still working in Los Angeles when cancer claimed his life in 1963.

THE INFORMER

1935 - USA - 91 MIN. - B & W - DRAMA

DIRECTOR JOHN FORD (1894–1973)
SCREENPLAY DUDLEY NICHOLS, based on the novel *THE INFORMER* by LIAM O'FLAHERTY
DIRECTOR OF PHOTOGRAPHY JOSEPH H. AUGUST EDITING GEORGE HIVELY MUSIC MAX STEINER PRODUCTION JOHN FORD for RKO.

STARRING VICTOR MCLAGLEN (Gypo Nolan), MARGOT GRAHAME (Katie Madden), J. M. KERRIGAN (Terry), HEATHER ANGEL (Mary McPhillip), UNA O'CONNOR (Mrs. McPhillip), WALLACE FORD (Frankie McPhillip), PRESTON FOSTER (Dan Gallagher), JOE SAWYER (Bartly Mulholland), DONALD MEEK (Peter Mulligan), D'ARCY CORRIGAN (Blind Man).

ACADEMY AWARDS 1935 OSCARS for BEST DIRECTOR (John Ford), BEST ACTOR (Victor McLaglen), BEST SCREENPLAY (Dudley Nichols), and BEST SCORE (Max Steiner).

"I didn't know what I was doing."

A man betrays his friend, is sentenced to death for it, and yet finds redemption – this is as John Ford as it gets. Among the director's "Irish" films, *The Informer* bears the most similarities to his Westerns: Ford's Catholicism never ran deeper. His protagonist, a sorry, dim-witted sinner, is played by Victor McLaglen, the typical hard-drinking Irishman to be found in so many Ford films.

McLaglen plays Gypo Nolan, a former member of the IRA, stumbling through foggy Dublin with no food in his belly and nowhere to go. The year is 1922. The IRA has expelled Gypo because he'd refused to kill an infiltrator. His girlfriend Katie (Margot Grahame) works as a prostitute. Sheer desperation and a twenty-pound reward cause Gypo to turn his old buddy Frankie McPhillip (Wallace Ford) in to the British forces. Twenty pounds is exactly the amount he needs to buy a ticket to the United States for himself

and Katie. At least that's what the poster of the shipping company claims, and Gypo keeps seeing it everywhere he goes. If he had any sense, he would buy a ticket for the very next sailing and escape the grim consequences of his betrayal. But Gypo has an even better plan – he walks straight into the next pub and gets blind drunk. On an extensive pub crawl through Dublin he buys drinks all round, and fish'n'chips for everyone in sight. Soon, they're calling him "King Gypo". Of course, it doesn't take long before the IRA gets wind of his sudden generosity. He protests his innocence, naturally, but in the light of the evidence against him, it seems almost touching that they actually grant him a trial.

Ford's heroes and their actions defy conventional logic, but the reasons for Gypo's tragic recklessness are easily named. His sorry attempts to offload

"Nolan commits his perfidious deed at about 6 p. m. of a foggy evening. He lives eight hours, or until about 2 a. m., during which span he goes through all the emotions from drunken boastfulness to stark terror to whimpering remorse. What makes the picture powerful is the faithful characterization of McLaglen as guided and developed by the direction of John Ford. Gypo is a blundering, pathetic fool who is not basically vicious yet is guilty of a truly foul betrayal." *Variety*

5

1　Every man has his price: Down and out IRA ruffian Gypo Nolan (Victor McLaglen) snitches on a comrade for a twenty pound reward only to fall victim to his conscience and former employers.

2　Eat your words: Frankie McPhillip (Wallace Ford) learns the hard way that one man's meal is another man's poison.

3　Ulysses: Gypo flees into the Dublin night to save his life and embarks on a spiritual odyssey.

4　Got him for a song: Gypo, however, soon changes his tune when the IRA seeks retribution.

the reward money as quickly and visibly as possible are his response to another poster, one that keeps nagging at his conscience: the 'Wanted' poster with Frankie's mug-shot. The British had finally caught Frankie and killed him in the ensuing skirmish. Even if Gypo fled the country, he could never escape his own guilt. Instead, he seeks out his punishment on a macabre triumphal march through the city.

McLaglen towers over this film, and not just because he stands two heads taller than any of the other actors. His portrayal of the thick-headed,

bullish, but pitiable traitor earned him one of the four Oscars awarded to the film. Gypo is a victim not only of his own folly but also of the poverty that Ireland was pushed into by the British occupation. John Ford's parents were Irish, and the director's sympathy for the Irish cause is never in doubt. But when the IRA is shown to tolerate a naive and garrulous character like Gypo Nolan in its ranks, this tells us more about Ford's delight in the Irish drinking culture than about the Irish Republican Army's strict code of conduct.

6

"The animal cunning of the man, his transparent deceits and naive belief in his powers of deception are woven into the fabric of a character worthy of the pen of a Dostoyevsky. Amid the murk and drizzly mists in which the drama is played out, he becomes some dreadful and pathetic creature of darkness. Although the photoplay makes you understand why informer is the ugliest word in the Irishman's vocabulary, there is a tragic quality in this man's bewildered terror." *The New York Times*

VICTOR MCLAGLEN
(1883–1959)

It never seemed to matter that this towering giant was born in England and the son of a Protestant parson – Victor McLaglen was Irish, at least in the world of John Ford's films. Coarse, loud, gregarious, and perpetually drunk – this was how Ford, the grand sentimentalist, had defined his ideal celluloid Irishman. With the Oscar-winning film *The Informer* (1935), Ford provided the former prizefighter McLaglen with an unexpected career in Hollywood. For *The Quiet Man* (1952), Ford reprised McLaglen's 'Irish' figure in the role of a jealous father-of-the-bride. In the intervening period, McLaglen had also starred successfully in George Stevens' adventure film *Gunga Din* (1938). In addition, he played supporting roles in numerous Westerns, including John Ford's Cavalry trilogy. In *Fort Apache* (1948), *She Wore a Yellow Ribbon* (1949) and *Rio Grande* (1950) McLaglen was never one to turn down bottles or even entire crates of "bad" whiskey, nor was he likely to abstain from a good punch-up. Legend has it that John Ford even encouraged the actor to 'prepare' for his roles with a drink or three. McLaglen's special gift was his ability to turn even the most unlikable and despicable of characters into audience favorites.

Victor McLaglen died of a heart attack in 1959. Five of his seven brothers also went into acting, and his son Andrew V. McLaglen became a director.

Drinking bouts and brawls are a recurring theme in the films of John Ford, who first came to critical attention with *The Informer*. Yet his visual language in this movie also shows some surprising foreign influences. Many of the cinematographic ideas, such as the suggestive dissolves between the 'Wanted' poster and Gypo's face, in fact came from Ford's favored scriptwriter, Dudley Nichols. *The Informer's* insistent symbolism, its menacing low camera angles and its dark atmosphere were direct references to recent masterpieces of German Expressionist film. When Gypo first recognizes the seriousness of his situation as he faces his IRA prosecutors, Ford borrows heavily from the trial of Peter Lorre's character by an underground court in Fritz Lang's *M* (1931). Gypo himself, the very image of a dejected giant, is almost a reincarnation of Franz Biberkopf in *Berlin Alexanderplatz* (1931), a character unforgettably embodied by Heinrich George. What makes this a typical Ford film is its sheer visual excess, the pervasive symbolism of night and fog that reflects Gypo's clouded state of mind, and of course the emblem of the cross, in the name of which Gypo is finally absolved by none other than the victim's mother. That might be the film's motto: Forgive them, o Lord, for they know not what they do.   PB

5   What goes around, comes around: IRA leader Dan Gallagher (Preston Foster) intends to give Gypo a trial by fire.

6   To forgive is divine: Katie (Margot Grahame) asks the rebellion council to spare Gypo's life and learns that her boyfriend doesn't have a prayer.

7   Nailed: After tearing himself apart for what he's done and making his peace with God, Gypo awaits his fate at a crossroads.

7

1935 - GREAT BRITAIN - 86 MIN. - B & W - SPY CAPER, THRILLER, LITERARY ADAPTATION

DIRECTOR ALFRED HITCHCOCK (1899–1980)
SCREENPLAY CHARLES BENNETT, ALMA REVILLE, based on the novel of the same name by JOHN BUCHAN
DIRECTOR OF PHOTOGRAPHY BERNARD KNOWLES EDITING DEREK N. TWIST MUSIC LOUIS LEVY PRODUCTION MICHAEL BALCON
for GAUMONT BRITISH PICTURE CORPORATION LTD.

STARRING ROBERT DONAT (Richard Hannay), MADELEINE CARROLL (Pamela), GODFREY TEARLE (Professor Jordan),
LUCIE MANNHEIM (Miss Smith), PEGGY ASHCROFT (Margaret), JOHN LAURIE (John), HELEN HAYE (Mrs. Louisa Jordan),
FRANK CELLIER (Sheriff Watson), WYLIE WATSON (Mister Memory), PEGGY SIMPSON (Maid).

"How far is Winnipeg from Montreal?"

Richard Hannay (Robert Donat) is caught between a rock and a hard place. Moments after leaving a vaudeville show with attractive secret agent Annabella Smith (Lucie Mannheim), the Canadian gentleman finds himself embroiled in international espionage, not romance, and fearing for his life inside his London apartment. Several frames later, the beautiful spy has been stabbed by two enemy assassins and is struggling to tell Hannay something before she breathes her last. Whether or not he got the message is unclear, but he grabs the map she was clutching in her fist and disappears into the night. Now all he has to do is get to Alt-Na-Shellach in the Scottish Highlands

uncover the mastermind of a criminal organization known as the 39 Steps, and make sure that Britain's most valuable secrets aren't sold to the highest bidder. A spy story, right? Well, actually not: master of suspense Alfred Hitchcock delivers something slightly different this time.

In *The 39 Steps*, one of Hitch's earlier hair-raising hot pursuit efforts, the caper aspect is almost incidental, and is simply there to bait the genre's fans. The same goes for the vaudeville boy wonder, Mister Memory (Wylie Watson), and for the secret formula, both of which only take on a more prominent role toward the film's conclusion. In Hitchcock's hands, the spy

movie is primarily a means of conjuring up a trademark deadly scenario to entrap an ordinary man, a two-bit romance that unfolds over an uncertain journey with a shot of black humor. For, as fans of film history will know, Hitchcock was a dab hand at blending and crossing genres, a popular conceit in the early days of cinema.

The fast-paced narrative, which hardly ever comes up for air, is peppered with clever cuts that provide a touch of comic relief while still hurrying the action on its way, as when a maid discovers Annabella's corpse and the director cuts to the whistle of a steam locomotive rather than letting us hear her screams firsthand, or when a bullet aimed at the protagonist is handily blocked by a hymnbook. The film deftly parries waves of action with crisp reactions, like the stoic railway waiters who don't bat an eyelid or drop

2

ROBERT DONAT (1905–1958)

British actor Robert Donat began his life as a thespian performing Shakespeare and other classics on the stage. Tall and dark with a smooth-sounding voice, he was quickly discovered by enthusiastic film producers who cast the actor in a number of romantic leading roles. No sooner had Donat become a household name throughout England than Irving Thalberg was eager to claim him for 'bigger and better' things. The actor, however, refused the offer and attained international fame for his role in *The Private Life of Henry VIII* (1933) under the direction of British filmmaker Alexander Korda. Donat went on to star in countless pictures like René Clair's *The Ghost Goes West* (1935). *Goodbye, Mr. Chips* (1939) brought him a long-awaited Oscar for Best Actor in a Leading Role. Unfortunately, Donat's failing physical and psychological health got the better of him and claimed his life at the age of 53.

1 From ordinary to extraordinary: Mild-mannered Richard Hannay (Robert Donat) gets tapped to be an operative in a secret mission of global proportions.

2 Cutting corners: Hannay's life depends on his winning a game of hide and go seek.

3 The dangers of nodding off: Hannay wakes up from a nap to discover Annabella Smith (Lucie Mannheim) out cold – permanently.

4 High anxiety in the highlands: Judging by the looks of it, these three characters know all too well that they're in a Hitchcock film.

3

"Hitchcock spent his fledgling years working in German silent cinema under greats like Friedrich Wilhelm Murnau. It was during their time together on Murnau's *The Last Laugh (Der letzte Mann,* 1924) that the future master of suspense learned to tell stories with the camera and come up with images that express a character's subjective reality." *Thomas Koebner, in: Filmklassiker*

a single tray of food when almost mown down by Hannay's pursuers in the train corridor. Delightful little moments abound, as when the master of ceremonies chides his spectators for not minding their manners with a firm yet civil reminder: "Gentlemen, please! You're not at home!" Hitchcock even takes a few stabs at ridiculous phrase-mongering created in the name of political correctness, while those moviegoers in need of a love story can revel in the scene in which the feisty yet lovely Pamela (Madeleine Carroll)

realizes, handcuffed to Richard Hannay, that the bungling idiot isn't that bad after all. Could there be a more effective means of defusing the first-rate Hitchcockian mêlée?

If you stop to blink along the way, you'll miss Mister Memory's answer about how far Winnipeg is from Montreal. And as for the contents of that stolen secret formula …

"It's a creamy role for Donat and his performance, ranging from humor to horror, reveals acting ability behind that good-looking facade." *Variety*

5   Cuff links: Hitchcock manages to find the humor in the stickiest of situations.

6   Headed north by northwest: Once strangers on a train, Pamela (Madeleine Carroll) and Dannay are now in the shackles of love.

MUTINY ON THE BOUNTY

1935 - USA - 132 MIN. - B & W - DRAMA, ADVENTURE MOVIE

DIRECTOR FRANK LLOYD (1886–1960)
SCREENPLAY TALBOT JENNINGS, JULES FURTHMAN, CAREY WILSON, based on the novels *MUTINY ON THE BOUNTY*
and *MEN AGAINST THE SEA* by CHARLES NORDHOFF and JAMES NORMAN HALL DIRECTOR OF PHOTOGRAPHY ARTHUR EDESON
EDITING MARGARET BOOTH MUSIC HERBERT STOTHART PRODUCTION IRVING THALBERG for MGM.

STARRING CHARLES LAUGHTON (Captain William Bligh), CLARK GABLE (Lieutenant Fletcher Christian),
FRANCHOT TONE (Midshipman Roger Byam), EDDIE QUILLAN (Thomas Ellison), DUDLEY DIGGES (Doctor Bacchus),
HERBERT MUNDIN (Smith), DONALD CRISP (Thomas Burkitt), BILL BAMBRIDGE (Chief Hitihiti), MOVITA (Tehanni),
MAMO CLARK (Maimiti).

ACADEMY AWARDS 1935 OSCAR for BEST PICTURE.

"I'll take my chance against the law. You'll take yours against the sea."

All great adventures on the high seas, from *Moby Dick* (1956) to *Master and Commander* (2003), owe a little something to the historical event popularized by the film *Mutiny on the Bounty*. The 1935 version of the tale was a seminal work in solidifying the standards of the genre. Here we see all that life at sea entails: from the spartan living conditions on board and the crew's back-breaking daily routine, to the watertight camaraderie among an odd bunch of social outcasts. What starts as an ordinary scientific mission quickly escalates into a compelling battle between good and evil, as high-ranking officers and crew on a British Marine frigate ask themselves what allegiance and duty really mean. No sooner has the question been posed than Captain Bligh has an uprising on his hands for having kept his crew under wraps with corporal punishment and a lack of nourishment. Leading the revolt is the valiant Fletcher Christian, who successfully sets the insidious captain and his cohorts adrift in a launch, before stealing away in the Bounty and founding a colony of exiles on Tahiti.

One of legendary MGM producer Irving Thalberg's final projects, this first sound version of *Mutiny on the Bounty* is the most revered cinematic adaptation of the historic sea epic. Marlon Brando's 1962 portrayal of Fletcher Christian and Mel Gibson's stab at the character in *The Bounty* (1984)

couldn't do a thing to change that; the pairing of Charles Laughton as Bligh opposite Clark Gable as Christian was simply unbeatable. To this day, Laughton's sadist remains one of movie history's most twisted villains. He is the embodiment of military discipline, complete with a downward-turned mouth, hands clasped behind his back, and a faint yet undeniable sneer. Only a tyrant as maniacal as he could regard his inhumanity – forty lashes per offense – as a service to the crown. But however despicable he may be, it's hard not to admire him when he manages to reach the coast by sailing 3,600 nautical miles in 50 days.

Christian's motives, by contrast, are less clear cut. In fact, it's left rather ambiguous whether his solidarity with the crew is really just a pretext for his desire to relocate to sweet Tahitian shores. On several occasions, the camera makes better arguments for mutiny than the ones Gable voices on board the ship as idyllic images of him basking in the sun with a perfectly bronzed and shaven chest fill the screen. And with those voluptuous Polynesian beauties beckoning in the wings, who could resist the thought of revolution?

In real life, Gable had wondered whether it was worth climbing aboard the Bounty at all. The Admiralty prohibited officers from wearing a mustache, which meant that the actor had to cut his off – a concession he would never

2

1   Batten down the hatches: Officer Fletcher Christian (Clark Gable) persuades the men of the Bounty to mutiny.

2   An aye for an aye: Navigational expert Captain William Bligh (Charles Laughton) doesn't even look at his men when handing out orders. Ironically,

Laughton was terrified of the ocean and violently seasick throughout most of the shoot.

"Mr. Laughton's performance as the incredible Bligh is a fascinating and almost unbearable portrait of a sadist who took rapturous delight in watching men in pain ... Bligh's reign of terror on the Bounty is described with such relish that in time you discover yourself wincing under the lash and biting your mouth to keep from crying out." *The New York Times*

agree to again. Others claim that his initial reticence to commit had more to do with the competition that stars Charles Laughton and potential shooting star Franchot Tone presented.

An actor who has all but faded into oblivion today, Tone plays midshipman Roger Byam, a man who urges a handful of British subjects to return home after Fletcher Christian persuades them to mutiny. Unfortunately, the group are picked up by a military search party and sentenced to death in a

court-martial. The film twists history a little at this point, allowing Byam to escape execution after he makes an impassioned speech before the sea tribunal. The film's sympathies clearly lie with the midshipman and his men, a fact not unrelated to the political interests of the anti-union MGM. By the same token, the picture readily damns the tyrannical Bligh, who in real life returned to England and continued his career in the Navy, and was even promoted to the position of Vice Admiral.

3 Calling a spade a spade: While the real life Roger Byam was the sole member of accused officers to be acquitted of the charges against him, he never held an impassioned appeal before the sea tribunal.

4 Chicken of the sea: Midshipman Byam (Franchot Tone) bends to the majority and concedes to mutiny.

5 Let's misbehave: The men of the Bounty tie up Captain Bligh and leave him to find his way back to England in a dinghy.

"He doesn't punish men for discipline. He likes to see men crawl."

Film quote: Lieutenant Fletcher Christian (Clark Gable)

6   Swab the deck: Does Fletcher Christian's role in
the mutiny give him the right to act as captain?

7   The quicker picker upper: Nothing can boost
Fletcher Christian's morale like the women of Tahiti.

All three of the picture's lead actors were pitted against one another for the Oscar – a fluke of Hollywood history that would never repeat itself. The fact that none of these fine performances earned the little golden guy prompted the creation of the Best Supporting Actor category for the following year's ceremonies.

Mutiny on the Bounty remains one of the few films to be awarded the Oscar for Best Picture and not so much as a booby prize for anything else.

Looking at the movie's production values, that meager haul was as shocking as Bligh's conduct on board. The two-million dollar budget that saw for an exact replica of the Bounty and a number of outside scenes made for unsinkable entertainment that continues to please. Then again, as is attested by the events that transpired on board the ship and the descendants of the Bounty themselves, who still inhabit the South Pacific, truth can be stranger than fiction.   PB

**IRVING THALBERG
(1899–1936)**

During his lifetime, few moviegoers were familiar with Irving Thalberg. This had much to do with the fact that the MGM producer never let his name appear in the credits. Within Hollywood, on the other hand, Thalberg was fondly referred to as the 'boy wonder.' Although diagnosed with a heart defect during childhood, this son of German immigrants advanced to one of the highest ranking creative positions in the Hollywood dream factory. A Brooklyn native, Thalberg got his start in film as an assistant to legendary Universal boss Carl Laemmle. Joining forces with Louis B. Mayer in 1924, the young producer contributed significantly to the initial formation of Metro-Goldwyn-Mayer studios. He is also believed to have played a fundamental role in shaping the production company's image. The name Thalberg stood for the pleasing combination of high profits and artistic standards. Furthermore, his watchful eye ensured that every aspect of production ran smoothly and effectively; the fact that the producer personally handled test screenings demonstrates the extent of his commitment.

Thalberg was also the man responsible for reviving *Greed*, Erich von Stroheim's colossal 1924 project, most of which had been shot at Universal, and streamlining it down to two hours at MGM. Classics like *Ben-Hur* (1925), *The Big Parade* (1925) and *Grand Hotel* (1932) followed.

Shortly after this period, however, Thalberg received specialized medical care abroad for his heart condition. By then Mayer had taken subtle steps to strip Thalberg of his power, effectively replacing him with producers David O. Selznick and Walter Wanger. The MGM mogul, it seemed, had been jealous of Thalberg ever since he married MGM actress Norma Shearer in 1927. Despite that, Thalberg still managed to turn out critically acclaimed hits like *Mutiny on the Bounty* (1935), *A Night at the Opera* (1935) and *Romeo and Juliet* (1936) in his less comprehensive role of "unit producer."

When Hollywood received word of Thalberg's death in 1936, work stopped at all of the big-name movie studios for five entire minutes. The Irving G. Thalberg Memorial Award was created the following year to commemorate producers with an outstanding body of cinematic achievement.

1935 - USA - 101 MIN. - B & W - MUSICAL, COMEDY

DIRECTOR MARK SANDRICH (1900–1945)
SCREENPLAY DWIGHT TAYLOR, ALLAN SCOTT, based on the play *THE GIRL WHO DARED* by ALEXANDER FARAGÓ
and ALADAR LASZLO DIRECTOR OF PHOTOGRAPHY DAVID ABEL EDITING WILLIAM HAMILTON MUSIC IRVING BERLIN, MAX STEINER
PRODUCTION PANDRO S. BERMAN for RKO.

STARRING FRED ASTAIRE (Jerry Travers), GINGER ROGERS (Dale Tremont), EDWARD EVERETT HORTON (Horace Hardwick),
ERIK RHODES (Alberto Beddini), ERIC BLORE (Bates), HELEN BRODERICK (Madge Hardwick), ROBERT ADAIR (Hotel Employee),
DENNIS O'KEEFE (Man in the Elevator), TOM RICKETTS (Waiter), LEONARD MUDIE (Flower Seller).

"Heaven, I'm in heaven ..."

American dance sensation Jerry Travers (Fred Astaire) taps his way to glory on the London stage. Life itself is a veritable performance for Jerry, who sings and sashays at the drop of a hat. So it follows that after a full night at the club, he pops by his manager's (Edward Everett Horton) hotel suite for a quick drink and suddenly finds himself giving an encore that could top his own stage show. Just as the spectacle reaches its climax, the camera follows Jerry's lead and breaks with reality. Down through the floor it goes, arriving at the room directly below, where the lovely Dale Tremont (Ginger Rogers) lies sprawled atop a lush white bed. Restless and robbed of shut-eye, she heads upstairs and tells the gentlemen to pipe it down. No sooner is she back in bed than Jerry is at it again. Only now that she's seen him, sleep is the last thing on her mind; for that dancing troublemaker is unquestionably the man of her dreams.

Destiny intervenes the very next day and the couple run into one another at a concert pavilion in the park, where they share in a dance and a fleeting embrace. Dale, however, still doesn't know exactly who her Romeo is. And it will take her over another hour to solve the mystery and get this picture to end happily. In the meantime, she'll mistake him for being married man Horace Hardwick – Jerry's manager from upstairs – and then run off to Italy to inform his wife Madge (Helen Broderick) of their London liaison. This, of course, prompts Jerry and Horace to track Dale down, which leads to further mishaps and a romantic resolution the only way Hollywood knows.

While *Top Hat* was indeed a crowd-pleaser, its popularity can't be attributed to the neatly contrived plot based on mistaken identity. The movie's magic lies instead in its ability to create an imaginary world governed entirely by rules of its own, which allow singing and dancing to kick in for any given situation. The musical's five Irving Berlin tunes provide a foundation for the various song and dance numbers: from Astaire's hotel room solo "I'm Fancy Free," via his theatrical revue piece "Top Hat," all the way to gliding duets with Rogers including both "Isn't This a Lovely Day to Be Caught in

"When *Top Hat* lets Mr. Astaire perform his incomparable magic or teams him with the increasingly dexterous Miss Rogers, it provides the most urbane fun you will find anywhere on screen." *The New York Times*

4

1 Movers and shakers: Ginger Rogers and Fred Astaire dance on air as twinkle-toed lovers Dale Tremont and Jerry Travers.

2 In good company: A top-notch dance chorus spins its way through a grand finale filled with ornamental top shots.

3 Footloose and fancy free: Ground level cameras let the audience in on all the elaborate moves of the "The Piccolino."

4 Bells and whistles: Fancy little frills can't make this Hollywood pairing any more perfect.

the Rain" and the evergreen "Cheek to Cheek." The icing on the cake is "The Piccolino," the grandest of musical finales in an era that was known for them.

Breaking the pattern established by the backstage musicals of the day, *Top Hat* limits its time at the theater to its title number. In the world of make-believe, the urge to sing and dance arises spontaneously, presenting itself as a logical means of moving the story forward: Jerry's first solo number sparks Dale's sexual interest; their first dance as a couple wins her affection, and the

one that follows has her making confessions of love once the chorus is in full swing. As Dale sings the praises of being "in heaven," the number crescendos in an opulent dream ballet that forecasts rainbow horizons for Rogers' and Astaire's characters.

More than just helping to interweave action, song and dance in this so-called integrated musical, *Top Hat's* artificiality acts like a guiding light that shines on nearly every aspect of the picture. Key in creating this illusion are

5

"Miss Rogers, improving magnificently from picture to picture, collaborates perfectly with Mr. Astaire in *Top Hat* and is entitled to keep the job for life."

The New York Times

the performances of supporting cast members such as Eric Blore (as Butler Bates) and Erik Rhodes (as Alberto, the Italian). Yet above all else, it is the result of the film's distinctly stylized *mise en scène*: interiors are noticeably bright, have unspeakably high ceilings and the dimensions of a ballroom; likewise, fantastically ornamental wall decorations and the opulent set dressing make for an all the more out-of-this world look.

Life has been reduced to a mere abstraction, having undergone streamlining that allows for things to appear as crisp and homogeneous as they might on a theatrical stage. This also holds true for the landscape, especially when the movie relocates to Venice for its second half. Suddenly, the ground is ornamented and polished to a pristine white, while the canals flow with a liquid black as ink. It's a parallel universe, whose inhabitants wouldn't be caught dead in anything other than top hats and tails or evening gowns. Here, music is in the air and the protagonists hear it all, swaying at even the most subtle lead-in and speaking in verse whenever possible. There need not be a piano or an orchestra in sight to warrant a song: somehow we just accept that invisible angels are behind it all. Given this, an absence of choreographed production numbers or performers as gifted as Ginger Rogers and Fred Astaire would be entirely unnatural.

Top Hat's director, Mark Sandrich, does an impeccable job of making this sort of dream-world logic work, and the movie became a paradigm that many pictures were to follow. This unforgettable film was the second of three Sandrich collaborations with the legendary dance team and remains the quintessential Rogers-Astaire musical. JS

6

5 Strictly business: Manager Horace Hardwick (Edward Everett Horton) hopes to put Jerry's affairs in order by tracking down Dale.

6 Sleepless beauty: Dale thought she was sore about being kept up by a dance rehearsal until she saw who was banging out the steps.

7 Testing his metal: Hansom Jerry tries to win over Dale by proving himself a man of many hats.

GINGER ROGERS (1911–1995)

Early talkies and musicals sent a young Ginger Rogers packing for Hollywood. Prior to that she was a regular of vaudeville stage and became a teen star with the Broadway musical "Top Speed" (1929–1930). Paramount then signed her on to a string of pictures that prompted Warner Bros. to pick her up for several choice supporting roles in Busby Berkeley song and dance extravaganzas like Lloyd Bacon's *42nd Street* (1933), and Mervyn LeRoy's *Gold Diggers of 1933* (1933). That same year, RKO, the studio that would offer Rogers a more permanent home as a headliner, tried pairing her with dance partner Fred Astaire in Thornton Freeland's *Flying Down to Rio* (1933). Swinging their way to super-stardom with the number "The Carioca," Rogers and Astaire stole the show from Dolores del Rio, the picture's intended lead. A series of RKO musicals would follow for the unstoppable dance team, including *The Gay Divorcee* (1934), *Top Hat* (1935), and *Shall We Dance* (1937) – all of which were directed by Mark Sandrich. When her legendary collaboration with Astaire eventually came to end, Rogers switched gears from musicals to comedies and dramas. Indeed, she was quite the actress. Her performance in Sam Wood's *Kitty Foyle* (1940) proved Oscar-worthy, and the crowds were still cheering her on in the 50s for her work in Howard Hawks' *Monkey Business* (1952). Around 1957, Rogers' screen appearances became infrequent. She went on to rejuvenate her career on the musical stage and penned an autobiography in her later years entitled "Ginger: My Story" (1991). A decade after her death in California in 1995, Ginger Rogers remains a great Hollywood legend.

1935 - USA - 119 MIN. - B & W - PIRATE MOVIE

DIRECTOR MICHAEL CURTIZ (1888–1962)
SCREENPLAY CASEY ROBINSON, based on the novel *CAPTAIN BLOOD: HIS ODYSSEY* by RAFAEL SABATINI
DIRECTORS OF PHOTOGRAPHY ERNEST HALLER, HAL MOHR EDITING GEORGE AMY MUSIC ERICH WOLFGANG KORNGOLD, FRANZ LISZT
PRODUCTION HAL B. WALLIS for FIRST NATIONAL PICTURES INC., COSMOPOLITAN PRODUCTIONS, WARNER BROS.

STARRING ERROL FLYNN (Dr. Peter Blood), OLIVIA DE HAVILLAND (Arabella Bishop), LIONEL ATWILL (Colonel Bishop),
BASIL RATHBONE (Captain Levasseur), ROSS ALEXANDER (Jeremy Pitt), HENRY STEPHENSON (Lord Willoughby),
ROBERT BARRAT (John Wolverstone), HOBART CAVANAUGH (Dr. Bronson), DONALD MEEK (Dr. Whacker),
GUY KIBBEE (Henry Hagthorpe), VERNON STEELE (King James II).

"Up the rigging, you monkeys! Break out those sails and watch them fill with the wind that's carrying us all to freedom!"

England, 1685. The despotic rule of King James the Second was firmly entrenched in the doctrines of Catholicism and the 'divine right' of absolute sovereignty. Subjects suspected of opposing of the regime had to reckon with the gallows – or worse still, slavery in the Caribbean. Anyone who survived the treacherous sea voyage to Jamaica's Port Royal found that life in the sugar plantations was a fate worse than death.

The noble-hearted Dr. Peter Blood (Errol Flynn) is one such involuntary colonist. No stranger to the face of war, he was a freedom fighter before deciding to enter the medical profession. But he never abandoned his ideals, and that eventually brought his downfall: if he hadn't insisted on treating a wounded rebel back in the isles, he never would have gotten banished in the first place. Still, he can consider himself one of the lucky few, as physicians are spared the toils of back-breaking physical labor. And Blood's privileges are many, seeing that he was the first man to rid Lord Willoughby (Henry Stephenson), the governor, of his chronic gout pains. Those special talents of his bring him further rewards, including the admiration of the enchanting Arabella (Olivia de Havilland), niece of the power-hungry Colonel Bishop (Lionel Atwill), who takes an instant liking to him and ensures that the brave Irish doctor is kept out of harm's way.

Despite Arabella's generosity, a cushy prisoner's life holds no allure for Peter Blood, so he plans his escape. When a Spanish frigate attacks the port city, a group of island exiles takes advantage of the ensuing chaos to hijack the ship and set sail for new horizons. Blood, naturally, is the mastermind behind it all. And no sooner is he at the helm than it becomes clear that the savvy crusader has switched sides once again: "the hunted have become the hunters!" he declares, as the crew raise a skull and crossbones atop the mast. For many Spanish and French seafarers, it's a chilling image that will mean certain death …

It might not have been the silver screen's first pirate movie (predecessors even included an identically titled silent from 1924), but *Captain Blood* did usher in the genre's golden age and provide it with a prototype that stood the test of time. At the center of the picture is a well-meaning outlaw bereft of greed and homicidal tendencies, forced into a life of piracy. It's the only means he has of rebelling against injustice until a more righteous regime comes to power. If he breaks the laws of the land, so be it. For there is no doubt about who the real rogues are: the corrupt minions of an incompetent ruler and the ostentatious Spaniards. In the waters of tyranny, Blood is a champion of goodness and truth, paving the way to a more promising future.

1 Pirate of the Caribbean: Dr. Peter Blood (Errol Flynn) leaves the operating room to take up work as an aquatic Robin Hood.

2 It's a living: Like Dr. Blood himself, most of these guys are actually former white-collar professionals who either suffered a nervous breakdown or just needed a change of pace.

3 Touch and go: Arabella Bishop (Olivia de Havilland) is less concerned about the schemes of duplicitous Captain Levasseur (Basil Rathbone, right) than with trying to pin down Captain Blood on matters of love and marriage.

"Oh those stunts! Director Michael Curtiz provides a rip-roaring adventure in those sequences, giving us booming battles that don't require crazy editing. Seeing those ships split apart and all those hands on deck, comprised of numerous stuntmen, is genuine excitement boosted by the thundering, sweeping music score of Erich Wolfgang Korngold, the greatest name in adventure music." *Rory L. Aronsky, in: Film Threat*

ERROL FLYNN (1909–1959)

Errol Leslie Thomson Flynn may not have known it at the time, but his character in the big-budget *Captain Blood* (1935) would be instrumental in determining the future course of his Hollywood career and the genre as a whole. The part, one of the first leads Flynn landed, fitted him like a glove; for in real life, the actor was just as much a go-getter, adventurer and ladies' man as the buccaneer he played. In fact, audiences found him so convincing in the role that he was unable to escape being typecast up until his sudden and fatal cardiac arrest in 1959.

A native Australian, Flynn tried his hand at gold prospecting, poaching, competitive sailing, journalism and acting for the theater before movie-star ambitions brought him to England in 1933. It was there that he made the acquaintance of Jack Warner, who promptly put him under contract and built him up as a Hollywood A-lister. Flynn enjoyed one hit after another in adventure movies like *The Adventures of Robin Hood* (1938) and *The Sea Hawk* (1940).

With the U.S. entry into World War II, interest in the genre's formula classics rapidly declined. Although Flynn tried to make a name for himself in Westerns and mysteries, audiences would have none of it. At around this time, disputes with directors (including names such as Michael Curtiz, with whom he shot a total of twelve pictures) took their toll on his career. Next came public scandal in the form of a rape charge that was eventually disproved. But by then, alcohol dependency had already claimed the upper hand, emerging as a major hurdle in his attempted return to the stage. Flynn's last resort was to circumvent the American film studio's no alcohol policy by sucking on vodka-drenched oranges between scenes. Yet in the end, he only succeeded in fooling himself.

Errol Flynn was married a total of three times. He never wedded the last love of his life, Beverly Aadland, who was just 15 years old when they met and shot the docudrama *Cuban Rebel Girls* (1959). By then, Flynn's best days were long behind him and his place as a swashbuckler had been reclaimed by the dashing Douglas Fairbanks.

In any case, thievery is only a temporary vocation for most of these protesters, given that most career pirates are eventually lured back ashore by marriage or steady work. Needless to say, those who fall victim to the seductive trappings of a lifetime at sea and see no higher purpose in it – like the wily Captain Levasseur (Basil Rathbone), whose word of honor is as thin as air – suffer dearly for it in the end. The inevitable day dawns when Arabella falls into the French pirate's fiendish hands and undying gratitude prompts Peter to liberate her and slay the brute responsible for her kidnapping.

Captain Blood delivers thrilling entertainment of the highest caliber. Casey Robinson's script dazzles the imagination with a fast-paced exposition teeming with twists and turns that climax in a heart-pounding final sea duel.

Equally impressive is Anton Grot's German Expressionist-inspired set decor, which subtly draws attention to the imbalance of the social order.

For the picture's score, Warner Bros. conducted some smooth wheeling and dealing and secured the world-famous Erich Wolfgang Korngold. Despite the studio system's grip on the industry, Korngold, whose move to Hollywood was inspired by Max Reinhard, managed to assert his independence until the end of his career, refusing to take on more than two projects a year. His work on *Captain Blood* produced a great dramatic score distinguished by its sophisticated instrumentation which delicately complement the visuals. As one might imagine, it was Korngold's gold standard that the big studios would quickly adopt as their own once scores began to gain importance in Hollywood.   EP

3

BRIDE OF FRANKENSTEIN

1935 - USA - 75 MIN. - B & W - HORROR MOVIE

DIRECTOR JAMES WHALE (1889–1957)
SCREENPLAY WILLIAM HURLBUT, JOHN L. BALDERSTON, based on themes and characters established
in the novel *FRANKENSTEIN OR THE MODERN PROMETHEUS* by MARY WOLLSTONECRAFT SHELLEY
DIRECTOR OF PHOTOGRAPHY JOHN J. MESCALL EDITING TED J. KENT MUSIC FRANZ WAXMAN
PRODUCTION CARL LAEMMLE JR. for UNIVERSAL PICTURES.

STARRING BORIS KARLOFF (The Monster), COLIN CLIVE (Doctor Henry Frankenstein),
ELSA LANCHESTER (The Monster's Mate / Mary Shelley), ERNEST THESIGER (Doctor Pretorius),
VALERIE HOBSON (Elizabeth Frankenstein), GAVIN GORDON (Lord Byron), DOUGLAS WALTON (Percy Shelley),
UNA O'CONNOR (Minnie), O. P. HEGGIE (Hermit), E. E. CLIVE (Burgomaster).

"Alone – bad. Friend – good!"

Dr. Frankenstein (Colin Clive) stands before the lab table of fellow scientist Dr. Pretorius (Ernest Thesiger) in utter disbelief. For arranged neatly atop it is a collection of bell jars, each with its own four-inch-tall 'human' chattering away at mouse pitch. One such jar houses a dancing ballerina, while an archbishop prays away in another. A third is home to the world's littlest queen, who expects a visit from her debonair husband. He, in turn, has already slipped through his jar's paper lid and now makes a mad dash across the table to reach her. None of this, however, is lost to Dr. Pretorius who, using a pair of tweezers, snatches up the escape artist by his ermine collar and deposits him back where he belongs.

Frankenstein lowers himself into the lab armchair, captivated and repulsed by the grotesque display before him. "This isn't science," he protests. "It's more like black magic." Dr. Pretorius responds that his creatures are nothing of the sort. As a matter of fact, his homunculi were grown from an original human seed using natural cultures and are perfect in every regard

except for size. Given Dr. Frankenstein's own success at animating larger beings, Pretorius sees potential for a collaboration. He sweetens the offer by suggesting that they start off by supplying Frankenstein's monster with a mate – an Eve who will mother a new and improved genetic race. After some hesitation, Frankenstein agrees to the plan. Then it's off to laboratory, where he and Pretorius start work on the so-called bride.

Bride of Frankenstein, the sequel to James Whale's *Frankenstein* (1931), picks up right where its predecessor left off. Whale thus introduces a prolog in which Mary Shelley (Elsa Lanchester) spends a stormy night telling her husband (Douglas Walton) and Lord Byron (Gavin Gordon) what happens to the monster (Boris Karloff) following the fire at the mill. It seems that after surviving the catastrophe by hiding in an underground niche of the mill, the stitched-up homunculus emerged determined to become human at all cost. Yet in the spirit of the story's first installment, basic misunderstandings and the callousness of his peers foil his attempts. Be that as it may, the monster does in fact

1   Here comes the bride: Dr. Frankenstein (Colin Clive) and Dr. Pretorius (Ernest Thesiger, right) declare mating season officially open.

2   Permanent fixture: Actress Elsa Lanchester gets kinky in a dual role as the monster's mate and Mary Shelley.

get a true taste of friendship in what is perhaps the film's most endearing and comical episode. While hiding out in the German forest, he stumbles upon a secluded cottage inhabited by a pious and blind hermit (O. P. Heggie). The elderly man warmly invites the 'mute traveler' into his home, cares for him and teaches him how to speak. Now fast friends, the men eat, drink and merrily while away the hours smoking and playing music. Unfortunately, their time together comes to an abrupt end when two hunters barge in on them and try to kill the monster. The cottage catches fire and the monster runs for his life, stopping only when he finds a new suitable hiding place – a cemetery crypt.

Following on from the original picture, director James Whale fills the synthetic man's tragic tale with distinctly Christian motifs. The fact that only a blind person is willing to befriend him is a clear comment on how the actions of ordinary mortals are dictated by surface appearances. Dr. Frankenstein, the man once bold enough to challenge the Creator, is coerced by the devilish Pretorius to do so again. Nevertheless, it is not these men of hubris who are ousted by society, but rather the product of their sins – a monster that makes mankind's innate imperfection painfully obvious. And the rejection this poor soul must endure is never-ending, for no sooner has

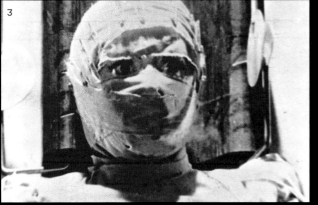

3 Nip and tuck: The bride gets all dolled up for her wedding. Brigitte Helm, the machine man in *Metropolis* (1926), originally signed on to play the role, but she was just too rusty.

4 The monster mash: If he can't be the smash of society, he'll just smash society altogether.

5 Can't warm up to him: The very thought of locking lips with her future husband leaves the bride stone cold.

"Runner-up position from an acting standpoint goes to Ernest Thesiger as Dr. Praetorius, a diabolical characterization if ever there was one ..." *Variety*

> # "... one of the finest productions to come out of the Universal lot for many a day. Mounted extravagantly, gorgeously photographed, excellently cast ..."
> *The Hollywood Reporter*

6 In bed with the chills: Stage actor Ernest Thesiger was James Whale's mentor before making Dr. Frankenstein mental as the diabolical Pretorius.

7 Tall, dark and back from the dead: Boris Karloff reprises his role as horror's prodigal son.

8 Gloom and doom in the bedroom: Elizabeth (Valerie Hobson) has good reason to worry. Within

two years of his second stint as Dr. Frankenstein, 37-year-old actor Colin Clive died of pneumonia aggravated by severe alcoholism.

the newly animated bride (Elsa Lanchester) felt the caress of his hand than she lets out a blood-curdling shriek. Tears stream down his cheeks as he realizes that even his own kind find him repulsive. In a fit of frustration, he grabs hold of a lever and blows the laboratory sky high, along with Dr. Pretorius and all his creatures.

Modern audiences tend to prefer *The Bride of Frankenstein* to the original for its emphatically comic tone. There's no stopping Whales' love for the outrageous in the sequences staged in Pretorius' laboratory. It's not enough

for the director to let his mad scientist have a miniature bishop keep a watchful eye over a potentially unchaste ballerina, king and queen; there simply has to be a bell jar with a lone mermaid twirling about a rock. Right next to her is the crowning achievement in this menagerie – a tiny devil complete with tail-coat and cape. Pretorius likes to be within close range of his favorite creation to provide him with a worthy example. After all, as the scientist goes to show, life might be a lot more interesting if the world were populated with little demons.　　　NM

> # "Mr. Karloff is so splendid in the role that all one can say is 'he is the Monster' ... James Whale, who directed the earlier picture, has done another excellent job; the settings, photography and the make-up ... contribute their important elements to a first-rate horror film."
> *The New York Times*

Many might argue that bombastic staging remained James Whale's calling card until his dying day. His death was no exception. Found drowned in his own swimming pool in 1957, the general consensus is that the filmmaker committed suicide in the wake of a disabling stroke. Two decades prior to this tragedy, James Whale had been one of Hollywood's most prominent directors. His *Frankenstein* pictures (1931, 1935) were a complete success and Whale was given an artistic *carte blanche* at Universal. That all changed when the studio was sold and he directed box-office flop *The Road Back* (1937), a loose sequel to *All Quiet on the Western Front* (1930). The project's fate cost him his independence, and Whale retired from film-making a few years later.

Briton James Whale was 39 when he came to the United States in 1928. Before, he had worked as an actor, theatrical set designer and director for the London stage. In 1930, he transformed his previous work as a theater director into his first Hollywood production, making a screen adaptation of the successful wartime drama "Journey's End." *Frankenstein* (1931) was his third project as a filmmaker. Although the occasional comedy or musical were also a part of his repertoire, Whale built his reputation on sensational displays of horror like *The Old Dark House* (1932), *Bride of Frankenstein* (1935) and *Invisible Man* (1933), a film he regarded as his personal best.

During his lifetime, Whale's openly gay lifestyle was a source of public scorn; today, it merely casts a different light on his work. Many people believe he drew on his own experiences of social ostracism for his direction of Frankenstein's monster. Throughout his lifetime, James Whale remained true to his British roots, as shown in Bill Condon's Oscar-winning *Gods and Monsters* (1997), a recent tribute to the early Hollywood filmmaker.

8

1936 - USA - 89 MIN. - B & W - LOVE STORY

DIRECTOR FRANK BORZAGE (1893–1962)
SCREENPLAY EDWIN JUSTUS MAYER, WALDEMAR YOUNG, SAMUEL HOFFENSTEIN, based on the play
"DIE SCHÖNEN TAGE VON ARANJUEZ" by HANS SZÉKELY, ROBERT A. STEMMLE DIRECTOR OF PHOTOGRAPHY CHARLES LANG
EDITING WILLIAM SHEA MUSIC FREDERICK HOLLANDER (= FRIEDRICH HOLLAENDER) PRODUCTION ERNST LUBITSCH,
FRANK BORZAGE for PARAMOUNT PICTURES.

STARRING MARLENE DIETRICH (Madeleine de Beaupré), GARY COOPER (Tom Bradley), JOHN HALLIDAY (Carlos Margoli),
WILLIAM FRAWLEY (Mr. Gibson), ERNEST COSSART (Aristide Duvalle), AKIM TAMIROFF (Police Official),
ALAN MOWBRAY (Dr. Pauquet), ZEFFIE TILBURY (Aunt Olga), ENRIQUE ACOSTA (Pedro),
STANLEY ANDREWS (Customs Official).

"What a time! What a place!"

1935. Master director Ernst Lubitsch, who'd brought many a sophisticated comedy to the screen, was tipped to become Paramount's head of production. It should have been the opportunity of a lifetime, but within a year Lubitsch was to have his promotion pulled out from under his feet. The problem, it seemed, was that the German-born whiz-kid tended to focus his entire efforts on one production and let all the others fall by the wayside – a policy that could have spelled disaster for Columbia.

Desire was one of those special projects he took under his wing during his stint as head of production. That unmistakable Lubitsch touch is everywhere in this romantic comedy about a slinky jewel thief whose love for a strait-laced American automotive engineer helps her turn over a new leaf. As director Frank Borzage was otherwise engaged for the initial weeks of the shoot, Lubitsch pitched in by staging a number of scenes in his absence. Chock-full of innuendo, these interludes in Desire play on the audience's expectations as only Lubitsch could. It begins right with the opening scene in which happy-go-lucky Detroit engineer Tom Bradley (Gary Cooper) talks something over with an off-screen person the spectator takes to be the manager of his company's Paris office. Employing an impressive range of persuasive words and imploring gestures, Bradley demands some time off for a trip to Spain. But as the camera pulls in closer, we suddenly see that Bradley is quite alone, merely rehearsing for the impending discussion. To Lubitsch's mind, one good turn deserves another. And so rather than giving the protagonist a chance to present the ins and outs of his case, the ace director has

the manager immediately approve his vacation as soon as he suggests it. What's more, his supervisor delivers the same arguments that Bradley had planned on using himself.

Desire keeps us on our toes by defying such expectations from beginning to end. Madeleine (Marlene Dietrich), a fast-talking con-artist, tries to cross the Spanish border undetected by slipping a stolen strand of pearls into the pocket of Tom's sports jacket. The customs, however, ignore Madeleine altogether and stop Tom, and fine him not for the jewelry, but for attempting to sneak some cigarettes into the country. This brand of absurdity sets the scene for what happens next as Madeleine flirts and makes small talk with Tom to get him to retrieve the coat containing the pearls from his car trunk. Just when she thinks she has him where she wants him, Tom grabs the wrong jacket and Madeleine drives off with his vehicle but without the goods. When she discovers her mistake, she has his vacation pictures developed in the hopes that a photo might lead her to him – but all that's on the roll are self-portraits from the neck down.

This love of lucre and the scramble for the pearls take a backseat in the second half of the picture when Madeleine discovers the value of true love. From here on, Desire takes on the traits of classic melodrama as Madeleine wrestles with the prospects of telling Tom the truth about herself and breaking off her business relationship with unsavory partners in crime Carlos (John Halliday) and Aunt Olga (Zeffie Tilbury), who might turn on her at any second. This general shift in tone comes as no surprise: the film's main director, Frank

Borzage, was far more at home with melodrama than light comedy. Consequently, many of *Desire's* gags lack that certain sizzle and precision which Lubitsch's best work is known for. The Borzage piece is too entrenched in the allure of its stars to come across as more than an entertaining farce. For despite Gary Cooper's valiant efforts at proving his comedic talents in a role that was neither strong nor silent, his co-star simply isn't up to the task. As always, eternal glamour girl Marlene Dietrich is too wrapped up in mink, feathers and glitter to concern herself with such trivialities – making her a downer in the laughter department but no less enjoyable than usual. On the other hand, the way she sports her *savoir faire* as a means of curbing Tom's rage is comedy at its finest. Ultimately, who has time to think about a stolen jalopy when Marlene is busy strutting her stuff in a half-open terrace doorway?

"The two stars, under the astute guidance of Ernst Lubitsch and Frank Borzage, work unusually well as a pair and carry out assignments that provide a fine fit for their talents. The direction is subtle and inspired, with many Lubitschian touches adding to the general appeal of the yarn and its plot." *Variety*

1 The world is their oyster: Automobile engineer Tom Bradley (Gary Cooper) and jewel thief Madeleine de Beaupré (Marlene Dietrich) leave their day jobs to light up the night.

2 Scrap heap: Getting his car back would make Tom happy as a clam. Maybe Madeleine will trade him for those pearls she so desperately wants.

3 The ones who got away: Madeleine's partner in crime, Carlos Margoli (John Halliday, center), is going to have a harder time than he suspects getting her to give up Tom.

4 Breakfast of champions: Tom and Madeleine start off their day on the right foot. They'll need all the energy they can get if they plan on outrunning the authorities.

**FRANK BORZAGE
(1893–1962)**

Originally from Salt Lake City, twenty-year-old Frank Borzage got his show-business start appearing in Westerns at Thomas H. Ince's production company. By 1916, the Utah boy had by and large switched to directing pictures for Mutual Studios. These were the days of the great Hollywood silents and approximately half the films Borzage made during his lifetime were without sound. Romantic melodramas were considered his specialty and his pictures generally incorporated contemporary themes, and emphasizing the fashions of the era.

Borzage was a critically acclaimed, master filmmaker. His picture *Seventh Heaven* (1927) garnered him the first ever Best Director Oscar; and he picked up another for his work on *Bad Girl* (1931). *Desire* (1936) was the first movie Marlene Dietrich starred in following her professional separation from director Josef von Sternberg, and it is said that Borzage was the only filmmaker at the time who had her confidence. Borzage was especially respected for the ease with which he created great human tragedies while avoiding the pitfalls of sentimentality.

The list of Borzage's standout productions goes on. Critics and audiences alike couldn't get enough of Gary Cooper and Helen Hayes as the American soldier and British nurse in Borzage's big-screen adaptation of *A Farewell to Arms* (1932), based on Hemingway's novel chronicling the throes of World War I. Also popular were the filmmaker's series of four melodramas starring Margaret Sullavan, which included a silver-screen version of Hans Fallada's novel *Kleiner Mann, was nun?* (*Little Man, What Now?*, 1934).

While pirate movies weren't the sort of thing that Borzage was known for, RKO still entrusted him to direct *The Spanish Main* (1945), the studio's first production made entirely in three-color Technicolor. The career of this great Hollywood master came to a definitive close in 1959 when his epic on Saint Peter, entitled *The Big Fisherman* (1959), flopped with audiences. Frank Borzage lost a battle with cancer in 1962.

"If it is a Lubitsch production, constantly highlighted by those indefinable touches of his, still one should not overlook the skill of its director, Frank Borzage, its excellent camera work, or the performances not only of Miss Dietrich, but of Gary Cooper, John Halliday, Ernest Cossart, Alan Mowbray and Akim Tamiroff. All were in the best comedy mood, and all contributed to one of the most engaging pictures of the season." *The New York Times*

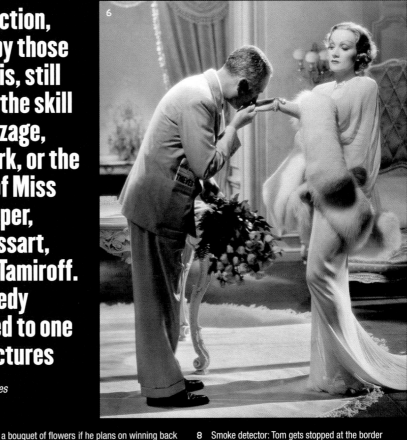

Knit one, pearl two: Marlene inspects her handiwork and decides she's done a flawless job.

Never a rose without the prick: Carlos will have to come up with more than blackmail threats and

a bouquet of flowers if he plans on winning back his accomplice.

7 Parting gifts: Madeleine tries to leave the jewelry store with a free sample.

8 Smoke detector: Tom gets stopped at the border for not declaring a pack of cigarettes. Little does customs – or he for that matter – know that he's carrying a strand of stolen pearls.

Arguably, the film's outcome caters more to Borzage's tastes than it goes to Lubitsch's. After all, why would the man responsible for the masterful *Trouble in Paradise* (1932), whose thieves remain as deliciously deviant as ever, opt for an ending in support of Hollywood's moral complacency? Production Code or not, the way Tom falls back on good old American values to defuse the situation with Madeleine's accomplices, return the pearls, save the female protagonist from doing time and pave the way for a white wedding all seems too cut and dry to be the work of Lubitsch.

Granted, the Hays Office, which had been active for two years, did insist that Madeleine get married rather than go to prison. Had they not, Tom and Madeleine could have just as easily returned the pearls to the jeweler and conned their way to America as originally planned. Unfortunately, by 1936 the motto "crime doesn't pay" and the legitimization of on-screen love affairs with nuptial rites had become as indispensable to a romantic caper as the crime itself.

LP

MODERN TIMES

1936 - USA - 87 MIN. - B & W - COMEDY

DIRECTOR CHARLES CHAPLIN (1889–1977)
SCREENPLAY CHARLES CHAPLIN DIRECTORS OF PHOTOGRAPHY ROLAND H. TOTHEROH, IRA H. MORGAN EDITING WILLARD NICO
MUSIC CHARLES CHAPLIN PRODUCTION CHARLES CHAPLIN for CHARLES CHAPLIN PRODUCTIONS, UNITED ARTISTS.

STARRING CHARLES CHAPLIN (A Factory Worker), PAULETTE GODDARD (A Gamine), HENRY BERGMAN (Café Proprietor),
STANLEY SANDFORD (Big Bill), CHESTER CONKLIN (Mechanic), HANK MANN (Burglar), LOUIS NATHEAUX (Burglar),
STANLEY BLYSTONE (The Gamine's Father), AL ERNEST GARCIA (President of the Electro Steel Corp.),
SAMMY STEIN (Turbine Operator).

> *"Se bella pui satore,*
> *je notre so catore,*
> *Je notre qui cavore,*
> *je la qu', la qui, la quai!"*

The first thing we see is a herd of sheep, then a quick cross-fade takes us to a herd of workers streaming into a factory. One of them is Charlie (Charles Chaplin). Our former Tramp is now standing at a conveyor belt. A slave to the rhythm of the machine, he tightens one bolt after another. As the tempo increases, he can't keep up, and the machine swallows him and spits him back out. Dazed, disoriented, almost entranced, he grasps his monkey wrench and tightens everything in sight: noses, buttons, whatever comes his way … In a bizarre, balletic sequence, he reduces the entire factory to chaos. They end up carting him off to the mental ward.

When the talkies were born in 1927, Charlie Chaplin was probably their most vehement opponent. Language, he believed, would destroy the universality of the cinema. By 1936, it was clear that the sound medium had triumphed; but with *Modern Times*, Chaplin created something that was neither talkie nor silent film. In the entire hour-and-a-half, the actors speak not a single understandable word, and the sound track consists solely of music, the racket of the factory machines, and commands from the boss

barked from enormous, futuristic screens. It's a sideswipe at the 'talking' cinema, which Chaplin thereby equates with the philistinism and brutality of the times.

This unconventional use of the sound is undoubtedly one reason why *Modern Times* is now regarded as one of the timeless masterpieces of the cinema. Like no other film character, Chaplin's Tramp gives touchingly comic form to humanity's existential struggle in a dehumanized world. Through no fault of his own, the little fellow is thrown into an industrialized world. Here, far from making the workers' lives easier, technology makes instruments of the workers themselves. The men are the meat part of a giant machine for manufacturing profit.

Yet it is also very clearly a film of its time: the Depression era. In contrast to Chaplin's earlier works, *Modern Times* presents the misery straight, without picturesque embellishment. At times, the camera work is almost documentary-like in its sober mustering of an impoverished environment. Chaplin is also alive to the political tensions of the period. In one scene, Char-

1   Homo faber: Charlie Chaplin shows technology
    who's boss in Modern Times and raises eyebrows
    in industrial America.

2   Here's mud in your eye: Charlie has better luck
    defending his individuality in the slammer than
    he does at the factory.

3   Getting the belt: Eight hours of mindless work is
    the worst whipping there is.

4   Interchangeable parts: Chaplin misuses his instru-
    ments and starts playing a silly symphony.

5   You want a knuckle sandwich? Charlie's co-
    workers don't tolerate mechanized behavior
    during lunch hour.

6   Get into gear: In one of the film's most beloved
    scenes, Chaplin is eaten alive by the machinery
    he services.

ie picks up a red flag that's fallen off the back of a passing truck. When a crowd of demonstrators appear around the corner, the police take Charlie for their leader and haul him off to jail.

Scenes like these reinforced Chaplin's reputation as a left-winger – thereby bolstering the animosity of right-wing Americans who had always had their suspicions about this immigrant Brit. In fact, the film's true position seems less socialist than profoundly humanist; for Charlie is innocent of the meaning of the red flag he picks up, and his wild dance in the factory is not the deliberate act of a machine-wrecker – it is his body that rebels, with the unconscious directness of genuine naivety. Even modern times can't turn the vagabond into a class-conscious proletarian. Kitted out as ever with his baggy pants, too-tight tailcoat, shabby shoes, black 'tache, walking stick and

"For those still unfamiliar with the picture, the first thing that needs to be said of *Modern Times* (1936) is that it's very funny and occasionally hilarious."
San Francisco Chronicle

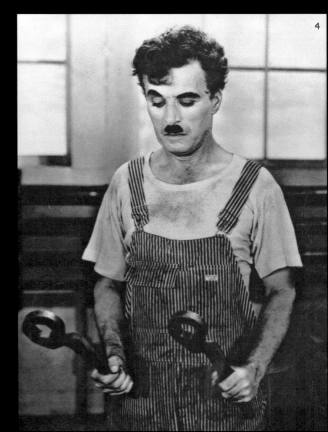

I go to a lot of movies, and I can't remember the last time I heard paying audience actually applaud at the end of a film. But this one did. And the talk afterward in the aisles, the lobby, and in line at the parking garage was genuinely excited; maybe a lot of these people hadn't seen much Chaplin before, or were simply very happy to find that the passage of time has not diminished the man's special genius." *Chicago Sun-Times*

7 Too pooped to pop: At the side of a gamine
(Paulette Goddard), a worn out Charlie falls in
love – and sleeps through the good parts.

8 Sneak attack: Staying true to his slapstick panto-
mime while giving a nod to innovation, Charlie
Chaplin shot *Modern Times* with a dialog-free

soundtrack. He did, however, have the Tramp sing
a bit towards the end – in garbledy gook.

bowler, he remains true to himself as a dandy in rags. Luxuriating in every tiny free space he can make for himself, the Tramp is his very own man – he is, quite literally, in a class of his own.

Back on the street, Charlie meets a young orphan (Paulette Goddard) who has stolen some bread. They flee the police together, and dream of a brighter future: of a country cottage, where you only have to reach out the window to find a bunch of grapes or fill your glass with milk from a friendly, passing cow. To achieve such a heaven on earth, Charlie is even prepared to go to work again – but everything he tries, from laboring to night-porter-ing, ends in disaster. For the first time, Chaplin provides his protagonist with an almost-equal partner, a kind of Trampess (so to speak). She is played by Paulette Godard, his companion of many years. It's this that makes the film, ultimately, an expression of optimism. The Tramp's love for the girl is so great that he even breaks his silence by getting up on stage in a dance hall and singing a song. And because he can't remember the words, he resorts to a kind of nonsensical Esperanto that's only comprehensible be-cause his gestures make it so. The song seems to indicate that Chaplin has made his peace with the talkies. The age of the Tramp was over. Yet there's something comforting about the little man's last exit: for the very first time, he's not walking that country road alone, but hand-in-hand with a pretty girl.

UB

PAULETTE GODDARD
(1911–1990)
Jean Cocteau once described her as "a little lion with a wild mane and splendid claws." The role of the lively vagabond in Charles Chaplin's *Modern Times* (1936) seemed tailor-made for Paulette Goddard, and they were in fact a couple at the time. Goddard grew up in poverty in New York City. Ambition and talent meant that she was already a Ziegfield girl by the time she was 14. Two years later, she married a wealthy playboy, divorced him, and went to Hollywood. There, she played minor roles until she met Chaplin in 1932. *Modern Times* made her famous, but her allegedly 'unofficial' marriage with Chaplin – it's said that they married for real in 1936 – was apparently not good for her career. Legend has it that David O. Selznick refused to cast her as Scarlett in *Gone with the Wind* (1939) because he feared bad publicity.
After *The Great Dictator* (1940), Chaplin and Goddard went their separate ways. In the years that followed, Paulette Goddard became a popular star of musicals and comedies for Paramount. Her performance as a nurse in Mark Sandrich's *So Proudly We Hail!* (1942) brought her an Oscar nomina-tion, though her title role in Jean Renoir's *The Diary of a Chambermaid* (1946) was a far more interesting piece of work. Thereafter, Paulette Goddard devoted more time to the theater. In the mid-50s, she emigrated to Switzerland and married the German writer Erich Maria Remarque. From then on, she rarely appeared on the screen.

SAN FRANCISCO

1936 - USA - 115 MIN. - B & W - DRAMA, DISASTER MOVIE, MUSICAL

DIRECTOR W. S. VAN DYKE (1889–1943)
SCREENPLAY ANITA LOOS, based on a story by ROBERT E. HOPKINS DIRECTOR OF PHOTOGRAPHY OLIVER T. MARSH
EDITING TOM HELD MUSIC EDWARD WARD, HERBERT STOTHART PRODUCTION JOHN EMERSON, BERNARD H. HYMAN for MGM.

STARRING CLARK GABLE (Blackie Norton), JEANETTE MACDONALD (Mary Blake), SPENCER TRACY (Father Tim Mullin),
JACK HOLT (Jack Burley), JESSIE RALPH (Mrs. Maisie Burley), TED HEALY (Mat), SHIRLEY ROSS (Trixie),
MARGARET IRVING (Della Bailey), HAROLD HUBER ('Babe', Blackie's Right-Hand Man), EDGAR KENNEDY (Sheriff Jim).

ACADEMY AWARDS 1936 OSCAR for BEST SOUND DESIGN (Douglas Shearer).

"Tim, I want to thank God, what do I say?" "Just say what's in your heart."

San Francisco, 1906. Neither riots nor unruly guests can make Blackie Morton (Clark Gable), the hardened manager of the Paradise Club, change his ways. Not even Mary (Jeanette MacDonald), a singer as attractive as she is talented, can soften him with her brilliant operatic voice. In fact, no sooner has she auditioned for him than the tough-as-nails Blackie gets Mary to sign a binding contract that keeps her under the same wraps as the rest of the club's personnel. Only childhood friend Father Tim Mullin (Spencer Tracy) can make him realize what a gem his new find really is and that hers is the voice of angels. By then, however, Jack Burley (Jack Holt), director of the Rivoli

Opera House, has come into the picture and is determined to claim Mary for himself. But all the fighting in the world can't determine whether Blackie or Jack is better suited for her. Indeed, it will take the forces of nature – and the aftermath of an earthquake that leaves the city in ashes – to bring this romantic drama to a conclusive, albeit abrupt, end.

The painstaking technical effort that went into staging *San Francisco's* cinematic recreation of the earthquake that struck the city on April 18, 1906 is just one of many reasons this film remains memorable. But it is director W. S. Van Dyke's finesse at conveying the human tragedy of the

1   Plush living: Caught between two men, Mary
    (Jeanette MacDonald) must decide between a
    cushy job and a fiery romance.

2   Counting their blessings: Mary and her boss Blackie
    (Clark Gable) share a moment of fleeting happiness
    before catastrophe strikes the City by the Bay.

shattering event that makes this 1.3 million dollar MGM production so spellbinding.

Anita Loos' razor-sharp script is a vital asset, poignantly capturing the extent of the devastation through the eyes of the meticulously drawn Blackie Norton. Paralyzed by the quake's power, the savvy night-club owner turns into a helpless victim as whole rows of houses collapse in front of him, and what were once family apartments are turned into grotesque dollhouses, deadly traps for their former occupants. Blackie can only watch on as these doomed souls plummet to their deaths. By stripping the self-made man

Blackie of his natural will-power and ability to assert himself, Loos deftly communicates the catastrophe's cataclysmic impact.

The disaster only has such a tremendous impact as its weight comes crashing down on the cast of fully developed characters and the 90-minute love story that precedes it. Adeptly equating the rift in the earth with the one in Blackie and Mary's relationship, the director ingeniously disrupts his staging and use of physical space. Before the quake, a structure of clearly defined acts and seamless scene transitions allowed the story to run like the proverbial well-oiled machine, with Van Dyke willingly transcending the established

3 Breaking engagements: Blackie wants his star singer to come back to him, but Father Mullin (Spencer Tracy, right) thinks that the voice of angels shouldn't be tied down by romance.

4 Stage door socialites: Mary becomes the talk of the town and hobnobs with San Francisco's elite.

5 The poor man's Aphrodite: Having a songbird on staff keeps Blackie's joint packed with admirers night after night.

"It is a shattering spectacle, one of the truly great cinematic illusions; a monstrous hideous, thrilling debacle with great fissures opening in the earth, buildings crumbling, men and women apparently being buried beneath showers of stone and plaster, gargoyles lurching from rooftops, water mains bursting, line wires flating, flame, panic and terror." *The New York Times*

6   Ruffled shirts and feathers: Many of these representatives of old San Francisco corruption will go down with the quake. Blackie, however, will get a chance to mend his ways.

7   Onwards and upwards: Blackie emerges from the rubble a different man and goes off in search of Mary and a new life.

8   Bet your bottom dollar: Prior to the quake, fame and fortune were the only things on Blackie's mind.

9   Premonitions on Portsmouth Square: Locals watch an apartment get devoured by a New Year's blaze as if seeing a preview of events in April.

"Spencer Tracy plays the priest and it's the most difficult role in the picture. It was a daring piece of writing to begin with and only the most expert and understanding handling could have kept it within the proper bounds. This man of cloth would not be unusual in real life, but on the screen he's a type never attempted before." *Variety*

floor plan in the interests of smooth storytelling. In a single scene, Father Mullin might thus be seen using the same door to enter a number of different rooms in the church, the dialog overriding these 'location changes' and ensconcing them in the story line. The fact that this highly creative approach to staging works as well as it does speaks for Van Dyke's exhilarating *mise en scène* and the high-caliber acting. When time gaps do occur, they are put down to the film's play-like structure, and bridged with soft fade-ins and fade-outs or lap dissolves.

Then, suddenly, the earth moves. Without warning, the narrative flow disappears altogether as shaky shots, blurred pans, cuts shown in rapid succession and even subliminal frames open the floodgates to total chaos. This jarring contrast makes Blackie's disorientation come across as a wholly sensory experience. The camera itself seems unable to process all the mayhem around him, as a sequence of disconnected hard cuts takes Blackie from one location to the next in his search for Mary.

Finally reaching his destination, Blackie has an epiphany while praying, and accepts that his destiny is in God's hands. Thoroughly humbled, Blackie sees the error of his ways and is able to start anew with Mary. While the film's moral agenda may be anything but subtle, the precision of its expert staging still makes it a captivating film to watch. *San Francisco's* fusion of drama and disaster supplied future films of the genre with a basic formula, and remains a fine example of how professional craftsmanship and artistic creativity went hand in hand in Hollywood's Golden Age.

DG

W. S. VAN DYKE (1889–1943)

Woodbridge Strong Van Dyke II learned directing from the ground up. He worked on *Intolerance* (1916) as D. W. Griffiths' assistant and, shortly thereafter, served as first assistant director for the silent film version of *Oliver Twist* (1916). During the 20s, Van Dyke went on to shoot a slew of quickie Westerns and other flicks for Paramount and Fox. He saved the troubled MGM production *White Shadows in the South Seas* (1928) and suddenly found himself among the ranks of Hollywood's most prominent filmmakers. 'One-Take Woody' remained under contract with MGM until 1942, where he was renowned for his efficiency, and ability to direct anything and everything. Master craftsmanship and an aptitude for getting a project in on time and under budget made him a favorite of producers. In fact, he was often brought in to save projects frivolous directors had nearly sucked dry. The high point of Van Dyke's career came in 1934 when he directed the first of the wildly popular *Thin Man* pictures, and he went on to lead the series for its next three installments, before eventually passing on the baton to Richard Thorpe in 1945. Other noteworthy Van Dyke movies like *Tarzan the Ape Man* (1932) and disaster extravaganza *San Francisco* (1936) demonstrate just how apt he was at blending innovative directing techniques with existing genre conventions. Even for the war drama *Journey for Margaret* (1942), Van Dyke's final picture, the director took special care with the performances and layered staging.

While Van Dyke may not have received the sort of artistic recognition enjoyed by his fellow MGM director George Cukor, his work was highly influential in shaping the general look of the studio's pictures during Hollywood's Golden Age. Van Dyke, a lifelong member of the Democratic Party, committed suicide on February 5, 1943.

FURY

1936 - USA - 90 MIN. - B & W - DRAMA, COURTROOM DRAMA

DIRECTOR FRITZ LANG (1890–1976)
SCREENPLAY BARTLETT CORMACK, based on the story "MOB RULE" by NORMAN KRASNA
DIRECTOR OF PHOTOGRAPHY JOSEPH RUTTENBERG EDITING FRANK SULLIVAN MUSIC FRANZ WAXMAN
PRODUCTION JOSEPH L. MANKIEWICZ for MGM.

STARRING SPENCER TRACY (Joe Wilson), SYLVIA SIDNEY (Katherine Grant), WALTER ABEL (District Attorney Adams), EDWARD ELLIS (Sheriff), WALTER BRENNAN (Deputy 'Bugs' Meyers), FRANK ALBERTSON (Charlie Wilson), GEORGE WALCOTT (Tom Wilson), BRUCE CABOT (Kirby Dawson), ARTHUR STONE (Richard Durkin), MORGAN WALLACE (Fred Garrett).

"In this country, people don't land in jail unless they're guilty."

When the Nazis came to power, Fritz Lang sought refuge in the U.S., where he eventually made most of his films. In the very first of them, Lang revisited the themes that had preoccupied him in *M* (1931) – the death penalty, lynching, and mass hysteria – and, once again, he presented his disturbing analysis in the form of a gripping drama. But *Fury* turns its gaze on America, the home of democracy, and Lang's hero is no driven, psychopathic child-killer but an innocent man played by Spencer Tracy, a man whose face was the very image of integrity. But the character he plays is a highly ambivalent one.

Joe Wilson is a decent, good-humored, thoroughly average American who might as well be called Joe Doe. These are the Depression years, though, and he's so poor he can't afford to get married. So he allows his fiancée Katherine (Sylvia Sidney) to take a job in a small town on the other side of the country. A year passes, and things have improved: Joe can now afford a car, and he uses it to visit Katherine. But on the way there, he's arrested, and a few peanuts in his pocket are enough to make him the main suspect in a kidnapping case. By the time the real culprits are found, it's too late: a lynch mob has long since passed judgment and set fire to the jail. Has Joe died in the flames? No, he's alive – but determined to keep it a secret. If Joe Wilson has his way, the 22 citizens who wanted to see him dead will hang for a murder that was never committed.

In the courtroom drama that follows, all parties involved do their best to present the evidence for their case, but none do it more successfully than Fritz Lang, the director. He dissects the value system of American democracy with the cool precision of a surgeon, and shows how it's threatened not only by the scandal of lynch justice, but by an archaic conception of law and justice. Should 22 people really die for a deed that can only be comprehended

2

1   Back and better than ever: After a lynch mob nearly kills him, Joe (Spencer Tracy) sets off to frame them for his murder.

2   From correctional facility to crematorium: Katherine (Sylvia Sidney) watches in disbelief as Joe's penitentiary is burnt to a cinder. Director Fritz Lang cast the actress, noted for having the saddest eyes in Hollywood, in three of his pictures.

as a phenomenon of mass psychology? Is the death penalty a suitable means of stilling the thirst for revenge? Surely not, when a jury can be impressed by such shockingly thin 'evidence.' To make it clear that he's dead, Joe sends an anonymous letter to the court; it contains his engraved engagement ring, which was allegedly found in the ashes. Lang never uses such symbols merely for their own sake; like the car and the peanuts, the ring plays an important role in the storyline.

Lang's portrayal of the transformation of a group of law-abiding citizens into a vicious mob is a brilliant piece of filmmaking. The constellation of characters and the build-up of the scene are strongly reminiscent of the corresponding sequence in *M*, and this is no accident. A deputy sheriff boasts about his "catch," a barber mouths platitudes about the criminal psyche then rushes off to tell his wife the news, and soon Joe's arrest is the talk of the town; the word goes round every shop and every bar, and this sequence is punctuated by shots of cackling hens. By the time the citizens have gathered at the courthouse, they've turned into apelike monsters, and the scene erupts into violence. In the courtroom, we'll see their contorted faces a second time, captured on film by a newsreel team; in this way,

"In graphic, relentless, brusquely literal sequences, the dialog and camera passages translate the sundry cross-section of the average American mentality, as belated justice seeks to square the debt. It seems curious that an Austrian director should so faithfully capture nuances that are so inherently American and attuned to the native mentality." *Variety*

3   Loud and clear: Citizens voice their disapproval of the American criminal justice system by storming a prison.

4   You're as bad as them: Joe's brothers denounce him when he asks them to take action against the men who lynched him.

5   Time for the big guns: Joe wants to see whether two wrongs make a riot.

6

**SYLVIA SIDNEY
(1910–1999)**

Film historian Ephraim Katz once described Sylvia Sidney as "the perfect screen heroine" for the Depression era. Sidney, with her sad, widely-spaced cat's eyes, was born into a Russian immigrant family in the Bronx in 1910, and was repeatedly cast as a hard-up 'working girl'. In her own sardonic words: "Paramount paid me by the tear." Having joined the studio in 1930 after big successes on Broadway, she went on to work with major directors such as Josef von Sternberg (*An American Tragedy*, 1931) and leading stars, from Gary Cooper (*City Streets*, 1931) to Humphrey Bogart (*Dead End / Cradle of Crime*, 1937). Fritz Lang cast her in three of his movies: *Fury* (1936), *You Only Live Once* (1936), and *You and Me* (1938). Though she yearned to escape typecasting, it was not to be. By the end of the 40s, this intelligent, humorous and indeed hugely popular actress was surplus to Hollywood's requirements. She continued working in the theater and on TV, but only in the 70s did she experience a kind of comeback in the movies. For her performance in *Summer Wishes, Winter Dreams* (1973), she received her first and only Oscar nomination. Later, Tim Burton cast her in his horror comedy *Beetlejuice* (1988) and created the role of Grandma Florence Norris in *Mars Attacks!* (1996) specially for her. It was the last film in a long, highly promising, but sadly frustrating career. In 1999 – after three failed marriages, and 12 years after the death of her only child – Sylvia Sidney died of throat cancer.

> "Joe Wilson, who had miraculously escaped, sits by his radio and hears them perjure themselves. His enjoyment is keen and his course of action clear to him: he is legally dead, legally murdered; he will let his legal killers stand a legal trial, get a legal sentence and a legal death." *The New York Times*

ang's very own medium satisfies the desire for justice *and* the lust for ensation.

Joe has seen the proof of this himself. In a memorable scene, he describes to his petty-criminal brother how he hid in a movie theater after the ailhouse fire: he had watched the same newsreel 20 times in a row – and een the audience applaud each time as they gaped at his apparent death in he flames. In the end, Joe comes to realize that his thirst for revenge has nade him no better than the mob that tried to kill him. Only he, as an indi-

vidual, can break the power of the mob – and he has to do it, though he's lost all faith in the law. It's the love of Katherine that shows him where he's gone wrong: in his embittered cruelty, he had allowed her to believe he was dead. The ending is idealistic, in a very American way, and it went a long way towards defusing the controversy surrounding the film. After a hard struggle, Fritz Lang had finally arrived in Hollywood – and in his next film, *You Only Live Once* (1936), he would take up the theme of the innocent suspect once again.

PB

6   Sugarcoated: Spencer Tracy is all the more riveting as a man on the rampage due to the wholesome sincerity he breathes into his character.

7   Sentenced to the chair: Some wives spend their nights wondering whether their husbands will ever come home at all.

8   Spencer for higher: Katherine's urging convinces Joe that he can do more good by sharing his story with the public than by slaying the men who wronged him.

THINGS TO COME

1936 - GREAT BRITAIN - 113 MIN. - B & W - SCIENCE FICTION, LITERARY ADAPTATION

DIRECTOR WILLIAM CAMERON MENZIES (1896–1957)
SCREENPLAY H. G. WELLS, LAJOS BIRÓ, based on the novel *THE SHAPE OF THINGS TO COME* by H. G. WELLS
DIRECTOR OF PHOTOGRAPHY GEORGES PÉRINAL EDITING CHARLES CRICHTON, FRANCIS D. LYON MUSIC ARTHUR BLISS
PRODUCTION ALEXANDER KORDA for LONDON FILM PRODUCTIONS.

STARRING RAYMOND MASSEY (John Cabal / Oswald Cabal), EDWARD CHAPMAN (Pippa / Raymond Passworthy),
RALPH RICHARDSON ('Chief'), MARGARETTA SCOTT (Roxana / Rowena), CEDRIC HARDWICKE (Theotocopulos),
MAURICE BRADDELL (Doctor Harding), SOPHIE STEWART (Mrs. John Cabal), ANN TODD (Mary Gordon),
DERRICK DE MARNEY (Richard Gordon), GEORGE SANDERS (Pilot).

"But that was only a beginning. There is nothing wrong in suffering if you suffer for a purpose."

The inhabitants of Everytown can't believe their ears: is that the sound of a *plane*? A black propeller aircraft emerges from the clouds, heralding the dawn of a new era. Everytown's mechanic had just been voicing his belief that man would never again be in a position to fly – for years, there's been no oil, and the old machinery is becoming harder and harder to repair. And now, a futuristic flying machine is landing right in front of him. A tall figure (Raymond Massey) with a huge helmet disembarks and introduces himself as a representative of "Wings over the World" – a group of scientists who wish to end the war and establish a new civilization. But the Chief of Everytown (Ralph Richardson) wants poison gas and airplanes rather than peace, so he takes the stranger prisoner.

The film is set nearly 40 years into the future, in the year 1970. After decades of war and a deadly plague, the world's population has been halved and Western civilization has collapsed into an assortment of quasi-medieval

"Typical Wellsian conjecture, it ranges from the reasonably possible to the reasonably fantastic; but true or false, fanciful or logical, it is an absorbing, provocative and impressively staged production ... *Things to Come* is an unusual picture, a fantasy, if you will, with overtones of the Buck Rogers and Flash Gordon comic strips. But it is, as well, a picture with ideas which have been expressed dramatically and with visual fascination." *The New York Times*

1 Fast forward: The future is ruled by barbaric warlords like the Chief of Everytown (Ralph Richardson). But all good things must come to an end.

2 Building a better future: Set director extraordinaire László Moholy-Nagy created an utterly sleek vision of the future.

3 Back in style: Hot pants, jousting suits and strap-up sandals are all the rage this 2036 fashion season. So much for the critics who claimed they were ancient history.

communities. Everytown, once a bustling modern city, is now little more than a giant ruin; where luxurious department stores once stood, potters and shoemakers now ply their trades. Only a few people can remember the period before the war, which had started in 1940 with bombardments from the air, and only the old can recall a time when automobiles were driven by fossil fuels rather than drawn by horses.

H. G. Wells' novel *The Shape of Things to Come* was published in 1933. It is a vision of the future, filled with grim forebodings. Almost to the year, he predicted the beginning of the next world war, and he also anticipated the enormous strategic importance of superior airpower. The producer Alexander Korda commissioned a screenplay, and Wells quickly wrote several drafts. When the film was made, it was one of the most ambitious and expensive British productions of the 1930s, with an army of extras, a spectacular set design and a plethora of complicated special effects.

The last third of the movie is particularly rich in memorable images, some of which are now regarded as milestones in the history of science fiction film. The captured pilot is freed by his comrades from "Wings over the World" and becomes the founding father of a rational society based

---

H. G. WELLS
(1866–1946)

It was a collaborative enterprise racked with difficulties: the author H. G. Wells went so far as to hand out notes on set, in which he announced his ideas on how his screenplay should be filmed. But producer Alexander Korda was prepared to put up with it, for Wells, after all, was one of the major literary visionaries of the age. His very name in the opening credits to *Things to Come* (1936) was a promise of thrilling futuristic worlds – and a guarantee of healthy takings at the box office.

Herbert George Wells is regarded as one of the founders of the science fiction genre. Born in Bromley, near London, in 1866, he worked as an auxiliary teacher, a draper, a scientist and a journalist. His very first novel, *The Time Machine* (1895), made him famous overnight. It now seems appropriate that it was published in the year the cinema was born, for Wells' original and spectacular tales were practically made for the silver screen. As early as 1902, with *Le Voyage dans la lune*, George Méliès had created a film adaptation of a Wells novel, *The First Men in the Moon* (1901); and *The Island of Dr. Moreau* (1896) was the subject of several screen adaptations.

Wells' novels precisely anticipate a number of inventions, including escalators, poison gas, and missiles driven by atomic power. Yet he was less interested in the inventions themselves than in their effects on the people who used them. For Wells, technology was merely a means of realizing his socialist ideals. In their socio-political dimension, his novels are fundamentally different from those of many other science fiction authors, including (for example) Jules Verne.

The Englishman's most famous work was *The War of the Worlds* (1898), and it too was the subject of two spectacular movie adaptations, in 1953 and 2005. Wells died in London in 1946, so he experienced neither of these films; but he dd hear of Orson Welles' sensational radio version, which frightened many listeners into fleeing their homes. Proof, if any were needed, that H. G. Wells' fantastic fictions are both immensely lively and disturbingly believable.

on science and technology. Beneath the old city of Everytown, gigantic machines create a completely new world, transparent and egalitarian. The people live in hi-rise structures like honeycombs; glass elevators glide up and down the buildings' exteriors; the apartments are furnished with flat screens, perspex fittings and shiny floors; and though these dwellings are windowless, each of them has a spacious, curved balcony facing out onto the city.

Yet despite the film's countless visual ideas – from nippy little helicopters to holographic TV – most critics of the day disliked it. Even today, this movie seems somewhat frigid and consciously constructed. This is partly because of the way it was directed by William Cameron Menzies, an Art Direction specialist who went on to work on movies such as *Gone with the*

Wind (1939) and *The Thief of Bagdad* (1940). Although his Wells adaptation is sensational to look at, the film's characters remain wooden and one-dimensional, and the dialog degenerates into a series of wordy monologs in which the great author proclaims his faith in science and technology. The root problem, however, is the film's basic conception: from the very beginning, Wells used the project as a personal counterblast to the skepticism about progress so prevalent amongst British intellectuals of the time – and against Fritz Lang's *Metropolis* (1926), which Wells had once castigated as banal, stupid, sentimental and cliché-ridden. In Lang's vision, machines enslave humanity; as Wells' saw it, technology would liberate mankind. The German film depicts scientists as hubristic fools, but the English movie presents them as pioneers of a world community ruled by reason, and while *Metropolis* is saturated with

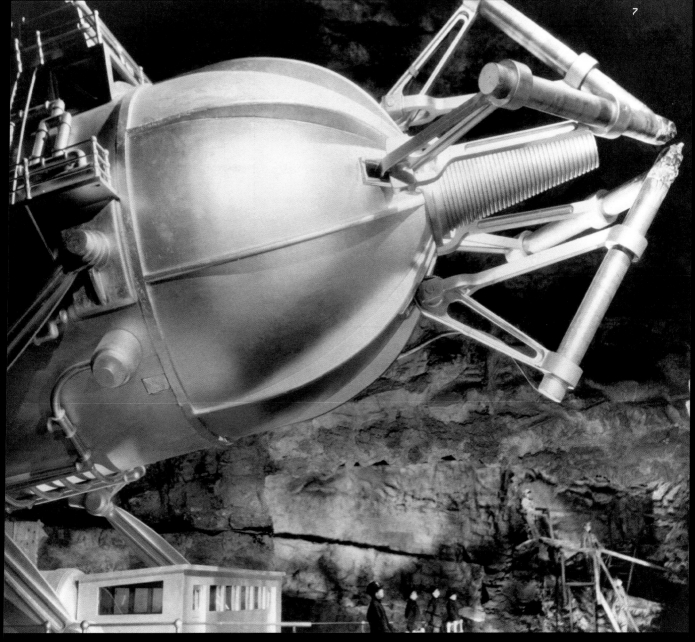

4 Welding a là Wells: Eat your heart out, Jennifer
   Beals.

5 Earthquake drill: William Cameron Menzie's special
   effects are what make Things to Come a memorable picture. Lewis Milestone (*All Quiet on the
   Western Front*, 1930) would have probably focused

   his attentions elsewhere, had he directed the project as planned.

6 The Geneva Convention: Cabal (Raymond Massey,
   left), the-soon-to-be founding father of a brave
   new world, tries to convince 'The Chief' to say
   farewell to arms.

7 Danger comes in all shapes and sizes: The new
   world leaders have put their faith in science and
   technology. If only someone could recall what
   caused the decades-long world war in the first
   place.

Christian and Biblical symbolism, *Things to Come* celebrates sober, instrumental rationality.

   As a positive utopian vision, this film is still almost unique in the history
of SF, a genre that is fascinated by the future but rarely trusts it. Profound
doubts have always accompanied the increasingly rapid progress in technological change, and in *Things to Come*, this skepticism is embodied in the

character of an artist, who starts a revolt in order to prevent the departure of
the first manned space flight. Yet 'the mob' fails to stop the launch of the
moon capsule, and the film ends with a view of a starry sky. The message is
clear: there are no limits to the development of mankind – at least in the eyes
of H. G. Wells.

NM

OLYMPIA – PART ONE: FESTIVAL OF THE NATIONS / PART TWO: FESTIVAL OF BEAUTY

Olympia – 1. Teil: Fest der Völker / 2. Teil: Fest der Schönheit

1936–1938 - GERMANY - 124 / 98 MIN. - B & W - DOCUMENTARY FILM

DIRECTOR LENI RIEFENSTAHL (1902–2003)
SCREENPLAY LENI RIEFENSTAHL DIRECTORS OF PHOTOGRAPHY WILLY ZIELKE, HANS ERTL, WALTER FRENTZ, GUZZI LANTSCHNER, KURT NEUBERT, HANS SCHEIB EDITING LENI RIEFENSTAHL, MAX MICHEL, JOHANNES LÜDKE, ARNFRIED HEYNE, GUZZI LANTSCHNER MUSIC HERBERT WINDT, WALTER GRONOSTAY PRODUCTION LENI RIEFENSTAHL for OLYMPIA-FILM GMBH.

SPEAKERS PAUL LAVEN, ROLF WERNICKE, HENRI NANNEN, JOHANNES PAGELS.

"To the honor and glory of the world's youth."

The ghosts of athletes past emerge from the ruins of ancient Olympia. Sculptures of gods awaken and become living athletes, embodiments of the Classical ideals of physical and spiritual perfection. From the temple of Zeus in Greece, the Olympic torch is carried to the German capital. Leni Riefenstahl's film of the 1936 Olympic Games begins with this solemn prolog. There is a bitter irony in the fact that these highly expressive images were probably not made by the director herself, but by the film artist Willy Zielke, who was later committed to a sanatorium and underwent forced sterilization by the Nazis. He never recovered from these experiences. Was he the victim of Riefenstahl's pathological ambition? It has never been proven, but the suspicion is certainly plausible, for she could tolerate no equal partner beside her.

Only a few minutes into the film, it's already apparent that Riefenstahl's work can hardly be viewed in isolation from her entanglement in the apparatus of National Socialist power, and from her responsibility for helping to spread its ideology – a responsibility she spent the rest of her life denying. Yet it is equally clear that the director of *Olympia* shaped modern sports-reporting like no other filmmaker before or since.

In keeping with the introduction, the first part of the film, *Festival of the Nations*, attends mainly to the classical Olympic disciplines, such as discus, javelin, and long jump, with the marathon presented as the supreme sporting challenge. Aesthetically, the camerawork and editing is in striking contrast to today's sports reporting. Rather than choosing the camera angles and posi-

1 Beauty to span the ages: Director Leni Riefenstahl evokes the spirit of the Olympic Games by filming godlike youths against a backdrop of ancient ruins.

2 Mass production: Unlike today's sports coverage, The Olympiad shows individual achievement as secondary to that of the whole team.

3 Wave to the fans: Riefenstahl documents the interaction of athletes and fans for maximum dramatic impact. The technique elevates the spectator's status to that of a player.

"*Olympia* is an elegy on the youth of 1936: here they are in their flower, dedicated to the highest ideals of sportsmanship – these young men who were so soon to kill each other." *The New Yorker*

4 Current trends: Given the number of extreme close-ups used in today's sports footage, it's easy to overlook what a feat it was to capture film like this in the 1930s.

5 In the swing of things: Riefenstahl's camera team set its own gold standard by documenting the games from all possible angles.

6 Dangerous liaisons: Nazi Germany portrayed itself as a country that wanted to foster impeccable relations with the nations of the world.

7 Ball of energy: Both the camera and the athletes always have their eyes on the prize.

8 Eternal flame: The Olympiad's imagery continues to inspire and provoke today's audience, especially in view of the political context.

tions best suited to an analysis of the sporting action, Riefenstahl always presents the athlete and his or her body in the most dramatic way possible. Commentaries are used only when absolutely necessary; usually, we are told nothing more than the name and nationality of the competitor shown.

Riefenstahl attempts to reflect the specific rhythm of each sport, using a completely different directing style for each Olympic discipline. The pole-

vault section, for example, begins with a sequence showing countless attempts in succession: then we see dark clouds forming, indicating that many hours of competition have passed, and that the victor will soon be crowned. Solemn music and a close-up of the Olympic flame against a black sky – the sporting event is presented as dramatically as possible, and such banal facts as the names of the athletes involved are of secondary interest at best.

"Suddenly it came to me, and I saw the ruins of the ancient Olympic stadiums emerge from nebulous fields, Greek temples and sculptures appear and disappear with Achilles and Aphrodite, Medusa and Zeus, Apollo and Paris, and then the discus thrower Myron. I dreamt how he became a man of flesh and blood and began to swing the disc in slow motion ..." *Leni Riefenstahl, Memoirs*

LENI RIEFENSTAHL

Leni Riefenstahl was born in Berlin in 1902. She began her career as a dancer. After suffering a knee injury, she moved on to film acting, under the influence of the director Arnold Fanck, whose *Mountain of Destiny / Peak of Fate* (*Berg des Schicksals*, 1923/24) had deeply impressed her. She played the female lead in Fanck's later films, which included *White Hell of Pitz Palu* (*Die weiße Hölle vom Piz Palü*, 1929) and *Avalanche / Storm over Mont Blanc* (*Stürme über dem Montblanc*, 1930). The first film she directed herself was *The Blue Light* (*Das blaue Licht – Eine Berglegende aus den Dolomiten*, 1931/32); and here, too, she played the leading role herself. Riefenstahl's work for the National Socialists began with her documentaries about the Nazi party rallies. With *Triumph of the Will* (*Triumph des Willens*, 1935), she made her name as a creator of a strongly aestheticized visual language, later perfected in her two films about the Berlin Olympics: *Festival of the Nations* and *Festival of Beauty* (*Fest der Völker* and *Fest der Schönheit*, 1936–1938).

Leni Riefenstahl was legendary for her refusal to compromise, not only in matters of artistic policy but when furthering the interests of her own career. As "the Fuehrer's favorite director," she even got her way against the Propaganda Minister, Joseph Goebbels. After the war, Riefenstahl was classified as a mere "fellow traveler" of the Nazi party, but she was unable to realize any film projects in the decades that followed. The sole exception was *Lowlands (Tiefland)*, which she had started in 1940 but completed only in 1953.

By the time she died in 2003, she had published several volumes of photography that brought her international recognition. While her personal role in the Third Reich is still the topic of controversy, her influence on contemporary visual language – both in art and in advertising – is now largely undisputed.

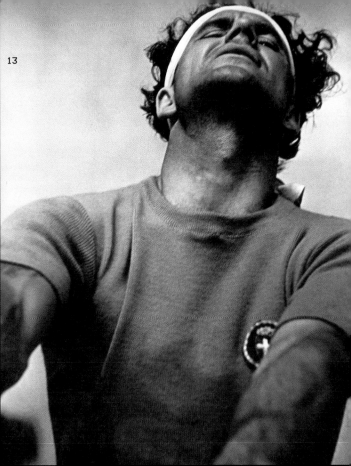

9 Love to see you smile: Nazi views on ethnicity make Riefenstahl's interest in the physiognomy of various ethnic groups all the more striking.

10 With your head held high: An athlete enjoys his one moment in time, which has been extended by the magic of the slow-motion camera.

11 Smooth sailing: The various Olympic disciplines are so meticulously catalogued that we could be watching a motion picture encyclopedia.

12 Sinewy sirens: More than just a celebration of the spirit and willpower, the symbolic and utterly aesthetic images of The Olympiad express the majesty of the human form.

13 Raising the bar: Time and again, the action documents athletes accomplishing heroic acts by sheer perseverance.

In strong contrast to this pathos, the film frequently cuts away to the spectators, emphasizing the happy "popular festival" atmosphere and the communal spirit of the nations taking part. This is the context in which Adolf Hitler appears. In her films of the Nazi party's meetings, Riefenstahl had shown Hitler as a charismatic leader; here, he's presented as a man of the people – visibly disappointed, for example, when the German women's relay team snatches defeat from the jaws of victory by dropping the baton. We also see this 'humanized' Hitler engaged in lively conversation with Göring and Goebbels as they watch the thrilling spectacle unfold.

In the second part of the film, *Festival of Beauty*, the dictator is nowhere to be seen. Riefenstahl focuses on the communal aspect of the Games, beginning with strongly aestheticized scenes of the teams' early-morning training sessions. Indeed, this part of the film shows only team sports. The painful effort of the individual is depicted in extreme close-ups of various body parts from the athlete's point of the view; and the individual's effort is rewarded by the shared success of the team, depicted (for example) in shots of hundreds of gymnasts moving in unison.

The sociologist Gunter Gebauer has said that the entire history of the modern Olympic Games is suffused by "the tension between unbridled nationalism and the egocentric exhibition of the self." In Riefenstahl's *Olympia* films, this thesis is vehemently confirmed. Not for nothing is the film dedicated to Pierre de Coubertin, the man who initiated the modern Olympics. Gebauer describes de Coubertin's "idea of ritualization, expressed in ceremonies, staged events, liturgical elements, diffuse messages, and finally in the production of communal experiences and exalted feelings." In Riefenstahl's *Olympia*, all this is omnipresent. With imagery that almost overwhelms the viewer, a sporting event is presented as a quasi-religious rite beyond the concerns of quotidian life. It was the perfect vehicle for a regime that wished to mobilize nationalistic feelings and glorify the idea of self-sacrifice for a 'great' cause.

SH

"A monumental event in every sense of the word." *Süddeutsche Zeitung*

MR. DEEDS GOES TO TOWN

1936 - USA - 115 MIN. - B & W - COMEDY

DIRECTOR FRANK CAPRA (1897–1991)
SCREENPLAY ROBERT RISKIN, based on the short story *OPERA HAT* by CLARENCE BUDINGTON KELLAND
DIRECTOR OF PHOTOGRAPHY JOSEPH WALKER EDITING GENE HAVLICK MUSIC HOWARD JACKSON PRODUCTION FRANK CAPRA
for COLUMBIA PICTURES CORPORATION.

STARRING GARY COOPER (Longfellow Deeds), JEAN ARTHUR (Louise 'Babe' Bennett), GEORGE BANCROFT (Mac Wade),
LIONEL STANDER (Cornelius Cobb), DOUGLASS DUMBRILLE (John Cedar), RAYMOND WALBURN (Walter),
H. B. WARNER (Richter May), RUTH DONNELLY (Mabel Dawson), WALTER CATLETT (Morrow), JOHN WRAY (Farmer).

ACADEMY AWARDS 1936 OSCAR for BEST DIRECTOR (Frank Capra).

"If that man is crazy, Your Honor, the rest of us belong in strait-jackets."

Simple Simon, whose selfless acts of kindness expose the baseness and insanity of 'decent' society, is far from being a modern Hollywood invention. Long before *Forrest Gump* (1994) made his way into the hearts of moviegoers, Frank Capra bestowed audiences with unlikely hero Longfellow Deeds, portrayed by Gary Cooper.

At the story's start, Mr. Deeds leads a modest existence in the small American town of Mandrake Falls, where he diligently practices his tuba and dreams up phrases for greeting cards. Life, however, takes an unexpected turn, when an uncle dies and wills him his millions. Suddenly, this simple Joe finds himself the master of a bourgeois New York mansion, but feels uncomfortable in its stony walls. To make things worse, Deeds is quickly made to look ridiculous for standing up to his uncle's lawyers and freeloaders of the estate. The person behind it all is Babe Bennett (Jean

Arthur), a newspaper reporter who wins her way into the "Cinderella Man's" heart only to then write about his embarrassing faux pas and futile attempts to live out childhood dreams during midnight excursions. After wising up to Babe, a disillusioned and deeply hurt Deeds decides he'd be better off without the fortune. Putting the money to good use, he buys land and apportions it to people the Depression has left unemployed so that they can start up small farms. The estate's corrupt attorneys view his impulsive behavior as an infringement of their interests and file suit to contest the will, claiming that Deeds is not of sound mind. Daunted by the prospect of defending himself in a court of law, the former country boy is ready to capitulate altogether and succumb to whatever punishment fate has in store for him. In the meantime, however, Babe is overcome with remorse and a sudden love for Deeds. She testifies in court on his behalf and pleads

1 Doer of good deeds: Mr. Deeds (Gary Cooper) marches to the tune of a different drum and helps his fellow man.

2 A point of error: Cedar (Douglass Dumbrille) wishes to make Deeds appear mentally incompetent to the court by turning his words around in his mouth.

3 Taking him for a ride: Babe Bennett (Jean Arthur) and Morrow (Walter Catlett) show Deeds the time of his life on an after-dark tour of New York.

with him to stick up for himself. A man transformed, he gives an impassioned speech before the court that wins him his freedom and the cheers of those he helped out financially.

Mr. Deeds Goes to Town is a social fairy tale that very much reflects the mood of its time. The story pulses with the blood of the 'New Deal,' a scheme engineered by President Franklin D. Roosevelt to combat the economic crisis that plagued the 1930s. Proclaiming the moral renaissance of the American people, his plan was to create jobs with the Works Progress Administration. Indeed, Mr. Deeds Goes to Town reads like a picture-book guide to the New

Deal as it spotlights the corruption and cynicism of the rich; people who help each other out in a fight against unemployment; an individual who champions the greater good, and last but not least, a renewed faith in government institutions, which in this case is that of justice.

While Frank Capra's previous work, It Happened One Night (1934) was a classic screwball comedy many would try to emulate, Mr. Deeds took the genre one step further by integrating strands of social criticism and melodrama in sync with the zeitgeist of the 30s. The plot also provided the foundation for two subsequent Capra undertakings: the emphatically patriotic

4 Poison pen: The provincial Deeds confesses his
   love to a journalist who has exposed his secrets to
   the whole of Manhattan.

5 Taking New York by the horns: Millionaire-in-the-
   making Longfellow Deeds leaves his hometown of
   Mandrake Falls for the big city.

**JEAN ARTHUR
(1900–1991)**

Jean Arthur left Plattsburgh, New York early in life and made her screen debut in John Ford's *Cameo Kirby* (1923). Within no time, the photographer's daughter had become a full-fledged supporting player in big pictures. In the 30s, she landed her first major role in another John Ford picture – this time a screwball comedy entitled *The Whole Town's Talking* (1934/35). It was the breakthrough Arthur needed to make it to the A list and she soon became known for her portraits of intelligent, well-meaning women. Her roles in two Frank Capra social comedies, *Mr. Deeds Goes to Town* (1936) and *Mr. Smith Goes to Washington* (1939), were no exception. In them, Arthur is the epitome of the hard-boiled, professional urbanite who teeters between cynicism, romance and her moral obligations. Characters like these and that of the disillusioned showgirl she depicted in Howard Hawks' *Only Angels Have Wings* (1939) went well with her tomboyish presence and distinctly sultry voice. While her career continued to thrive through the mid-40s, *A Foreign Affair* (1948) and *Shane* (1953) were her only big-screen projects once World War II was over. After that, Arthur appeared in a short-lived television program entitled *The Jean Arthur Show* (1966), which was broadcast in the 60s. Jean Arthur died in 1991 in Carmel, California.

6 A pillar of strength: Although Babe Bennett nearly ruins Deeds by humiliating him in her column, she will ultimately emerge as his rock of support.

7 Chin up: Babe gives Longfellow a much-needed boost and helps him defend his actions to his peers.

8 And the little guy stands tall: Deed is proclaimed to be of sound mind and America's small farmers retain control of the land he has given them.

Mr. Smith Goes to Washington (1939) and the somewhat more dejected *Meet John Doe* (1941), in which only the love story ends happily.

Nearly 60 years after *Mr. Deeds* premiered, the Coen Brothers deconstructed Capra's film with *The Hudsucker Proxy* (1994). Their plot also dealt with a simple man's unanticipated rise, fall, and resurrection, as well as a lady journalist who initially betrays him only to end up falling for him head over heels in grand Hollywood style. Yet despite this, the Coens expose the fairy tale for what it is by literally having an angel float down from heaven at the last minute to set things right. While their post-modernist use of such a *deus ex machina* was undoubtedly meant in jest, Capra knew exactly how to key into his audience's very genuine hopes and dreams with a sweepstake turn of events. François Truffaut venerated the so-called 'miracle worker' for this particular talent, saying that, "the Italian (Capra), born in Palermo, brought the *commedia dell'arte* to Hollywood. He could steer his protagonists into the darkest depths of human desperation (the tragic moments in Capra's tragedies have reduced me to tears many a time) to then swing the boat round and let a miracle run its course. And when the lights came up, the audience would make its way out of the theater, taking a new faith in life with them."   JS

"... the picture moves easily into the pleasant realm reserved for the season's most entertaining films." *The New York Times*

A DAY IN THE COUNTRY
Une partie de campagne

1936 - FRANCE - 44 MIN. - B & W - LITERARY ADAPTATION, MELODRAMA

DIRECTOR JEAN RENOIR (1894–1979)
SCREENPLAY JEAN RENOIR, based on the novella of the same name by GUY DE MAUPASSANT
DIRECTOR OF PHOTOGRAPHY CLAUDE RENOIR EDITING MARGUERITE RENOIR, MARINETTE CADIX MUSIC JOSEPH KOSMA
PRODUCTION PIERRE BRAUNBERGER for PANTHEON-PRODUCTION.

STARRING SYLVIA BATAILLE (Henriette Dufour), GEORGES D'ARNOUX (Henri), JANE MARKEN (Madame Juliette Dufour),
ANDRÉ GABRIELLO (Monsieur Dufour), JACQUES B. BRUNIUS (Rodolphe), PAUL TEMPS (Anatole),
GABRIELLE FONTAN (Grandmother), JEAN RENOIR (Poulain), MARGUERITE RENOIR (Maid).

"How amazing the country is!
Every blade of grass hides a tiny, living thing."

France, 1860: on a beautiful midsummer Sunday, Parisian ironmonger Dufour (André Gabriello) borrows a milk truck and treats his family and his assistant Anatole (Paul Temps) to a day out in the country. They stop and take a break at an inn, idyllically located on the banks of a river. There, the Dufours meet Henri (Georges D'Arnoux) and Rodolphe (Jacques B. Brunius), two wealthy playboys who take a lively interest in Madame Dufour (Jane Marken) and her daughter Henriette (Sylvia Bataille). They 'generously' offer the men the use of their fishing rods, and invite the two ladies to take a boating trip. The naive Dufour and his slow-witted assistant – a duo reminiscent of Laurel and Hardy – give their foolish consent to this proposal, and while they're angling on the river bank, Rodolphe and Henri seduce the mother and daughter. Years later, Henri and Henriette meet once again at the riverbank, where they wistfully remember their afternoon of love.

Having started as a comedy, the film develops a dreamlike quality before ending on a melancholy note. Jean Renoir's romantic images of the river landscape lend a powerfully poetic flavor to the satirical tale told by Guy de Maupassant. Renoir's exterior shots are both simple and artful. Une partie de campagne is clearly a tribute to his father, the great painter Pierre-Auguste Renoir, who often painted en plein air on the banks of rivers. The atmosphere, the motifs, the very poses of the figures – everything recalls the Impressionist painters, with their love of light and water. In one scene Renoir even brings his father's painting "The Swing" (1876) to life: like the woman in the picture, Henriette stands on the seat of a swing suspended from a tree, and the sunlight filtered through the branches throws dancing points of light onto her white summer dress. Yet Renoir is not content with a mere reproduction, and

actually succeeds in heightening the lyricism of the original by allowing us to join the young lady on the swing (so to speak!). The camera shows us her ecstatic face in close-up, while heaven and earth rush past her.

For the audience, it's a moment of magic. Even some passing priests are enchanted by the sight of Henriette smiling radiantly on the swing. Rodolphe, too, is watching lecherously, and he's delighted when she finally sits down, allowing him to catch a tantalizing glimpse of her underwear. Henriette, played wonderfully by Sylvia Bataille, is the film's main character, and Renoir frames her perfectly in a series of skillful transitions from long shot to medium shot to close-up. But the center of the film's attention is the river with which it begins and ends. It is a symbol of life itself. "I cannot imagine film without water," said Jean Renoir. "Cinematic movement has something inexorable, like the flowing of a river."

There was certainly no shortage of water while the film was being made. On the contrary: it rained so mercilessly that location shooting, scheduled to last eight days, dragged on for several weeks. The crew had to spend an age waiting in hotels for the sun to shine, and this led to tension and strife. Things might have been even worse if the film team hadn't consisted mainly of Renoir's friends and family: his nephew Claude was the cameraman, his wife Marguerite played the maid, and the director himself had the role of the jovial innkeeper. Although this way of working cut costs, filming took so long that Renoir eventually ran out of money and interrupted filming in order to a start a new project. The producer Pierre Braunberger wanted to release the film anyway, but all he had was a rough cut prepared by Marguerite Renoir and lasting around 40 minutes. Braunberger hoped to im-

"This lyric tragedy rates with Renoir's greatest."

Pauline Kael, in: Kiss Kiss Bang Bang

prove his chances of marketing the film by using the available material as the basis for a full-length feature; but despite producing several draft screenplays, he never succeeded in persuading Renoir or any other director that this would be a good idea.

During the German occupation of France, the first rough cut of the film was destroyed. Marguerite Renoir and her sister Marinette Cadix then went back to the negatives and cut a new version based on the original script. Certain scenes were missing – before the money ran out, the plan was to shoot these in the studio – and the sisters simply filled the gaps with linking captions. Joseph Kosma, who had already provided the music for other Renoir films, composed catchy melodies that underline the lyrical and melancholy flavor of the images while binding the loose sequence of scenes into an integrated whole.

At the premiere in Paris in 1946, the critics' response was wholly positive; but when the film reached the cinemas a few weeks later, moviegoers reacted with sheer delight. After the misery of the war years, this romantic day in the country was like a breath of fresh air.

Ever since then, *Une partie de campagne* has been one of Renoir's most popular movies. Its visual qualities are impressive in their very simplicity, and they still have a powerful impact. Years before Orson Welles, Renoir was creating compositions with astonishing sharpness and depth of field. Take the famous scene in which Rodolphe and Henri are sitting at the breakfast table: when Rodolphe opens the shutters, light floods the room – and instantly, the interior space is nothing more than a frame for the garden outside, where Henriette, the very image of *joie de vivre*, is flying through the air on her swing. The spirit of summer has never been captured more hauntingly.   OK

1   The thrill of it all: Henriette (Sylvia Bataille) swings her way to happiness under the Renoir family tree in a moment inspired by the director's father, Impressionist painter Pierre-Auguste Renoir. The artist's grandnephew Claude was the picture's cinematographer.

2   These magic moments: Henri (Georges D'Arnoux) and Henriette spend the afternoon in a veritable Garden of Eden and eat of the forbidden fruit.

3   Foreplay or satyr play? Rodolphe (Jacques B. Brunius) puts on quite the show for Madame

Dufour (Jane Marken) complete with flute and tantalizing innuendo.

POETIC REALISM

In the 1930s, the introduction of sound coincided with some serious economic and political crises. This moved a number of young French filmmakers to focus more strongly on social conditions. These directors worked in a number of different genres, and from 1933 onwards, they were described as "poetic realists" – a term already familiar from art and literature. Their films usually depict an unhappy love affair combined with a detailed study of a working-class milieu – a typical example is Marcel Carné's drama *Daybreak* (*Le Jour se lève*, 1939). Julien Duvivier's *Pépé le Moko* (1936/37) is an equally 'dark' film – a fascinating study of the fatal consequences of falling in love.

The most productive representative of the genre was Jean Renoir, whose films constituted a trenchant critique of French society. But with works such as *The Bitch* (*La Chienne*, 1931), *Toni* (1934/35), *The Grand Illusion* (*La Grande Illusion*, 1937) and *The Rules of the Game* (*La Règle du jeu*, 1939), he also impressed filmmakers around the world like no other director outside Hollywood. His films were largely shot on location, integrating the natural landscape and deploying natural light, featuring carefully choreographed long takes and making revolutionary use of the extreme focal depth offered by new camera technology. Renoir had a lasting influence on naturalistic filmmakers, and he was a role model for many directors of the Nouvelle Vague.

LA HABANERA

La Habanera

1937 - GERMANY - 100 MIN. - B & W - MELODRAMA

DIRECTOR DETLEF SIERCK (= DOUGLAS SIRK) (1897–1987)
SCREENPLAY GERHARD MENZEL DIRECTOR OF PHOTOGRAPHY FRANZ WEIHMAYR EDITING AXEL VON WERNER
MUSIC LOTHAR BRÜHNE PRODUCTION ERICH HOLDER, BRUNO DUDAY for UFA.

STARRING ZARAH LEANDER (Astrée Sternhjelm), FERDINAND MARIAN (Don Pedro de Avila),
KARL MARTELL (Dr. Sven Nagel), JULIA SERDA (Aunt Ana Sternhjelm), BORIS ALEKIN (Dr. Luis Gomez),
PAUL BILDT (Dr. Pardway), EDWIN JÜRGENSEN (Shumann), CARL KUHLMANN (Prefect),
MICHAEL SCHULZ-DORNBURG (Juan), ROSITA ALCARAZ (Spanish dancer), LISA HELWIG (Old servant).

"Everything is strange."

Young Swede Astrée Sternhjelm (Zarah Leander) and her grumpy Aunt Ana (Julia Serda) are on a luxury liner. Destination: Puerto Rico. Astrée feels as if she's landed in paradise, but her Aunt has nothing but contempt for the place: "wild," "barbaric" and "filthy" are among the more harmless adjectives she applies to everything from bullfighting to the song "La Habanera." Then Ana meets the wealthy nobleman and landowner Don Pedro de Avila (Ferdinand Marian). It's love at first sight. Just as the ship is about to depart, she dashes down the gangway to join him. They marry and have a son (Michael Schulz-Dornburg), and Astrée breaks off all contact with her family.

Ten years later, in 1937, Aunt Ana has become the chairperson of the Swedish Tropical Institute, and she sends physician Sven Nagel (Karl Martell) and his Brazilian colleague Luis Gomez (Boris Alekin) on an expedition to Puerto Rico. Their mission is to combat the "Puerto Rican fever," which is raging there, and to find out what's become of Ana's niece. It turns out that the corrupt government and local scientists are trying to hush up the epidemic in order to avoid economic sanctions. Eventually, the influential Don Pedro invites the two physicians to visit him at home, so that the police can search their hotel rooms at leisure and prepare their arrest. Sven, who is an old schoolfriend of Astrée's, discovers that she is practically being held prisoner by her domineering husband. But luck is on her side: Don Pedro falls ill, lapses into a coma and dies. Sven, Astrée and her son return to Sweden, happily united as a new family.

Melodrama was one of the preferred genres in Nazi Germany. In this particular example, the theme is *Heimat* – home. Don Pedro is revealed to be a cold-blooded feudal lord who controls the entire island, including the government, the police and the hospital, while forcing Astrée to exist in a gilded cage. She forms a symbiosis with her strikingly blond, pale-skinned son, whose name – Juan – seems strangely inappropriate. Even in the hottest

1 Pent up and pissed off: Astrée Sternhjelm (Zarah Leander) would rather fall victim to a deadly epidemic than spend another minute with her husband, Don Pedro.

2 A step down: Astrée may seem high and mighty, but she is by no means above melodrama.

3 Hanky panky: During a bullfight, Don Pedro de Avila (Ferdinand Marian) meets the woman of his dreams – and proceeds to make her life a nightmare.

weather, Astrée wears white fur, and sings her child songs about the beauty of snow. Unable to forget Sweden, she is now completely alienated by the island she once saw as a tropical paradise. But *La Habanera* isn't just a film about homesickness; it is also permeated by a diffusely racist fear of the foreign, and the foreigner, *per se*. While Astrée and Sven – "Aryans" in the Nazi ideology of the period – seem ageless, immune to the passage of time, Pedro goes gray and succumbs to the disease that's ravaging the island. The film suggests that certain nationalities are inherently better than others; thus, when Sven plays with little Juan, he immediately comes across as the 'natu-

ral' father figure. The case becomes clear when we look at the bacteriological mission that forms such a large part of the film. South America is the source of an infectious disease that threatens the world: from the ports of this island, ships depart with fruit in their holds ... Finally, the doctors identify the cause of the disease: pathogens in the blood that carry the infection. Sven refers to these microbes as "murderers," and says he would like to exterminate them. Today, it's hard not to associate this rhetoric with the Nazis' racial ideology, and to see it as a harbinger of the war of extermination they would soon unleash upon the world.   PLB

4 Lady of pain, I abhor you: Once all the guests have
left their lavish wedding, Pedro shows his Swedish
bride around his cozy citadel.

5 Bolero: Astrée and Don Pedro's relationship is
a dance in which the wrong move could bring
the kiss of death.

ZARAH LEANDER   Actress and singer Zarah Leander was born on March 15, 1907, in Karlstad, Sweden. Her real name was Sara Stina Hedberg. Famed for her deep, 'hermaphroditic' voice, Leander signed a contract with UFA in Berlin in 1937, and went on to become one of the biggest stars in Germany during the Nazi era. This was partly due to the fact that actresses such as Marlene Dietrich had left the country after the Nazis came to power. Leander's best-known films include *La Habanera* (1937), *To New Shores* (*Zu neuen Ufern*, 1937), *Magda* (*Heimat*, 1938) and *The Great Love* (*Die große Liebe*, 1941/42). In melodramas such as these, she embodied a suffering femme fatale, a figure with whom German women on the home front could identify. The Propaganda Ministry repeatedly suggested that Leander be made a *Staatsschauspielerin* (state actress), but Hitler rejected the proposals. In 1943, Zarah Leander broke her contract and returned to Sweden. After the war, she was forbidden to perform in Germany from 1945 until 1948. From then on, she was better known as the author of several volumes of autobiography, and above all as a singer and musical star. She died in Stockholm on June 23, 1981.

LOST HORIZON

1937 - USA - 132 MIN. - B & W - ADVENTURE MOVIE, LITERARY ADAPTATION,

DIRECTOR FRANK CAPRA (1897–1991)
SCREENPLAY ROBERT RISKIN, based on the novel of the same name by JAMES HILTON DIRECTOR OF PHOTOGRAPHY JOSEPH WALKER
EDITING GENE HAVLICK, GENE MILFORD MUSIC DIMITRI TIOMKIN PRODUCTION FRANK CAPRA for COLUMBIA PICTURES
CORPORATION.

STARRING RONALD COLMAN (Robert Conway), H. B. WARNER (Chang), JANE WYATT (Sondra),
EDWARD EVERETT HORTON (Alexander P. Lovett), JOHN HOWARD (George Conway), THOMAS MITCHELL (Henry Barnard),
ISABEL JEWELL (Gloria Stone), MARGO (Maria), SAM JAFFE (High Lama), HUGH BUCKLER (Lord Gainsford).

ACADEMY AWARDS 1937 OSCARS for BEST EDITING (Gene Havlick, Gene Milford), and BEST ART DIRECTION / SET DECORATION
(Stephen Goosson).

"A scurrying mass of bewildered humanity crashing headlong against each other, compelled by an orgy of greed and brutality."

The stakes were high. Hoping to join the ranks of Hollywood's "Big Five," Columbia Pictures put its money on Frank Capra's *Lost Horizon*, a project with a 2.5 million dollar price tag. When it was ready to be unveiled, test audiences panned the three-hour-plus opus and left Capra with no other alternative but to scrap a good third of the picture. Then, lo and behold, *Lost Horizon* opened to enthusiastic critics and prestige smiled on Columbia Pictures. Still, the response at the box office was somewhat sub-par. The reputation Capra's film enjoys today as an adventure classic actually came much later, once audiences began to see just how prophetic and alarmingly mystical the piece really was …

The story begins in the war-torn Chinese city of Baskul, where British diplomat Robert Conway (Ronald Colman) and four civilians manage to flee an angry lynch mob by plane. No sooner are they airborne than the aircraft is hijacked and the passengers find themselves about to crash-land somewhere in the snow-covered Himalayas. But rather than perishing on impact or suffering from the brutal elements, help reaches the party in the form of the friendly Mr. Chang (H. B. Warner). At his urging, the survivors journey to the secluded mountain village of Shangri-La, hidden in one of the mountain range's most fertile valleys. For hundreds of years, residents of the ancient settlement have led a peaceful existence by following the teachings of the gentle High Lama (Sam Jaffe), who upholds order from the great temple. While the outsiders initially believe themselves to have found heaven on earth, they come to suspect that the mysterious civilization is more than just coincidentally connected to their hijacking.

Much like the portentous *Things to Come* (1936), *Lost Horizon* is one of the movies of the 30s that addressed the harrowing political climate then

2

"... there is no denying the opulence of the production, the impressiveness of the sets, the richness of the costuming, the satisfying attention to large and small detail which makes Hollywood at its best such a generous entertainer." *The New York Times*

1 Hero's welcome: If this is the way the Chinese greet people they like, British diplomat Robert Conway (Ronald Colman) would hate to see how they treat their enemies.

2 Dungeons and dragons: Art Director Stephen Goosson won an Oscar for designing the Himalayan prison paradise.

3 Run that by me again: When initial test audiences responded poorly to the movie, Capra sacrificed *Lost Horizon's* framing story and its first two reels to the cutting room floor.

4 Angel eyes: One look at the Shangri-La's radiant residents and Robert Conway (right) is hypnotized.

5 They're old in them thar hills: The soft-spoken Mr. Chang (H. B. Warner) maintains his health by shielding himself from the outside world and its reprehensible ways.

"Is it ... that you fail to recognise one of your own dreams when you see it?"

Film quote: Chang (H. B. Warner)

prevailing in Europe. British writer James Hilton, who also wrote the novel on which the film is based, displays an astute ability to interpret the signs of the times, such as the scene in which the High Lama shares a haunting vision of the future with Conway. In this exchange, the sage claims to have foreseen the total destruction of human culture and heritage at the hand of war-faring nations. A former Belgian monk, he has been importing cultural artifacts from the outside world for the past 200 years, to preserve the achievements of mankind and share them with future generations. And yet despite his astounding age, this Methuselah is not immortal. He has thus chosen Conway to uphold his legacy and help turn Shangri-La into the cultural Mecca as mankind approaches the dawn of a new age.

Although Conway is a character unburdened by the hardships of the American Depression, he still has all the traits of the filmmaker's preferred style of hero: part admirable, starry-eyed idealist, part voice of reason, Ronald Colman couldn't be better as the visionary entrusted to maintain the Arcadian idyll. Needless to say, the part contains a kernel of irony that becomes a hotbed for comedy in Capra's hands. More explicitly intended to provide comic relief, however, are the sardonic paleontologist Alexander P. Lovett (Edward Everett Horton) and the crooked fugitive swindler Henry Barnard (Thomas Mitchell), whose verbal stabs at one another make for one of the film's most entertaining digressions.

To this day, *Lost Horizon* serves as a source of inspiration for numerous filmmakers. Traces of the story can be found in pictures like Steven Spielberg's *Indiana Jones and the Temple of Doom* (1984) or even in releases as modern as *Sky Captain and the World of Tomorrow* (2004), in which

6

**JAMES HILTON
(1900–1954)**

English novelist and screenwriter James Hilton wrote his first book *Catherine Herself* while still a teenager and got it published by 1920. His best-known work, *Goodbye, Mr. Chips* (1934), was adapted for the screen in the widely successful 1939 Sam Wood production of the same name. Indeed, less than four years after Hilton's 1935 arrival in Hollywood, he had already become one of the American cinema's favorite sons.

Director George Cukor's picture *Camille* (1936), starring Greta Garbo, was among the very first classics Hilton composed for the screen. By 1943, his collaborative writing effort on William Wyler's homefront melodrama *Mrs. Miniver* (1942) had won him an Oscar. It was just one of many credits in Hilton's extensive resumé that proved him a master of World War II dramas and other war-related subject matter. From 1948 to 1953, Hilton trod new waters as host of CBS radio's "Hallmark Playhouse." Despite being a diversion from his writing career, the move was indicative of the professional versatility he demonstrated as both Vice President of the Screen Writers Guild and an active member of the Academy of Motion Picture Arts and Sciences.

At the height of America's involvement in World War II, he teamed up with Frank Capra on the scripts for the propaganda series *Why We Fight* (1942–1945), a project that Hilton and many other creative minds never received credit for. Fellow sentimentalists Hilton and Capra were however linked officially by Columbia Pictures' *Lost Horizon* (1937), a Capra adaptation of Hilton's identically titled 1933 novel. Interestingly, the piece's popularity prompted United States President Franklin D. Roosevelt to introduce Hilton's term "Shangri-La" into several public addresses and the word quickly found its way into everyday conversation as a synonym for Utopia. At the age of 54, Hilton lost his life to cancer in Long Beach, California.

Jude Law goes off on his own search for the legendary village of Shangri-La. Yet none of the works that tried to emulate it could top *Lost Horizon's* Oscar-winning set design. The temple's monumental architecture astonishingly fuses Buddhist ornamentation with the functionalism of Frank Lloyd Wright and a sober organically-based objectivity, creating a harmonious whole reminiscent of Le Corbusier's Villa Savoye. Given the visionary magnitude of the set pieces and the awe-inspiring backdrops, one could feasibly cite German producer Joe May's various escapist adventures made in the 1910s and early 20s as forerunners of this Capra piece. As far as the American cinema goes, *Lost Horizon* would lay the foundation for the Hollywood action-adventure movie.

DG

7

"*Lost Horizon* can take its place with the best prestige pictures of the industry. It is also a cinch for money, but with such an overhead Columbia can call Capra a miracle man, as well as 'genius', if this one gets out from under." *Variety*

6   Airplane on the rocks: Willing to go to extremes to give *Lost Horizon* a documentary feel, Capra had his actors work on a refrigerated set. Quote: "The actors' breath MUST SHOW."

7   Sir Hillary I presume: Although known for his skill with comedy and social dramas, Capra proved to be an ace adventure filmmaker, producing some of the classic cinema's most gripping action sequences.

8   Just visiting: Conway (pictured) manages to escape Shangri-La by the skin of his teeth, while the townswoman who comes along with him succumbs to the elements once outside the city walls.

8

PÉPÉ LE MOKO
Pépé le Moko

1936/37 - FRANCE - 94 MIN. - B & W - GANGSTER MOVIE, LITERARY ADAPTATION

DIRECTOR JULIEN DUVIVIER (1896–1967)
SCREENPLAY HENRI JEANSON, ROGER D'ASHELBÉ [= HENRI LA BARTHE], JACQUES CONSTANT, JULIEN DUVIVIER, based on the novel of the same name by ROGER D'ASHELBÉ [= HENRI LA BARTHE]
DIRECTORS OF PHOTOGRAPHY JULES KRUGER, MARC FOSSARD EDITING MARGUERITE BEAUGÉ MUSIC VINCENT SCOTTO, MOHAMED YGUERBUCHEN PRODUCTION ROBERT HAKIM, RAYMOND HAKIM for PARIS FILM.

STARRING JEAN GABIN (Pépé le Moko), MIREILLE BALIN (Gaby Gould), LINE NORO (Inès), GABRIEL GABRIO (Carlos), LUCAS GRIDOUX (Inspector Slimane), FERNAND CHARPIN (Régis), SATURNIN FABRE (Le Grand Père), GILBERT GIL (Pierrot), ROGER LEGRIS (Max), MARCEL DALIO (L'Arbi).

"With you, it's like being in Paris."

Women, freedom, suicide – these three words could sum up the fate of Pépé (Jean Gabin), a professional crook whose story forms the basis for Julien Duvivier's outstanding French thriller. Ever since fleeing France, Pépé has been hiding out in the Kasbah in Algiers. Here, in the Old Town's warren of alleys and side streets, the law has no hope of apprehending him – he simply has too many informers and too many places to hide. Even Inspector Slimane (Lucas Gridoux), who sees him day in, day out, doesn't dare arrest him; for here, Pépé is the uncontested king of the criminals. Instead, Slimane cultivates Pépé's trust, meeting him every day for a drink or a falafel and a chat. Yet, although they clearly respect each other, Slimane leaves no one in any doubt that he'll never miss an opportunity to get Pépé behind bars. He circles round his prey, always waiting, always smiling: the spider and the fly. In this bizarre situation, the spectator can barely discern the boundary between good and evil.

It's Slimane who introduces the fugitive to a beautiful tourist called Gaby (Mireille Balin). At first, Pépé is only interested in her jewelry, but things change when he learns that she's from Paris – and, indeed, from the same *quartier* as he is. Just as Pépé's dealings with Slimane are governed by ideas of honor, his relationship to Gaby is marked by his hunger for freedom. Every street name she mentions strengthens his yearning for another life; after two years in the Kasbah, Pépé often feels like a tiger in a cage. "They want to jail you," says his mistress Inès (Line Noro), "but you're already locked up."

The atmospheric intensity of the Kasbah is largely the work of the set designer Jacques Krauss, who reconstructed this urban labyrinth in the

Julien Duvivier was born in Lille in 1896. After graduating from school there, he attended university for a short time before heading to Paris to study acting. Following drama school, he played a few professional roles and then turned his attention to directing, He worked as an assistant to André Antoine and eventually decided to seek employment in the film business, which he felt offered greater creative opportunities than the theater. In the 20s, he directed a large number of silent films, in genres ranging from comedy to melodrama and documentary. His first big success came in 1930 with his sound-film premiere: *David Golder* (1930/31), the story of an old Jewish financier who is abandoned by his family and friends. There followed films such as *The Red Head* (*Poil de carotte*, 1932), a study of a maltreated child, and *Behold the Man* (*Golgotha*, 1935), in which Jean Gabin played Pontius Pilate. With *They Were Five* (*La belle équipe*, 1936) and *Pépé le Moko* (1936/37), Duvivier made his mark on the French cinema of the 30s and stamped Gabin's image as a tough guy with a heart of gold. Julien Duvivier reached the pinnacle of his success with *Un Carnet de Bal* (1937), which was released under a variety of English titles, including *Christine* and *Dance of Life*. It tells the story of a young widow who resolves, out of pure nostalgia, to seek out her dance partners from her very first ball. The consequence is disillusionment: not one of those hopeful young men had made his dreams come true. After making this film, Duvivier went to Hollywood, where he was unable to repeat his European success. In the post-war period, he directed several box-office hits in France, including his two world-famous adaptations of the Don Camillo books: *The Little World of Don Camillo* (*Le petit monde de Don Camillo / Il piccolo mondo di Don Camillo*, 1952) and *The Return of Don Camillo* (*Le Retour de Don Camillo / Il ritorno di Don Camillo*, 1953). By now, however, his style seemed to belong to a bygone age. Julien Duvivier died in a car accident in 1967.

oinville studios. Combined with only a few real exterior shots and the dynamic camerawork so typical of Duvivier's films, this studio set is transformed into a vibrant Oriental metropolis. As in many French films of the era, most of the takes are longer than in the average Hollywood film, but clever editing and artful panning shots ensure that the tempo never drags. Thus, the spectator becomes an invisible gang-member, strolling through the exotic alleyways, past the chattering people on the street, up staircases and round corners, squashing up against Pépé and Inspector Slimane at a falafel stand to allow a herd of sheep to pass.

In stark contrast to these bustling street scenes are the interiors, atmospherically lit and shot from high and low angles, making the film a forerunner of film noir. The camera passes repeatedly through dark passageways, heading for a sepulchral bar or a seedy separée. One striking feature of the lighting is Duvivier's skilful use of the Kasbah's architectural peculiarities. When Pépé plays cards in the bar, for instance, his foster son Pierrot (Gilbert Gil) warns him that Régis (Fernand Charpin) is cheating: there's a point of light in his eyes, but the rest of his face is lost in the shadows. And when Inès jealously watches her Pépé talking to Gaby, we at first see the couple flirting through an arabesque window shutter; then the counter shot shows us Inès' striking face criss-crossed by the same diamond lattice. The effect is strange and disturbing. With such methods, Duvivier sustains the tension and supports the actors' performance.

Pépé le Moko is often described as one of the first French gangster films. It was unmistakably influenced by such American classics as Josef von Stern

1   Was it good for you, too? Inès (Line Noro) the gypsy and Pépé the gangster (Jean Gabin) like life to be hard and heavy.

2   White and blue-collar gangsters: Carlos (Gabriel Gabrio, right) lets his fists do the talking, whereas Pépé makes a statement with a freshly pressed suit.

3   You're a better man than I am, Gunga Din: Every day Inspector Slimane (Lucas Gridoux) crosses over into Pépé's turf to chew the fat with his rival on neutral territory.

4   Pearls before swine: The refined Gaby Gould (Mireille Balin) wastes her charms on the thugs of Paris.

berg's *Underworld* (1927), William A. Wellman's *The Public Enemy* (1931) and Howard Hawks' *Scarface* (1932). Duvivier's film also focuses on the weird communal life of the gangsters, men who hide guns in the pockets of their elegant suits. But in contrast to the denizens of Hollywood's underworld, Pépé is no action hero; he doesn't use the Kasbah for chases, bomb attacks or brutal assassinations. There is only one shoot-out in the course of the whole film, and tellingly, Pépé aims at the policemen's legs. Algiers' "King of the Underworld" is not so much a proactive hero as a man who waits patiently, and the film pays only passing attention to his criminal acts.

Duvivier dilutes the violence of the book he's adapting, and focuses instead on the atmosphere of the city and the emotions of his protagonist. Though Pépé is a man on the run from the police, he's driven in a far more essential sense by his own powerful longings. All the other men in the film pale in comparison to him and Inspector Slimane; and the women seem only to be there in order to push the men towards certain ruin. This is a scenario firmly in the tradition of the gangster movie, with its iron androcracies. It's the death of Pierrot, then, that brings the decisive change: though Pépé revenges the boy's killing, he is so shocked that he leaves the Kasbah and resolves to go to Paris with Gaby. The victory of love … In a magnificent closing sequence, Duvivier fully exploits the possibilities of the sound film: at the docks, Pépé's desperate cry of love is drowned out by the deafening drone of the ship's horn, while Gaby (who can't see him) is covering her ears in pain. Pépé is arrested, but has the last laugh – regaining his liberty by pulling a blade and taking his own life.   OK

"I cannot remember a picture which has succeeded so admirably in raising the thriller to a poetic level."

Graham Greene, in: The Spectator

SNOW WHITE AND THE SEVEN DWARFS

1937 - USA - 83 MIN. - COLOR - CARTOON, FAIRY TALE

DIRECTOR DAVID HAND (1900–1986)
SCREENPLAY TED SEARS, OTTO ENGLANDER, EARL HURD, DOROTHY ANN BLANK, RICHARD CREEDON, DICK RICKARD, MERRILL DE MARIS, WEBB SMITH, based on the fairy tale of the same name by the BROTHERS GRIMM
DIRECTOR OF PHOTOGRAPHY MAXWELL MORGAN **MUSIC** FRANK CHURCHILL, LEIGH HARLINE, PAUL J. SMITH
PRODUCTION WALT DISNEY for WALT DISNEY PICTURES.

ACADEMY AWARDS 1938 HONORARY OSCAR for A SIGNIFICANT ACHIEVEMENT IN FILMMAKING (Walt Disney).

"Magic Mirror, on the wall, who is the fairest of them all?"

Vanity has made her rotten to the core. And as queen, she has no qualms about consulting her most trusted adviser – a magic mirror – while her fair-skinned stepdaughter is away on errands more suited to a peasant. Unable to lie, mirrors are usually great conversationalists. Only hers has reminded her that her days as the land's most ravishing creature are numbered; for said stepdaughter, young Snow White, is becoming more beautiful with each passing day.

Her Majesty promptly hires a hunter to axe the competition. But he can't go through with it and, instead, urges the sweet princess to disappear into the woods, where animals guide the girl to a cottage inhabited by seven dwarfs. This is where Snow White makes a home for herself, keeping house in exchange for board and lodging, until she samples a poisoned apple. Now, only true love's kiss can break the spell of sleeping death. Luckily, Prince Charming will be only too happy to oblige …

Arguably the most beloved of all the fairy tales jotted down by German storytellers the Brothers Grimm, *Snow White and the Seven Dwarfs* is the one story everybody knows. For precisely that reason, Walt Disney chose to adapt

it into the first-ever feature-length cartoon. His hope was that audience familiarity with the material would offset the risk of relocating animation from its established place in the world of shorts to the realm of main attractions. The straightforward plot also allowed plenty of room for creative license where narrative curlicues, musical intermezzos and the curiosities of the seven dwarfs were concerned.

It was a gamble that more than paid off. The one-and-a-half million dollars it took to make *Snow White*, a sum that nearly drove Disney's studio into the ground, were instantly recouped in ticket sales. By the end of 1938, the picture had already grossed approximately eight million dollars. And this figure is just a fraction of what it has earned since, especially when factoring in the *Snow White* merchandising campaigns and royalties, which continue to bring in revenue.

It's incredible just how well the first full-length animated feature has stood the test of time. Then again, few cartoons have produced such hypnotic and surreal imagery: from Snow White's perilous journey through the forest, via the dwarfs *heigh-hoing* their way home from the diamond mines, all

"Never before has the history of cinema seen anything like Disney's *Snow White and the Seven Dwarfs* – a whole seven reels of Technicolor cartoon that provide interesting and at times genuinely compelling entertainment. The illusion is so perfect and the romance so emotional that the interaction between the characters acquires a truly human depth." *Variety*

1 With a smile and a song: *Snow White and the Seven Dwarfs*, the world's first feature-length cartoon, drew in more moviegoers than anyone imagined possible.

2 Warning: Excessive drinking can cause premature aging.

3 Fair to one and all: Snow White has an ear for all the woodland creatures and even takes time to hear the grass grow.

the way to the queen's violent metamorphosis. One can only imagine how taxing it must have been for dwarf animators like Shamus Culhane to not only make sure that the characters could march through the woods convincingly, but that each of them also had his own distinct personality, including a specific gait and set of mannerisms.

An estimated 750 people helped bring *Snow White* to life. With so many hands at work, the animators were divided into teams that handled individual characters. The result is that noticeable stylistic and qualitative differences among artists gave the film a patchwork quality — something

many critics sight as a major flaw. In particular, the naturalistic Snow White and Prince Charming seem to clash with the film's basic concept, whereas the woodland creatures read like a prototype for the cartoon animals that have distinguished the Disney screen and other animated productions ever since.

Snow White also marked the first time Disney could put his multiplane camera to the test. First implemented earlier that year for *The Old Mill*, the 70,000 dollar, 4.2-meter-tall apparatus gave cartoon animation a new degree of spatial complexity. Up to seven layers of transparencies could be

4   Someday her prince will come: Just not today.

5   With true love's kiss the spell shall break: Prince Charming saves Snow White from sleeping death with a little help from seven overjoyed admirers.

6   Dancing queen: Doc, Happy and Bashful celebrate the good times with Snow White and keep her out of harm's way.

7   Not one for small talk: Dopey doesn't have to say a word to let Snow White know that he loves her.

8   In the wee small hours of the morning: Snow White wakes up to find seven dirty old men staring her down in bed – and promptly makes them wash!

9   Just whistle while you work: The Disney animals are all too happy to help clean up Snow White's act. Oftentimes they seem more human than either she or Prince Charming.

individually lit and placed during filming, which lent sequences like the evil queen's midnight departure from her castle an unprecedented illusory depth.

While *Snow White and the Seven Dwarfs* may not be as crisp as its successor *Pinocchio* (1940) or as visionary as *Fantasia* (1940), it was nonetheless Disney's most daring undertaking and the greatest triumph of his career. Without it, the cartoon medium would have undoubtedly embarked on a very different course. Indeed, *Snow White and the Seven Dwarfs* is just as much a cinematic landmark as D. W. Griffith's *The Birth of a Nation* (1915) or Orson Welles' *Citizen Kane* (1941). Disney left that year's Academy Award ceremonies with his hands full, having been presented with one large and seven miniature statuettes for "a significant screen innovation which has charmed millions and pioneered a great new entertainment field."   SH

THE BIRTH OF ANIMATION English physiologist Peter Mark Roget (1779–1869) is credited with having discovered that minute differences in a series of still images will be perceived as movement if shown in a logical sequence at a rapid rate. Whether or not this illusion is created by means of drawings or photography is
relatively insignificant; either way the product can be categorized as a 'motion picture.' In 1877, Emile Reynaud used his praxinoscope to produce
the first of these for a cinematic medium and the cartoon was born. At the turn of the 20th century, James Stuart Blackton impressed audiences by
using a stop-motion technique to combine hand-drawn sketches with photographs of three-dimensional objects. In 1914, Earl Hurd invented the so-
called cel animation technique, allowing individual elements to be painted on transparencies placed atop one another. This would serve as the basis
for the multiplane cameras invented at Walt Disney's studio, which could film and light up to seven separate layers of flat artwork simultaneously.
Disney had already proven himself an industry pioneer back in 1928, when he completed his first sound cartoon and secured the exclusive rights to
the Technicolor three-color process.
While *Snow White* may have been the first full-length cartoon feature animated with moving illustrations, director Lotte Reiniger specialized in an
alternative form of animation that arguably beat Walt to the punch: made entirely of cut-out silhouettes, the hour-long *Adventures of Prince Achmed*
(*Die Abenteuer des Prinzen Achmed*, 1923–1926) reached audiences in 1926.
In 1951, a group of innovative technicians from Boston's MIT gave U.S. TV audiences a first taste of a craze that would eventually take the cartoon
by storm: computer animation.

THINK FAST, MR. MOTO

1937 - USA - 67 MIN. - B & W - DETECTIVE CAPER

DIRECTOR NORMAN FOSTER (1900–1976)
SCREENPLAY NORMAN FOSTER, HOWARD ELLIS SMITH, CHARLES KANYON, based on the serial installment of the same name by JOHN P. MARQUAND DIRECTOR OF PHOTOGRAPHY HARRY JACKSON EDITING ALEX TROFFEY
MUSIC SAMUEL KAYLIN PRODUCTION SOL M. WURTZEL for 20TH CENTURY FOX.

STARRING PETER LORRE (Mr. Moto), VIRGINIA FIELD (Gloria Danton), THOMAS BECK (Bob Hitchings), SIG RUMAN (Nicholas Marloff), MURRAY KINNELL (Mr. Joseph Wilkie), LOTUS LONG (Lela Liu), JOHN ROGERS (Carson), GEORGE COOPER (Muggs Blake), J. CARROL NAISH (Adram), GEORGE HASSELL (Mr. Hitchings).

"Strange people, these Americans."

Japanese detective Mr. Moto would have never gotten his Hollywood green card had it not been for the popularity of Charlie Chan. Having struck cinematic gold in the 1930s with the series of pictures featuring the Chinese snoop, 20th Century Fox was eager to expand its share of Asian private eyes. Two elements were of major concern as development proceeded for the new protagonist: first, the audience needed to readily identify the established Chan plot format; second, the fresh new face in crime-fighting, to be based on a character appearing in a *Saturday Evening Post* serial by John P. Marquand, needed to differ significantly from Chan in terms of personality and modus operandi.

It followed that Mr. Moto was anything but the family man that Swedish actor Warner Oland had made Charlie Chan out to be, and instead took the guise of a shifty loner. The audience knew very little about his background and habits – except that he enjoyed drinking milk. He was patient and reserved when dealing with his peers, yet could bump off an opponent without a tinge of remorse. In *Think Fast, Mr. Moto*, for instance, he hurls one of his

unsavory enemies overboard during a pleasure cruise, then cynically speculates as to the man's whereabouts the following day. Moto's tactics attest to a degree of physical fitness far superior to the borderline sedate Charlie Chan. Furthermore, the Japanese master of disguise versed in Ju-Jitsu could handle a gun more competently than most people can tie their shoes.

The role itself presented pros and cons for actor Peter Lorre, who had suffered from years of typecasting after bowling over audiences as a homicidal maniac in Fritz Lang's *M* (*M – Eine Stadt sucht einen Mörder*, 1931). Critics were especially curious to see what Lorre would do with the role; for much more than being a cold-blooded assassin, Moto was first and foremost a likable guy. Lorre, however, made no secret about how indifferent he felt about playing yet another 'exotic' character. And, considering the usual quality of B-movies, the actual content would be thin at best.

'Incoherent' is more like it. The first of what became a series of eight pictures, *Think Fast, Mr. Moto* focuses on glamorous locales and personalities while fumbling through a plot about a smuggling ring that hides dia-

monds and narcotics in various East Asian antiques being shipped to the U.S. The audience is often left guessing who's doing what where and why, with the actual story proving to be little more than an excuse for prolonged suspense. In fact, the viewer is neither exactly clear about who Mr. Moto really is nor what prompts him to act as he does until shortly prior to the film's conclusion.

Aside from Lorre himself, whose layered performance must have exceeded the writer's wildest dreams, the saving grace of this film is a cavalcade of memorable villains. These auxiliary characters adhere to the character formulas utilized by the Charlie Chan flicks with at least one terribly suspicious eccentric and a seemingly innocent party who is ultimately unmasked as the guilty culprit by the detective. Subsequently, Mr. Wilkie

"In fairness to J. P. Marquand, it should be said that the screen story follows his original mystery serial along only the most general sort of outlines. Mr. Lorre is certainly the man for Mr. Marquand's Mr. Moto; maybe Mr. Lorre and Alfred Hitchcock can get together on the next Moto assignment." *The New York Times*

1 Don't underestimate me: Mastermind Nicolas Marloff (Sig Ruman, left) often doesn't notice that Mr. Moto (Peter Lorre) is around, let alone think that he could pose a threat to his double dealings.

2 Huey, Dewey and Screwy: Mr. Moto sobers up a couple of American practical jokers with a few martial arts moves.

3 Never misses a deadline: Even when shopping for antiques, Mr. Moto never fails to find a fresh corpse.

4 Whatever floats your boat: Lovers Bob Hitchings (Thomas Beck) and Gloria Danton (Virginia Field) may have some exotic tastes, but they don't include being tied up by third parties.

(Murray Kinnell), the utterly average representative of an American liner based in Shanghai, is exposed as a veritable 'Dr. Evil,' whereas German-born actor Sig Ruman – a.k.a. 'Concentration Camp' Ehrhardt from Ernst Lubitsch's anti-Nazi farce *To Be or Not to Be* (1942) – is perfect as the man believed to be a criminal mastermind. Ruman's performance as smuggler Nicholas Marloff in *Think Fast, Mr. Moto* congenially fuses an element of danger with comic know-how. A scene featuring Marloff playing a game of poker with his right-hand man Max sums up his con-artist disposition better than any adjectives might: while Max believes to be holding an unbeatable full-house with three jacks and two queens, Marloff trumps him with a full house of three queens and two jacks – leaving his dumbfounded opponent to wonder how five queens and five jacks made it into the deck.   LP

NORMAN FOSTER (1900–1976)

Richmond, Indiana native Norman Hoeffer started out in show business as a stage actor before switching to the cinema with Millard Webb's *Gentlemen of the Press* (1929). For many years thereafter, 'Foster' seemed to have his foot in the door at nearly every studio in Hollywood, but remained unable to land a role that could launch him to stardom. This career roadblock prompted him to assume the director's chair for the melodrama *I Cover Chinatown* (1936). From there, Foster agreed to shoot a planned series of B capers about Japanese detective Mr. Moto for 20th Century Fox producer Sol M. Wurtzel as a means of establishing himself in Hollywood.

Think Fast, Mr. Moto (1937) was a hit with audiences and Foster stayed on board the project until 1939, directing and co-writing five further installments of the eight pictures in which Peter Lorre played the protagonist from the Orient. When Fox decided to discontinue both the Moto and Charlie Chan series in response to wartime America's sudden xenophobia regarding Asians, Foster was in immediate need of finding a new type of project that could re-root him within the industry. The answer to his dilemma presented itself in not one, but rather a number of genres. Indeed, Foster went on to shoot everything from Westerns like *Rachel and the Stranger* (1948) to film noir pieces including *Kiss the Blood Off My Hands* (1948), and even had a long-standing engagement at Disney (1954–1961) as a director of live action movies and television.

But Foster wasn't destined to become one of the Hollywood Dream Factory's premier filmmakers. His pictures were simply too impersonal for him to make the grade. Beyond the Mr. Moto series, his name will be forever associated with the noir espionage piece *Journey Into Fear* (1943). Ironically, however, Foster entered the project as a replacement hitter for auteur Orson Welles, who had not only adapted Eric Ambler's novel for the screen with favorite co-writer Joseph Cotten, but also left his indelible mark on the film's direction.

5 Romance against the railing: Bob discovers that being heir to an immense fortune can work wonders when it comes to dating.

6 Chariots of Feng Shui: Mr. Moto doesn't need state-of-the-art technology to beat the bad guys to the punch.

"Lorre's new characterization, that of an educated Japanese merchant and amateur sleuth, gets away from the grim villainy of his previous film efforts. An air of mystery surrounds his activities for story purposes but he's developed humanly. He no longer is a bogey man. When he smiles, it is not a wry, warped grimace. The new Peter Lorre probably will be rated as a find by others who heretofore knew him only as a dyed-in-wool villain." *Variety*

"Aren't they just sweet?"
"Sure, but only from a distance."

Dead End's opening shot of the glorious New York skyline is deceptive: the camera quickly pans down window fronts and fire escapes to arrive in one of the countless dirty dead-end streets by the East River. It's a dreary area, but this hasn't stopped some of the wealthier New Yorkers from getting their slice of waterfront life. Elegant apartment buildings rise above the slums so new residents can enjoy the view, while the surrounding brick houses are still home to the poverty and despair of the Depression. The neighborhood consists of two social strata that are worlds apart, providing the setting for three intertwined stories – stories of crime, love and hope.

First up we have "Baby Face" Martin (Humphrey Bogart), a notorious killer wanted all over America. Baby Face has recently returned to the slums of his childhood to revisit his mother (Marjorie Martin) and first love (Claire Trevor). Then there's his old sidekick Dave (Joel McCrea), who has grown into a good-looking man and an ambitious architect. If he could, Dave would demolish the whole area and rebuild it from scratch, but he's just not getting the contracts. Although his neighbor, the working girl Drina (Sylvia Sidney), is in love with him, Dave has his sights set higher, on the rich but elusive Kay (Wendy Barrie). Taking center stage, however, is the hood's teenage gang, headed by Drina's brother Tommy (Billy Halop). These bored kids spend their lives in the street, dipping into the River when they're hot and talking trash to anyone who'll listen.

The three plot lines weaving through the film share a single critical perspective. In contrast to the then prevalent belief that crime was the sole responsibility of the criminal – who is justly punished for his deeds with a prison sentence – *Dead End* puts the blame squarely on social conditions. Teens who grow up the East River slums are almost inevitably caught up in street crime. Drina will always fail in her attempts to keep her brother out of trouble; when one of the wealthy residents tries to get his hands on Tommy after his son was attacked by the gang, the boy stabs him with a knife – more out of fear than anger. As a consequence, he is facing arrest and relocation to a reformatory, which would spell the start of a criminal career proper. Even Baby Face Martin was a decent guy once, as his childhood friend Dave remembers. Dave decided against a life of crime long ago, finished school and went to college. But he never managed to beat poverty, and he is full of sym-

2

1   Road to nowhere: Producer Samuel Goldwyn wanted director William Wyler to make the slums look
less like a Dead End, but the filmmaker refused to
clean up the streets for the audience's sake.

2   Holmes and the Baker Street Boys: "Baby Face"
Martin (Humphrey Bogart) grooms young neighborhood gangsters in street smarts and survival.

3   Water under the bridge: Can't wash away the
sewage, dirt and grime.

pathy for the kids in his neighborhood: "What chance do they stand in a place like this? They've got to fight for their playgrounds, they've got to fight for every bit of bread. They've got to fight for everything!"

In 1930s Hollywood, social criticism like that usually provided ample grounds for the censors to ban a film from general release. *Dead End* overcame that hurdle thanks to the diplomatic actions of producer Samuel Goldwyn, who toned down the plot and the action at many crucial turns. Baby Face is thus never seen to kill a cop, and the syphilis afflicting his ex-lover is never mentioned by name. Director William Wyler was not allowed to film on location, as this would have shown the misery of the slums too realistically; instead,

Goldwyn had the eponymous dead-end street rebuilt in his studio for the grand sum of $100,000 and personally ensured that the set never looked too dirty.

The fact that the film still managed to convey a sense of authenticity is largely attributable to the cinematography, particularly the long focal lengths employed by cameraman Gregg Toland. Wyler's illusion of slum realism was reinforced by a constant whirl of background activity. Extras would be posing on the street corners, taking out the trash, closing their curtains – a mosaic of movement to animate the street. Wyler's camera perspectives are usually very detached, so medium and long shots dominate throughout. Visual drama is nevertheless granted thanks to Wyler's careful composition of the shots,

---

**SAMUEL GOLDWYN
(1882–1974)**

"I was a rebel, a lone wolf. My pictures were my own. I financed them myself and answered solely to myself." As fitting as Goldwyn's self-assessment may be, it very much understates the achievements of this extraordinary man who was born in 1882 in Warsaw, Poland, and buried in Beverly Hills in 1974. His career as one of the first independent producers of the U.S. film industry to be successful outside of the major studios is the story of a self-made man living the American Dream.

Samuel Goldfish, as he was then known, arrived in the U.S. at the age of 16 and started working part-time at a glove-making factory. Within a few years, the ambitious Goldwyn had already become a part owner in the company. It was only by chance and in the later stages of his life that he was actually introduced to the film business – by his brother-in-law Jesse L. Lasky. Unlike many of his producer colleagues, Goldwyn was interested not only in the financial side of the business, but also in the marketing, casting, and the quality control. After going through several partnerships, a stubborn Goldwyn decided to go solo – he opened his own studios on Santa Monica Boulevard.

Box-office hits like *Wuthering Heights* (1939) and William Wyler's award-winning *The Best Years of Our Lives* (1946) were produced here; Samuel Goldwyn believed in quality, not quantity, always selecting the best actors and directors for his films. His annual output of films was low but widely acclaimed. In Hollywood, the "Goldwyn touch" soon became synonymous with productions that were both intelligent and entertaining.

"Samuel Goldwyn's screen transcription of *Dead End*, as it came to the Rivoli Theatre last night, deserves a place among the important motion pictures of 1937 for its all-out and well-presented reiteration of the social protest." *The New York Times*

4 Schoolmarm: Drina (Sylvia Sidney) does her best to steer brother Tommy (Billy Halop) away from vice, but the kid is unwilling to take a lesson from his big sister.

5 Swimming upstream: By expressing a belief in Middle American values, Drina and Dave (Joel McCrea) make themselves unpopular in their own neighborhood.

6 All wet: Will these kids still want to be treated like men when they get into hot water with the law?

evident for example in his arrangement of the streetkid characters among the planks and fire ladders of the set. Wyler's idiosyncratic way of staging the cast, a style the French film critic André Bazin described as "styleless," is strong and subtle, and provides a wonderful framework for the film's story-line and dialogs. The gang slang delivered by the youth actors impressed audiences greatly, sounding surprisingly authentic despite scriptwriter Lillian Hellman's many grammatical corrections. In fact the responses were so pos-

itive that the *Dead End* ensemble of teens, already a hit in the stage production, was re-cast in several other films.

The real star of the film, however, remains Humphrey Bogart, in one of his first gangster roles as pensive killer Baby Face Martin. His surgically altered face may suit his nickname, but ironically, it makes him unrecognizable even to his friends. Together with his old face, Martin seems to have lost his penchant for crime. "You must've changed more on the inside than on the

7 Empty nest: Mrs. Martin (Marjorie Main) disowns her son and robs him of all hope. Director William

Wyler often used stairs in his films to play up the drama of a turning point.

8 Pecking order: The law-abiding citizen on the left is the lowest walk of life in this neighborhood.

outside," concludes fellow gangster Hunk (Allen Jenkins) when Baby Face tells him that he's stopped caring about money. Obviously, the facelift – an attempt to throw the police off his trail – has deeply unsettled Martin. Looking for mental peace, the killer has returned home to seek out his mother and old girlfriend. The mother, however, slaps Martin straight in his altered face when he visits and disowns him on the spot. Set in the downtrodden staircase of the parental home, this is a seminal film noir scene. Martin's former girlfriend Francey is delighted to see the gangster and welcomes her long-lost lover with open arms. Sadly, she has turned into a disease-ridden prostitute and Martin cannot picture a future together with her. Rejected, repelled and disillusioned, he re-embraces crime in a blind rage, provoking his own death in the process. In the classic gangster shoot-out between Martin and Dave at the end, Wyler once more evokes the vivid authenticity of the depicted milieu with a number of masterfully composed crowd scenes; in comparison, the closing happy-end of Dave and Drina – united at last – seems like a mere nod to Hollywood convention. OK

"Wyler's direction is faultless." *Variety*

THE GRAND ILLUSION
La Grande Illusion

1937 - FRANCE - 114 MIN. - B & W - DRAMA, WAR FILM

DIRECTOR JEAN RENOIR (1894–1979)
SCREENPLAY CHARLES SPAAK, JEAN RENOIR DIRECTOR OF PHOTOGRAPHY CHRISTIAN MATRAS EDITING MARGUERITE RENOIR
MUSIC JOSEPH KOSMA PRODUCTION FRANK ROLLMER, ALBERT PINKOVITCH for R. A. C. – RÉALISATIONS D'ART
CINÉMATOGRAPHIQUE.

STARRING JEAN GABIN (Maréchal), PIERRE FRESNAY (Capt. de Boeldieu), ERICH VON STROHEIM (Capt. von Rauffenstein),
DITA PARLO (Elsa), MARCEL DALIO (Lt. Rosenthal), JULIEN CARETTE (Cartier, the actor), GASTON MODOT (The Engineer),
JEAN DASTÉ (The Teacher), JACQUES BECKER (An English Officer), GEORGES PÉCLET (A French Soldier).

"There's the border, designed by men – but nature doesn't give a damn!"

Captain de Boeldieu (Pierre Fresnay) and Lieutenant Maréchal (Jean Gabin) – the former an aristocrat, the latter a proletarian – are shot down in a plane during World War I. Captured and imprisoned in a German POW camp, the two French soldiers find themselves amongst a mixed bag of compatriots who form a real community despite their differences. Their solidarity is strongest in the shared enterprise of digging a tunnel; but before it can be used as an escape route, the men are transferred to a different camp. Following the failure of further escape attempts, Maréchal and de Boeldieu eventually end up imprisoned in a castle, where the commanding officer, Captain von Rauffenstein (Erich von Stroheim), immediately pays his respects to his fellow aristocrat. But instead of taking the opportunity to enjoy the privileges of rank, Boeldieu resolves to help Maréchal and his Jewish comrade Rosenthal (Marcel Dalio) in yet another bid for freedom. By creating a distraction, he confuses the guards and forces von Rauffenstein to shoot him. As de Boeldieu dies, Maréchal and Rosenthal make good their escape.

When *La Grande Illusion* premiered in 1937, a new world war was already in the air. Jean Renoir's film didn't just hit a nerve with the French public; it also attracted the attention of politicians all over Europe. The movie's pacifist stance led to its being banned in the Fascist countries, and Germany's Propaganda Minister Goebbels went so far as to call it "Cinematic Enemy No. 1." In the U.S., however, Franklin D. Roosevelt vehemently defended the movie, saying that every democrat should see it. In fact, *La Grande Illusion* is one of the few anti-war films that truly deserves to be called great, not least because it keeps its distance from the stereotypes and the all-too-easy spectacle of the battlefront. Renoir refused to subject his audience to an orgy of "thrilling" bloodshed; and just as he declined to exploit the spectacle of war, he was also only marginally interested in the story's potential for suspense. The escape scenario intrigued him for another reason: it gave him an opportunity to share his perspective on the world – a world in which nations and the conflicts between them

seem merely arbitrary, and in which the real barriers are those between classes.

Thus, Renoir arranges the microcosm of the prison camp as a kind of cross-section of society. Alongside Maréchal and de Boeldieu, this enforced community includes an engineer, a somewhat naive schoolteacher, a Jewish banker's son, and an actor. What's astonishing is that one hardly notices how schematic this arrangement is. On the contrary: the ensemble is refreshingly lively and absolutely credible – even when the film is emphasizing the subtle signs by which the men's social ranking is made manifest. The characters are never reduced to mere types or given crude psychological motivations. Renoir leaves the actors time and space enough to do their work, and if the performances sometimes seem exaggerated, then this too

"Jean Renoir tells his story with an almost unbelievable sense of balance. There are no monsters in the ranks of soldiers, not even among the Germans. All of them are – to a certain extent – the victims of their particular circumstances ... Renoir focuses more on the differences between social classes than on differences between nationalities. A man's way of yawning tells us more about him than his uniform, or the fact that he wears white gloves." *die tageszeitung*

1 Am I seeing things? Nazi propaganda minister Joseph Goebbels detested *The Grand Illusion* for allowing a regular working-class guy like Maréchal (Jean Gabin, left) to befriend the son of an affluent Jewish banker (Marcel Dalio). Goebbels confiscated the film's print as soon as Germany occupied France.

2 It takes all kinds: War proves to be the great social equalizer when a commoner, an aristocrat, a black man and a Jew find themselves on equal footing at a prison camp.

3 You and who's army: Rather than assuming the off-screen command of *The Grand Illusion*, actor-director Erich von Stroheim settles for calling the shots in the role of Capt. von Rauffenstein and graces the cinema with one of his finest performances.

4 No such thing as a free lunch: *Grand Illusion* director Jean Renoir would never have been able to secure his producer had he not sparked French star Jean Gabin's interest in the project first.

as its reasons. It's one of the mysteries of Renoir that his obvious sympathy for the art of acting is precisely the means by which life itself enters his films. So, although *La Grande Illusion* is regarded as a classic of cinematic realism, it does have a peculiarly larger-than-life quality, and yet it never descends into cliché. Renoir can indicate the absurdity of war through various grotesque situations without ever disrupting the rhythm of the film.

In one scene, for example, a soldier tries on a suit of women's clothes for a stage appearance – and his comrades respond to this feeble imitation of femininity with an embarrassed silence.

There is one surprisingly melodramatic thread in the film: the relationship between Rauffenstein and de Boeldieu. Renoir directs it like a love story with a tragic ending. When the Frenchman dies of his bullet wound, th

5 No tongues: French soldier Maréchal and German
Fräulein Elsa (Dita Parlo) communicate through
glances and body language.

6 Take the bait: Capt. de Boeldieu (Pierre Fresnay)
diverts the guards' attentions so that his friends
can escape unscathed.

7 Put a spike in my vein: Jean Renoir depicts the
friendship between bluebloods Rauffenstein and
de Boeldieu much like a tragic love story.

8 Wash my feet: In *Grand Illusion*, actors like
Carette, Dalio, Modot and Gabin demonstrate
their grandeur in front of the camera.

German places a flower on his lifeless body. It is the only flower in the whole
castle. This pathos-laden gesture is not merely Renoir's tribute to the actor
Erich von Stroheim, one of the great film directors of the silent era, but also
signifies the feeling for social class that links men across national boundaries.

As in *The Rules of the Game* (*La Règle du jeu*, 1939), Renoir depicts the
aristocracy as a species heading for extinction – while other classes remain.

And when Maréchal, the metalworker, and Rosenthal, the Jewish *grand bourgeois*, trudge side-by-side through the snow towards Switzerland, it's no accident that we are reminded of the famous finale of Chaplin's *Modern Times*
(1936). For this odd couple, it seems, there is no room in cold reality; their
friendship is an illusion, but a great and beautiful illusion.

JH

"From the first image to the last, the picture not only sustains but intensifies its grip on the audience. The film is 'orchestrated,' conducted, and we are left with an extraordinary impression of a realism that is powerful and compelling, stripped of any vestige of classicism and orthodoxy." *Cinémonde*

MARCEL DALIO
(1900–1983)

Small, dark, mercurial and elegant, Marcel Dalio seemed predestined for roles such as the Jewish banker's son Rosenthal in *The Grand Illusion* (*La Grande Illusion*, 1937). Yet Dalio, born in Paris to a Romanian Jewish family, was too good an actor to be typecast as he was. In *The Rules of the Game* (*La Règle du jeu*, 1939), another of Renoir's masterpieces, he gave a brilliant performance as the vain but sensitive aristocrat Robert de la Cheyniest. Marcel Dalio was one of the most instantly recognizable actors in the French cinema of the 30s, appearing in famous films such as Julien Duvivier's *Pépé le Moko* (1936/37) and Robert Siodmak's *Mollenard / Capitaine Corsaire* (1937), yet only *The Rules of the Game* provided him with a truly important leading role. In 1940, he fled France when the Germans invaded, and this undoubtedly saved his life: the Nazis even used his portrait for their anti-Semitic propaganda. Dalio went to Hollywood, where he suffered the fate of many immigrants from the European film industry. As a supporting actor in anti-Nazi films, he was generally cast as a cultivated Frenchman with a charming accent. Thus, he appeared alongside Humphrey Bogart as the croupier in Michael Curtiz's *Casablanca* (1942) and as the proprietor of a bar in Howard Hawks' *To Have and Have Not* (1944). After the war, Dalio worked on both sides of the Atlantic, but he rarely found films that did justice to his talent. Nonetheless, Dalio was capable of wryly parodying his own image, as he did in the Louis de Funès vehicle *The Adventures of Rabbi Jacob* (*Les Aventures de Rabbi Jacob*, 1973).

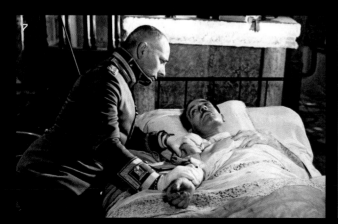

THE ADVENTURES OF ROBIN HOOD

1938 - USA - 102 MIN. - COLOR - ADVENTURE MOVIE

DIRECTORS MICHAEL CURTIZ (1888–1962), WILLIAM KEIGHLEY (1889–1984)
SCREENPLAY NORMAN REILLY RAINE, SETON I. MILLER **DIRECTORS OF PHOTOGRAPHY** SOL POLITO, TONY GAUDIO **EDITING** RALPH DAWSON
MUSIC ERICH WOLFGANG KORNGOLD **PRODUCTION** HAL B. WALLIS for WARNER BROS., FIRST NATIONAL PICTURES INC.

STARRING ERROL FLYNN (Robin Hood), OLIVIA DE HAVILLAND (Maid Marian), BASIL RATHBONE (Sir Guy of Gisbourne),
CLAUDE RAINS (Prince John), PATRICK KNOWLES (Will Scarlett), EUGENE PALLETTE (Friar Tuck), ALAN HALE (Little John),
MELVILLE COOPER (Sheriff of Nottingham), IAN HUNTER (King Richard the Lionheart), UNA O'CONNOR (Bess).

ACADEMY AWARDS 1938 OSCARS for BEST MUSIC (Erich Wolfgang Korngold), BEST EDITING (Ralph Dawson),
and BEST ART DIRECTION (Carl Jules Weyl).

"You've come to Nottingham once too often!"

Imagine James Cagney in the role of Robin Hood. The audacity and impudence of the character would perfectly suit Cagney's Irish-American 'tough guy' persona, but would he be convincing as the noble and visionary English freedom fighter we associate with Robin Hood? It's difficult to picture Cagney as the elegant hero of a cloak-and-dagger drama, but believe it or not, he was Warner Bros.' first choice for the role when they tried to make *The Adventures of Robin Hood* in 1935.

Australian-born Errol Flynn, on the other hand, was already an established capacity in the field. Having celebrated his first big on-screen success in the title role of *Captain Blood* (1935), a pirate film directed by Michael Curtiz, Flynn epitomized the figure of the swashbuckler. With his good looks, athletic physique and stage presence, it wasn't long before he was Warner Bros.' most popular action star. Seeing that Cagney had fallen out with the studio, Flynn was the obvious choice for the role of Robin Hood.

The first screenplay for the film, written by author and director Rowland V. Lee, saw the characters speaking an especially lyrical and antiquated language. While very poetic, Lee's interpretation of the classic story did not meet

with much sympathy at Warner Bros; Seton I. Miller and Norman Reilly Raine were commissioned to write a new screenplay. The producers wanted to see action, and plenty of it. The basic plot outline of the resulting script was lifted from the Sir Walter Scott classic *Ivanhoe* – the Robin Hood story set against the backdrop of a bloody conflict between the Normans and the Saxons in England following the capture of King Richard the Lionheart by Leopold of Austria, and the usurpation of the throne by Richard's treacherous brother, Prince John. A Robin Hood operetta from the 19th century provided the second strand of the story, which sees Robin competing with the villainous Sir Guy of Gisbourne for the hand of the fair Maid Marian.

Shooting of the ambitious production – at two million dollars Warner's most expensive to date – began in September 1937 with a spurt of on-location filming to capture the Sherwood Forest scenes in Bidwill Park, Chico, California. However when the film team, directed by William Keighley, returned to Hollywood in November, the producers decided to drop him, claiming his action scenes were insufficiently spectacular. This was to be remedied by Michael Curtiz, a filmmaker renowned for his dynamic directing techniques

Marian and her merry man: Maid Marian (Olivia de Havilland) loves reaping the emotional benefits of Robin's (Errol Flynn) pillaging.

2 Seven with one blow: Robin Hood's marksmanship gives rich men a heart attack.

3 Don't come knocking: Robin Hood has a sure-fire way of keeping solicitors out of the castle.

Curtiz replaced the former Directooor of Photography Tony Gaudio with Sol Polito, who captured his footage in the intensely saturated hues of Technicolor. Curtiz directed all of the film's studio scenes. He is further credited for the climactic archery competition, filmed in Busch Gardens in Pasadena, as well as other exterior shots used to supplement and liven up Keighley's footage. A number of additional scenes that did not feature the lead actors were filmed by William Dieterle and by stunt action expert B. Reeves Eason.

Amazingly, there are no perceptible rifts in style between the different directors' shots – proof of the excellent craftsmanship and sophisticated division of labor in the classic Hollywood studio system. Indeed it's difficult to imagine how *Robin Hood* could have been improved at all. The film wonderfully juxtaposes its impertinent comic elements – such as the scenes where Robin first meets thickset Little John (Alan Hale) and ever-hungry Friar Tuck (Eugene Pallette) – with the engaging love story of Robin and Marian. Viewers found the romantic element of the film particularly captivating as the character of Marian (Olivia de Havilland) is assigned an active and dramatic role in Robin's struggle for justice, rather than being relegated to a passive love interest.

"Few storybooks have been more brilliantly brought to life, page for page, chapter for chapter, derring-do for derring-do than this full-colored recounting of the fabulous deeds of legend's arch-archer, Sir Robin of Locksley." *The New York Times*

OLIVIA DE HAVILLAND

According to Olivia de Havilland, her acting career can be divided into two stages: the seven years from 1935–1943, which she spent under contract to Warner Bros. – starring alongside Errol Flynn in eight movies, as well as in many other parts – and the years after 1945, when she was no longer bound by a studio contract, and able to pick her own, frequently more interesting roles.

De Havilland's career in film began in 1935, when she was offered the role of Hermia in William Dieterle and Max Reinhardt's screen adaptation of Shakespeare's *A Midsummer Night's Dream*. The actress, born in 1916 in Tokyo to British parents, had previously played the same part in a Reinhardt stage production. The stunning nineteen-year-old soon became one of Warner Bros.' most sought-after starlets, but she quickly tired of her roles – more often than not, de Havilland was cast as the pretty-but-passive love interest of the male lead in Westerns and cloak-and-dagger films. One of Olivia de Havilland's best roles in the Warner Bros. years was that of Melanie in Victor Fleming's *Gone with the Wind* (1939) opposite the more assertive, but also more unsettled Scarlett O'Hara. Not surprisingly, she literally had to beg Jack Warner to be allowed to take part in Selznick's production. The contractual relationship between de Havilland and Warner ended in 1943 with a protracted legal battle, in which the actress fought against some of the more binding obligations that came with the standard seven-year contracts issued in Hollywood. She won the case and gained unprecedented artistic independence.

De Havilland was not allowed to work during the legal proceedings, which took three years, but once she was back in front of the camera, her career soared. De Havilland increasingly focused on complex and challenging characters and was awarded two Oscars – one for her portrayal of a mother who lets go of her child in Mitchell Leisen's *To Each His Own* (1946), and the other for her role as the hapless victim of a dowry hunter in the screen adaptation of Henry James' *The Heiress* (1949, directed by William Wyler).

In the latter stages of her career, de Havilland was also able to explore the darker aspects of her characters: she received critical acclaim for her double role as a good and evil twin sister in Robert Siodmak's psychological thriller *The Dark Mirror* (1946) as well as for her portrayal of a psychiatric patient in Anatole Litvak's *The Snake Pit* (1948). Olivia de Havilland moved to Paris in the late 1950s. After 1960, she only sporadically starred in feature films.

The film's most striking feature is undoubtedly its mass of breathtaking action sequences. Errol Flynn alone has five extensive action scenes, including Robin's escape from the Castle of Nottingham and the final duel with Sir Guy of Gisbourne (Basil Rathbone). With its dynamic interplay of light and shadow, this last scene is especially characteristic of Michael Curtiz' bold cinematography.

It was a stroke of scriptwriting genius to pit Robin Hood against not one but three adversaries – the smooth and slippery Prince John (Claude Rains), who hides his rotten morals behind his elegant mannerisms; Sir Guy, who takes care of the convincingly staged physical attacks on Robin's life (Basil Rathbone was known as one of Hollywood's best fencers); and the boastful yet cowardly Sheriff of Nottingham (Melville Cooper), who provides the necessary comic relief.

Robin Hood as we know him would be inconceivable without the vibrant score of renowned Austrian composer Erich Wolfgang Korngold, who assigned highly recognizable signature melodies and motifs to the film's main characters. Initially, the composer had rejected the studio's offer to write the soundtrack, claiming he did not want to provide mere musical illustrations for an action movie. However, when Austria was annexed by Nazi Germany, Korngold was forced into exile. In his chosen new homeland of America, he did finally accept the Warner Bros. offer – and received an Oscar for his pains. On the subject of *The Adventures of Robin Hood*, which has become one of the milestones in the history of cinema, Korngold had but one thing to say: "Robin Hood saved my life."

LP

6

"The film is done in the grand manner of silent day spectacles with sweep and breadth of action, swordplay and hand-to-hand battles between Norman and Saxon barons. Superlative on the production side." *Variety*

4   Standing room only: Prince John (Claude Rains, left) and Sir Guy (Basil Rathbone) think that they can capture Robin Hood if Maid Marian will agree to perform a venomous act.

5   I dub thee: King Richard (Ian Hunter) proves he is all heart by knighting Robin.

6   Guess who's coming to dinner? Robin, however, passes on a second helping.

7   Horse sense: Robin enters an archery tournament in disguise to humiliate Prince John and satisfy his vanity in one fell swoop.

ALEXANDER NEVSKY

Aleksandr Nevskiy

1938 - USSR - 108 MIN. - B & W - HISTORICAL DRAMA

DIRECTOR SERGEI M. EISENSTEIN (1898–1948)
SCREENPLAY SERGEI M. EISENSTEIN, PYOTR PAVLENKO DIRECTOR OF PHOTOGRAPHY EDOUARD TISSÉ
EDITING ESFIR TOBAK, SERGEI M. EISENSTEIN MUSIC SERGEI PROKOFIEV PRODUCTION I. BAKAR for MOSFILM.

STARRING NIKOLAI CHERKASOV (Prince Alexander Nevsky), ANDREI ABRIKOSOV (Gavrilo Oleksich),
DMITRI ORLOV (Ignat, the Master Armourer), VARVARA MASSALITINOVA (Amelfa Timofeevna),
VERA IVASHOVA (Olga, a Maid of Novgorod), ALEKSANDRA DANILOVA (Vasilisa), NIKOLAI ARSKY (Domash),
SERGEI BLINNIKOV (Tverdilo), LEV FENIN (Archbishop), NAUM ROGOZHIN (Monk).

"He who comes to us sword in hand, by the sword shall perish."

The Russian national hero Alexander Nevsky was seventeen when his father appointed him Prince of Novgorod in 1236. Four years later came his first great challenge, when a Swedish army invaded Russia from the north. Alexander confronted the Nordic forces, which significantly outnumbered his own, by the Neva River, and defeated them. For this display of bravery he became known as "Nevsky," in reference to the site of his victory. Peace proved difficult to uphold, however, not least due to the numerous attacks from the region's warring Mongol tribes. The next major threat from the West came a mere two years after the Swedish were thwarted – the Teutonic Knights, under the guise of missionary goodwill, closed in on the flourishing merchant city of Novgorod. The wealthy citizens of Novgorod had successfully extracted themselves from the control of the Grand Duke of Kiev, instating their own mayor and largely relegating the functions of the Prince to military protection. At the beginning of Eisenstein's film, we thus find Nevsky outside the city walls as the law did not permit him to settle within its confines.

Although historical accuracy is granted throughout, we would do well to remember that Alexander Nevsky is first and foremost a propaganda film. Eisenstein tapped into the centuries-old myth of the national hero Alexander, while wholly omitting his significance as a saint of the Orthodox Church – a historical aspect irreconcilable with the anti-religious stance of the Soviet regime. Throughout Russian history, the heroic figure of Alexander Nevsky had been deployed to warn of Russia's vulnerability to the West, and in 1938, this was the case once more. The Germans had signaled their intention to expand eastwards, and the pact between Hitler and Stalin was yet to be made.

However, Alexander Nevsky also aimed to expose the enemy within. Eisenstein depicted Novgorod as a haven of submissive collaborators, where the merchants in particular would sooner give in without a fight than endanger their personal profits. Looking at such telling historical precedents, the opposing forces targeted by the Stalinist regime here are easily identified: Trotskyites and capitalists.

No city dweller but leading the life of a simple fisherman in the rare times of peace, Nevsky is at one with the Russian land and rural population, and thus commands sufficient respect to rally the region's peasants against the German invaders. Eisenstein depicts the cruel deeds of the Germans in drastic images, such as the scene in which a Teutonic Knight throws a naked young Russian boy into the flames, and becomes the personification of the crimes the Germans perpetrated against the Russian people in the process.

With his superlative use of images and the power of suggestion, Eisenstein masterfully translates his propagandistic guidelines into the medium of film. In an epic 35-minute battle sequence set on the frozen Lake Peipus, the director preempts much of what we have now come to regard as the defining elements of a well-staged battle scene, be it in the works of Akira Kurosawa or Ridley Scott. Countless rows of warriors advancing over the horizon, extreme close-ups that make us feel the hoarse breath of the warriors on our faces, a series of jarring, fast-paced hard cuts, and devastated postdiluvian battle landscapes: Eisenstein laid the foundations for a long tradition of war filming that continues down to the present day. These scenes in which the horrors of warfare are shown in all their gory detail is perhaps the only moment in which Eisenstein managed to transcend the

"A splendid historical pageant which shows the director at his most inventively pictorial and climaxes in a superb battle sequence using music instead of natural sound." *Halliwell's Film and Video Guide*

1 Get off your high horse: Director Sergei Eisenstein presents the Grand Prince of Novgorod and Vladimir as a just and worldly ruler in some of medieval Russia's most trying times. Nikolai Cherkasov as Alexander Newsky.

2 Set the world on fire: With Alexander's help, Russia bands together to defend against foreign aggressors.

3 A slick victory: Nevsky crushes the Teutonic Knights during the so-called Battle of the Ice. Eisenstein set new stylistic standards in epic filmmaking with his depiction of the massacre, which spans more than thirty minutes of screen time.

film's rigid political brief in favor of a more pacifist perspective. The Germans aren't simply the enemy in *Alexander Nevsky*; they represent everything that is evil. This is made especially clear when they are finally vanquished by Nevsky's motley crew: not only are the Teutonic Knights defeated, they are literally swallowed up by the lake. True to historic accounts of the battle, Eisenstein shows us how the ice breaks under the Germans' heavy armor and the knights drown – elegantly symbolizing how even the Russian soil supports the cause of national defense.

A visionary piece of Soviet propaganda, *Alexander Nevsky* went down in film history as a work of great artistry, a counterpart to Leni Riefenstahl's equally propagandistic *Olympia* films (1936-38) that were produced in Nazi Germany at the same time.   LP

SERGEI SERGEIVICH PROKOFIEV	Born in Moscow in 1891, Russian pianist and composer Sergei Prokofiev left his home country in 1918 after scoring a number of early successes. His travels took him to Japan, America, and Europe, and he became internationally renowned for his ballets and operas, which included *A Love for Three Oranges* (*Ljubov' k trem apel' sinam*, 1919/21). Prokofiev returned to the USSR in 1933, which signified a change of musical direction and a return to his musical roots – the Russian folk music of the 19th century. This aesthetic shift made the composer compatible with the ideas of Socialist Realism, and Prokofiev was eventually teamed up with filmmaker Sergei Eisenstein. Eisenstein's epic tale of Russian nationalism, *Alexander Nevsky* (*Aleksandr Nevskiy*, 1938), profited greatly from Prokofiev's score, which combined neoclassical, folkloristic and experimental elements to produce an overwhelming sense of musical drama. Prokofiev, who also wrote operas based on Russian novels such as Dostoyevsky's *The Gambler* (*Igrok*, 1915–1916, 1927-28) and Tolstoy's *War and Peace* (*Wojna i mir*, 1941–1953) as well as numerous vocal works, was a master beyond compare in his ability to blend music with narrative structures. Prokofiev again collaborated with Eisenstein on *Ivan the Terrible I & II* (*Ivan Groznyj I, II*, 1944/46) as well as several other films. The evocative power of the composer's work also led to a collaboration that was literally worlds removed from the ideology of Stalinist Russia: in 1946, Walt Disney adapted Prokofiev's musical setting of the Russian folk tale *Petja i volk* (1936) for his animation classic *Peter and the Wolf*.

4 Fired by faith: Eisenstein creates images as powerful as religious artwork to show Russia at war with its Western enemies.

5 Alexander the Great: In the spirit of Robin Hood, Nevsky is a champion of the common man, who fights off opportunists in the interest of the common good.

THE LADY VANISHES

1938 - GREAT BRITAIN - 97 MIN. - B & W - THRILLER, COMEDY

DIRECTOR ALFRED HITCHCOCK (1899–1980)
SCREENPLAY FRANK LAUNDER, SIDNEY GILLIAT, based on the novel *THE WHEEL SPINS* by ETHEL LINA WHITE
DIRECTOR OF PHOTOGRAPHY JACK E. COX EDITING R. E. DEARING, ALFRED ROOME MUSIC LOUIS LEVY, CHARLES WILLIAMS
PRODUCTION EDWARD BLACK for GAINSBOROUGH PICTURES.

STARRING MARGARET LOCKWOOD (Iris Henderson), MICHAEL REDGRAVE (Gilbert Redman), DAME MAY WHITTY (Miss Froy),
PAUL LUKAS (Dr. Hartz), BASIL RADFORD (Charters), NAUNTON WAYNE (Caldicott), CECIL PARKER (Eric Todhunter),
LINDEN TRAVERS (Margaret), MARY CLARE (Baroness), GOOGIE WITHERS (Blanche), CATHERINE LACEY (Nun).

"I was having tea about an hour ago with an English lady. You saw her, didn't you?"

Young, refined Englishwoman Iris Henderson (Margaret Lockwood) is returning home from her holiday in Southern Europe to marry her fiancé. While riding the trans-European railway, Iris befriends Miss Froy (Dame May Whitty), a charming elderly compatriot seated in her compartment. Curiously, however, the little old lady is nowhere to be found after Iris awakes from a brief nap. Concerned about her traveling companion's whereabouts, the young woman goes off in search of her, only to find that no one on board recalls ever having seen Miss Froy. Among the passengers, only folkloric musicologist Gilbert Redman (Michael Redgrave) believes, as Iris does, that there really was a Miss Froy at all, and that she must have been kidnapped. Not only are they right, but their meddling soon plummets them into an international espionage scandal and quite as much danger as the missing lady.

Most film buffs are familiar with director Alfred Hitchcock's legendary obsession with trains. Whether it was the sexually suggestive ending to *North by Northwest* (1959), the death of his widow-killer in *Shadow of a Doubt* (1942) or the fatal encounter in *Strangers on a Train* (1951), the master of suspense always had a way of incorporating his preferred means of transport into pivotal scenes. Nonetheless, *The Lady Vanishes* is the sole picture of his career that is set almost exclusively on a locomotive from start to finish, with only the opening and closing sequences set elsewhere. Confining the action to this setting enabled Hitchcock to bring an unlikely hodgepodge of characters face to face in a powder keg of suspense with the greatest of ease. The technical challenge of staging a mainstream film on a set of no more than 30m_ is probably what appealed most to Hitchcock about the project. Here, in his penultimate British production prior to relocating to

"Just in under the wire to challenge for a place on the year's best ten is *The Lady Vanishes*... the latest of the melodramatic classics made by England's greatest director, Alfred Hitchcock. If it were not so brilliant a melodrama, we should class it as a brilliant comedy." *The New York Times*

1 Now you see me, now you don't: Did these suspicious-looking train passengers (Linden Travers and Cecil Parker) have anything to do with the sudden disappearance of a woman on board?

2 Connecting the dots: Unlikely lovebirds Gilbert (Michael Redgrave) and Iris (Margaret Lockwood) are going to make a very handsome couple by the end of the picture.

3 Bad medicine: Is Dr. Hartz (Paul Lukas, second from the left) abiding by the Hippocratic oath or is he just a big hypocrite?

4 Fahrvergnügen: If Dr. Hartz's strange accent isn't a dead giveaway that he's up to no good, his German getaway car is.

Hollywood, the filmmaker proved himself a maven of minimalism: the train car set was built at the small Islington Studios in London, and the rest of the cinematic illusion was achieved through rear projections and models with sterling results.

The Lady Vanishes is a zippy and sophisticated film full of surprises, charades and unpredictable twists of fate. It's a thriller-meets-comedy in which a seemingly dotty old woman turns out to be an agent on Her Majesty's Secret Service, and a sheltered young lady loses her heart to an accident-prone beau while saving the day. Hitchcock delights in undermining the suspense with cheeky movie clichés like flowerpots that fall from overhead, via knockout drops to nun costumes. He's just as shameless in playing up the national stereotypes of the train's passengers, especially when it comes to the two British sportsmen Charters (Basil Radford) and Caldicott (Naunton Wayne), whose sole concern is arriving in London before the final day of a crucial cricket match.

With all these lighthearted touches, it's easy to overlook the fact that Hitchcock gracefully weaves in his trademark phobias and themes. Iris fills the role of the unsuspecting protagonist who gets lured into a potentially deadly scheme, and the fact that nobody believes her story about Froy's disappearance and everyone doubts her sanity is a signature Hitchcockian nightmare.

The Lady Vanishes also subtly comments on the European political backdrop of the day. For starters, the choice to have the story open in an

overbooked hotel that is a veritable Tower of Babel is clearly symptomatic of the explosively chaotic era. Likewise, the detached passengers who either tune out of the conspiracy altogether or secretly fuel it, reflect the attitudes that the various European governments had towards Hitler's political actions. This parallel becomes particularly evident when a cagey doctor (Paul Lukas) with a German surname is unmasked as an enemy spy and mastermind of the kidnapping. But those political concerns are best taken with a pinch of salt, as they are primarily a means of evoking suspense in what can be seen as a coming-of-age story *à la* Hitchcock. One might even say that the lady who vanishes is none other than the prim young Iris as she matures into a tender and loving woman.

JH

5   A date with destiny: Michael Redgrave and Margaret Lockwood went on to become favorites of the British screen after charming audiences a là Hitchcock.

6   Sister act: Given his experiences at Catholic school, Alfred Hitchcock must have taken particular delight in gagging this poor excuse for a nun.

7   Starter pistols: Sports fans Charters and Caldicott (Basil Radford and Naunton Wayne) are not about to let an international espionage operation prevent them from attending the cricket game on time.

"This early Hitchcock is a treat for the connoisseur, who will experience a delight akin to that of a collector who stumbles upon a curious old Art Nouveau armchair or a kitschy turn-of-the-century gramophone and things long superseded at an antiques fair ... An enchantingly silly old relic." *Abendzeitung*

**PAUL LUKAS
(1887–1971)**

When Paul Lukas made it to Hollywood in 1928, he already had a ten-year career as a stage and film actor under his belt. Born in Budapest when it was still part of the Austro-Hungarian Empire, Lukas had a chiseled look to him that was perfectly suited to the role of the cultivated European and debonair seducer in the early days of sound. His role as a mob boss in Rouben Mamoulian's *City Streets* (1931) gave him the opportunity to briefly depart from his established screen persona.

It was during his professional sojourn in England that Lukas landed the part of a diabolical spy disguised as a neurosurgeon in Alfred Hitchcock's *The Lady Vanishes* (1938). From this point forward, it would have been only natural for Lukas to portray one generic Nazi villain after another. Yet while he played such a character for Anatole Litvak's early Anti-Nazi manifesto *Confessions of a Nazi Spy* (1939), the actor was soon given the opportunity to approach the subject matter from a different angle altogether In *Watch on the Rhine* (1943). Lukas bowled over audiences with an Oscar-winning leading role as a fighter against fascism. This performance paved the way for him to breathe life into a number of similar screen heroes. Still, every so often, Lukas reverted to stepping into the shoes of the psychopaths he had embodied in earlier days as was the case for Jacques Tourneur's *Experiment Perilous* (1944).

After the war had ended, Lukas became a regular supporting player for projects like Tourneur's notable thriller *Berlin Express* (1948) in which he plays a politician marked for assassination.

1938 - USA - 58 MIN. - B & W - COMEDY

DIRECTOR JOHN G. BLYSTONE (1892–1938)
SCREENPLAY CHARLEY ROGERS, FELIX ADLER, JAMES PARROTT, HARRY LANGDON, ARNOLD BELGARD
DIRECTOR OF PHOTOGRAPHY ART LLOYD EDITING BERT JORDAN MUSIC MARVIN HATLEY PRODUCTION HAL ROACH for HAL ROACH STUDIOS INC.,
STAN LAUREL PRODUCTIONS.

STARRING OLIVER HARDY (Ollie), STAN LAUREL (Stan), PATRICIA ELLIS (Mrs. Gilbert), MINNA GOMBELL (Mrs. Hardy),
JAMES FINLAYSON (Mr. Finn), PATSY MORAN (Lulu), SAM LUFKIN (Veteran), JEAN DEL VAL (French Pilot),
HARRY STRANG (Clerk), KARL 'KRACHY' KOSICZKY (Midget), BILLY GILBERT (Mr. Gilbert).

"You remember how dumb I used to be?"
"Yeah?"
"Well, I'm better now."

Trench warfare gets off to a bang in 1917 for friends Stan (Stan Laurel) and Ollie (Oliver Hardy). After months of toughing it out in the pits of "Cootie Avenue," the soldiers suddenly experience a bizarre cease-fire. Ollie and the rest of the unit venture up to the outside world to assess the situation, leaving Stan alone to defend their position. Twenty years later, he's still holding the fort. Decades of systematic pacing and a towering wall of the empty food cans have deepened the hole he calls home, but otherwise, little has changed. Then the day comes when he is discovered by a private plane flying overhead and is informed of something his battalion neglected to mention so many moons ago: namely that the Great War is no more and everybody's gone home.

Though the news is not exactly current, it is still cause for a celebration and buddy Ollie is eager to share in the festivities. Back in the United States,

he's learned the hard way that dodging ammunition can be a lot less dangerous than maintaining peace and domesticity with the little woman (Minna Gombell). No sooner does Ollie read about how the friend he thought dead has taken up residence at a nearby veterans' hospital than he's off to visit him instead of celebrating his first wedding anniversary. It's only natural. After all, this is a Laurel & Hardy picture, which means that women will have to play second fiddle, if they even get to play at all.

And so it goes: the two pals are reunited and the dam of propriety caves into a series of non-stop gags. One of the lengthiest bits involves Ollie first laying eyes on his long-lost friend, who's sitting in a wheelchair with one leg crossed under. Misinterpreting the situation, he runs to the aid of his 'amputated' buddy: eagerly pushing the chair, carrying him, and acting as a pillar of

1   Lightening the load: Considering the number of ac-
cidents he and Stan (in the driver's seat) get into,
you'd think Oliver Hardy (parked on the ground)
would have gotten rid of his spare tire by now.

2   In the army now: Soldiers Stan and Ollie are put
in the front lines of battle in the hopes that the
enemy might gun them down.

3   Junk in the trunk: Mr. Gilbert (Billy Gilbert) is
shocked to find a little something extra in his
neighbor's luggage – namely his wife. Patricia
Ellis as Mrs. Gilbert.

"Laurel & Hardy easily made the transition from their silent classics to the sound films, but, in most of their sound pictures their material never equalled that of their great silents. *Block-Heads* is an exception and features a few sequences that are among the duo's best."

Motion Picture Guide

LAUREL & HARDY

In *The Battle of the Century* (1927), they drive an entire neighborhood to a cake fight that ends with more than 3,000 confectionery casualties. In *The Music Box* (1932), their shenanigans as piano movers reduce a baby grand to plywood. And in *Big Business* (1929), they take revenge on anyone brazen enough to belittle the sale of Christmas trees in July.

The 25-year collaboration between rascals Stan & Ollie left a dent on the cinema that generations of aspiring numbskulls have taken a lesson from ever since. As masters of the slow burn, they'd start off cool and collected in stressful situations and then slowly build up to that explosive boiling point where there was no alternative but to pay the piper.

Between 1926 and 1951, Laurel & Hardy appeared before the camera together on more than 100 separate occasions. Both feature films like *The Battle of the Century* and shorts like *Big Business* or *The Music Box*, which won an Oscar for producer Hal Roach, were an essential part of their repertoire. Many fans prefer the team's shorts over their features, arguing that the format allows for a more concentrated form of tomfoolery. The full-length features redirect the focus elsewhere: for example, the period piece *The Devil's Brother / Fra Diavolo* (1933) brings ancient versions of their alter-egos to life whereas *Way Out West* (1937) showcases their flair for vaudevillian song and dance.

The legendary screen collaboration came into being about 15 years after Englishman Stan Laurel (1890–1965) decided to professionally tour the United States. The trip prompted him to take up residence among the Yanks, which panned out into his finding work as a film actor and gag writer for producer Hal Roach. It was through Roach that Laurel got to know American funnyman Oliver Hardy (1892–1957). The two men first appeared together in *A Lucky Dog* (1921), but not as a comedy duo. Together, Laurel & Hardy went on to become one of the all-time most successful oddball pairings, inspiring later teams like Bud Spencer and Terence Hill. The golden era for Hollywood's favorite fat and skinny combo came to end in 1940 when Hal Roach jumped ship. From then on, their careers would consist of modest screen appearances and numerous stage tours.

Stan Laurel withdrew from the movie industry altogether following Oliver Hardy's 1957 death. Four years later, Laurel was presented with an honorary Oscar in recognition of his innovative work in big-screen comedy.

moral support. When the moment comes for the Good Samaritan to help Stan up onto his feet again, he is flabbergasted to discover that both are intact.

With this little ice-breaker out of the way, the real demolition work can begin. Car, garage, apartment and happy marriage are totaled in record time by what should have been an ordinary drive home. Needless to say, it's not the damage itself but rather the gusto with which it is executed that continues to win the hearts of even contemporary audiences. Social conventions and the innovations of modern technology crumble in the wake of Laurel &

Hardy, who go about their business with the guilelessness and relentlessness of children.

Few would disagree that Stan Laurel is anything other than an overgrown baby. He is ungraceful, gullible, and doesn't have a dishonest bone in his body. Taking everything at face value, he is prone to misunderstandings that can lead to catastrophes like 20 wasted years in the trenches.

Oliver Hardy, on the other hand, tries his damnedest to be a man: he caresses his wife, plays house and even flirts with the neighbors. He knows

4   Keep it under your hat: Ollie's not-so-secret ad-
     mirer Lulu (Patsy Moran) has written him a letter
     that his wife had better not ever see.

5   Replacement killer: It seems Mrs. Hardy (Minna
     Gombell) feels more threatened by her predeces-
     sor Stan than she does by other women.

6   Pleased as punch: After Ollie's wife moves out, he
     and Stan are free to inaugurate their bachelor pad
     as they see fit.

exactly how adults behave and fails miserably trying to conduct himself accordingly. As if this weren't bad enough, he takes great satisfaction in pulling
the wool over other people's eyes. There's just no telling how unpleasant he
might be if Stan weren't there to perpetually burst his bubble and pin him
down. In the words of the German weekly *Die Zeit*, "Stan Laurel is Oliver
Hardy's tragedy and the salvation of his soul."

Yet beyond the spiritual, Stan's talents also extend to the metaphysical –
something he demonstrates at Ollie's apartment building on an endless stair-

well journey. Thoroughly annoyed by the teasing – almost mocking – silhouette of a window-shade on the interior far wall, Stan reaches into the realms
of the shadows and pulls down on the blind's cord. Ollie attempts to do the
same, but he just doesn't have the magic touch. Stan outsmarts reality on yet
another occasion by making a pipe with his fist and proceeding to smoke out
of it without burning himself. Isn't it just like a kid to show us what the imagination is capable of?

HJK

"It has no plot, but Laurel & Hardy had never needed plots, and their worst films were those with the most story."

William K. Everson, in: The Films of Laurel & Hardy

PORT OF SHADOWS
Quai des brumes

1938 - FRANCE - 91 MIN. - B & W - DRAMA, THRILLER

DIRECTOR MARCEL CARNÉ (1909–1996)
SCREENPLAY JACQUES PRÉVERT, MARCEL CARNÉ, based on the novel of the same name by
PIERRE MAC ORLAN [= PIERRE DUMARCHAIS] DIRECTOR OF PHOTOGRAPHY EUGEN SCHÜFFTAN EDITING RENÉ LE HÉNAFF
MUSIC MAURICE JAUBERT PRODUCTION GREGOR RABINOVITCH for CINÉ-ALLIANCE.

STARRING JEAN GABIN (Jean), MICHÈLE MORGAN (Nelly), MICHEL SIMON (Zabel), PIERRE BRASSEUR (Lucien),
RAYMOND AIMOS (Tramp), ROBERT LE VIGAN (Painter), EDOUARD DELMONT (Panama), JENNY BURNAY (Lucien's
Girlfriend), RENÉ GÉNIN (Doctor), MARCEL PÉRÈS (Chauffeur), ROGER LEGRIS (Hotel Page).

"Life's a bitch."

In a grubby dockside bar in Le Havre, a deserter named Jean (Jean Gabin) meets Nelly (Michèle Morgan), a young runaway. He's looking for a ship that will save him by getting him out of France. She wants to get away from her home and her guardian Zabel (Michel Simon), who watches over her jealously. The two of them fall in love, without any prospect of a shared future. Through his relationship with Nelly, Jean gets drawn into the conflict between Zabel and the would-be gangster Lucien (Pierre Brasseur), who suspects the shady old man of being responsible for the disappearance of his buddy Maurice – Nelly's former lover. As matters come to a head, Jean succeeds unexpectedly in gaining a berth on a cargo ship bound for South America. All that remains to the couple is one last night of love in a hotel. Next morning, just as the ship

is about to depart, Jean makes a fateful decision: he disembarks, in order to see Nelly one last time.

The deserter, the girl and the *tristesse* of the docklands: with its atmosphere of melancholy, fatalism and romance, *Port of Shadows* now seems to embody the essence of French pre-war film. This was the country's first cinematic Golden Age, the period of Poetic Realism. Dark melodramas depicted the tragic fates of mainly proletarian heroes, telling tales of man's existential loneliness in a corrupted world, and depicting the futility of all attempts to achieve happiness. Marcel Carné was only 28 when he made *Port of Shadows*, and it established his reputation as a master of these shadowy love dramas. The films that followed – *Hôtel du Nord* (1938) and *Daybreak (Le Jour*

"It's a thorough-going study in blacks and grays, without a free laugh in it; but it's also a remarkably beautiful motion picture from a purely pictorial standpoint and a strangely haunting drama." *The New York Times*

1   When the fog clears: Jean Gabin and Michèle Morgan emerged from the *Port of Shadows* as the premiere romantic pairing of the French screen.

2   Bear hug: Small-minded Zabel (Michel Simon) needs to get a grip.

3   Do you see what I see? Preoccupation prevents these guys from recognizing that they're in a fog.

4 Lost and gone forever: Cinematographer Eugen Schüfftan paints a portrait of love that is doomed from the get-go.

5 Over the moon: This couple was too busy playing hey diddle diddle to notice that the dish ran away with the spoon.

6 Welcome to our world of toys: Alexandre Trauner's set design shows how lonely it can be when you have to play by yourself.

se lève, 1939) – were no less pessimistic, yet all three of them now come across as the work of a great ensemble working in perfect accord.

The singularly poetic character of *Port of Shadows* is largely due to the tension between everyday realistic elements and a perceptible stylization that removes events from their temporal and spatial context. This is particularly apparent in Jacques Prévert's characteristically sharp dialog, which moves effortlessly between authentic argot and polished literariness, while Alexandre Trauner's wonderfully artificial sets form a fascinating contrast to the establishing shots filmed on location in the docklands. That the film

retains its integrity as a work of art despite these apparently disparate aesthetic tendencies is due not least to Eugen Schüfftan's camerawork. It bathes the story in a mysterious, diffuse light, so that the film's melancholy atmosphere acquires an attractive and positively sensual quality. All this is supported by Maurice Jaubert's music. Today, *Port of Shadows* affects those who see it as strongly as it did when first released.

But we shouldn't forget that it is also beautifully acted. At the center stands Jean Gabin, at that time the unrivalled star of the French cinema. The character he plays is a man of the people: rough, tough and easily angered,

"This film is among the few that simply do not age. This ballet of the docklands, this story of a deserted soldier, is as timeless as the fog, as lostness, crime and love. All this is as intertwined and hauntingly present in the landscape of faces violent and beaten, hunted and pure, drunken and dreaming as in the mist-wrapped images of quays and streets." *Der Tagesspiegel*

7　Chill factor: While a bit premature, Jean Gabin foresees the Cold War.

8　Throwing caution to the wind: French icon Michèle Morgan struts her stuff as the pin-up of the prairie in a raincoat and beret.

yet vulnerable inside and essentially a very good guy. This made him a cinematic hero of the progressive *Front Populaire* – a man who insists on his dignity whatever life happens to throw at him. Gabin had already made his name as a tragic lover in Julien Duvivier's *Pépé le Moko* (1936/37), but it was only after *Port of Shadows* that he truly became an icon of the cinema. This has something to do with the presence and charisma of his co-star Michèle Morgan, who seems immune to the damp shabbiness of her surroundings, and perfectly indifferent to it in her raincoat and beret. With her legendary pale eyes gazing vaguely into the distance, she forms a focal point for Jean's diffuse yearning. Michel Simon, by contrast, embodies the obstacle that blocks their innocent happiness. He lends Zabel the distorted visage of a monstrous petit bourgeois, trapped in bigotry, self-pity and a kind of joyfully celebrated nastiness. When Jean returns to Nelly, he catches the old man trying to rape her. Senseless with rage, he batters Zabel to death with a brick. Nelly urges her lover to flee, but Jean will never reach the ship: outside on the street, Lucien, the gangster, is waiting with a gun. Jean is shot in the back, and dies in Nelly's arms.

JH

MICHÈLE MORGAN Born in 1920, she made her film debut at the age of 15, and it wasn't long before her beauty attracted the attention of Marc Allégret, who offered her a leading role in *Heart of Paris* (*Gribouille*, 1937). One year later, Michèle Morgan was Jean Gabin's partner in Carné's *Port of Shadows* (*Quai des brumes*, 1938) and a new star of the French cinema. Her reputation was sealed as the most radiant beauty of Poetic Realism, as "the Greta Garbo of the *banlieues*." In the years that followed, her clear, melancholy face shone in a series of equally romantic films: most brightly, however, in Jean Grémillon's *Stormy Waters* (*Remorques*, 1939–1941), with Jean Gabin as her co-star once again. During the war, Morgan went to Hollywood. There, she was cast as a Frenchwoman in a number of propagandist films. She was Humphrey Bogart's partner in *Passage to Marseille* (1944), for instance – the follow-up to *Casablanca*. When the war ended, she returned to France, where she immediately landed a big success with Jean Delannoy's melodramatic Gide adaptation, *La Symphonie pastorale* (1946), a role for which she was named Best Actress at Cannes. Following this, she went on to play the title heroine in Alessandro Blasetti's kitschy historical drama, *Fabiola* (1948/49), in which she was partnered by her third husband, the athletic Henri Vidal. She also gave a convincing performance in Carol Reed's *The Fallen Idol* (1948).
In the 50s, Michèle Morgan was usually cast as a woman tragically in love, often in historical settings. As her reputation grew, she was cast in such roles as Josephine in Sacha Guitry's *Napoléon* (1955) and Marie Antoinette in Delannoy's *Shadow of the Guillotine* (*Marie Antoinette reine de France / Maria Antonietta regina di Francia*, 1956). It has to be said that the young filmmakers of the Nouvelle Vague saw her as a leading representative of the *cinema de qualité* they so detested; and it may have been an impulse of sly mischievousness that led Claude Chabrol to cast her nonetheless – as one victim of the serial murderer in *Bluebeard* (*Landru*, 1962).

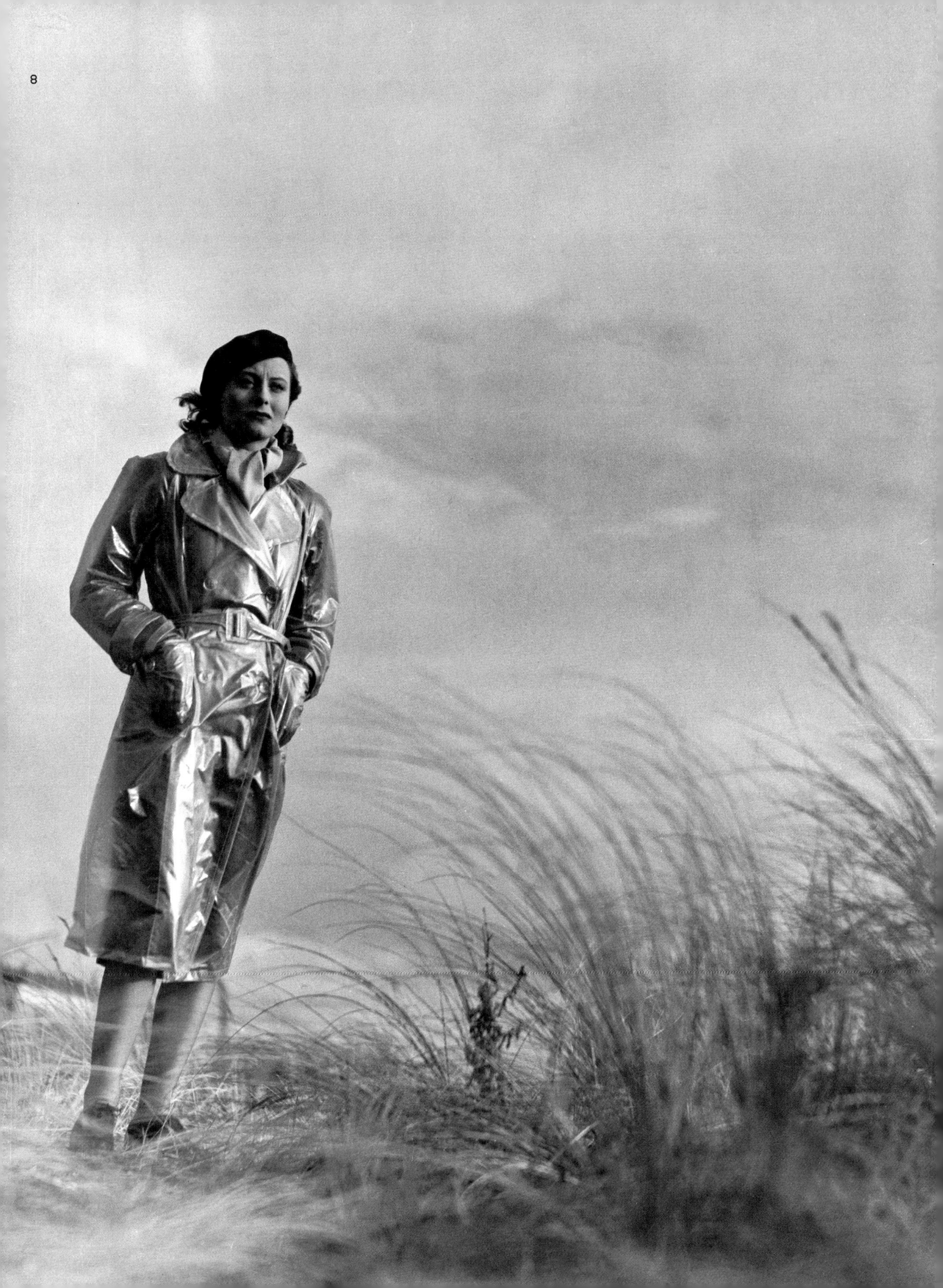

BRINGING UP BABY

938 - USA - 102 MIN. - B & W - SCREWBALL COMEDY

DIRECTOR HOWARD HAWKS (1896–1977)
SCREENPLAY DUDLEY NICHOLS, HAGAR WILDE **DIRECTOR OF PHOTOGRAPHY** RUSSELL METTY **EDITING** GEORGE HIVELY **MUSIC** ROY WEBB
PRODUCTION HOWARD HAWKS for RKO.

STARRING KATHARINE HEPBURN (Susan Vance), CARY GRANT (Dr. David Huxley), MAY ROBSON (Aunt Elizabeth Random), CHARLES RUGGLES (Major Horace Applegate), WALTER CATLETT (Constable Slocum), FRITZ FELD (Dr. Fritz Lehman), VIRGINIA WALKER (Alice Swallow), BARRY FITZGERALD (Mr. Gogarty), GEORGE IRVING (Mr. Peabody), JOHN KELLY (Elmer).

"Well, the love impulse in men very frequently reveals itself in terms of conflict."

Bespectacled paleontologist David Huxley (Cary Grant) of the Stuyvesant Museum of Natural History contemplates the brontosaurus skeleton before him. For the past four years, he's dedicated his life to the mammoth project of piecing the dinosaur back together, and there's still one bone missing. Just as Huxley begins to accept the fact that his work will probably never reach completion, his assistant, Alice Swallow (Virginia Walker), comes running in with a telegram, claiming that the missing intercostal clavicle has been found! Now, it looks like Alice and David will really have something to celebrate at their wedding tomorrow. Only rather than popping open a bottle of champagne, the no-nonsense bride puts a damper on the occasion by exhorting her disappointed fiancé to forget about honeymoons and offspring altogether – the brontosaurus will be their 'child,' the result of their union. Alice then reminds David that he mustn't neglect his golf engagement that afternoon with Mr. Peabody (George Irving), a lawyer who represents a wealthy woman eager to donate a million dollars to the museum.

Metaphorically, the opening scene shows how the scientist's life is as stripped-down, calcified and dead as a brontosaurus skeleton. Wearing a white museum smock tightly wrapped around him along with the ridiculous sort of glasses that silent-era comedian Harold Lloyd was famous for, Cary Grant's character is the embodiment of a stiff thinker who just can't let loose. That all changes, however, when David swings his nine iron at Peabody's side and gets mixed up with the free-spirited Susan Vance (Katharine Hepburn). After relieving the scientist of his golf ball, the young heiress sets her sights on his automobile, followed by the remains of his male pride. Only hours after having made Vance's acquaintance, David finds himself on all fours in the woods, digging up bones hidden by the Vance

family dog and chasing wild leopards through suburban Connecticut. As if this weren't humiliating enough, the scientist ends up meeting the philanthropist interested in his museum while clad in a frilly, fur-trimmed woman's dressing gown. While it's certainly unfortunate that the wealthy woman is offended by Huxley's shameful display, it's worse that she also happens to be Susan's aunt. Is it Miss Vance's sudden love for David that prompts him to go to such extremes? No. He does it all in the name of situational irony and side-splitting laughter.

Apart from being one of Howard Hawks' great masterpieces, *Bringing Up Baby* is the definitive screwball comedy. The picture's underlying comic anarchy is the result of both Grant and Hepburn's infallible performances and a perfectly constructed script. The duo's non-stop mayhem never lets up with their comments flying at each other, past each other, and oftentimes over each other. Hawks speeds things up even more by cutting off an action before it can reach completion and then starting up with something else. It goes without saying that oil-and-water lovers like David and Susan are as integral to the genre as the missing bone is to the brontosaurus; and yet seldom has the pairing led to as many misunderstandings, embarrassments and indignities as it does here. Regardless of what Susan does, she always manages to steer David straight into harm's way.

Having recognized that these two crazy kids are desperately in need of a psychiatrist, Hawks supplies the picture with Dr. Lehman (Fritz Feld) whose professional maxim that "all people who behave strangely are not insane" could be taken as a convenient disclaimer for his own neuroses. And indeed, the film wouldn't be what it is without eccentric supporting characters like him or the petulant Aunt Elizabeth (May Robson) and her dinne

1 A leopard can't change its spots: Susan Vance (Katharine Hepburn) fears she'll never be able to change her mischievous nature.

2 Unlimited ammunition: Game hunter Major Applegate (Charles Ruggles, second from the right) tracks down wild animals in a Connecticut yard

and proves that nuts aren't an endangered species.

3 I've got a bone to pick with you: While David Huxley (Cary Grant, right) always makes a spectacle of himself when Susan is around, tonight she's the one who is going to get caught with her pants down.

4 Sticky fingers: Susan accidentally rips David's dinner jacket while trying to steal his heart.

5 Digging up funny bones: George (Asta) has buried David's intercostal clavicle somewhere on Aunt Elizabeth's grounds and Susan is determined to help him find it.

"*Bringing Up Baby's* slapstick is irrational, rough-&-tumble, undignified, obviously devised with the idea that the cinema audience will enjoy (as it does) seeing stagy actress Hepburn get a proper mussing up." *Time Magazine*

companion Major Applegate (Charles Ruggles), a seasoned game hunter who can imitate the leopard's cry.

Much to Applegate's surprise, Elizabeth's estate boasts two of them – one wild and one tame. As one might suspect, only one of these beasts can be soothed by music and the sound of its name – "Baby." Still, neither of them is king of this picture's jungle. That title is reserved for Susan, the most dangerous of all cat women in what is surely Katharine Hepburn's most purr-fectly seductive role. As an irreverent non-conformist with flowing red hair, she is the exact opposite of David's rigid girlfriend. Naturally, Susan's plan is to prevent the marriage from taking place and make a man out of the dinosaur doctor while she's at it. Playing a ball of yarn to Hepburn's cat, Grant shines as the guy who just can't say no. In fact, in what is perhaps the crowning achievement of all Susan's bungling schemes,

David gets caught wearing her muumuu and defends himself by claiming in jest to have gone 'gay' all of a sudden. It was a historic occasion; for this marked the first time on screen that the word gay was used to mean homosexual.

The reversal of gender roles, the subtle use of sexual innuendo in references like lost 'bones', and the barrage of slapstick gags attest to just how far ahead of his time director Howard Hawks actually was. And given the boldness of the film, its no wonder that it failed miserably at the box office. A good, old-fashioned man's man, Hawks took the blame upon himself, attributing the movie's poor reception to its lack of normal characters. On the other hand, funnyman Harold Lloyd, on whom Dr. David Huxley is based, dubbed the picture "the best comedy of all time and an instant classic." Clearly, the man knew what he was talking about.   PB

**ROY WEBB
(1888–1982)**

Few people today are familiar with the name Roy Webb, a Hollywood legend born the same year as his famous friend and fellow composer Max Steiner. The irony is that Webb was responsible for creating more than 300 movie scores that included classics like *The Seventh Cross* (1944), *It's a Wonderful Life* (1946), *Notorious* (1946) and *Marty* (1955). When he was a child, his mother took him to the New York Metropolitan Opera to nurture his passion for music. As a young adult, Webb studied at the Art Student's League in Manhattan and got a degree in music from Columbia University. It was by route of Broadway that the composer eventually made it to RKO, where Steiner would later join him, a man who played an instrumental role in convincing skeptical studio bosses of the importance of atmospheric music in the burgeoning world of talkies. Webb's understated arrangements became a trademark of the RKO pictures, whereas Steiner at Selznick International Pictures and later at Warner Bros., became known for his bombastic flair. It was the subtlety and suggestiveness of Webb's work that made him the ideal choice for RKO's B-horror flick scores and many milestone film noir productions. The 40s were perhaps his most prosperous decade, producing scores for films including *Cat People* (1942), *I Walked with a Zombie* (1943), *The Seventh Victim* (1943), *The Curse of the Cat People* (1943), *The Spiral Staircase* (1945) and *Out of the Past* (1947). Over the course of his prestigious career, Roy Webb was nominated for a total of seven Oscars – none of which he was awarded. Indeed, longevity proved to be the greatest reward for the conductor, who died at the age of 94. A remastered compilation of Webb's many compositions for classic horror movies was recently released on CD.

JESSE JAMES

1938/39 · USA · 106 MIN. · COLOR · WESTERN

DIRECTOR HENRY KING (1888–1982)
SCREENPLAY NUNNALLY JOHNSON DIRECTOR OF PHOTOGRAPHY GEORGE BARNES, W. HOWARD GREENE
EDITING BARBARA MCLEAN MUSIC LOUIS SILVERS PRODUCTION DARRYL F. ZANUCK for 20TH CENTURY FOX.

STARRING TYRONE POWER (Jesse James), HENRY FONDA (Frank James), NANCY KELLY (Zee), JOHN CARRADINE (Bob Ford), RANDOLPH SCOTT (Will Wright), HENRY HULL (Rufus Cobb), SLIM SUMMERVILLE (Jailer), J. EDWARD BROMBERG (Mr. Runyan), BRIAN DONLEVY (Barshee), DONALD MEEK (McCoy).

> "We ain't ashamed of him – I don't know why but I don't think even America is ashamed of Jesse James. Maybe it was because he was bold and lawless like all of us like to be sometimes, maybe it's because we understand a little that he wasn't altogether to blame for what his times made him."

A shadow trails a moving locomotive in the dead of night. Just as it catches up with the caboose, a figure swoops over the top of the car and makes its way forward – undetected against the whistle's blare. From inside the train's brightly lit compartments, sharply clad passengers are too preoccupied with themselves or the newspapers they read to notice a thing. Now in the engine room, the black silhouette reveals his identity with those career-making words: "stick 'em up!" Jesse James (Tyrone Power) is an outlaw beyond compare and the train robbery in this early cinematic version of his tale is one of the most visually spectacular moments in this seminal Old Hollywood Western. Taking us back to 1868, the semi-biographical account of outlaw brothers Frank (Henry Fonda) and Jesse James begins at a time long before their names had become synonymous with lawlessness. Indeed, the picture opens on another sort of villain altogether – the agents of the Midlands Railroad Company, who are threatening to uproot the West by forcing farmers to sell their land for a song in the interests of transcontinental transportation. When the conniving corporation finally claims the last breath of a woman in failing health – none other than Mama James – her boys retaliate by opening fire and embarking on a life on the wrong side of law and order.

According to the movie, the rift between social classes is the cancer at the core of the James' criminality, a stance often adopted in the capers and social dramas of the 20s and 30s. Unlike big-city gangsters, men like Frank and Jesse were never members of the mob, and their motives were very different from the corruption and thirst for political influence that fueled organized crime. The duo were perceived as individuals, crusading for the common man, whose interests they defended in the spirit of Robin Hood. It was a message that rang true with audiences. So true in fact that Jesse James served as the blueprint for countless other flicks about historical U. S. outlaws. And given the political crisis brewing in Europe, Hollywood recognized the domestic market's growing need for subject matter with an American focus.

Historical truth, however, often fell by the wayside in this genre, even if – as was the case for Jesse James – the picture introduced actual documentation and snapshots in the opening shots. Truth be told, Mother James outlived both her sons, whereas the real Jesse joined a gang of bandits of his own accord at age 16 and was responsible for eleven deaths. Director Henry King managed to wipe Jesse's murderous slate clean for the cinematic telling of his story by limiting the robberies to newspaper headlines instead of staging them. According to a statement made by Jesse James' granddaughter at the movie's premiere, "the only similarity between grandfather and that man on screen is that both of them could ride a horse."

1 The man with the golden gun: Wholesome Henry Fonda finds ways to lift the spirits of a depressed economy as down-and-dirty outlaw Frank James.

2 Breaking with convention: Straight-laced Zee (Nancy Kelly) understands how being bad can feel

so good now that she and Jesse James (Tyrone Power) are a couple.

3 Bang, bang! He shot me down: But as long as there's a horse nearby, Frank and Jesse James still have a chance of making a daredevil escape.

4 Preaching to the converted: Jesse and his men know how to make believers of secular folk.

Nonetheless, the picture's thrilling and novel direction, very much a product of Nunnally Johnson's glorious screenplay, still succeeds in capturing viewers' imaginations. Action sequences, gripping dialog, and Jesse and Zee's (Nancy Kelly) romance all feed into the grand cinematic divide between the march of progress and the Wild West's anarchic spirit. On one side stand the country's honest farmers and Jesse, a man forced to hide out in a cave and secretly meet Zee along a picturesque riverbank. In diametric opposition to this is the railroad and all that comes with it. Made out by the opening sequence as a virtual leviathan, its minions are mainly city folk like the

president of the Midlands Railroad Company, Mr. McCoy (Donald Meek), who guarantees Jesse a fair trial only to then fervently motion for the bandit's execution following his arrest. Zee, the sole character capable of moving in both worlds, symbolically bridges these polar opposites; for after marrying Jesse and taking up with him as an outcast, the birth of her son makes her realize that she's not cut out for life on the lam.

The viewer, conversely, can't get enough of the James brothers' daredevil attempts to flee the law, including two sensational stunts on horseback: the first, a ride through the storefront window of the town haberdashery

**HENRY KING
(1888–1982)**

While still in his youth, Henry King joined a traveling theater company and went on a professional tour of the United States. A performer with quite a range, he took to Shakespeare as readily as he did contemporary crowd-pleasers, and also enjoyed success in the circus and vaudeville circuits. He switched to film in the 1910s, with his directorial debut coming in 1915. After making a string of Westerns and melodramas, King established himself as a filmmaker with the hit army comedy *23 1/2 Hours' Leave* (1919). He then won critical acclaim for *Tol'able David* (1921), a laconic and witty David and Goliath allegory that unfolds in awe-inspiring American landscapes. Although sweeping visuals of this sort became a fixture in King's work, the director never reached the ranks of the great auteurs. Nor did he want to. Instead, the favorite son of the studios built his career on an ability to infuse even second-rate material with a grandeur and humor that registered with audiences. Mood and story were the main focuses of King's direction. He took a decidedly pragmatic approach to his work, declaring that: "the mood is written into the story, there isn't much you can do but just handle it in a very natural, normal way, just like a carpenter saws a board." Cinematic history is thus perhaps justified in viewing King as an artisan rather than an artist. Nevertheless, pictures like *Jesse James* (1938/39), the revisionist Western forerunner *The Gunfighter* (1950), the gripping melodrama *The White Sister* (1923) and literary adaptations like *The Song of Bernadette* (1943) and *The Snows of Kilimanjaro* (1952) attest to directing skills that far exceed the requirements of commercial entertainment.

"An authentic American panorama."

The New York Times

store, and the second a 60-foot mounted free-fall off a cliff that ends with a splash landing. Equally effective, though significantly more subtle, is the atmospheric landscape photography. An example of Technicolor at its finest, these shots had one German film critic conclude that *Jesse James* was the American answer to the *Heimatfilm*, and that "Henry King has shown just what this genre is capable of when taken seriously."

Jesse James was one of the first color Westerns born of the studio system to impress with state-of-the-art sound effects and a star-studded cast. The death of the protagonist at the story's conclusion was a particularly innovative feature. Ironically, it was the one aspect of the picture that producer Darryl F. Zanuck insisted on revamping. The studio, however, eventually felt obliged to go with the director's original cut as test audiences rejected out-

right Zanuck's formulaic Hollywood ending. And so, instead of a happy ending, a heartfelt eulogy held at Jesse's grave by newspaper editor and former mayor Rufus Cobb (Henry Hull) closes the picture on an optimistic note.

Looking back on the project, director Henry King stated that "Jesse James was one of our most successful pictures. It just proves that on some occasions it's better to use a little common sense than a lot of manufactured fiction." How right he was. For in the greater scheme of things, his movie and others like John Ford's *Stagecoach* (1939), Cecil B. DeMille's *Union Pacific* (1939) and Michael Curtiz's *Dodge City* (1939) fostered the renaissance of a genre threatened by extinction and exhibited a cinematic grandeur later Westerns could seldom match.

OK

THE WIZARD OF OZ

939 - USA - 101 MIN. - COLOR - MUSICAL

DIRECTOR VICTOR FLEMING (1883–1949)
SCREENPLAY NOEL LANGLEY, FLORENCE RYERSON, EDGAR ALLAN WOOLF, based on the novel *THE WONDERFUL WIZARD OF OZ* by L. FRANK BAUM **DIRECTOR OF PHOTOGRAPHY** HAROLD ROSSON **EDITING** BLANCHE SEWELL **MUSIC** HERBERT STOTHART, HAROLD ARLEN (Songs) **PRODUCTION** MERVYN LEROY for LOEW'S INC., MGM.

STARRING JUDY GARLAND (Dorothy Gale), FRANK MORGAN (Professor Marvel / Emerald City Doorman / Cabbie / Wizard's Guard / Wizard of Oz), RAY BOLGER (Hunk / Scarecrow), BERT LAHR (Zeke / Cowardly Lion), JACK HALEY (Hickory / Tin Man), BILLIE BURKE (Glinda / Good Witch of the North), MARGARET HAMILTON (Miss Gulch / Wicked Witch of the West / Wicked Witch of the East), CHARLEY GRAPEWIN (Uncle Henry), PAT WALSHE (Nikko, the Winged Monkey), CLARA BLANDICK (Auntie Em).

ACADEMY AWARDS 1939 OSCARS for BEST MUSIC (Herbert Stothart), and BEST SONG: "Over the Rainbow" (Music: Harold Arlen; Lyrics: E. Y. Harburg).

"Somewhere over the rainbow"

Kansas seems a very dull place indeed as Dorothy Gale's (Judy Garland) life on Auntie Em's (Clara Blandick) farm unfolds in monochrome, sepia-stained imagery. Then one day young Dorothy's dog Toto wanders into neighbor Miss Gulch's (Margaret Hamilton) garden, and the girl decides it's time for her and her pet to abandon their dismal world, ere the animal is put to sleep. Just outside of town, the runaways cross paths with traveling miracle worker Professor Marvel (Frank Morgan), who appeals to Dorothy's conscience and convinces her to return to her family. Getting back to Auntie Em and friends, however, quickly turns into an adventure beyond compare when a tornado lifts girl, dog and farmhouse up over the rainbow to a magical land called Oz.

Shortly after landing, Dorothy learns from Glinda the Good Witch that she has been proclaimed a national hero for having rid Oz of the Wicked Witch of the East – the airborne farmhouse having killed the wretch on touchdown. And yet despite the girl's spectacular flight, a journey home seems impossible without a visit to the wonderful Wizard of Oz (Frank Morgan), who resides in the distant Emerald City. Perils abound, but with the help of new friends Scarecrow (Ray Bolger), Tin Man (Jack Haley) and Cowardly Lion (Bert Lahr), Dorothy emerges victorious: first obliterating the dreaded Wicked Witch of the West (Margaret Hamilton) and then standing up to the obstinate wizard. In exchange for these acts of valor, the Scarecrow

1 A long way from Kansas: Dorothy (Judy Garland) and her trusty companions brave the unknown in the wonderful land of Oz.

2 Are you a good witch or a bad witch? Glinda (Billie Burke) informs Dorothy that she has freed Munchkinland from the oppression of the East.

3 Weak in the knees: It's still going to take a bit of convincing before the Scarecrow agrees to follow the yellow brick road.

"The *Wizard of Oz* has a dreamlike quality and a tremendous emotional power."

David Lynch

awarded a brain, the Tin Man a heart, the Cowardly Lion his courage – and Dorothy discovers that getting back to Kansas is as easy as a click of the heels.

The Wizard of Oz is based on Lyman Frank Baum's novel *The Wonderful Wizard of Oz*, first published in 1900. The screen adaptation is an American fairy tale in its own right that continues to influence U.S. pop culture as it wins over coming generations of moviegoers. Indeed, it is as if by magic

that the picture uses a combination of Baum's story, Technicolor and song and dance numbers to paint a dazzling tale of its own about the unlimited potential of motion-picture photography.

It's no exaggeration to say that the film itself can be understood as a grand meditation on the cinema. The first real taste of this comes as Professor Marvel pretends to draw on televisory powers to see into the future via a crystal ball. Nonetheless, no one is as apt at manipulating these powers

LYMAN FRANK BAUM American author Lyman Frank Baum (1856–1919) was born in Chittenango, New York on May 15, 1856. Prior to his official start in writing, Baum worked in a variety of areas and published a catalog for window dressers. *Mother Goose in Prose* (1897) marked his debut in fiction. The follow-up volume, *Father Goose: His Book* (1899), quickly became a bestseller. Indisputably, nothing he wrote received as much public attention as *The Wonderful Wizard of Oz* (1900). Readers and critics alike instantly proclaimed it the first full-fledged American fairy tale. In fact, the tale was so popular that a musical version already had hit stages by 1902. Although Baum also wrote plays that appealed to more mature audiences, it was his children's books that made him an American icon. A total of thirteen additional novels would eventually join the Oz series, including titles like *The Patchwork Girl of Oz* (1913). On many occasions, Baum adopted pen names such as "Schuyler Staunton" and "Floyd Akers" for his works of literature. Incidentally, he also wrote more than twenty books under the pseudonym "Edith Van Dyne" to win the allegiance of female readers. He died in Hollywood on May 6, 1919.

"A fairybook tale has been told in the fairybook style, with witches, goblins, pixies and other wondrous things drawn in the brightest colors and set cavorting to a merry little score." *The New York Times*

4   Garland's travels: Young Judy learns what it's like to be a big star playing opposite a bevy of bit actors.

5   Opium den: Dorothy and friends fall asleep in a poppy field surrounding the Emerald City.

6   Up, up and away: After Oz has been saved, its wizard (Frank Morgan) heads somewhere over the rainbow without Dorothy.

7   No more tears: Dorothy wonders whether the Cowardly Lion (Bert Lahr) will ever stop consulting with the rain.

"There's an audience for *Oz* wherever there's a projection machine and a screen." *Variety*

as the adventurous Dorothy herself. After her own overactive imagination literally takes her by storm – in the form of an oncoming tornado that knocks her out and deposits her in bed – she is free to dream to her heart's content. As feverish images flash above Dorothy's face, the film suddenly assumes a more experimental format. With her eyes now open, she shifts focus to the free-floating window frame at her bedside and peers into the outside world through what proves to be a dynamic movie screen. Trick photography continues to overrule the doctrines of science as familiar faces enter the window frame only to be placed in contexts that make them seem entirely out of place.

When the spinning visions stop, Dorothy's world will have been turned upside-down, and only a trip to the wizard can untangle all the knots. The great irony of the matter, as we'll discover en route, is that women seem to

hold all the power in Oz. The wizard himself is merely a technician, who operates light projections, levers, fire and colored smokes to appear almighty – in essence nothing more than an illusionist. It is actually the good witch who ultimately provides Dorothy with crucial pieces of advice to help her along her journey and return home.

Back in the real world however, a simple girl's imagination is no weapon against the powers that be and certainly not one that can overrule parents. As we are reminded, the magic words that promise love and order are "there's no place like home." And so Dorothy will have to make do with Professor Marvel's reports of breathtaking mountains, unexplored oceans and far-off places; for when the story was written, most young women could only dream of such things.

PLB

NINOTCHKA

1939 - USA - 110 MIN. - B & W - COMEDY

DIRECTOR ERNST LUBITSCH (1892–1947)
SCREENPLAY CHARLES BRACKETT, BILLY WILDER, WALTER REISCH, based on a story by MELCHIOR LENGYEL
DIRECTOR OF PHOTOGRAPHY WILLIAM H. DANIELS EDITING GENE RUGGIERO MUSIC WERNER RICHARD HEYMANN
PRODUCTION ERNST LUBITSCH for LOEW'S INC., MGM.

STARRING GRETA GARBO (Nina Ivanovna Yakushova, Ninotchka), MELVYN DOUGLAS (Count Léon d'Algout),
INA CLAIRE (Grand Duchess Swana), SIG RUMAN (Iranoff), FELIX BRESSART (Buljanoff), ALEXANDER GRANACH (Kopalski),
BELA LUGOSI (Commissar Razinin), GREGORY GAYE (Count Alexis Rakonin), ROLFE SEDAN (Hotel Manager),
EDWIN MAXWELL (Mercier, the Jeweler), RICHARD CARLE (Gaston, the Butler).

"Don't make an issue of my womanhood."

How can political satire and romantic comedy be united in a single film? Easy: by presenting a clash of ideologies as a battle of the sexes. That's what Ernst Lubitsch does in *Ninotchka*. The woman is a committed communist (Greta Garbo); her opponent is Count Léon d'Algout (Melvyn Douglas), a representative of capitalism in its final decadence. The two must come together, in breach of the rules of Marxism-Leninism and the etiquette of the haute-bourgeoisie; and not for nothing does this class struggle take place in Paris, the city of love and luxury.

Comrade Nina Ivanovna Yakushova ("Ninotchka") couldn't care less about either of those things. A staunch Party member, she's been sent to the French capital to pull three weak-willed comrades into line. Soviet emissaries Iranoff (Sig Ruman), Buljanoff (Felix Bressart) and Kopalski (Alexander Granach) had been given the task of exchanging the jewelry confiscated from a Russian Grand Duchess for hard currency, but the splendor of Paris has turned their heads. Should the Soviet people starve, just because a trio of would-be playboys would rather play Big Spender in the city's most ex-clusive hotel than do their duty? For cases of this kind, there are show trials

taking place in Moscow at this very moment … and Ninotchka sees them as a great success: "There are going to be fewer but better Russians." Naturally, no one yet dares to call this stern lady "Ninotchka." Her manner is cool, chaste and utterly humorless, and her delinquent comrades are understandably intimidated.

Nina Ivanovna is a political animal *par excellence*, and she forbids any references to her gender. Only a casual acquaintance named Léon sees the woman beneath the guardian of the Russian revolution. Are clothes, jewelry and romantic street-lighting nothing but "a waste?" Is love really just "a chemical reaction?" At first, she's curt in her rejection of his gallant bourgeois flattery, telling him that his type will soon be extinct. But this charming snob achieves the impossible: he makes her laugh. What a pity that he turns out to be the lover of the Duchess whose jewels Ninotchka and her comrades are so determined to sell …

A heartwarmingly silly hat is now regarded as a milestone in cinematic history. At first, Ninotchka sees it as the end of civilization, but eventually she seals her transformation by placing it on her head with incomparable grace

and panache. In the 30s, though, the real sensation was the change of image undertaken by the Swedish Diva: "Garbo laughs!" – just once, when Léon, frustrated by the failure of his attempts to breach her reserve by telling bad jokes, falls off his chair. The audience, by contrast, has been having a wonderful time since the film began, not least because Lubitsch plays with Garbo's unearthly image in his own way. When she laughs, she laughs like a beginner; when she celebrates her asceticism with tight lips and a monotonous vocal delivery, she comes fascinatingly close to self-parody. As so often, Lubitsch's stylistic brilliance manifests itself in the way he chooses an elegant artificiality rather than a banal naturalness. In this case, it wasn't a hard choice. Lubitsch is said to have remarked: "I think she is the most inhibited person I have ever worked with."

"A streamlined screenplay, literally sparkling with brilliant dialog, tests the mettle of this duo, with the result that the widely vaunted Lubitsch touch of yore asserts itself with new mastery. Garbo finds herself in an entirely new type of role, one which prescribes the more difficult nuances of sophisticated comedy, and while she rises to the situation nobly, her elegance remains undeniable, and she carries herself with proud assurance of her talents."

Boxoffice Magazine

1 Many roads to romance: Soviet secret weapon Ninotchka (Greta Garbo) goes kablooey after meeting the debonair Léon (Melvyn Douglas).

2 Strictly ballroom: The representatives of two opposing political systems do a little two-step and enter into a very attractive peace agreement.

3 Standing up for democracy: Léon cuts the political red tape for his Soviet comrades.

4 Pushing the envelope: Ninotchka goes against her principles and cracks a smile for capitalism – even if it only is a little one.

4

MELVYN DOUGLAS (1901–1981)

In numerous comedies of the 30s, this tall, distinguished actor embodied witty, worldly and slightly blasé gentlemen. In this way, Melvyn Douglas established himself as a charmer alongside Gloria Swanson, Myrna Loy and Irene Dunne. His ability to deliver well-written lines perfectly made him an ideal actor for Ernst Lubitsch, who cast him beside Marlene Dietrich in *Angel* (1937) and *That Uncertain Feeling* (1941). After *Ninotchka* (1939), he was stuck with the label of "the man who made Garbo laugh." They were co-stars again shortly after, but *Two-Faced Woman* (1941) was a flop, and it ended Garbo's career.

Douglas himself quickly grew tired of his roles, but his ten-year absence from the screen in the 50s also had something to do with the political climate. His wife, Democratic Congresswoman and former actress Helen Gahagan, was lambasted as a communist by Richard Nixon, and Melvyn Douglas himself was politically active enough to be classed a suspicious person. In the 60s and 70s, he experienced a rebirth in a range of demanding father roles. He won an Oscar for his performance in *Hud* (1963) as the disappointed father of an amoral rancher played by Paul Newman. *The Candidate* (1972) featured Douglas as the father of the hero played by Robert Redford. At the age of 79, he picked up his second Academy Award, as Best Supporting Actor, for his performance in Hal Ashby's brilliant satire, *Being There* (1979). Douglas played the naive tycoon who helps Peter Sellers' Mr. Chance – a slow-witted gardener and an inexhaustible source of popular pseudo-profundities – to acquire extraordinary political power. Sadly, Melvyn Douglas was unable to pick up the prize in person: he died in 1981 at the age of 80.

"Ernst Lubitsch, who directed it, finally has brought the screen around to a humorist's view of those sobersided folk who have read Marx but never the funny page, who refuse to employ the word 'love' to describe an elementary chemico-biological process, who reduce a spring morning to an item in a weather chart, and who never, never drink champagne without reminding its buyer that goat's milk is richer in vitamins." *The New York Times*

5

5 Can't judge a book by the covers: Is Léon really
in love with Ninotchka or does he just want to put
communism to bed?

6 Wearing your teacher's hat: Ninotchka, or Nina
as she now prefers to be called, has taken to
capitalism like a fish to water.

But the famous "Lubitsch touch" was also partly the work of his pupil
Billy Wilder. His screenplay is not just filled with gags that cleverly contrast
two opposing political systems; it also confronts ideology with the human
weaknesses of those who have to live with it. The understandable desire to
enjoy the freedom and wealth of a city like Paris is more than Comrades Iranoff, Buljanoff and Kopalski can bear. For their greatest 'stupidities' they will
find no forgiveness in Moscow; but the same system offers them the perfect
excuse, at least for each other: "Who said we were supposed to think?" Like
Lubitsch and Wilder, the actors Sig Ruman, Felix Bressart and Alexander

Granach were exiles. Their awareness that their home countries were without freedom lends a melancholy flavor to the comedy.

Ninotchka was the first of Lubitsch's films to make explicit reference
to contemporary international politics. It enjoyed a friendlier reception than his
next movie, the anti-Nazi satire *To Be or Not to Be* (1942), but it only became
a much-loved classic long after the war. After the news of the Hitler-Stalin
pact, Lubitsch felt that he had been too gentle in his depiction of the communists. Nonetheless, the communists banned the film, as expected. In the end,
Ninotchka brought Garbo no luck: it was to be her penultimate film.   PB

THE WOMEN

1939 - USA - 133 MIN. - B & W / COLOR - COMEDY, DRAMA

DIRECTOR GEORGE CUKOR (1899–1983)
SCREENPLAY ANITA LOOS, JANE MURFIN, based on the play of the same name by CLARE BOOTHE LUCE
DIRECTOR OF PHOTOGRAPHY OLIVER T. MARSH, JOSEPH RUTTENBERG EDITING ROBERT KERN MUSIC DAVID SNELL, EDWARD WARD
PRODUCTION HUNT STROMBERG for MGM.

STARRING NORMA SHEARER (Mary Haines), JOAN CRAWFORD (Crystal Allen), ROSALIND RUSSELL (Sylvia Fowler),
JOAN FONTAINE (Peggy Day), PHYLLIS POVAH (Edith Potter), MARY BOLAND (Countess Flora DeLave),
PAULETTE GODDARD (Miriam Aarons), VIRGINIA WEIDLER (Mary's Daughter), LUCILE WATSON (Mrs. Moorehead),
HEDDA HOPPER (Dolly Dupuyster), DENNIE MOORE (Olga).

"There is a name for you, ladies. But it isn't used in high society ... outside of a kennel."

Norma Shearer is a doe, Rosalind Russell a cat, Joan Crawford a cougar, Joan Fontaine a lamb and so on. This is how director George Cukor describes his actresses in the opening sequence to *The Women*. If the monikers sound sexist, wait until you hear what these ladies have to say about the men – or rather the rats and skunks – in their lives. Doubly despicable is the fact that these guys don't even get to defend themselves. For not a single one is to be found in Cukor's outrageous and absolutely on-the-money cinematic original, starring 135 of Hollywood's finest man-eaters. New York's Park Avenue with its boutiques and perfumeries serves as the stomping ground of these wild beasts. And zookeeper Cukor is more than content to let them have free reign as they gab, gossip and scratch each others' eyes out to their hearts' content.

The story begins at a beauty parlor, where married women with time to spare gather under the sun lamps or pamper themselves with mud packs and facials. In front of the shop, we get a taste for what lies in store as a cat-fight brews among two poodle owners and their respective pets – all of whom are, of course, bitches. Back inside the shop, we are introduced to Sylvia (Rosalind Russell) just as she finds out during a manicure that her friend Mary (Norma Shearer) has been played for a fool. As Sylvia soon divulges to the rest of her crowd while nursing a glass of sherry, Mary's husband has been going astray with a young shop girl named Crystal (Joan Crawford). The unsuspecting wife is of course the last person in the city to find out.

Having sprung the news on her, the vultures feast their eyes on Mary, who is sure to crack at any second. After all, what else is a woman in her situation to do? Sylvia entreats Mary to defend her dignity as a woman and file for divorce, whereas the poor creature's mother thinks it better to turn

a blind eye. Mary herself sees no reason to destroy her life for what she assumes is just an insignificant fling. The final decision, however, is not to be hers – for she is literally at the mercy of her friends.

Mary soon finds herself taking a train for Reno and setting the wheels of divorce in motion. Confidantes Sylvia and Peggy (Joan Fontaine) have come along to support her – and make sure she redesigns herself according to plan. The focus of the story then shifts slightly when a floozy named Miriam (Paulette Goddard) tries to take up with Sylvia's ex-spouse. Needless to say, Cukor gives the audience ringside seats to one of the most unforgettable grudge matches in Hollywood history.

Damning rumors, devilish schemes, alligator tears, acts of spite, hair pulling, kicks in the ass, you name it – the malevolence of these ladies knows

> **"This ensemble classic from 1939, re-released as part of the George Cukor retrospective at the NFT, has gaiety, charm and a heartfelt belief in monogamous love. Only women appear, and the movie playfully leaves us to decide whether that means we're getting half, or, for the very first time, the whole story."** *The Guardian*

1 Hostile takeovers: Crystal (Joan Crawford) knows that you don't have to watch Dynasty to have an attitude.

2 Always the last to find out: Dutiful Mary (Norma Shearer) always thought she had a loving husband – she just didn't know how much.

3 I don't believe in fretting and grieving: Sylvia (Rosalind Russell) and Peggy (Joan Fontaine) use shopping's restorative powers to make a new woman out of Mary.

4 Animal crackers: Catty Sylvia informs dear Mary that her husband is a cheetah.

no limit. Naturally, only Hollywood's finest were considered for the job. Still, with the exception of Myrna Loy and Greta Garbo, MGM turned down a number of big-name actress eager to get in on the action. The project itself was a consolation prize of sorts for those snubbed by David O. Selznick's much publicized "Search for Scarlett O'Hara" – nearly all the ladies interested in *The Women* had auditioned for the lead in *Gone with the Wind* (1939). Cukor gave them the opportunity to parody prevalent female archetypes and their own Hollywood images: the overbearing Russell as the cunning cur, Fontaine as Goodie Two Shoes and gossip columnist Hedda Hopper as herself. As usual, Norma Shearer played the hopeless – and gullible – romantic, who this time round gets a rude awakening from real-life rival Joan Crawford. It comes as the down-and-dirty diva slaps the retort, "Thanks for the tip. But when anything I wear doesn't please Stephen, I take it off." In a movie loaded with great one-liners, these words were the icing on the cake.

NORMA SHEARER (1902–1983)

Apart from being the first true MGM starlet, Norma Shearer was also the wife of studio producer and film industry 'boy wonder,' Irving Thalberg. He discovered the actress and did everything in his power to build up her career, although Shearer didn't become the embodiment of feminine elegance and cultural refinement simply by virtue of marriage. Well before she met Thalberg, this Montreal native was a beauty queen, at the tender age of 14. By 1920, Shearer's mother Edith had made sure both Norma and sister Athole had a foothold in motion pictures.

1927 proved a landmark year in the young actress' life: apart from marrying Thalberg, she also gave a star-making performance in Ernst Lubitsch's *The Student Prince in Old Heidelberg* (1927). The romantic characters she went on to play brought her five Oscar nods – with a win for her work in *The Divorcee* (1930). Shortly thereafter, Clark Gable got his big break, appearing opposite Shearer in *A Free Soul* (1931). Five years later, she lit up the screen at Leslie Howard's side in *Romeo and Juliet* (1936), although both of them were actually far too old for their respective roles. Shearer's fellow actresses, especially Joan Crawford, viewed her with a certain degree of disdain. When asked by the press whether she considered Shearer a rival, Crawford simply said: "How am I supposed to compete with her? She sleeps with the boss."

Thalberg's premature death in 1936 left his wife at an utter loss and determined to retreat from the industry. Shearer, however, was bound by her contract to make six more pictures before retirement. These included blockbusters like *Marie Antoinette* (1938), *Idiot's Delight* (1938/39) opposite Clark Gable and George Cukor's *The Women* (1939). Following short-lived affairs with men as dissimilar as Mickey Rooney and George Raft, she left show business for good in 1942. Although she was happily married to a ski instructor 20 years her junior until her death in 1983, every now and then Norma Shearer would still accidentally refer to him as Irving.

5 Grin and bear it: Mary meets Crystal and takes infidelity with a gracious smile. Behind the scenes, however, rival actresses Norma Shearer and Joan Crawford hardly made their hate for one another a secret.

6 Gild the lily: A little bow here, some Chanel there – anything to make him notice me.

7 Backlash: After admiring Sylvia's claws from afar, Mary grows some of her own.

8 Male polish remover: A gossiping manicurist inadvertently exposes the true colors of Mary's husband to her.

Just whether Mary's fickle husband or the other men these ladies fight over are really worth the trouble, we'll never know. For men are absolutely incidental to this sophisticated Cukor work in which it is the privilege of a paid servant to recount the juicy details of nuptial warfare. Less discreet are the costumes of world-famous designer Adrian, whose creations are a true match for Cukor's sizzling direction. In fact, a fashion show even provides a brief cinematic interlude in rainbow colors, which the director of this other-wise black-and-white piece had no qualms about. And why should he have? After all, it was *The Women's* across-the-board garishness that made it one of the first great milestones of pop culture. Indeed, by the end of the picture, Mary herself has been successfully indoctrinated: having grown her own claws and painted them jungle red, she is ready to fight back and dig them into her husband's unfaithful flesh.

PB

THE ROARING TWENTIES

1939 - USA - 104 MIN. - B & W - GANGSTER MOVIE

DIRECTOR RAOUL WALSH (1887–1980)
SCREENPLAY JERRY WALD, RICHARD MACAULAY, ROBERT ROSSEN, based on the story "THE WORLD MOVES ON" by
MARK HELLINGER DIRECTOR OF PHOTOGRAPHY ERNEST HALLER EDITING JACK KILLIFER MUSIC HEINZ ROEMHELD, RAY HEINDORF,
LEO F. FORBSTEIN PRODUCTION HAL B. WALLIS for WARNER BROS.

STARRING JAMES CAGNEY (Eddie Bartlett), PRISCILLA LANE (Jean Sherman), HUMPHREY BOGART (George Hally),
GLADYS GEORGE (Panama Smith), JEFFREY LYNN (Lloyd Hart), FRANK MCHUGH (Danny Green),
PAUL KELLY (Nick Brown), ELISABETH RISDON (Mrs. Sherman), EDWARD KEANE (Pete Henderson),
JOE SAWYER (Sergeant).

"He used to be a big shot."

New York, 1919. When Eddie (James Cagney), George (Humphrey Bogart) and Lloyd (Jeffrey Lynn) come home from World War I, each of the three buddies has his own plans. While Lloyd dreams of his own law practice and George is hoping to get rich quick, Eddie just wants to get back to work as an auto mechanic. Soon, he's forced to realize that it's not going to be easy to survive as a civilian. His old job has been given away, and no one else seems to need a returning hero. Eventually, Prohibition offers him a way out of his misery: Eddie joins the alcohol-smuggling industry, and his fortunes improve radically. Very soon, he's doing a roaring trade in illicit booze. Even Brown (Paul Kelly), the boss of a rival gang, can't stop him — and George, meanwhile, has become his indispensable right-hand man. Eddie teams up with this old pal from army days, hires Lloyd as a legal advisor, and builds up a powerful organization. The three veterans of the trenches are soon on a roll, but it can't last forever … George's brutal methods and Eddie's jealousy of Lloyd, who's

stolen his girl, lead to the collapse of their friendship – and when Wall Street crashes in 1929, Eddie falls lower than he ever could have imagined.

In the 30s, with each of the three major Hollywood studios cultivating its own style, Warner Brothers developed a masculine image with a slew of fast, raw, realistic and highly entertaining movies. Harry, Jack, Sam (died in 1927) and Albert Warner ran a very tight ship, and they became famous above all for their gangster films. With hits like *Little Caesar* (1930) and *The Public Enemy* (1931), they established the Golden Age of the genre, and when the original formula began to pall, Warners brought the decade to a brilliant climax with *The Roaring Twenties*.

The film was based on the story "The World Moves On" by Mark Hellinger, who was notorious for his private dealings with Mafia bigshots, and the story, as Hellinger explains in a foreword, was itself based on real-life events. This was not the least of the reasons why *The Roaring Twenties*

attracted so much attention, and the film disappoints no one who's expecting something close to the real deal. It's not just because the sets, costumes and music convincingly revive the era of gang wars and speakeasies. The film is also littered with high-tempo semi-documentary sequences that drive the plot ahead while also embedding the movie firmly in the period it depicts: Eddie's rise and fall is seen to take place in the context of victory parades, drinking joints, police raids, tumultuous scenes at the Stock Exchange, and the election of Franklin D. Roosevelt. Thus, *The Roaring Twenties* amounts to a critical reflection on an epoch of the very recent past – the post-war decade in which American mobsters had risen to power and wealth with dizzying speed, and which had ended, with a sickening thump, on Black Friday, October 25, 1929.

"This film is a memory and I am grateful for it." *Mark Hellinger*

1 Feather weight: Humphrey Bogart may look like he's flying high in this picture, but back in the 30s, he was still a "second banana gangster" to Warner Bros. favorite tough guy James Cagney (right).

2 Blonde on board: Ditzy Jean (Priscilla Lane) doesn't realize how severely she is toying with Eddie's emotions. But it's no surprise as Cagney's characters often got the short end of the stick when it came to romance.

3 Love don't live here anymore: Convinced that he's no Casanova, Eddie fails to hear the knock of opportunity until it is too late. Gladys George as Panama.

4 Double-breasted double-crosser: George (Humphrey Bogart) makes it clear to former friends Eddie and Lloyd (Jeffrey Lynn) that his loyalties lie with the highest bidder.

4

It also marks the beginning of Raoul Walsh's lengthy collaboration with Warner Brothers. Already an experienced hand in the business, Walsh proved himself the ideal director for this movie. He worked rapidly and efficiently, as the studio demanded; and his films themselves were fast, direct, and rhythmically faultless. These are the qualities that make *The Roaring Twenties* so gripping to watch, even seven decades after it was made. Above all, Walsh coaxed outstanding performances from his stars – especially James Cagney, whose business-savvy gangster seems like the quintessence of all his previous bad guys. He's really a good guy at heart, though, animated by the American spirit of honest diligence, and tempted from the path of virtue only by exceptionally tough circumstances. Bogart, by contrast, plays a man whose taut self-possession makes him seem eerily untrustworthy. He's the real bad guy

here – a cynic whose own deeds repeatedly confirm him in his negative view of the world. "He doesn't trust his friends," says George at one point in the film. Inevitably, therefore, he and Eddie are going to end up deadly enemies.

The Roaring Twenties didn't just crown the classical era of the gangster film: it also allowed the genre to re-align itself, as Walsh's later work demonstrated. An interesting transformation in the characters played by Bogart and Cagney can be traced in these movies: in *High Sierra* (1940), Bogart's cynic is first seen as a tragic romantic hero, while *White Heat* (1949) explains the vitality of Cagney's bandit as a consequence of morbid mother-love. In *The Roaring Twenties*, however, there was as yet no hint of such deformations: Eddie expires on the steps of a church, repenting his sins as he dies in the arms of a woman whose love he has come to recognize too late.   JH

MARK HELLINGER (1903–1947)

Probably no one else was capable of writing with such spellbinding authenticity about the great age of American gangs. Mark Hellinger was a famous man in his time, working as an author, journalist, Broadway columnist and eventually as a film producer – and he was personally acquainted with several legendary Mafiosi, including Al Capone, Lucky Luciano and Bugsy Siegel. It's said that Dutch Schultz gave him an armored white Rolls Royce as a present.

Hellinger was a gifted storyteller who loved drinking and gambling. Originally, he was closer to the theater than the movies, though he had been writing screenplays since the early 30s; but he only became a true Hollywood man after penning the story that formed the basis for *The Roaring Twenties* (1939). The film's success motivated Warner Brothers to hire him as an Associate Producer. In this capacity, he worked on three films with Raoul Walsh, including *High Sierra* (1940), which made Bogart a star, and *Manpower* (1941).

From 1941 onwards, Hellinger worked as a producer himself, changing studios several times over in the process. During WW II, he spent some months as a war correspondent in the South Pacific. Finally, he went to Universal, where he produced *The Killers* (1946), one of the masterworks of film noir. Today his name is associated above all with two classics of the semi-documentary crime genre: *Brute Force* (1947) and *The Naked City* (1948). In the latter, he can also be heard as the voice of the off-screen commentator. Shortly after the film was completed, Mark Hellinger, only 44 years old, suffered a heart attack and died. His dazzling personality inspired Richard Brooks to write the novel *The Producer* (1951). A large theater in New York is named after him.

1939 - USA - 92 MIN. - B & W - SCREWBALL COMEDY

DIRECTOR HOWARD HAWKS (1896–1977)
SCREENPLAY CHARLES LEDERER, based on the play "THE FRONT PAGE" by BEN HECHT and CHARLES MACARTHUR
DIRECTOR OF PHOTOGRAPHY JOSEPH WALKER EDITING GENE HAVLICK MUSIC MORRIS STOLOFF PRODUCTION HOWARD HAWKS for
COLUMBIA PICTURES.

STARRING CARY GRANT (Walter Burns), ROSALIND RUSSELL (Hildegaard 'Hildy' Johnson), RALPH BELLAMY (Bruce Baldwin),
GENE LOCKHART (Sheriff Peter B. Hartwell), PORTER HALL (Murphy), ERNEST TRUEX (Roy V. Bensinger),
CLIFF EDWARDS (Endicott), CLARENCE KOLB (Fred, the Mayor), ROSCOE KARNS (McCue), FRANK JENKS (Wilson),
REGIS TOOMEY (Sanders).

"Madam, you are a cock-eyed liar!"

It all starts with a routine kiss-off. The day before she is due to get remarried, Hildy Johnson (Rosalind Russell) meets up with newspaper editor Walter Burns (Cary Grant), her former husband and boss. While reliving old times, Walter remarks that he's sorry to see her throwing in the towel on her journalism career. Yet, there's something in his tone that suggests his agenda where Hildy is concerned might be more than purely professional. The couple's stroll down memory lane comes to an abrupt stop as Hildy's fiancé, Bruce Baldwin (Ralph Bellamy), a soldier and mild-mannered insurance salesman, stops in at the newspaper offices. The brief exchange of gestures and quips between past and present beaus make one thing clear to audience and bride alike: compared to the fast-talking Burns, Baldwin is just a tongue-tied oaf. After assessing this himself, the groom exits the office, and leaves Hildy to 'defend his honor' in a battle-of-the-sexes style debacle full of verbal affronts and side-stabs. The fiery discussion, however, is cut short yet again as Burns receives word that a murderer sentenced to capital punishment has escaped and agreed to grant him an exclusive interview. Before long the journalists realize that they're sitting on the story of a lifetime as new evidence in the case suggests an unsubstantiated conviction and the possibility that the corrupt mayor's intended to exploit the execution in the upcoming elections. The painstaking hunt for breaking news suddenly has the press waging war against the big-wigs in the local political machine. And Hildy, pumped with adrenalin, forgets about both Bruce and their honeymoon as she hands

1 Wide-eyed receivers: A good journalist never lets wires cross when getting the scoop.

2 Woodward and Boobstein: Hildy (Rosalind Russell) and Walter (Cary Grant) are an unbeatable team – both in and out of the newsroom.

3 Wonder woman: Nothing gets between Hildy and front-page news.

4 Won't take this sitting down: Walter butts heads with ex-wife Hildy to get her all fired up about him again.

"It takes you by the scruff of the neck in the first reel and shakes you madly ... for the remaining six or seven. Before it's over you don't know whether you have been laughing or having your ears boxed." *The New York Times*

over what is sure to be a front-page article. To cap it all, getting bitten by the journalism bug suddenly reminds her of what she used to see in Walter ...

A veritable roller-coaster ride of a film, *His Girl Friday* is rooted in the American mindset and mythology of the 30s. The escalation of corruption and Mafia activity during the Great Depression clearly left its mark on the film's cold view of the world. In an era of pervasive sobriety, the fast-paced, no-nonsense newsroom resembled the gangster movie genre in providing a window to a darker underworld. As a result, the inner-workings of the newspaper business were the subject of countless reporter movies. In response to the burgeoning women's movement, Hollywood began filling many reporter roles with actresses by the mid 30s, launching them into an arena where they could interact on equal footing.

"... the maddest newspaper comedy of our times."

The New York Times

In 1931, nearly a decade prior to *His Girl Friday*, Lewis Milestone had brought Ben Hecht and Charles MacArthur's hit play "The Front Page" to the screen; the production bore the original title and starred two male actors, Adolphe Menjou and Pat O'Brien, rather than a man and a woman. Howard Hawks' twist on the tale shows how dramatically the zeitgeist had changed, as 'Hildy' was no longer a nickname for Hildebrand, but rather for Hildegaard. What was once a story about two at-odds 'newspapermen' morphed into a

he-says-she-says screwball. Very much on a par with Hawks' previous work *Bringing Up Baby* (1938), *Friday* is considered the quintessential example of this once wildly popular genre, which the director himself helped to create. Much of the success of this "comedy of re-marriage," a sub-genre which dealt with conflicts related to gender equality, rides on Rosalind Russell and Cary Grant's ability to turn high anxiety, overlapping dialog and rapid verbal exchanges into an art form. Whereas pieces of this nature, especially in early

4

Hollywood, normally ended up with the wife abandoning her professional ambitions, Hawks' Hildy has to decide in favor of hers to secure a marital reconciliation.

Countless remakes and variations on *His Girl Friday* attest to both the story's longevity as well as its roots within American mythology. More than forty years after the original picture's release, Billy Wilder redesigned *The Front Page* (1974) as a Watergate-inspired comedy featuring magnificent performances by Jack Lemmon and Walter Matthau. Ted Kotcheff's recent *Switching Channels* (1988) reset the focus again to one of love, marriage and career – this time in the modern age of broadcast news.

JS

"You know, I always have a candle in the window for you."
"I jumped out of that window long ago."

Film quote: Walter Burns (Cary Grant) and Hildy Johnson (Rosalind Russell)

5   Not up to snuff: Hildy begins to rethink her engage-
    ment when her future husband starts smelling like
    yesterday's news. Ralph Bellamy as Bruce.

6   Blindsided: Apparently, local politics is full of things
    too gruesome for a woman's eyes.

7   Second thoughts: Even with fiancé Bruce standing
    before her real as life, all Hildy can think about is
    her love for journalism – and Walter.

ROSALIND RUSSELL
(1907–1976)

The fourth of seven children in an affluent Connecticut family, Rosalind Russell was strongly encouraged by her mother to study acting at the American Academy of Dramatic Art in New York. Russell had the good fortune to instantly land a seven-year contract with MGM, which brought her the lead in Edwin L. Marin's *The Casino Murder Case* (1935) and a number of prominent supporting roles. In 1939, George Cukor cast her in *The Women* and Russell was instantly applauded for her comic genius. That same year, she dazzled audiences as a fast-talking reporter opposite Cary Grant in *His Girl Friday*. Quick on her feet, with the ability to throw lines like daggers, Russell became the face of the self-assured woman in big screen farces, musicals and lighthearted comedies alike.

Her Hollywood career continued to thrive throughout the 1950s. Yet her more traditional, dramatic roles in pictures like *Mourning Becomes Electra* (1947) didn't win the same audience response that had made Russell a star. Then came the two-year original Broadway run of "Auntie Mame," arguably the actress' most revered vehicle. A 1958 screen adaptation of the show followed in which Russell recreated the magic for moviegoers. *Mrs. Pollifax – Spy* (1971), directed by Leslie H. Martinson, marked her final screen appearance. Rosalind Russell died in Beverly Hills, five years after retiring from show business.

WUTHERING HEIGHTS

1939 - USA - 103 MIN. - B & W - DRAMA, LITERARY ADAPTATION

DIRECTOR WILLIAM WYLER (1902–1981)
SCREENPLAY CHARLES MACARTHUR, BEN HECHT, based on the novel of the same name by EMILY BRONTË
DIRECTOR OF PHOTOGRAPHY GREGG TOLAND EDITING DANIEL MANDELL MUSIC ALFRED NEWMAN PRODUCTION SAMUEL GOLDWYN
for SAMUEL GOLDWYN COMPANY.

STARRING MERLE OBERON (Cathy), LAURENCE OLIVIER (Heathcliff), DAVID NIVEN (Edgar Linton), GERALDINE FITZGERALD (Isabella Linton), FLORA ROBSON (Ellen), HUGH WILLIAMS (Hindley), DONALD CRISP (Doctor Kenneth), LEO G. CARROLL (Joseph), CECIL KELLAWAY (Mr. Earnshaw), SARITA WOOTON (Cathy, as a child), REX DOWNING (Heathcliff, as a child), DOUGLAS SCOTT (Hindley, as a child)

ACADEMY AWARDS 1939 OSCAR for BEST CINEMATOGRAPHY (Gregg Toland).

"Oh Cathy, I never broke your heart. You broke it!"

Blazes of passion stormed over *Wuthering Heights* both before and during the legendary shoot: Laurence Olivier was headstrong about having his fiancée, Vivien Leigh, cast in the role of Cathy and found that expressing affection for leading lady Merle Oberon was a true test of his acting abilities. David Niven didn't want to be a part of the production at all, and producer Samuel Goldwyn insisted that the story end happily, which nearly had director William Wyler packing his bags. Against all expectations, everyone was thoroughly satisfied with the outcome: Leigh signed on to play Scarlett in *Gone with the Wind* (1939), Olivier and Niven became international superstars, and Wyler's film was not only deemed the definitive screen adaptation of Emily Brontë's literary masterpiece, but also hailed as one of the cinema's greatest and most tragic romances – a status it enjoys to this day.

The story itself takes us almost 200 years back in time to the wild moors of Yorkshire, where the estate of Wuthering Heights juts to the heavens like the formidable rock of Gibraltar. The lord of the manor, Mr. Earnshaw (Cecil Kellaway), divides his family in two when he returns home one day with a dark-haired orphan boy he has taken to calling Heathcliff (Rex Downing). While Earnshaw's daughter, Cathy (Sarita Wooton), quickly develops affection for the impetuous young brute, her older brother Hindley (Douglas Scott) regards him with disdain. When Earnshaw dies several years later, Hindley (Hugh Williams) becomes master of the house and reduces his surrogate sibling to a stable hand. As a secret love builds between the quickly maturing Cathy (Merle Oberon) and Heathcliff (Laurence Olivier), class differences threaten to drive them apart. When Cathy finally decides to marry affluent neighbor Edgar Linton (David Niven), a humiliated Healthcliff vanishes into the night. Three years later, Heathcliff returns just as unexpectedly as he left. Only now, he's "Mr. Heathcliff" – a man who uses wealth as a weapon for revenge...

Filling this Hollywood production with a British ensemble – all of whom were unknowns apart from Oberon and Olivier – was a triumph in casting. No actor could have made the plight of servitude more mortifying than the utterly aristocratic Olivier. Deliciously reminiscent of Richard III, a role Olivier knew like the back of his hand, Heathcliff allows his compatriots to mistake his inward rage for humility. Likewise, Oberon performs a masterful balancing act as the complex Cathy, equally driven by an unbridled passion for the gypsy-like Heathcliff and a shallowness that cannot refuse Linton's material wealth. Then there's Niven, who holds his own as what is undoubtedly the story's most thankless character – for how could a man as tame as Edgar ever conquer the heart of a wildcat like Cathy? Stiff competition on Oscar night prevented any of these dazzling portrayals from being duly rewarded. Indeed

with films like *Gone with the Wind*, *Stagecoach*, *The Wizard of Oz*, and *Mr. Smith Goes to Washington* also up for numerous nominations, many critics consider 1939 to be the "greatest year in film history."

The sole trophy *Wuthering Heights* picked up at the awards ceremony was for Gregg Toland's camera work, which demonstrated mastery of the medium's recently developed deep-focus cinematography. Toland's commitment to visual precision was capable of making a replica of the Yorkshire moors constructed in the San Fernando Valley look like the real thing. Furthermore, Orson Welles was so convinced by the images of the Linton estate that he went on to team up with Gregg Toland two years later for *Citizen Kane* (1941). One need but look to the scene in which Cathy and Edgar are trapped in the foreground while Heathcliff approaches from the horizon like

"William Wyler has directed it magnificently, surcharging even his lighter moments with an atmosphere of suspense and foreboding, keeping his horror-shadowed narrative moving at a steadily accelerating pace, building absorbingly to its tragic climax. It is, unquestionably, one of the most distinguished pictures of the year."

The New York Times

1   Grab his soul away: Edgar (David Niven) loves wife Cathy (Merle Oberon) utterly and completely. She, however, will never shut Heathcliff out of her heart.

2   A temper like her jealousy: Heathcliff's (Laurence Olivier) rage blazes more brightly than the fire that warms him.

3   Let me in-a-your window: Edgar's sister Isabella (Geraldine Fitzgerald) marries Heathcliff only to be disowned by her family and sacrificed like a pawn by the man she loves.

4   Love on the wily, windy moors: In their younger years, Heathcliff and Cathy roll and fall in green.

a human maelstrom to understand *Wuthering Heights'* connection to the later picture.

William Wyler's direction is also worthy of recognition. Like Emily Brontë's 1847 novel, the only one of her career, the movie remains morally ambivalent toward its main characters. Although certainly not a source of public scandal as the book had been in its day, Wyler's work was often criticized for its impartiality. Yet had he not been neutral, this pearl of melodrama would have undoubtedly sunk in a sea of schmaltz. Ironically, one of the film's most winning directing moves was executed against Wyler's wishes. Using extras, producer Samuel Goldwyn filmed a 'happy ending' without his director, showing the romantic leads at peace in the great beyond. While Brontë herself may have opted for another conclusion, the sequence does in fact do justice to the romantic leads: doomed to eternal separation on Earth, Cathy and Heathcliff finally find each other in death. PB

"I cannot live without my life! I cannot die without my soul."

Film quote: Heathcliff (Laurence Olivier)

> "A celebration of depth of field, permanently worrying us with the question of what goes where. Will the neighbor be received, and if so — where? Who will watch by the sheep? Who will spend the night at the hearth in the kitchen? Who will sleep in the stable, in the living room, or in the princely four-poster bed? The camera incessantly discovers new levels of backgrounds and perspectives and tries to make things speak." *epd Film*

5 Stormy weather: The opposing forces of nature so brilliantly depicted in Emily Brontë's literary masterpiece come alive on the silver screen.

6 Terror made me cruel: Whether as a stable hand or lord and master of Wuthering Heights, Laurence Olivier's Heathcliff is a larger-than-life character who lives by Machiavellian doctrines.

7 Joined in law, but not in spirit: If Heathcliff has to endure Cathy and Edgar's lifelong devotion to one another, he can at least ensure that their time one earth together will be brief.

DAVID NIVEN (1910–1983)

Born into a Scottish family of professional soldiers, the urbane David Niven wowed big-screen audiences as the ever-so-eccentric British gent. His father died when he was five years old, and young David followed family tradition by going to military school and in due course becoming an officer on the island of Malta. Niven's journey to becoming a Hollywood actor was eventful to say to the least: yet neither his brief stints picking racehorses in New York nor his time training the revolutionaries of Cuba to overthrow the regime proved lucrative career choices. By 1935, Niven was working consistently as a Tinseltown extra and had become a dependable supporting player in films like William Wyler's *Dodsworth* (1936). He took some convincing to team up again with the "total despot" for a meatier role in *Wuthering Heights* (1939) but, ironically, *Heights* was the film that would bring Niven his first real taste of success. He returned to his military roots with the outbreak of World War II, and attained the rank of colonel while serving with British commandos. Between maneuvers, he did his part to boost the morale of his fellow countrymen by appearing in propaganda films like Leslie Howard's *The First of the Few / Spitfire* (1942) and Carol Reed's *The Way Ahead* (1944). Commuting between American and British movie studios gradually became routine. Once the war had ended, Niven revived his acting career by starring as a Royal Air Force pilot in the Pressburger/Powell picture *A Matter of Life and Death* (1946). Whether in a lead or supporting role, the wavy-haired charmer left his mark on every film production that welcomed his talents. His performance as Phileas Fogg in Michael Anderson's *Around the World in Eighty Days* (1956) is one of his most well-known and most beloved. Two years after helping bring Jules Verne's masterpiece to the screen, Niven earned an Oscar for his work in *Separate Tables* (1958). Even in the twilight of his career, David Niven continued to shine as the master thief Sir Charles Lytton in *The Pink Panther* (1963/64), and two of the series' further installments. The actor, who fondly laughed at the shortcomings of his profession in two sets of memoirs, died in Switzerland in 1983.

THE HUNCHBACK OF NOTRE DAME

1939 - USA - 118 MIN. - B & W - DRAMA, LITERARY ADAPTATION

DIRECTOR WILLIAM [=WILHELM] DIETERLE (1893–1972)
SCREENPLAY SONYA LEVIEN, BRUNO FRANK, based on the novel *NOTRE-DAME DE PARIS* by VICTOR HUGO
DIRECTOR OF PHOTOGRAPHY JOSEPH H. AUGUST EDITING WILLIAM HAMILTON, ROBERT WISE MUSIC ALFRED NEWMAN
PRODUCTION PANDRO S. BERMAN for RKO RADIO PICTURES.

STARRING CHARLES LAUGHTON (Quasimodo), MAUREEN O'HARA (Esmeralda), THOMAS MITCHELL (Clopin),
CEDRIC HARDWICKE (Frollo), EDMOND O'BRIEN (Gringoire), HARRY DAVENPORT (King Louis XI),
ALAN MARSHAL (Phoebus), KATHARINE ALEXANDER (Madame de Lys), MINNA GOMBELL (Queen of Beggars),
GEORGE ZUCCO (Procurator), WALTER HAMPDEN (Archdeacon).

"Why was I not made of stone – like thee?"

Paris, at the end of the 15th century: the dawn of a new era. Gutenberg's printing press is a recent and dazzling technological innovation, and now rumors are circulating that the earth is not flat; a fellow called Columbus, it's said, is planning to reach India by sailing westwards. The world is ablaze with a new spirit of restless curiosity – but the common people are still mired in ignorance and superstition. As ever, they stream in their thousands to the square in front of Notre Dame cathedral, to enjoy the jesters, the jugglers, the floggings, and the executions. In the midst of this everyday pandemonium, one man is mocked and feared in equal measure: Quasimodo (Charles

Laughton), the grotesquely deformed cathedral bellringer. Abandoned as a baby, he was adopted and brought up by the sinister Archdeacon Frollo (Cedric Hardwicke), to whom he is still cringingly devoted. Until, that is, the appearance of a stranger in the city rocks their relationship to the core: Esmeralda (Maureen O'Hara) is a dancer with a troupe of gypsies and Frollo is smitten by her charms. Possessed by desire for this dark and sensuous beauty, he murders a rival in a fit of jealousy. Worse: in order to cover up the deed and free himself from his obsession, he has Esmeralda hauled up in court for witchcraft and murder. She is sentenced to burn at the stake – but

"Look at those sets! Whole streets of 15th-century Paris, water-spouting gargoyles, mighty bells, and entire stories of Notre Dame Cathedral recreated with the most exacting precision! And the extras! Half Hollywood was kitted out with doublets, caps and puffed sleeves. The costume designers must have worked round the clock to equip the throngs of bearded, stubbly, one-eyed, toothless, haggard and gouty faces that crowd the screen." *Der Spiegel*

Quasimodo, who has also fallen for her hopelessly, frees the girl at the last moment and spirits her away to the belltower of Notre Dame.

Among the many film adaptations of Victor Hugo's *Notre-Dame de Paris* (1831), William Dieterle's version has probably most successfully captured the tension at the heart of the novel: the ideals of the Enlightenment in a gruesome mediaeval atmosphere.

Dieterle was an erstwhile apprentice of the legendary Berlin theater impresario Max Reinhardt, and his earliest experiences in cinema dated from the era of German Expressionist silent film. In *The Hunchback of Notre Dame*, Expressionist style is a means of rendering the gloomy atmosphere of the pre-war 30s; see the dramatically effective treatment of light and shade, the creepy Gothic architecture and the carefully choreographed crowd scenes.

3

1   Just a hunch: Something tells gypsy beauty
    Esmeralda (Maureen O'Hara) that poet Gringoire
    (Edmond O'Brien) will only be writing love songs
    from now on.

2   Putting the cart before the horse: Believing her to
    have murdered one of their own, the Paris troops
    mount up in full regalia for Esmeralda's execution.

3   Testing the waters: When the rest of the land
    torments Quasimodo (Charles Laughton) for his
    hideousness, Esmeralda demonstrates a drop of
    compassion.

4   Belle tower: Quasimodo snatches Esmeralda out
    of death's hands and opens up his home to her.

5   Riding the Lord's coattails: No matter how much
    sympathy Frollo (Cedric Hardwicke) shows towards
    the hunchback, he never forgets that he is above
    him.

The acting, too, is mercurial in a way that emphasizes the power of the irrational, and even the bizarre make-up (for certain characters) is less Hollywood Realist than German Expressionist.

The Hunchback of Notre Dame is a typical example of the allegorical costume dramas in which 1930s Hollywood encoded its response to contemporary events in Europe – and thereby maintained its neutrality, at least nominally, as the U.S. government (still) demanded. Though the film functions perfectly as a movie entertainment in its combination of horror and romance, Dieterle's political stance is unmistakable. His film quite clearly characterizes the advance of fascism as an atavistic return to the violent obscurantism of the Middle Ages; thus the brutal suppression of the gypsies inevitably reminds us of the Nazis' racial policies and the brutality of their

6   Keeping the faith: All King Louis XI (Harry Davenport) and the Archdeacon (Walter Hampden) can do to stop Frollo from going too far is pray for a little divine intervention.

7   Touch of evil: Esmeralda thinks she's getting closer

to God. Little does she know that she's dancing with the devil.

8   You can ring my bell: Charles Laughton's portrayal of Quasimodo chimed perfectly with the way Victor Hugo had written the character. Actors Lon Chaney,

Anthony Quinn and Anthony Hopkins are among the other great who have played the role.

9   Festival of Fools: Too bad the aristocracy has no idea that they're the stars of the show.

"We prefer to avert our eyes when a monstrosity appears, even when we know he's a synthetic monster, compounded of sponge rubber, greasepaint and artifice. Horror films have their following, but children should not be among them. The Music Hall is no place for the youngsters this week. Take heed!" *The New York Times*

uniformed hordes. When the Hunchback carries Esmeralda off to the cathedral, where she is safe from the clutches of the witch hunters, he triumphantly cries out to the crowd: "Sanctuary! Sanctuary!" We should remember that the film was made at a time when European refugees from fascism were not welcomed by everyone in the United States.

With his courageous action, Quasimodo demonstrates his full humanity. Until then, the Hunchback is merely a pitiable creature; but the deed transforms him into a tragic hero. Though Charles Laughton's face was almost immobilized by the heavy make-up, his performance is unforgettably moving.

Essentially, the poet Gringoire (Edmond O'Brien) fights a no less heroic battle. In a world ruled by torture, hysteria and hatred of strangers, this character can be seen as the voice of the Enlightenment – and it's his untiring

faith in the power of language and the triumph of justice that ultimately saves Esmeralda's life. (Here, the film diverged notably from the plot of Hugo's novel.)

Dieterle's film came at the end of a decade in which the horror-film genre had acquired an unprecedented popularity. It might be said that *The Hunchback of Notre Dame*, for all its Enlightenment impulses, is a little too interested in grabbing its audience with an opportunistic depiction of grotesque ugliness. At the very least, though, Dieterle does hint at the self-reflective attitude that distinguishes Victor Hugo's novel: when the King watches the antics of the populace at the annual Coronation of the Fool, he notes that such grotesque spectacles satisfy the people's hunger for sensation. His observation is undoubtedly directed at us, too – the moviegoers.

UB

WILLIAM (WILHELM) DIETERLE (1893–1972)

In the 30s, Warner Bros. saw the director William Dieterle as a specialist for film biographies of Great Men. Warner were best known for churning out reliably entertaining movies, and it was hoped that Dieterle's biopics would bring the studio a certain cachet – which they did. *The Story of Louis Pasteur* (1935) and *The Life of Emile Zola* (1937) each won three Oscars, and the latter even walked off with Best Film. It can fairly be said, then, that Dieterle was the only German director besides Lubitsch to gain a firm foothold in Hollywood. Yet his name is decidedly less familiar to film fans today, and this may be because Dieterle was never identified as an *auteur*. Instead, he is stuck with an unglamorous reputation as a solid craftsman with a penchant for pathos and a 'message' laid on with a trowel. Perhaps, too, it has something to do with the fact that he always saw himself as essentially a man of the theater, despite having directed movies as impressive as *The Hunchback of Notre Dame* (1939).
Wilhelm (William) Dieterle was born in Ludwigshafen, Germany, and spent nearly two decades working as a theater actor. One of the directors who most influenced him was the legendary Max Reinhardt. Dieterle also appeared in numerous silent movies and began directing films in 1923. Having enjoyed considerable success in Germany, he traveled to Hollywood in 1930 to direct German-language versions of sound films for Warner. Though aware of the importance of cinematography, Dieterle always regarded the actors as the heart of any movie. During his years in Hollywood, he also provided personal support to many refugees and distinguished himself as a committed anti-Nazi. In the 1950s, he returned to his native country.

THE SHOP AROUND THE CORNER

1939 - USA - 99 MIN. - B & W - COMEDY, LOVE STORY

DIRECTOR ERNST LUBITSCH (1892–1947)
SCREENPLAY SAMSON RAPHAELSON, based on the play "PARFUMERIE / ILLATSZERTAR" by NIKOLAUS LASZLO
DIRECTOR OF PHOTOGRAPHY WILLIAM H. DANIELS EDITING GENE RUGGIERO MUSIC WERNER RICHARD HEYMANN
PRODUCTION ERNST LUBITSCH for LOEW'S INC., MGM.

STARRING MARGARET SULLAVAN (Klara Novak), JAMES STEWART (Alfred Kralik), FRANK MORGAN (Hugo Matuschek),
FELIX BRESSART (Pirovitch), JOSEPH SCHILDKRAUT (Ferencz Vadas), SARA HADEN (Flora Kaczek),
WILLIAM TRACY (Pepi Katona), INEZ COURTNEY (Ilona Novotny), CHARLES HALTON (Detective), CHARLES SMITH (Rudy).

"Psychologically, I'm very confused … But personally, I don't feel bad at all."

In an idyllic Budapest, far from the political turmoil of the age, stands a little shop owned by Hugo Matuschek (Frank Morgan). It could be anywhere — Vienna, Paris, or a studio lot at MGM — because people the world over have much the same problems: money, job security, and daily hassle with the boss. Most importantly, they're all in business, and they have to sell things. In this particular case, the wares are leather goods, high-class gifts for the wealthy haute bourgeoisie. Like everyone else, of course, the salesmen at Matuschek's have to sell themselves a little, too, and Alfred Kralik (James Stewart) seems pretty good at it. When it comes to selling, and buying, he's the undisputed authority, and he's trusted by his employer one hundred percent. But lately, he's been looking less than happy. A wage rise is long overdue but nowhere in sight, and the boss has grown strangely distant from his number-one salesman. What's more, Alfred's new colleague Klara (Margaret Sullavan) is making his life even harder with her catty remarks. In any case, he feels called to higher things. For weeks now, he's been engaged in an intense discussion of matters cultural with a mysterious female pen-friend. Who on earth can the mystery woman be? On the very day of his first rendezvous after finishing work, he finishes work for good: Matuschek fires him. And Alfred hasn't the slightest idea that the boss thinks he's been having an affair with his wife …

Ernst Lubitsch regarded *The Shop around the Corner* as the best of his "human comedies." In a time of crisis, he wanted to get away from the stylized high-class milieus of his previous films, and a little closer to the nitty gritty of ordinary life. To some extent, he was trying to escape from the "Lubitsch touch;" but fortunately, he also knew where his qualities lay: in the end, the milieu was the only thing he really did change.

The microcosm of Matuschek's shop is populated by thoroughly average people. But like the protagonists of Lubitsch's glamorous sex comedies, they too have only one means of measuring the quality of their lives and their current exchange value: money. In both cases, they have Lubitsch's full sympathy and understanding. Like Alfred, the director preferred a reassuringly full wallet to a cigarette box that plays a nice tune when you open it.

Now, as then, the fundamental things apply, as was demonstrated when the movie was remade in the 1990s. In *You've Got Mail* (1998), Tom Hanks and Meg Ryan played two rival scriptwriters who hated each other's guts in real life while cultivating an intimate romance with each other's pseudonyms in cyberspace. Back in the 30s, Alfred and Klara were doing it equally anonymously with the help of post-office boxes. Naturally, the mysteriously alluring unknown woman is Klara the shopgirl; but the problem for both of them at the workplace is that they can only see each other as un-

**FELIX BRESSART
(1892–1949)**

In art and in life, there was always an air of tragedy about him. But the shy klutziness of his manner and the physical comedy of his performances did make people laugh. Jewish character actor Felix Bressart was born in East Prussia, an area of present-day Poland that at that time belonged to Germany. He acted at various theaters in Germany and Austria, including a spell in Vienna under Max Reinhardt, before making his film debut in 1928. German moviegoers soon got to know him as the most hopeless doofus in the battalion: in a whole bunch of movies set in army milieus, it was Bressart's thankless task to sweeten the pill of a dubious militaristic message. When the Nazis seized power in 1933, he fled, first to Austria, then to Switzerland, and finally to the U.S.A.

He fared better in Hollywood than many other exiles, for his talents were quickly recognized. This was due largely to Ernst Lubitsch, a fellow East Prussian who immediately cast him in three of his best comedies. In *Ninotchka* (1939), Bressart was one of the three communists seduced by the charms of Paris; in *The Shop Around the Corner* (1939), he played the little shop assistant Pirovitch, who's constantly trying to evade his boss; and in the Anti-Nazi satire *To Be or Not to Be* (1942), he memorably embodied Greenberg, the Jewish bit-player who gives the role of his life as Shakespeare's Shylock.

Felix Bressart was always restricted to supporting roles, but in the Lubitsch films, it's his characters above all that embody the characteristic tension between absurd humor and European melancholy. Until his early death in 1949, he appeared in comedies, musicals and war films, including Fred Zinnemann's *The Seventh Cross* (1944).

1 Window shopping: Frank Morgan gets in the Christmas spirit as capitalist Hugo Matuschek.

2 Serves you right: Klara Novak (Margaret Sullavan) still has a few things to learn about being a sales-girl.

3 Employee of the month: Alfred Kralik (James Stewart, second from the right) is always on Matuschek's bestseller list.

4 Shop around: Although Alfred is in desperate need of additional personnel, he's not sure that Klara will be of any real help.

derpaid flunkies. When Alfred finally discovers the identity of his intellectual correspondent, he begins a desperate game of hide-and-seek. It's cruel for him, because he feels forced to become the rival of his 'other' pen-and-ink self. How could a lowly shop assistant possibly match up to Klara's beautiful illusion?

Lubitsch's feeling for human weaknesses is supported by an excellent cast, and the result is a wonderful combination of romance and razor-sharp analysis that evades the twin traps of kitsch and cynicism. Besides the wonderfully gloomy James Stewart and the snippy Margaret Sullavan, Felix Bressart gives a brilliant performance as the humble Pirovitch. Not only does he serve as Matuschek's valued window dresser, he also does a sterling job as Alfred's secret go-between. Joseph Schildkraut plays Valas, a vain and unpopular colleague who is the real reason his boss has marital troubles. Frank Morgan's Matuschek is a jovial despot whose personal problems and insecu-

"You know, people seldom go to the trouble of scratching the surface of things to find the inner truth."

Film quote: Alfred Kralik (James Stewart)

"It's a marvelously delicate romantic comedy, very moving, with the twisted intrigues among the staff also carrying narrative weight, Morgan's cuckolded proprietor being especially affecting. Thoroughly different from *To Be or Not to Be* but just as exhilarating, it's one of the few films that truly justify Lubitsch's reputation for that special 'touch.'" Time Out Film Guide

5   How do you like the sound of that? Lubitsch favorite Felix Bressart emerges as the voice of reason. His character Pirovitch assists Alfred in reading between the lines of Klara's love letters.

6   Melody time: In Klara's hands, a little wind-up box is hardly frivolous – it's music to a lonely customer's ears.

7   Getting the sack: Everyone is shocked to learn that Ferencz Vadas (Joseph Schildkraut, second from the right) is nothing more than a self-interested basket case.

8   You've got mail: Klara and Alfred's relationship works much better on paper than it does in person – at least initially.

"There is such subtleness about it: the actors towards their characters, the director towards the supporting cast! Lubitsch has an implicit trust in his actors and the intelligence of his audience, giving us plenty of room to sit back and enjoy!" *Le Monde*

rity soften our judgment of his management style. Nothing is more dreaded in the shop than his demand: "Give me your *honest* opinion!"

The technical challenge for Lubitsch was to keep things moving in a tiny space. So the shop's personnel are constantly racing up and down ladders, or – like Pirovitch whenever a confrontation with the boss looks imminent – using the spiral staircase as a means of escape. Lubitsch was known as "the master of doors," and here too they inevitably have a major role to play. As soon as the last customer has left the shop, the superb dialog changes in tone, and smooth sales professionals are transformed back into people like you and me. Which doesn't mean they ever stop *performing* …

Lubitsch was never closer to Frank Capra than this, and on Christmas Eve, everything turns out happy. Admittedly, Matuschek's marriage is finished, but his face lights up like a Christmas tree when a steady throng of festive shoppers keeps the cash registers ringing. The staff get the bonuses they so richly deserve and Alfred finally plucks up the courage to reveal his true identity to Klara. Surprise, surprise – she's nowhere near as disappointed as he'd feared, but simply very confused. If there's one thing Lubitsch can teach us, it's that happiness is not to be found in books; but maybe, if we open our eyes, we can find it in the shop around the corner.

GONE WITH THE WIND

1939 - USA - 222 MIN. (ORIGINAL RELEASE) / 238 MIN. (RESTORED VERSION) - COLOR - DRAMA, LITERARY ADAPTATION

DIRECTOR VICTOR FLEMING (1883–1949)
SCREENPLAY SIDNEY HOWARD, based on the novel of the same name by MARGARET MITCHELL
DIRECTOR OF PHOTOGRAPHY ERNEST HALLER **EDITING** HAL C. KERN, JAMES E. NEWCOM **MUSIC** MAX STEINER
PRODUCTION DAVID O. SELZNICK for SELZNICK INTERNATIONAL PICTURES.

STARRING CLARK GABLE (Rhett Butler), VIVIEN LEIGH (Scarlett O'Hara), LESLIE HOWARD (Ashley Wilkes), OLIVIA DE HAVILLAND (Melanie Hamilton), THOMAS MITCHELL (Gerald O'Hara), BARBARA O'NEIL (Ellen O'Hara), EVELYN KEYES (Suellen O'Hara), ANN RUTHERFORD (Carreen O'Hara), HATTIE MCDANIEL (Mammy), OSCAR POLK (Pork), BUTTERFLY MCQUEEN (Prissy), RAND BROOKS (Charles Hamilton), CARROLL NYE (Frank Kennedy), LAURA HOPE CREWS (Aunt Pittypat Hamilton).

ACADEMY AWARDS 1939 OSCARS for BEST PICTURE (David O. Selznick), BEST DIRECTOR (Victor Fleming), BEST ACTRESS (Vivien Leigh), BEST SUPPORTING ACTRESS (Hattie McDaniel), BEST ADAPTED SCREENPLAY (Sidney Howard), BEST CINEMATOGRAPHY (Ernest Haller, Ray Rennahan), BEST EDITING (Hal C. Kern, James E. Newcom), and BEST ART DIRECTION / INTERIOR DECORATION (Lyle R. Wheeler).

"After all ... tomorrow is another day."

In Hollywood, greatness is written on the wind. And grand sweeping statements can hit like a tempest as early as the opening titles. Their message: *Gone with the Wind* was and is the most magnificent of all epics, a triumph in moviemaking, and an ode to the Old South unlike any other. Return to a world upheld by masters and slaves, where chivalry has yet to die. Hear the Civil War cannons roar as they crumble the walls, but not the foundations of a great society. And see it all as only novelist Margaret Mitchell could tell it.

Able to spot a hit from a mile off, producer David O. Selznick paid a then incredible 50,000 dollars to secure the rights to adapt the story for the cinema. The year was 1936, and the novel – the only own Mitchell would ever write – had been in print for approximately a month. Immediately, Selznick launched a publicity campaign that transformed the book into a bestseller.

A media-propagated 'search for Scarlett' would follow, although the decision already had been made: Vivien Leigh, a virtually unknown British actress, had signed on to play the shameless Southern Belle. A bold heroine

in an era when Hollywood preferred to see women as meek, Scarlett braves an inferno for her Tara home and a shot at true love with the wrong man. Between Secession and Reconstruction, her obstinacy will have worn down as many husbands as the filming of her story did directors: personal differences with male lead Clark Gable caused George Cukor to jump ship; and Victor Fleming suffered fits of exhaustion that forced him temporarily pass the baton to Sam Wood. Then again, sleep deprivation and frayed nerves seem a small price to pay in exchange for over three-and-a-half hours of the finest cinema the world had ever seen.

At the center of this Technicolor extravaganza of magnolias and antebellum estates is the larger-than-life Scarlett. Desperately in love with foolish dreamer Ashley Wilkes (Leslie Howard) from the moment they meet, the pampered plantation owner's daughter simply won't take no for an answer. And until shortly before the curtain falls, neither Ashley's happy marriage to his cousin Melanie (Olivia de Havilland) nor the cunning advances of war-

1   Well, I'll be damned: Heartthrob Clark Gable sizzles things up down South as dashing rogue Rhett Butler.

2   Little whore on the prairie: For a long time, Rhett feels more at home in the hands of a working girl than he does in the company of a fine lady. Yet even he is prone to a change of heart.

3   A very civil war: Many a fine suitor will vie for the hand of young Scarlett O'Hara (Vivien Leigh). But it will ultimately take more than gentlemanly tactics to conquer her.

4   A walk in the park: Melanie (Olivia de Havilland) and Ashley (Leslie Howard) have a picture-perfect romance that knows not the sound and the fury of Scarlett and Rhett.

5   Tara firma: In just a few years time, the life Scarlett so loved as a child will be but a distant memory.

horse Rhett Butler (Clark Gable) can steer Scarlett's heart from its path. While Rhett alone sees her for the wolf she is, even he underestimates the extent of her singled-mindedness; for no matter whom she marries, she'll relinquish her sexual autonomy to no one. Melanie respects her for it, whereas Rhett claims not to "give a damn." How telling it is that male and female viewers also tend to differ in their interpretations of the film.

From today's standpoint, *Gone with the Wind's* romance may seem trite and its attitude towards slavery questionable at best. The picture, however, presents us with two very 'real' characters. Scarlett is the first. Beyond good and evil, and riddled with flaws, she seems infinitely more human than the angelic Melanie. Mammy (Hattie McDaniel), the story's second great heroine, gains depth through a resoluteness that commands more respect than all the

"*Gone with the Wind* presents a sentimental view of the Civil War, in which the 'Old South' takes the place of Camelot and the war was fought not so much to defeat the Confederacy and free the slaves as to give Miss Scarlett O'Hara her comeuppance. But we've known that for years; the tainted nostalgia comes with the territory. Yet as *Gone with the Wind* approaches its 60th anniversary, it is still a towering landmark of film, quite simply because it tells a good story, and tells it wonderfully well." *Chicago Sun-Times*

7

"Sir, you are no gentleman."
"And you, Miss, are no lady."

Film quote: Scarlett O'Hara (Vivien Leigh) and Rhett Butler (Clark Gable)

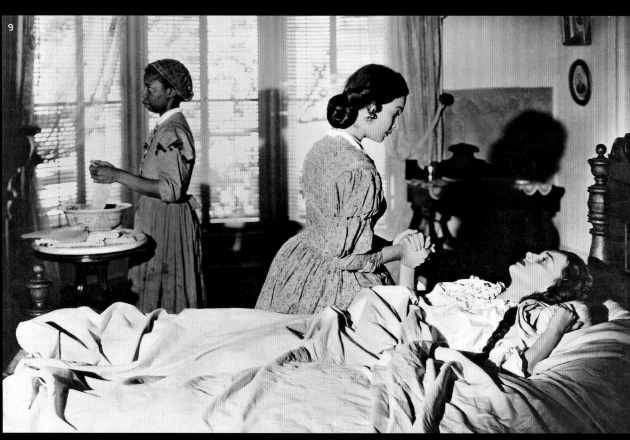

6 Standing grand: Gunrunner and adventurer Rhett Butler doesn't flinch in the face of adversity.

7 Pride and prejudice: Vivien Leigh embodies the legacy of the Antebellum South as the steadfast Scarlett O'Hara.

8 Bonnie and blithe: Rhett and Scarlett are overjoyed by the birth of their daughter.

9 I don't know nothing about birthing no babies: Although Prissy (Butterfly McQueen, left) often doubts herself in emergencies, Scarlett always rises to the occasion.

10 As God is my witness, I'll never be hungry again: Scarlett may not have to endure poverty again, but only time will tell whether or not she'll end up love-starved.

other characters put together. It was a poignant performance that made history as Hattie McDaniel became the first black actress to receive an Oscar.

Beyond the characters themselves, uncompromising images of the Civil War continue to breathe life into this epic as the camera chronicles the burning of Atlanta in blood-red. From here, a panoramic crane shot reveals a field hospital where limbless and fallen soldiers reach as far as the eye can see. Such gruesome confrontations with American history, in particular with the Civil War, were categorically regarded as box-office poison prior to *Gone with the Wind*. And nobody, other than Selznick himself, reckoned with a hit.

Star appeal, color symbolism – green for Scarlett, black for Rhett, ash yellow for Ashley etc. – and the fusion of individual destiny with historical

10

**CLARK GABLE
(1901–1960)**

Ohio native Clark Gable was born the son of a freelance oil driller. Several small stage appearances sparked the future star's lifelong interest in theater and prompted him to seek out professional acting training. His coach, Josephine Dillon, an actress who was 17 years his senior, soon become the first Mrs. Clark Gable.

MGM took the screen hopeful under contract in 1930 and proceeded to make a leading man out of him. In no time flat, the sly dog with Mickey Mouse ears and pomade mustache had become what every woman of the era was looking for. Nonetheless, it wasn't until MGM lent Gable to the smaller Columbia for Frank Capra's hit comedy *It Happened One Night* (1934) that the actor won his first Oscar.

Numerous adventure picture roles followed, with Gable often being paired opposite leading ladies like Jean Harlow or Myrna Loy. His most memorable performance in the genre came as Lieutenant Fletcher Christian in *Mutiny on the Bounty* (1935), rated by many fans as a highlight in his career. Later, when David O. Selznick needed someone to play Rhett Butler in *Gone with the Wind* (1939), Gable was the only man the producer so much as considered.

In 1942, after losing third wife Carole Lombard in a plane crash, the man nicknamed the "King of Hollywood" was overcome by depression and enlisted in the army. Well over 40, Gable carried out missions over Nazi Germany as a U.S. fighter pilot and returned home a war hero. Despite enjoying the respect of the entire industry, it was clear that his Hollywood heyday was behind him. Be that as it may, the never-say-die Gable still insisted on performing his own daredevil stunts for his final film, John Huston's *The Misfits* (1960). In all likelihood, the strain was too much for him. Two days after wrapping up the shoot, he suffered a heart attack that claimed his life two weeks later.

477

"As God is my witness, as God is my witness they're not going to lick me. I'm going to live through this and when it's all over, I'll never be hungry again. No, nor any of my folk. If I have to lie, steal, cheat or kill. As God is my witness, I'll never be hungry again."

Film quote: Scarlett O'Hara (Vivien Leigh)

11 Southern gentleman gone south: Knowing that he could never live up to Scarlett's expectations, Ashley (Leslie Howard) rejects her in no uncertain terms.

12 Mass exodus: Atlantans evacuate the town to escape the wrath of the Union Army.

13 Sherman's March to the Sea: In one of the most infamous acts in United States history, the Northern troops sweep over Georgia like a ball of fire.

14 Life under glass: Having faced war head-on, Scarlett emerges from a purple haze with new-found humanity.

events created a blueprint for what would become the gold standard in filmmaking. Even so, the then astronomical four-million dollar budget did more to end an era in filmmaking than usher in a new one. The fact that *Gone with the Wind* continues to bowl over contemporary audiences as a total work of art of Wagnerian complexity is the single-handed accomplishment of old-school producer David O. Selznick. He was the one who effectively pulled all the strings in terms of directing, screenwriting, and editing. Forget the director's cut, Selznick knew exactly what he wanted from start to finish and sat at editor Hal C. Kern's side to get a perfectly mastered negative. Needless to say, *Gone with the Wind* was made at a point in time prior to the creation of unions and workers' rights. Eight Oscars and gross U.S. ticket sales totaling 200 million dollars made it one of the most impressive undertakings in cinematic history and attest to the majesty of a production that could never be replicated today.

PB

14

"Scarlett is at once despicable and admirable. One of our greatest challenges is to sort out whether she is ultimately good, bad, or simply a flawed person like the rest of us." *Apollo Movie Guide*

THE RULES OF THE GAME

La Règle du jeu

939 - FRANCE - 91 MIN. (PREMIERE VERSION) / 106 MIN. (INTEGRAL VERSION) - B & W - DRAMA, TRAGICOMEDY

DIRECTOR JEAN RENOIR (1894–1979)
SCREENPLAY JEAN RENOIR, CARL KOCH **DIRECTORS OF PHOTOGRAPHY** JEAN BACHELET, JACQUES LEMARE, JEAN-PAUL ALPHEN, ALAIN RENOIR **EDITING** MARGUERITE RENOIR, MARTHE HUGUET **MUSIC** WOLFGANG AMADEUS MOZART, PIERRE-ALEXANDRE MONSIGNY, FRÉDÉRIC CHOPIN, CAMILLE SAINT-SAËNS, JOHANN STRAUSS **PRODUCTION** JEAN RENOIR, CLAUDE RENOIR for LA NOUVELLE ÉDITION FRANÇAISE.

STARRING MARCEL DALIO (Robert de la Chesnaye), NORA GRÉGOR (Christine de la Chesnaye), ROLAND TOUTAIN (André Jurieux), JEAN RENOIR (Octave), MILA PARÉLY (Geneviève de Marras), PAULETTE DUBOST (Lisette, Mme. la Chesnaye's chambermaid), GASTON MODOT (Schumacher, the gamekeeper), JULIEN CARETTE (Marceau, the poacher), PIERRE NAY (Monsieur St. Aubin), CLAIRE GÉRARD (Madame de la Bruyère).

"The most terrible thing in the world is that everyone has his reasons."

Regularly included in lists of the ten best films ever made, *The Rules of the Game* is positively revered by French cineastes. At first glance, however, it may appear to be nothing more than a fairly trivial social comedy. A crowd of wealthy guests out for a good time arrive at the country house of a French aristocrat. Entertainment has been arranged: a foxhunt, a festive dinner, and an improvised theater performance. The fine folks eat, laugh and flirt; it seems that each of them is at least a little in love with all the others. And what about the lower orders? The staff, too, have their love affairs … Comedy turns into slapstick when a furious gamekeeper chases his rival across the entire estate, wantonly eliminating the barrier between Upstairs and Downstairs. Anyone who's seen Robert Altman's *Gosford Park* (2001) will see where he got his inspiration.

If you believe them, all the directors of the Nouvelle Vague have seen this film at least ten times – and with very good reason, as we'll recognize when we take that second glance. What's astonishing about this movie is the perfection with which Jean Renoir sets up and presents his 'game.' The cinematography, the editing and the dialog transport a narrative that flows with almost magical ease, yet is beautifully complemented and completed by more somber sequences shot with immense depth of field. One scene shows the host in the foreground singing the praises of friendship – which is so much more reliable than love … while the very friend he's eulogizing is

running off with his wife in the background. In reality, *nothing* can be relied on here. The rules of the game – or the breaking of them – lead to intrigues, betrayal and murder.

In all this, Renoir demonstrates his mastery of character, his profound knowledge of the human psyche. All of the figures depicted in this film are fascinating, and most of them are introduced in the opening sequence. After a flight across the Atlantic lasting 23 hours, the pilot André (Roland Toutain) is given a hero's welcome. In the world of Jean Renoir, however, there are no heroes. The reporters hold out their microphones and André laments the non-appearance of the woman for whose sake he had undertaken the whole adventure. Christine (Nora Grégor) is listening to the broadcast, as is her husband, the Marquis de la Chesnaye (Marcel Dalio), in another room. He confronts her, they talk, and it soon becomes clear that the rules of the game, in these circles, also include promiscuity. Octave (Jean Renoir), a friend who lives with them, is another of Christine's secret admirers; he brings the despairing André to the Marquis' house party in order to smooth the waves.

What's it all about, though? What are the rules of the game? Many things can only be understood intuitively. Not a single word reveals the political significance of this film, merely the year in which it was produced: shortly after the Munich Agreement and just before the outbreak of the Secon

1   Game face: Lisette (Paulette Dubost) knows that the rule number one of love and marriage is never to kiss and tell.

2   The games people play: Many moviegoers felt that having Austrian actress Nora Grégor (seated) in the role of Christine de la Cheyniest would make the film a decidedly political spectacle.

3   There there now: Despite the way things look, Octave's need for comfort isn't a sign that actor-director Jean Renoir felt less at ease in front of the camera than he did behind it.

4   Skeleton dance: This brief interlude from the main story is less an innocent diversion than a commentary on the dangers of infidelity.

5   You can either watch or wonder what happened: The Marquis Robert de la Chesnaye (Marcel Dalio, right) and his poacher Marceau (Julien Carette) don't believe their eyes.

World War, Renoir shows us a doomed civilization. In the famous hunting scene, a dozen rabbits suffer an agonizing death; a rural idyll transformed into a battlefield. At the end of the film, after his unfortunate change of clothing, André will die in precisely this way. No one wanted this death, and the Marquis calls it "a regrettable accident." But in view of what has happened, that is of little significance. And the death of André is caused by Octave, of all

people – André's friend, and one of the most lovable characters ever to appear in a film.

Renoir himself played Octave, and he described the character as the wedge one places under a piece of furniture so that it doesn't wobble. Octave, who introduces practically every scene, pursues his own policy of appeasement to ensure that the rules of the game are observed. He does so

JEAN RENOIR
(1894–1979)

As a young director, he would sell one of his father's paintings whenever he needed to finance a film. Jean Renoir, born in Paris in 1894, was the son of the Impressionist painter Pierre-Auguste Renoir. Impressionism and Naturalism also left their mark on his early silent films, which he made to further the career of his wife, actress Catherine Hessling. He himself soon enjoyed general recognition as the most important French film director of the age. Renoir's work influenced at least two generations of filmmakers in France and abroad, who idolized him as a realist, humanist, moralist and pacifist.

His films *Toni* (1934/35) and *The Crime of Monsieur Lange* (*Le Crime de Monsieur Lange*, 1936) were forerunners of Italian Neorealism. *The Grand Illusion* (*La Grande Illusion*, 1937) is still one of the best antiwar films ever made. Renoir had a perceptive eye and a deep understanding for the people around him, and he also had the ability to express his insights in films of formal perfection. He was a master of lighting, and a pioneer of deep-focus cinematography and the mobile camera; and in everything he did, he was a perfectionist. He reached the highpoint of his artistic career with *The Rules of the Game* (*La Règle du jeu*, 1939), but the film's lack of success moved him to emigrate to the U.S.A. He once joked that no Frenchman could produce anything worthwhile unless he had a bottle of wine and piece of Brie in easy reach. In fact, he had little success in Hollywood, though he revered American films, especially those of Charles Chaplin. Nonetheless, he did receive an Oscar nomination for *The Southerner* (1945). In 1955, he scored another major success in France with *French Cancan*. Jean Renoir died in Beverly Hills in 1979.

5

with growing helplessness, spending a large part of the film in a bear costume. He is a key character, but not a leading one, in a magnificent ensemble. Renoir approaches each and every one of them with endless sympathy and without an ounce of malice, but they resemble the mechanical effigies collected by the melancholy Marquis. In 1939, moviegoers understood this metaphor instantly. There were furious protests at the premiere, and the film was widely regarded as "demoralizing". Renoir was shocked, and made some very substantial cuts in the film, but his days as an independent director were numbered. The film was banned. Only in 1965, after enthusiastic admirers had lovingly restored the film, was *The Rules of the Game* shown in Paris again.

PB

6   A sight for sore eyes: Christine looks through a pair of binoculars and catches her husband playing the field.

7   Watch me pull a rabbit out of my hat: Marceau's gradual shift from poacher to gamekeeper is more than a sleight of hand.

8   You win some, you lose some: Octave and his lovesick pal André (Roland Toutain) can't resist a bit of fun and games with an attractive woman.

"It excels in every area. The camera work is innovative but also part of the narrative. The exposition – the bane of all writers – is exquisite. Eight characters, all unique, are set in motion; each interacts in a different way with the others … At the end of an era (the eve of WW II), Renoir took a dying genre (the bedroom farce) and used it to define the world." *Paul Schrader, in: The Rules of the Game – The Criterion Collection DVD*

1939 - USA - 97 MIN. - B & W - WESTERN

DIRECTOR JOHN FORD (1894–1973)
SCREENPLAY DUDLEY NICHOLS, based on the short story *STAGE TO LORDSBURG* by ERNEST HAYCOX
DIRECTOR OF PHOTOGRAPHY BERT GLENNON EDITING DOROTHY SPENCER, OTHO LOVERING MUSIC RICHARD HAGEMAN,
W. FRANKE HARLING, JOHN LEIPOLD, LEO SHUKEN, LOUIS GRUENBERG PRODUCTION WALTER WANGER for
WALTER WANGER PRODUCTIONS, UNITED ARTISTS.

STARRING JOHN WAYNE (Henry a. k. a. 'The Ringo Kid'), CLAIRE TREVOR (Dallas), JOHN CARRADINE (Hatfield),
THOMAS MITCHELL (Doc Boone), ANDY DEVINE (Buck Rickabaugh), GEORGE BANCROFT (Marshal Curly Wilcox),
DONALD MEEK (Samuel Peacock), BERTON CHURCHILL (Henry Gatewood), LOUISE PLATT (Lucy Mallory),
TOM TYLER (Luke Plummer), TIM HOLT (Blanchard).

ACADEMY AWARDS 1939 OSCARS for BEST SUPPORTING ACTOR (Thomas Mitchell), and BEST MUSIC (Richard Hageman,
W. Franke Harling, John Leipold, Leo Shuken).

"There are some things a man just can't walk away from."

A stagecoach carrying eight passengers from Tonto to Lordsburg heads through Indian territory; a cowboy avenges the murder of his father and brother. That's all there is to the story, and all John Ford needs to create a powerhouse of a Western. The bare bones of the plot have inspired countless analyses and eulogies. What's more, the film attached to them claimed two Oscars – and this in 1939, when the movie counted pictures like *Gone with the Wind* (1939) among its rivals.

The appeal of this Western has its roots in the myths and legends of young America and its early settlers. It's a movie that deals with the Wild Frontier, and the invisible border that separates civilization from savagery and the unknown, which the stagecoach has to cross as it passes through Indian territory en route to its destination. A further focus is the age-old image of the lonesome cowboy, that noble figure of few words embodied by the Ringo Kid (John Wayne), whose self-belief enables him to overcome any obstacle. And ultimately, *Stagecoach* is about the notion of unlimited freedom symbolized by the nation's once uncharted reaches, the clouds in the sky and the majestic rocks known as Monument Valley.

Stagecoach was the first John Ford film to be shot in this valley, a location that would become central to his work. This milestone motion picture also marked the first true 'John Ford – John Wayne' collaboration, despite the fact that it was already the actor's 80th appearance in front of the camera, including productions that had involved bit and walk-on parts in Ford films in the late 20s and early 30s. Wayne's stardom and the indelible impact he was to make on the Western began with his role as the Ringo Kid. In this film, both the actor and the genre were reinvented by Ford, putting a welcome end to the decade's cookie-cutter B-movies and their hordes of singing cowboys. With *Stagecoach*, cinematic greatness finally rode out onto the prairie.

French film theorist André Bazin is the man who elevated *Stagecoach* to the Mount Olympus of Westerns, a status it still enjoys today. He compared the picture to a perfectly fashioned wheel that maintains an ideal balance between modern myths, historical reconstruction, psychological truth and traditional subject matter. But even at the time of its release, critics were already hailing *Stagecoach* as an instant classic, admiring its unity of time and space, its poetic backdrops, masterful composition and crisp narrative structure.

"In one superbly expansive gesture, which we ... can call *Stagecoach*, John Ford has swept aside ten years of artifice and talkie compromise and has made a motion picture that sings a song of camera."

The New York Times

5

1 Fleshed out characters: The Ringo Kid (John Wayne) and Dallas (Claire Trevor) spice up life in the Wild West as Hollywood's favorite outlaw and hooker.

2 Highway patrol: The Sheriff pulls over a Lordsburg-bound stagecoach believed to be transporting outlaw Ringo Kid.

3 Geronimo! With *Stagecoach's* revolutionary chase sequence, John Ford transformed the daily strife between cowboys and Indians into warfare of epic magnitude.

4 Cutting the cord: The last chapter opens on the Wild West when Lucy's baby is born at the Apache Wells outpost and civilization comes marching in.

5 Honest John: Dallas always welcomes customers who can ease her pain. Actor Thomas Mitchell won a Best Supporting Actor Oscar for his performance as Doc Boone.

Ford's staging is characterized by a brilliant economy of direction. Only in a limited number of scenes does the director unleash the camera, but when he does, you really feel the force of it, as in the almost eight-minute-long action sequence when the Apache ambush the stagecoach, or the daring river crossing for which two logs have to be strapped to the wagon's wheels.

Naturally, the camera also swings into action when John Wayne first appears on screen. The legendary scene starts with the cowboy firing his gun and forcing the stagecoach to a stop, his weapon twirling about his finger, his saddle swung loosely over his shoulder. The camera pulls in toward his young, determined face, as his eyes go wide with disbelief. For seated beside the wagon's driver (Andy Devine) is the marshal (George Bancroft), who's been hunting him down. It seems to be the end of the line for the Ringo Kid, an escaped convict who just a minute ago was headed to Lordsburg for a showdown with the Plummer Brothers. Now a prisoner, he continues his journey alongside the coach's six other travelers. These include a corrupt banker

YAKIMA CANUTT (1896–1986)

His are the first words spoken in *Stagecoach* (1939). An army scout, he alerts the company to the nearby Apache. Later – he was a full-blood Apache himself – he leaps from the back of his horse to the one at the head of the stagecoach. John Wayne shoots him in the back, he falls to the ground and is trampled to a pulp first by horses' hooves and then by the wheels of the cart. Whenever there was a scene featuring horses, chases or fighting scenes, Yakima Canutt was the man to call. If he wasn't so already, *Stagecoach* clinched his status as Hollywood's most popular stuntman.

A former rodeo rider, Canutt entered Tinseltown during the late 1910s by means of screen cowboy Tom Mix. He soon became a permanent fixture in Westerns as both an actor and stuntman. Rather than going to the trouble of describing detailed action sequences, his screenwriters often jotted down a mere: "Action by Yakima Canutt." The daredevil doubled for names like Gene Autry, Roy Rogers and John Wayne, with whom he shot over 30 pictures. Together they came up with a standard choreography for fist fights that is still used in movies today. Beyond this, Canutt also did behind-the-scenes work and was a valued second unit director. But it was the feast of a chariot race he staged for *Ben-Hur* (1959) that ultimately confirmed his status as an out-and-out Hollywood legend.

Although his job required guts few people had, Canutt left nothing up to chance. Indeed, he even set the safety standards for future stuntmen and was presented with an honorary Oscar in 1967 for his life's work. In 1986, Yakima Canutt died in Hollywood at the age of 90.

6

"One of the greatest of all Westerns. And one of the most interesting Hollywood possibly could have for study ... We have the feeling all the time that we are pressing onward with the characters, going with them on their perilous journey, hoping with them that they will reach their destination in safety. And for that, we have John Ford to thank." *The Hollywood Spectator*

6   Crazy horse: While the Indians in Stagecoach are portrayed with dignity, they are, to a great extent, stylized warriors.

7   John Ford Country: The Monument Valley portion of the shoot lasted for only forty-seven days. Nonetheless, the region's imagery defines the look of the entire film.

(Berton Churchill), a bashful whiskey salesman who later musters up some gumption (Donald Meek), a lush of a doctor who is still able to practice his craft despite his habit (Thomas Mitchell), a Confederate gambler who proves to be of noble origin (John Carradine), an uppity society lady who keeps her pregnancy a secret (Louise Platt), and a prostitute (Claire Trevor) who steps in as the woman's midwife.

The ensemble as a whole has often been seen as a microcosm of the civilization of the Old West, which valued appearances over honesty, and hypocrisy over human decency. Whether the film actually intended to present such a critical view of American society remains a matter of debate. But what is clear is that John Ford's sympathies lie with the outsider, the lonesome dove for whom society has no place. Thus it is the Ringo Kid, i. e. the wanted man, and the prostitute who eventually find happiness as they ride off together towards the outlaw's little ranch. Only there, far beyond the reaches of the city, do people like them have a real chance to live life the way they want to. It's a utopian view of the great wild yonder, which *Stagecoach* presents more strikingly than any picture that came before.

NM

REBECCA

1940 - USA - 130 MIN. - B & W - THRILLER, LITERARY ADAPTATION

DIRECTOR ALFRED HITCHCOCK (1899–1980)
SCREENPLAY ROBERT E. SHERWOOD, JOAN HARRISON, based on the novel of the same name by
DAPHNE DU MAURIER DIRECTOR OF PHOTOGRAPHY GEORGE BARNES EDITING HAL C. KERN, W. DONN HAYES
MUSIC FRANZ WAXMAN PRODUCTION DAVID O. SELZNICK for SELZNICK INTERNATIONAL PICTURES.

STARRING JOAN FONTAINE (The Second Mrs. de Winter), LAURENCE OLIVIER (Maxim de Winter),
GEORGE SANDERS (Jack Favell), JUDITH ANDERSON (Mrs. Danvers), NIGEL BRUCE (Major Giles Lacey),
GLADYS COOPER (Beatrice Lacey), REGINALD DENNY (Frank Crawley), C. AUBREY SMITH (Colonel Julyan),
MELVILLE COOPER (Coroner), FLORENCE BATES (Mrs. Van Hopper).

ACADEMY AWARDS 1940 OSCARS for BEST PICTURE (David O. Selznick), and BEST CINEMATOGRAPHY (George Barnes).

"You thought I loved Rebecca? You thought that? I hated her!"

A young woman employed as a travel companion (Joan Fontaine) falls in love with wealthy widower Maxim de Winter (Laurence Olivier) in romantic Monte Carlo. The two marry and retreat to Manderley, the de Winters' familial estate located on the coast of Cornwall. But what starts off as a fairy-tale romance for the new Mrs. de Winter soon spirals into a nightmare when the shadow of her husband's former spouse, Rebecca, begins to tighten its grip on the timid lady of the manor. At the heart of the matter is housekeeper Mrs. Danvers (Judith Anderson), who remains loyal to her previous mistress' memory. Indeed, beyond treating the new madam as an intruder, the servant even goes so far as to insinuate that Maxim de Winter's lingering love for his dead wife is causing him to lapse into trances. Then, one stormy night, the situation is turned on its head as a wrecked ship containing Rebecca's corpse washes ashore and Maxim is suddenly suspected of foul play …

Rebecca marked the beginning of an exciting eight-year collaboration for director Alfred Hitchcock and legendary Hollywood producer David O. Selznick. The studio executive had originally lured the British filmmaker across the Atlantic with a proposal to adapt the sinking of the Titanic for the screen. However, the financial burden of realizing such a project caused the pair to jump ship for Daphne Du Maurier's best-selling novel. It was to be a change of course with complications of its own as the men's differing visions for the screen version of the story proved to have little in common: whereas Hitchcock saw the manuscript as a starting point to embark on his own interpretation of the story, Selznick was determined to give audiences a picture that was uncompromisingly true to the hit novel, as was the case with his previous and hugely popular cinematic endeavor, *Gone with the Wind* (1939).

"Although it wasn't really Hitchcock's kind of story, the film still bears his unmistakable signature."

Le Figaro littéraire

1 Last night I dreamt I went to Manderley again: Home life is horrible for the second Mrs. De Winter (Joan Fontaine), a woman who lives in the shadow of her predecessor, Rebecca.

2 Courting catastrophe: Another inquest is ordered after a boat containing Rebecca's body washes ashore near the mansion and foul play is suspected.

3 Bringing down the house: Maxim de Winter and his new bride won't live at Manderley for long if Mrs. Danvers (Judith Anderson) has any say about it.

4 A hairy situation: Chills run down Mrs. De Winter's spine as she begins to comprehend that Mrs. Danvers was more in love with Rebecca than Maxim was.

5 Good help is hard to find: Horror's favorite housekeeper tries to convince her new mistress to resign, but misses her mark.

Despite being not at all accustomed to production executives meddling in his affairs, Hitchcock found himself with no choice but to concede to Selznick's wishes. *Rebecca*, as a result, breaks dramatically with his previous films. Cast and locale provide for the director's signature British flair, but gone are Hitch's trademark humor and brilliant dramatic irony. Instead, an atmosphere of bewildering darkness and solemnity gradually transforms the psychodrama into a thriller singularly preoccupied with Rebecca's mysterious death. The film rarely leaves the side of its heroine, the story's first-person narrator, who ensures that the audience experiences her character's perpetual state of distress with the same intensity as she does. Little by little, Manderley assumes the character of a prison, as expressive displays of shadow and light imbue the mansion with a horrific life of its own. And by

4

**JUDITH ANDERSON
(1898–1992)**

Her portrayal of the housekeeper with the heart of stone is unforgettable. Rarely do we see her enter or exit in *Rebecca* (1940); somehow she just seems to materialize as if she could predict the camera's every move. Eerie isn't the word to describe the black-uniformed servant with the drawn face and tautly pulled back hair. Inhuman is more like it. The mere fact that no one else has ever managed to hold an icy stare without flinching for so long earns Mrs. Danvers a place among Hollywood's most sinister villains. And for Australian stage actress Judith Anderson, the Oscar-nominated role was to be one of the greatest she'd ever portray on the silver screen.

Still in her homeland when she broke into theater, Anderson was Broadway-bound by 1918. In no time, the actress was celebrated as one of New York's shining stars. Yet despite Anderson's ability to dazzle live audiences as Lady Macbeth, Hollywood seemed altogether unaware of existence. It wasn't even her first appearance behind the camera in 1933, but rather her role in *Rebecca* seven years later that first won her cinematic acclaim and credibility. She soon became a Hollywood favorite, praised for just about everything other than her looks.

Utterly versatile, Anderson was a perfect addition to the illustrious group of eccentrics in *Laura* (1944) as a neurotic jet-setter. More characteristic, however, were the rigid and overbearing mothers she was so apt at playing in Lewis Milestone's black melodrama *The Strange Love of Martha Ivers* (1946) and Raoul Walsh's psychological Western *Pursued* (1947). Anderson also appeared in high-profile, prestigious pieces such as Jean Renoir's *The Diary of a Chambermaid* (1946) and Richard Brooks' *Cat on a Hot Tin Roof* (1958). She survived well into her nineties and remained active on stage, television and film. A career landmark came in 1960 when Queen Elizabeth made the actress a Dame Commander of the British Empire.

"What seems to have happened, in brief, is that Mr. Hitchcock, the famous soloist, suddenly has recognized that, in this engagement, he is working with an all-star troupe. He makes no concession to it and, fortunately, vice versa." *The New York Times*

6   Healthy, wealthy and wise: Worldly Maxim de Winter (Laurence Olivier) falls in love with a woman who lacks the savoir faire of his first wife. In real life, however, he thought that actress Joan Fontaine was a touch too green to play the role.

7   Maid of honor: Mrs. Danvers remains true to the spirit of former mistress Rebecca by making the new Mrs. De Winter feel inadequate.

6

"Possibly it's unethical to criticize performances anatomically. Still we insist. Miss Fontaine has the most expressive spine – and shoulders! – we've bothered to notice this season."

The New York Times

he end of the film, Manderley seems less a place that can be objectively experienced than the very image of a tortured soul.

While the Master of Suspense openly treated *Rebecca* like an unwanted child throughout his career, all the shunning still can not refute the fact that the film ultimately bears his signature. Regardless of how literary the picture's tone may seem to be, it is actually the Hitchcockian visuals that tell the story. To a much greater extent than his British productions, *Rebecca* reveals just how heavily influenced the director was by German silent cinema. More living shadow than human, Mrs. Danvers creeps around Manderley much like Murnau's Nosferatu did in his haunted castle. Nor do the film's similarities with the rest of the master's oeuvre end there. Not only can Mrs. Danvers be seen as a prototype of the many tyrannical mother figures that allowed, but the film was weighted with a feeling of doom, arguably un-

known to Hitch's British period, that would eventually reach its culmination in *Psycho* (1960) some twenty years later. Leitmotifs that would gain importance in future masterpieces also make their debut appearance here. One might even say that Mrs. Danvers' worship of her deceased employer nearly resurrects Rebecca as effectively and surreally as *Vertigo*'s (1958) Scottie does Madeleine Elster.

Ironically, for all Hitchcock's eagerness to take artistic license with the original story, the sole moment the movie succeeds in doing so was entirely beyond his control. Instead, it was work of the censors at the Hays Office who decided that Du Maurier's choice to have Maxim de Winter murder his first wife was unacceptable for viewers. And so, against his better judgment, David O. Selznick allowed for one significant amendment to the original story and had Rebecca lose her life in a tragic fluke accident.

THE PHILADELPHIA STORY

1940 - USA - 112 MIN. - B & W - SCREWBALL COMEDY

DIRECTOR GEORGE CUKOR (1899–1983)
SCREENPLAY DONALD OGDEN STEWART, based on the play of the same name by PHILIP BARRY
DIRECTOR OF PHOTOGRAPHY JOSEPH RUTTENBERG **EDITING** FRANK SULLIVAN **MUSIC** FRANZ WAXMAN
PRODUCTION JOSEPH L. MANKIEWICZ for MGM.

STARRING KATHARINE HEPBURN (Tracy Lord), CARY GRANT (C. K. Dexter Haven), JAMES STEWART (Macaulay Connor),
RUTH HUSSEY (Elizabeth Imbrie), ROLAND YOUNG (Uncle Willie), JOHN HOWARD (George Kittredge),
JOHN HALLIDAY (Seth Lord), MARY NASH (Margaret Lord), VIRGINIA WEIDLER (Dinah Lord), HENRY DANIELL (Sidney Kidd).

ACADEMY AWARDS 1940 OSCARS for BEST ACTOR (James Stewart), and BEST ADAPTED SCREENPLAY (Donald Ogden Stewart).

"I'm testing the air.
I like it but it doesn't like me."

Society weddings have a way of attracting the tabloids like flies to honey. And at the Lord family estate, the final preparations are being made for what will hopefully be Tracy's final march down the aisle. Tracy (Katharine Hepburn), the elder Lord daughter, intends to cast away life as a divorcee and settle down with self-made millionaire George Kittredge (John Howard) – starting tomorrow. However, by the time the sun has set and risen again, a full-blown charade and series of white lies will have turned the young bride's world upside down and put a new slant on the festivities at her Uncle Willie's (Roland Young) pre-wedding party.

No sooner has the audience been briefed on the plot than Tracy's ex-husband C. K. Dexter Haven (Cary Grant) arrives on the scene with Macaulay Connor (James Stewart) and Elizabeth Imbrie (Ruth Hussey), whom he introduces as "intimate friends of Junius," Tracy's absent brother in South America. In truth, however, the uninvited strangers are undercover reporters on assignment for the trashy "Spy Magazine." But before they can pop the cork on her, Tracy feels the sobering after-effects of that pre-ceremonial bubbly and realizes that while it is indeed marriage she seeks, good old George is not the man of her dreams …

The Philadelphia Story was a smash-hit production that brought together many big names under one roof. Not only did it mark the fourth time that Cary Grant and Katharine Hepburn starred opposite one another, but the piece was also under the supervision of master director George Cukor – who had impressed audiences with his juicy comedy The Women (1939) just one year earlier. The Philadelphia Story would also turn out to be the picture that garnered an up-and-coming James Stewart his sole Oscar for Best Actor. But there's no doubt about which of its stars the film really belongs to: Hepburn, the outspoken actress, who had been a Hollywood fixture for over eight years, and who had been branded box-office poison prior to her work in Philadelphia. In a shrewd move that saved her career, Hepburn took a break from life in California and went to New York in search of a play that would provide her with a suitable vehicle. She found it thanks to playwright Philip Barry, who came up with the idea for the stage version of "The Philadelphia Story." With Hepburn's financial support, Barry tailored a play to suit her and succeeded in bringing the greatest stage success of the actress' career to Broadway. The original cast, which also starred Joseph Cotten (as Haven) and Van Helfin (as Connor), performed the production 417 times together.

1 The whole kid and caboodle: Tracy (Katharine Hepburn) gives young Dinah (Virginia Weidler) a few pointers in etiquette. But behind closed doors, the would-be role model is more swinging sister than sophisticated socialite.

2 Big mouths: Reporter Macaulay Connor (James Stewart, left) and Tracy's ex-husband C. K. Dexter Haven (Cary Grant) compare notes on their favorite filly.

3 In with the in laws: Dexter worms his way back into the hearts of Tracy's mother Margaret (Mary Nash, second from the left) and younger sister Dinah.

4 Bottoms up: After accompanying Tracy on a mad-cap drinking binge, Macaulay returns the runaway bride to suitors Dexter and George (John Howard, far left).

5 Snap out of it: George has good reason to believe that his fiancée's heart now belongs to another man. But it remains to be seen whether she has eyes for Dexter or Macaulay.

"It is the personality of Tracy Lord that compels: a character compounded of beauty, brains, wit, wealth, pedigree, position and, eventually, vulnerability."

Sunday Telegraph

REPORTERS IN THE MOVIES "So I'm to be examined, undressed, and generally humiliated at fifteen cents a copy," asks Katharine Hepburn, a. k. a. Tracy Lord in *The Philadelphia Story* (1940) of the two journalists sent to invade her private life. It's a comment with a grain of truth that still applies today. Back when Hepburn made the observation, classic Hollywood was fond of investigating journalism in movies. One might say that the occupation, at least in its modern incarnation with tabloid tactics and the paparazzi, was hardly any older than the motion pictures themselves. In general the typical 'Hollywood reporter' was cosmopolitan yet quite as ruthless as the ones in *The Philadelphia Story*. Here, James Stewart plays a journalist who'd rather be a respectable writer than take advantage of other people's misfortunes; still, while he hates both his job and boss, his work pays the bills. One need only look to the titles of pictures like *Nothing Sacred* (1937) and *Ace in the Hole / The Big Carnival* (1951) to understand the low esteem in which Hollywood often held these professionals. That attitude, however, changed dramatically during the 70s when dedicated investigative reporters began to win over audiences in films like *All the President's Men* (1976), about Woodward and Bernstein's unmasking of the Watergate scandal. The focus shifted again during the 90s when media companies moved into the spotlight once reserved for individual reporters with their power to make, break or annihilate news as they and their backers saw fit. No film makes a better case for this than *Wag the Dog* (1997) in which a staged war is waged to detract the media's attention from the questionable moral conduct of a U.S. President.

> **"Considering the talkative nature of the film, it moves marvelously and the performances would be very hard to beat because they are based on the wit of character rather than lines."** *The Guardian*

Knowing she had something big on her hands, Hepburn secured the rights to the piece, which she proceeded to sell to Louis B. Mayer for a whopping 250,000 dollars and a few lucrative extras: besides ensuring that the actress would star in the screen adaptation of the show, their agreement also gave her a hand in shaping the screenplay and the right to handpick her director and co-stars. Cukor was an obvious choice to lead the project, given

that he was her favorite director, and that she had already worked on four pictures with him, including *Little Women* (1933). Grant and Stewart, masters of understatement, were equally opportune choices as men who could shine without stealing her limelight.

Together, the dream team cooked up one of Hollywood's greatest classic screwballs. The popular 1956 musical remake, *High Society*, starring

6 Ring toss: Tracy gladly accepts jewelry from her ex-husband, fiancó and reporter boyfriend.

7 But surely, you jest: Could a woman as resolute as Tracy truly be satisfied with a happy ending this tame?

Grace Kelly and Bing Crosby, speaks for the film's staying power and charm. The picture was an instant hit upon its premiere. Much of this success is owed to Donald Ogden Stewart's Oscar-winning script, which set the scene for the outrageously comic conflicts that entangle the many protagonists. All the characters live in the lap of luxury – except the two reporters who have to work hard for a living. And all of them, even Tracy's precocious younger sister, are certifiable eccentrics – again excluding the reporters. Yet despite this, even the level-headed Connor develops a taste for extravagant living over the course of the film. Everyone considers Tracy to be a snooty ice

princess – except, of course, for Connor, who simply refuses her on the basis of good principle. True to its theatrical roots, snappy dialog is the backbone of *The Philadelphia Story*, a picture brim full of razor-sharp wit, with panache, smarts and sweetness to match. For in this frivolous world of fun and games there is but one capital offender – boredom. And so, the only character left holding the short end of the stick at the film's conclusion is the guy Haven refers to as Mr. "broad shoulders and narrow-mindedness." You guessed it – George the groom.

HJK

1940 - USA - 120 MIN. - COLOR - CARTOON

DIRECTORS SAMUEL ARMSTRONG (1893–1976) [SEGMENT 1, 2], JAMES ALGAR (1912–1998) [SEGMENT 3],
BILL ROBERTS, PAUL SATTERFIELD [SEGMENT 4], HAMILTON LUSKE (1903–1968), JIM HANDLEY, FORD BEEBE
(1888–1978) [SEGMENT 5], T. HEE (1911–1988), NORMAN FERGUSON (1902–1957) [SEGMENT 6], WILFRED JACKSON
(1906–1988) [SEGMENT 7]
SCREENPLAY LEE BLAIR, ELMER PLUMMER, PHIL DIKE [SEGMENT 1], SYLVIA MOBERLY-HOLLAND, NORMAN WRIGHT,
ALBERT HEATH, BIANCA MAJOLIE, GRAHAM HEID [SEGMENT 2], PERCE PEARCE, CARL FALLBERG [SEGMENT 3],
WILLIAM MARTIN, LEO THIELE, ROBERT STERNER, JOHN MCLEISH [SEGMENT 4], OTTO ENGLANDER, WEBB SMITH,
ERDMAN PENNER, JOSEPH SABO, BILL PEET, VERNON STALLINGS [SEGMENT 5], CAMPBELL GRANT, ARTHUR HEINEMANN,
PHIL DIKE [SEGMENT 7] DIRECTORS OF PHOTOGRAPHY MAXWELL MORGAN, JAMES WONG HOWE MUSIC JOHANN SEBASTIAN BACH
[SEGMENT 1], PIOTR ILYICH TCHAIKOVSKY [SEGMENT 2], PAUL DUKAS [SEGMENT 3], IGOR STRAVINSKY [SEGMENT 4],
LUDWIG VAN BEETHOVEN [SEGMENT 5], AMILCARE PONCHIELLI [SEGMENT 6], MODEST MUSSORGSKY [SEGMENT 7],
FRANZ SCHUBERT [SEGMENT 7] PRODUCTION WALT DISNEY for WALT DISNEY PICTURES.

SPEAKER LEOPOLD STOKOWSKI (Himself), DEEMS TAYLOR (Narrator), WALT DISNEY (Voice of Mickey Mouse).

ACADEMY AWARDS 1941 HONORARY AWARD for THE OUTSTANDING CONTRIBUTION TO THE ADVANCEMENT OF THE USE OF
SOUND IN MOTION PICTURES (Walt Disney, William E. Garity, J. N. A. Hawkins), and HONORARY AWARD for UNIQUE
ACHIEVEMENT IN THE CREATION OF A NEW FORM OF VISUALIZED MUSIC (Leopold Stokowski and his associates).

"Congratulations to you, Mickey!"

Two hours of classical music and often abstract visuals isn't exactly a recipe for a Hollywood blockbuster. Still, prior to *Fantasia* (1940), no one had ever attempted to make a film along those lines. Walt Disney originally dreamed up the concept for the picture with his studio's music director, Carl W. Stalling, back in 1929 – long before the cartoon mogul's astounding success with the world's first full-length animated feature *Snow White and the Seven Dwarfs* (1937) and its successor *Pinocchio* (1940). Ten years later, Leopold Stokowski, the director of the Philadelphia Orchestra, suggested to Disney that he combine a number of the animated shorts known as "Silly Symphonies" in a single concert-length production. *Fantasia* began to take shape, and Disney had plans to regularly update it with new pieces that reflected current trends and innovations in animation. Sixty years later, that dream finally became a reality with the Walt Disney Company's release of *Fantasia 2000*.

For the version completed in his lifetime, Disney chose Bach's "Toccata and Fugue in D minor" to initiate the viewer into the action. The orchestra, first seen in colorful silhouette, quickly evolves from an assembly of stylized instruments into an array of ever-shifting graphic images. Waves, clouds and other natural shapes visually depict musical sounds and vibrations but soon dissolve into utterly abstract representations. Avant-garde filmmaker Oskar Fischinger helped created these images, which are at times reminiscent of the work of expressionist painter Wassily Kandinsky. Unfortunately, the uncompromising Fischinger, who had directed his own abstract animated shorts, left the project disillusioned as later segments began to resemble more traditional cartoons. In fact, during the very next sequence, the audience is presented with a rendition of Tchaikovsky's "Nutcracker Suite" packaged as a fairy ballet that climaxes in a mushroom dance. And from here on, *Fantasia's* music almost exclusively relies on concrete and often kitschy illustrations.

"Yesterday night's long-awaited world premiere of Disney's *Fantasia* at the Broadway Theatre went down in film history. Let us all agree, like almost everyone who was there, that Mickey Mouse, Snow White and the assembled darlings of animated film created something that throws tradition overboard and takes film in quite a new direction. The simple verdict is: *Fantasia* is fantastic." *The New York Times Directory of the Film*

2

3

1　Disney's greatest star: Fantasia is a fireworks display of classical music and animation. "The Sorcerer's Apprentice" sequence is one of the film's many highlights.

2　Fetch a pail of water: Mickey learns that working magic can be a chore.

3　From one maestro to another: Philadelphia Orchestra conductor Leopold Stokowski collaborates with pop culture icon Mickey Mouse on a full-length cartoon symphony.

In the central and undoubtedly most famous segment of the film, Mickey Mouse magically commands a broom to carry buckets of water for him as Paul Dukas' "Sorcerer's Apprentice." Things, however, soon get out of control when the broom inadvertently causes a flood while performing the chore, leaving the sorcerer to intervene and clean up the mess, a mishap that gives rise to a whole range of water images that bear witness to the impeccable artistry and boundless creativity of the Disney animators.

The fourth segment, occupied by Igor Stravinsky's "Rite of Spring," documents the history of the earth from the planet's cosmic – and thus necessarily abstract – infancy to the age of dinosaurs. For this piece, the initial images of life's violent beginnings are in fact so awe-inspiring that the ensuing prehistoric fight for survival is almost anticlimactic in comparison.

Following a light-hearted intermezzo in which various musical sounds are illustrated by a moving line, the mood changes again as the film leads into Beethoven's "Pastoral Symphony." Instead of its original setting of Heiligenstadt, Austria, the piece is relocated to the heights of Mount Olympus, where it now chronicles the flirtations of centaurs. This altogether 'free' interpretation of the musical composition had some music aficionados up in arms, as did the Stravinsky segment which preceded it. Still, Disney took just as much artistic license with his adaptation of Ponchielli's "Dance of the Hours," which he staged as a parodic animal ballet starring hippos and crocodiles.

SILLY SYMPHONIES　Fantasia (1940) was by no means the first of Walt Disney's cartoons to be so in tune with its music. Unlike Fantasia, however, the point of Walt's Silly Symphonies series (1929–1939) was to build a short cartoon around a musical score. The symphonies were the brainchild of Disney musical director Carl W. Stalling, a former silent movie pianist. Kicking off the series was The Skeleton Dance (1929), a piece Ub Iwerks animated to match a Stalling composition inspired by the work of Edvard Grieg. Silly Symphony Flowers and Trees (1932) was the first cartoon ever to be shot in three-color Technicolor, and went on to win an Oscar for Best Animated Short. Disney turned the cartoon into an art form of its own by inspiring his animators to use music and a wide range of artistic techniques to breathe life into the inanimate. Indeed, Disney's experiments with music in the cinema's early days of sound set motion picture standards for animation and live-action films alike. Over the course of its ten-year run, the Silly Symphony series served as a great creative outlet for animators and helped foster new techniques in the field. A number of beloved Disney characters, such as Donald Duck, also got their start thanks to these shorts. The final cartoon in the series, Ugly Duckling (1939), an animated adaptation of the Hans Christian Andersen fairy tale of the same name, was recognized with an Oscar in 1940. That same year, Fantasia, which was awarded two honorary Oscars, marked both the zenith and the grand finale of Disney's revolutionary project.

4 The devil made me do it: The Lord of Darkness hosts the soirée of the century atop Bald Mountain.

5 The land of milk and honey: Despite its symbolic imagery and Art Deco décor, many defenders of art found Disney's film to be an insult to high culture. The Hollywood censors, however, had no objection to mixing cartoon centaurs with Stokowski – as long as the female characters wore fig-leaf pasties.

6 Mule-tilated: Regardless of what the photo may suggest, it was not Disney's intention to make asses of the great masters of classic music.

7 I'll be hard to handle: Mickey learns that you should never send a broom to do a mouse's work.

8 The wind beneath my wings: Beethoven's "Pastorale" reaches new heights through color animation.

> **"It is this faith in the discrimination of the average person that led us to make such a radically different type of entertainment as *Fantasia*. We simply figured that if ordinary folk like ourselves find entertainment in these visualizations of so-called classical music, so would the average person."** *Walt Disney, in: Robert D. Feild, The Art of Walt Disney*

The film concludes with a wonderful grand finale, Mussorgsky's "Night on a Bare Mountain" and Schubert's "Ave Maria." The fusion of these two musically contrasting pieces is among *Fantasia's* most extraordinary technical and artistic achievements. The medley begins with the Prince of Darkness conjuring up an army of demonic creatures for the highly expressionistic Mussorgsky piece, images which are replaced by an angelic procession of lantern bearers and souls floating up to heaven against a foggy backdrop as "Ave Maria" announces the dawn of a new day.

Perhaps inevitably, *Fantasia* was snubbed by audiences of the day. Advocates of high culture claimed it defiled classical music, whereas the general public found it overwhelming – even after it was later shortened by more than forty minutes. Disney's vision of reconciling popular and elite culture had failed for the time being. He was, nonetheless, convinced that education entails the "freedom to have faith in one's own choices, and to read, think and express whatever one wishes." *Fantasia* is the artistic expression of Walt Disney's commitment to these liberties.   SH

THE BANK DICK

1940 - USA - 72 MIN. - B & W - COMEDY

DIRECTOR EDWARD F. CLINE (1892–1961)
SCREENPLAY MAHATMA KANE JEEVES [= W. C. FIELDS] DIRECTOR OF PHOTOGRAPHY MILTON R. KRASNER EDITING ARTHUR HILTON
MUSIC CHARLES PREVIN PRODUCTION CLIFF WORK for UNIVERSAL PICTURES.

STARRING W. C. FIELDS (Egbert Sousé), CORA WITHERSPOON (Agatha Sousé), UNA MERKEL (Myrtle Sousé), EVELYN DEL RIO (Elsie Mae Adele Brunch Sousé), GRADY SUTTON (Og Oggilby), SHEMP HOWARD (Joe), PIERRE WATKIN (Mr. Skinner), HARLAN BRIGGS (Doctor Stall), FRANKLIN PANGBORN (J. Pinkerton Snoopington), JESSIE RALPH (Mrs. Hermisillo Brunch), DICK PURCELL (Mackley Q. Greene).

"Shall I bounce a rock off his head?"
"Respect your father, darling ... What kind of a rock?"

Egbert Sousé is a misanthropic small-town grouch who's always 'looking' for work and somehow landing up in the bar instead. One day, he catches a bank robber without even trying, or wanting to, and is rewarded with a job as a detective at the selfsame bank. He makes a ham-fisted attempt to swindle his new employers, but saves his skin by arresting yet another bank robber, who would have been better off without Egbert as his getaway driver. In this way, he acquires further rewards and even gains the respect of his unruly family.

This is the paper-thin storyline of *The Bank Dick*, a star vehicle for the immortal W. C. Fields. He sways through the movie in a kind of a daze, from which he awakes at regular intervals to issue another of his barbed one-liners. The result is exactly what you'd expect: a classic American film comedy. Anti-hero Egbert Sousé is practically indistinguishable from his legendary creator; either that, or else he's a brilliant caricature of W. C. Fields' public image as the world's grumpiest lush. From what we know of Fields, both interpretations have a lot going for them. Sousé's natural enemies include children, women, everyone else, and of course himself. His only friend is the bar-

man at the Black Pussy Café, the epicenter of his (anti-)social life. This is where he comes to escape the hell he calls 'home.' His mother-in-law wants him to stop smoking and drinking, his daughter keeps throwing things at his head, and his wife despises him with a passion.

At the Black Pussy Café, Sousé is talked into participating in a crooked piece of business with some stocks and shares; in the same establishment, he slips the bank manager a brain-blowing cocktail, to hinder any investigations; and it's to the Black Pussy that he'll ultimately return, when disaster, as ever, has been averted in the nick of time with the help of some highly improbable luck.

When the man with the cauliflower nose was hitting the bottle, nothing and nobody could stop him – not even Universal Pictures, which had asked him to remain on the wagon for the duration before giving him unprecedented control over the entire movie. (The screenplay is credited to one "Mahatma Kane Jeeves," whose identity is not hard to guess.) The conditions were ideal for this brilliant comedian, and *The Bank Dick* displays him at the top

of his game, i. e. shortly before he crashed. Fields cocks a snook at continuity, trusting to his own talents in a loosely improvised string of scenes. Watch that repeated and weirdly elegant trick with the scrunched-up paper napkins, which Fields tosses over his shoulder, catches with the heel of his shoe, and kicks over the bar, or see the scene that comically anticipates Robert De Niro's Travis Bickle, in which Egbert practices with his guns in front of the mirror. *The Bank Dick* was directed by Edward F. Cline, a former member of Mack Sennett's Keystone Kops, and we're reminded of that when the movie climaxes in a marvelous chase scene. When it comes to the script, though, Fields is free to do whatever the hell he wants with it; and he does so, with a vengeance. Many of his best lines are not so much understated as under-mumbled, and some of the most memorable scenes result from his un-

1   Jeepers creepers: Egbert Sousé W. C. (Fields) and his buddy are notorious for being town peepers.

2   Gunsmoke: Two bank robbers are about to find out that Egbert Sousé's incompetence packs a wallop no firearm can match.

3   Kid tested, mother disapproved: W. C. Fields teaches the local youth things they shouldn't know.

4   Now you're talking: Even a jigger's worth of truth serum can't bring a foul-mouthed Sousé to say nasty things to an enchanting young woman.

"There is not a single Fields film that 'must' be seen in order to qualify as a literate movie lover, and yet if you are not eventually familiar with Fields you are not a movie lover at all." *Chicago Sun-Times*

gentlemanly habit of leaving his colleagues waiting for their cue. All of these qualities are exemplified in a mercilessly funny sequence that also gives a fair idea of Fields' actual working methods. While propping up the bar in the Pussy one day, Sousé is hired to direct a movie at very short notice; the real director is even drunker than he is, and completely incapable of going to work. Egbert arrives on the set, makes a few minor changes to the script ("Instead of it being an English drawing room drama, I've made it a circus picture …"), baffles everybody in sight with his directing notes, and vamooses again at the earliest opportunity.

Our hero is supported by a gaggle of supporting characters who are, without exception, thoroughly unsympathetic: an incompetent film producer, a slimy bank manager, Sousé's loveless wife, his egotistical daughter and her fool of a fiancé. But it's not these people who are the target of Fields' japes; the butt of most of them is the outsider Sousé himself, an ultimately pitiable figure. And if the film is actually milder than Fields' early short features, or *Never Give a Sucker an Even Break* (1941), it is still a joy to watch – surreal, original, and wonderfully witty.

PB

UNIVERSAL STUDIOS Universal Studios is an industry giant and the world's oldest movie studio still in operation today. The tale of its birth, however, is decidedly more modest. In 1915, Carl Laemmle merged his Independent Moving Picture Company of America with five other production companies and purchased a plot of land near Los Angeles. The name Universal soon became synonymous with low-cost Westerns, comedy flicks and adventures. Erich von Stroheim's *Foolish Wives* (1921) was among the few prestigious pictures to come out of the studio during its infancy. While Universal's *All Quiet on the Western Front* (1930) did manage to secure an Oscar for Best Picture, the general quality of that year's nominees was substandard. To generate additional revenue, Laemmle opened his studio to the public and began to charge admission. This practice, however, was discontinued with the advent of the talkies as the crowd-pleasing tours created unwanted noise on the film sets. Thankfully, by this time, Universal was cranking out a slew of big-screen money-makers including the many W.C. Fields' pictures and the studio's legendary Universal monster movies: *Frankenstein* (1931), *Dracula* (1931) and *The Mummy* (1933).

Lew Wasserman took over the company in 1946, and a noticeable improvement in production standards followed. During the 1960s, Universal produced a number of Hollywood classics such as *To Kill a Mockingbird* (1962) and Alfred Hitchcock's *The Birds* (1963). Just as popular were its many Doris Day movies and the string of blockbusters in the disaster genre such as *Airport* (1970). Then came the 1973 gangster movie *The Sting*, which generated a wave of public and critical ovations and raked in nearly 160 million dollars in U.S. ticket sales alone.

Steven Spielberg's involvement with Universal, a source of unfathomable earnings, proved a windfall par excellence. The acclaimed director-producer got his start at the studio in the late 60s and soon began making one record-breaking hit after another including *Jaws* (1975), *E.T. – The Extra-Terrestrial* (1982), *Schindler's List* (1993) and *Jurassic Park* (1993).

Since the 1940s, the studio has changed hands several times, with one-time owners including International Pictures, Decca Records, MCA, Seagram and other corporations. Today, it is a subsidiary of the NBC television network. The original property site in Southern California is now home to the Universal Studios Theme Park, a major Disneyland competitor where the once beloved set tours continue to thrive in a more elaborate form.

THE MARK OF ZORRO

1940 - USA - 94 MIN. - B & W - ADVENTURE MOVIE, WESTERN

DIRECTOR ROUBEN MAMOULIAN (1897–1987)
SCREENPLAY JOHN TAINTOR FOOTE, GARRETT FORT, BESS MEREDYTH, based on the novel *THE CURSE OF CAPISTRANO*
by JOHNSTON MCCULLEY DIRECTOR OF PHOTOGRAPHY ARTHUR MILLER EDITING ROBERT BISCHOFF MUSIC ALFRED NEWMAN
PRODUCTION DARRYL F. ZANUCK for 20TH CENTURY FOX.

STARRING TYRONE POWER (Don Diego Vega / Zorro), LINDA DARNELL (Lolita Quintero), BASIL RATHBONE
(Captain Esteban Pasquale), GALE SONDERGAARD (Inez Quintero), EUGENE PALLETTE (Fray Felipe),
J. EDWARD BROMBERG (Don Luis Quintero), MONTAGU LOVE (Don Alejandro Vega), JANET BEECHER
(Señora Isabella Vega), GEORGE REGAS (Sergeant Gonzales), BELLE MITCHELL (Maria de Lopez).

"Sometimes, one must fight fire with fire!"

A masked horseman gallops down Main Street, scattering squawking chickens and tearing bewildered locals from their afternoon siestas. Having reached the local notice board, the rider comes to an abrupt halt and uses his rapier to relieve two soldiers of a freshly posted tax law notice. He replaces it with a decree of his own, announcing that rebellion has begun. It's a crystal-clear statement of intent from the black-clad renegade determined to liberate the oppressed Indian farmers of Los Angeles from their shackles. Then he's off – vanishing as quickly as he came and leaving no clue to his identity other than a "Z" he carved with his blade.

So begins the legend of Zorro, the vigilante who cannot be unmasked. The avaricious Don Quintero (J. Edward Bromberg) and his accomplice Captain Pasquale (Basil Rathbone) would give an arm to know the real name of the man who threatens their dominion. No one, however, can reveal it to them: even those closest to the bandit must endure his charade and haven't the foggiest notion who he is, for it would seem that the real mask this man wears is not one of cloth, but a mixture of deception and disguise – a meticulously constructed persona.

Only the viewer is privy to the truth, namely that this champion of the people is none other Don Diego Vega (Tyrone Power), the son of former governor Don Alejandro Vega (Montagu Love), who was unjustly ousted from office. Having enjoyed the privileged life of a cavalryman in Madrid, Don Diego plays up his reputation as an effeminate dandy to prevent anyone from wising up to his secret identity. The act is so convincing that even the ungentlemanly Fray Felipe (Eugene Pallette), a cinematic twin of Robin Hood's Friar Tuck, doesn't suspect that the lily-livered Diego and Mr. Z are one and the same.

Drawing on his theatrical roots, *Mark of Zorro* director Rouben Mamoulian expertly combines his tricks of the trade with the natural grace of Tyrone Power to turn Diego's cloak and dagger activities into a first-rate comedic spectacle full of surprises for enemies and audience alike. Combined with

"**Power's performance as the fearless master of the art of fencing, who returns to California from Madrid and sets out to right the wrongs that afflict the poor farming folk, is resolute and utterly convincing.** *The Mark of Zorro* **is a movie in the best sense of the word.**" *Rob Wagner's Script*

ZORRO ON SCREEN

To movie buffs around the globe, Zorro will forever be the great masked avenger in black who marks his conquests by carving a signature Z with a rapier or the tip of his bullwhip at the scene of the crime or on the torso of the enemy. What few people realize, however, is that the character created by writer Johnston McCulley in 1919 actually debuted on the pages of a pulp fiction magazine. Within a year of his inception, McCulley's champion of the weak had been adapted for director Fred Niblo's silent picture *The Mark of Zorro* (1920). Here, Douglas Fairbanks rode onto the screen and into audiences' hearts with daredevil stunts and awe-inspiring agility. Needless to say, the character's Hollywood image was instantly set in stone. Five years later, Fairbanks gave an encore performance as the early California hero in Donald Crisp's *Don Q Son of Zorro* (1925).

By the mid-30s, Robert Livingston became the second Hollywood icon to assume the role and, like his predecessor, enjoyed two stints as the crusader. Soon Zorro was developed as an ongoing serial, the first of which was John English and William Witney's twelve-part project *Zorro Rides Again* (1937). The character's popularity in this format continued into the 40s with director Fred C. Brannon – who was partial to switching his leading man midstream – shooting a twelve-parter of his own entitled *Ghost of Zorro* (1949). Among the best of all the dramatizations were Lewis R. Foster and Norman Foster's 82 installments of *Zorro* starring Guy Williams, televised between 1957 and 1959. Eight of the episodes were later edited into the feature film *The Sign of Zorro* (1958).

Western fans on the other side of the Atlantic, especially the Italians, Spaniards and French, began to warm to the mysterious man in black in the late 60s and early 70s. It was also at around this time that Mexico began producing Zorros more quickly than many countries were producing cars. European pop culture aficionados will be interested to know that French star Pierre Brice, who became inordinately popular in Germany as the big screen's Chief Winnetou, tried his hand at playing the Latino Robin Hood in the Italian *Samson and the Slave Queen* (*Zorro contro Maciste*, 1963). More than ten years later, the actor's compatriot Alain Delon could have passed for his spitting image in Duccio Tessari's *Zorro* (1975). In the early 90s, France collaborated with the United States on yet another American television series that broadcast as *Zorro* or *Les nouvelles aventures de Zorro* (1989–1993). In his most recent incarnation, the unforgettable defender of liberty and justice was played by Spanish-born heartthrob Antonio Banderas in *The Mask of Zorro* (1998).

1 The game is afoot: Don Diego Vega (Tyrone Power, left) teaches Captain Esteban Pasquale (Basil Rathbone) not to go snooping around in other people's business.

2 Total indulgence, zero guilt: Lolita (Linda Darnell) has always considered herself a good Catholic, but she's not about to protest a little reformation.

3 A show of hands: Zorro's enemies unanimously decide to surrender to the masked avenger without putting up a fight.

stylish images, the result is a sleek and rhythmic tribute to the classic brand of romance adventures that were such a popular product of Hollywood's golden age. Tyrone Power shines as a daredevil rider and fencer, proving himself a worthy successor to former Zorro star Douglas Fairbanks, who had died the previous year. The picture climaxes with a momentous duel to the death between Diego and Captain Pasquale, an acoustic and visual triumph of big-screen battle sequences. We can only imagine how speechless the first *Zorro* audiences must have been upon seeing the mounted hero ride his horse clear off a bridge and drop 30 feet to land softly in the river below.

The man behind this battery of stunning images was legendary cinematographer Arthur Miller, who succeeded brilliantly in bringing Mamoulian's vision to the screen. In order to maximize the dramatic impact of shadow and light, the two men decided to shoot in black-and-white. Dramatically embodying the uncompromising nature of a Hollywood battle between good and evil, the images also play on the contrast between the beauty of nocturnal obscurity and the glaring pretense of daylight.

The eloquent economy with which the film tells its story is due to innovative editing techniques rather than gratuitous flourishes. With the greatest

"Mamoulian took the material and made a film that is quite different from the average adventure flick. It is a film whose action sequences are not decorative stunts, but arise naturally from the situation ... It is a film that displays a complete mastery of its genre, and goes way beyond its confines." *Frankfurter Allgemeine Zeitung*

6

4 Left holding the chick: Much to Don Quintero's
   chagrin, his wife Inez (Gale Sondergaard) has
   taken a fancy to gentleman Don Diego.

5 Nothing up my sleaze: There's no telling how far
   Don Luis Quintero (J. Edward Bromberg) would
   go to own a set of threads as nice as Don Diego's.

6 Supper club: Fray Felipe (Eugene Pallette) thinks
   he's stumbled upon an innocent little gathering at
   the home of Don Alejandro Vega (Montagu Love).
   If only he knew what these conniving souls were
   really cooking up.

7 Finishing touches: After winning a decisive battle
   against Captain Esteban Pasquale, Don Diego
   moves in for the kill.

"Every film star had his own individual style, with Fairbanks excelling in acrobatic élan, while Tyrone, the more handsome of the two, was both romantic and dashing."

James Robert Parish, Don E. Stanke, in: The Swashbucklers

of ease, Zorro sashays past the details of minor plot elements that explain themselves in the context of subsequent scenes. This efficient style of story-telling gives the picture an additional agility, elegantly parrying the rhetorical finesse Zorro later uses to coerce the despotic Quintero into abdicating.

While there's no mistaking the thematic parallels between Mamoulian's film and the Warner Bros. Technicolor extravaganza *The Adventures of Robin Hood* directed by Michael Curtiz two years earlier, *The Mark of Zorro* capital-izes on a sense of irony altogether absent from the other picture. This is made apparent on two separate occasions when the protagonist's weapon emerges as an unlikely symbol of peace: upon his departure from the Madrid

military academy at the beginning of the film and after his final victory at the story's conclusion, Diego thrusts his rapier into a ceiling joist. "Leave it there," he beseeches his fellow soldiers in Madrid. "And when you see it, think of me in a land of gentle missions, happy peons, sleepy *caballeros* and everlasting boredom." But we're left guessing whether the world across the Atlantic ever proves to be the place Diego once toasts to as a country "where a man can only marry, raise fat children and watch his vineyards grow" as the picture ends with Diego a.k.a. Zorro riding off into a Hollywood-style happy ending with true love Lolita (Linda Darnell).

SR

THE GRAPES OF WRATH

1939/40 - USA - 128 MIN. - B & W - DRAMA, LITERARY ADAPTATION

DIRECTOR JOHN FORD (1894–1973)
SCREENPLAY NUNNALLY JOHNSON, based on the novel of the same name by JOHN STEINBECK
DIRECTOR OF PHOTOGRAPHY GREGG TOLAND EDITING ROBERT L. SIMPSON MUSIC ALFRED NEWMAN
PRODUCTION DARRYL F. ZANUCK for 20TH CENTURY FOX.

STARRING HENRY FONDA (Tom Joad), JANE DARWELL (Ma Joad), JOHN CARRADINE (Casy),
CHARLEY GRAPEWIN (Grandpa Joad), DORRIS BOWDON (Rosasharn), RUSSELL SIMPSON (Pa Joad),
O. Z. WHITEHEAD (Al Joad), JOHN QUALEN (Muley Graves), EDDIE QUILLAN (Connie Rivers),
ZEFFIE TILBURY (Grandma Joad), FRANK DARIEN (Uncle John Joad).

ACADEMY AWARDS 1940 OSCARS for BEST DIRECTOR (John Ford), and BEST SUPPORTING ACTRESS (Jane Darwell).

"I'll be all around in the dark – I'll be everywhere."

The Grapes of Wrath opens and closes with protagonist Tom Joad (Henry Fonda) solitarily crossing a vast expanse of land. The first time, Tom has just been released from prison and is headed for his family's farm in Oklahoma. Fighting exhaustion, he walks along a deserted country road studded only with lopsided power lines. Little does he suspect that his home is now nothing more than a memory. By the film's end, Tom is alone again, having fatally bludgeoned the deputy responsible for the death of his friend, Casy (John Carradine). And although Tom's story closes with him fleeing over the California horizon beneath a foreboding night sky, there's something about the scene that makes it seem as if he were crossing into undiscovered country.

Between these two scenes lie a 1,000-mile adventure and 124 minutes of uncompromising cinema. The film tells the incredible story of the twelve-member Joad family as they leave their farm in Oklahoma and drive out to California in a beat-up pick-up truck. The road taking them through the American Southwest to a new life is riddled with potholes, and hard times and barred doors are just about all the Joad family find …

John Steinbeck's fictitious Joads were representative of the thousands of Oklahoma tenant farmers, often referred to as Okies, whom the Great Depression robbed of house and home. During the 1930s, many of these people headed west on Route 66, hoping to arrive at a better life somewhere down the line.

Filmmaker John Ford put his heart into adapting Steinbeck's piece of social criticism for the screen. The director saw parallels between the situation in Oklahoma and the Great Famine that swept over Ireland in the middle of the 19th century, which forced many families to give up their property and leave the country. One of those families was Ford's own, who emigrated to

"The whole thing appealed to me – being about simple people – and the story was similar to the famine in Ireland, when they threw the people off the land and left them wandering on the roads to starve. That may have something to do with it – part of my Irish tradition – but I liked the idea of this family going out and trying to find their way in the world. It was a timely story. It's still a good picture – I saw part of it on TV recently." *John Ford interviewed by Peter Bogdanovich*

1 Left turn at Albuquerque: Life becomes a series of bitter detours when Tom Joad (Henry Fonda) and his family are forced to take up life as migrant farmers.

2 Plowed down: Things go from being bad to worse for Tom, Casy and Muley. From left – Henry Fonda, John Carradine and John Qualen.

3 Flyers and liars: A group of farmers examines a poster advertising work in California, but aren't so sure that the state is as golden as it claims to be.

4 Out of gas: The Joads take their share of kicks on Route 66.

the United States in the aftermath of the famine before the filmmaker or any of his many siblings were born.

Unlike Ford's later Welsh family drama, *How Green Was My Valley* (1941), which chronicled decades of life in a sharply divided coal-mining community, this Steinbeck adaptation unfolds across a seemingly endless cinematic space within a relatively short period of time.

Needless to say, the Joads' dreams are not destined to come true. The older family members die of exhaustion before reaching the promised land, and once there, the remaining Joads discover that only a limited number of seasonal workers are needed to work the fertile Californian fruit farms. The harsh living conditions in the transient migrant camps they call home are reflected with uncompromising realism in the black-and-white cinematogra-

phy of cameraman Gregg Toland, who clearly references the work of renowned photojournalist Dorothea Lange. Little by little, the film becomes an allegory of Biblical magnitude told through overpoweringly naturalistic imagery. This piece of filmmaking, which was rewarded with an Oscar for best direction, is a testament to John Ford's legendary abilities.

While the story's outcome may be far from cathartic, its grandeur lies in the Joads' enduring struggle. Here, the path that must be taken is dictated by the march of capitalism, which makes millionaires of some people while leaving others to reap nothing but the grapes of wrath. Unlike Steinbeck, whose novel offers little promise of redemption, Ford asserts that the government should keep capitalism's random voracity in check to keep the balance among the nation's people.

5 Killjoy: Traveling man Casy (John Carradine) uplifts the poor with the word of Lord, but ends up biting the bullet for his beliefs.

7 Soup's on: No sooner have the Joads finished setting up camp than Ma brings a smile to their faces with the magic of a midday meal.

6 Expiry date: Ma Joad (Jane Darwell) fears that the end is near for Grandpa Joad (Charley Grapewin, lying down).

8 Sold at cost: After being released from jail, Tom Joad finds out that his family has been evicted from their land and left penniless.

"Seems like the government's got more interest in a dead man than a live one."

Filmzitat: Tom Joad (Henry Fonda)

JOHN CARRADINE
Richmond Reed Carradine was born on February 5, 1906 in Greenwich Village, New York City. His acting career started off on the theatrical stage during the mid–1920s, and positive public response led to a professional tour of the American South. It wasn't long before Carradine was playing Shakespeare coast-to-coast and earning himself quite a reputation: indeed, his tendency to advance towards the front of the stage and walk among the audience during longer monologs won him the title "The Bard of Boulevard." Carradine soon went on to land himself roles in big-screen epics like *The Sign of the Cross* (1932) and *Cleopatra* (1934), both directed by the legendary Cecil B. DeMille.

Adopting the stage name John Peter Richmond, the New York actor appeared opposite Boris Karloff in horror films like Edgar G. Ulmer's *The Black Cat* (1934) and James Whale's *Bride of Frankenstein* (1935). During the mid–1930s, he abandoned that name once more and set out to conquer Hollywood as John Carradine.

In 1935, Carradine teamed up with John Ford and it wasn't long before he had become a familiar face in his pictures. Classic Westerns like *Stagecoach* (1939), *Drums Along the Mohawk* (1939), *The Last Hurrah* (1958), *The Man Who Shot Liberty Valance* (1962) and *Cheyenne Autumn* (1964) are among the more noteworthy titles of the eleven films the two men shot together.

During World War II, Carradine played Nazi officer Reinhard Heydrich in Douglas Sirk's *Hitler's Madman* (1943). A long line of further featured roles in pictures like Fritz Lang's *The Return of Frank James* (1940), Nicholas Ray's *Johnny Guitar* (1954) and Cecil B. DeMille's *The Ten Commandments* (1956) consolidated Carradine's reputation as one of Hollywood's most gifted supporting actors. Sadly, his career ended without him ever having received an Academy Award. While his depiction of the soothsaying former priest Casy in *The Grapes of Wrath* (1940) was certainly worthy of such an honor, Jane Darwell's portrayal of Ma Joad was the only performance in the film to claim an Oscar.

Today, the Carradine legacy continues to thrive. Sons David, Keith and Robert as well as granddaughter Martha Plimpton all grew up to become respected actors. John Carradine, the man with those unforgettable chiseled features and that rich, smoky voice died on November 27, 1988.

Coming full circle for its conclusion, the picture ends at a crossroads of uncertainty and possibility. Given this, it's no wonder that the film's production title was originally "Highway 66" after that endless stretch of road that permanently alters the Joad's faith in their fellow men. But although the experience of so much poverty and so many losses may have stripped the family of its former innocence, it also gave them an invaluable experience of life.

And if hardships are worth their weight in gold, no one is richer than Tom Joad. By the end of the story, he is forced to abandon his family in order to keep them out of harm's way. Although he is now a social outcast facing an uncertain future, Tom does have a sense that there must be something out there that makes life worth living. "Maybe it's like Casy says. A fellow ain't got a soul of his own, just little piece of a big soul – the one big soul that belongs to everybody," he tells Ma Joad (Jane Darwell) as he leaves her for the last time. "Wherever you can look – wherever there's a fight, so hungry people can eat, I'll be there."

While Ma Joad seems not to immediately understand the meaning of her son's words, she herself waxes existential in the following scene, explaining to her husband that "We keep a-comin', Pa. Cuz we're the people that live." And so the Joad's beat-up truck rattles its way up north to take advantage of the twenty days of solid work supposedly waiting to be had in Fresno. It's practically a cause for celebration and the surviving family members couldn't be in better spirits. The scene fades to black just as the vehicle passes a power line from which a "No help wanted" sign hangs.

SR

"All the AI guys are gone, or in Alcatraz. All that's left are soda-jerks and jitterbugs."

After eight years in jail, Roy Earle (Humphrey Bogart) has only one thing on his mind: pulling off one last heist and settling down to a new life. But times have moved on in the outside world. Earle's boss, Big Mac (Donald Mac-Bride), is now an ailing old man, and all his best "workers" are either dead or behind bars, so when Earle resolves to rob a luxury hotel on the edge of the desert, the best Big Mac can offer in the way of assistance is a couple of in-experienced wise guys: Babe (Alan Curtis) and Red (Arthur Kennedy). It gets worse: these two petty crooks are accompanied by a dame, and a very at-tractive one at that – Marie (Ida Lupino), who's tired of making a living as a dancer in two-bit dives. She falls for Earle, but he's planning to wed a poor farmer's daughter, a girl he'd met on his way to California. The girl is lame, and Earle enables her to undergo an expensive operation, but he's soon forced to admit that she doesn't really love him. Then the heist goes disas-trously wrong, and Red and Babe are burned to death in the car, along with most of the loot. All Earle can do now is flee – with Marie at his side.

High Sierra is mainly famous for being the film that made Bogart a star. Though he'd been in the business for a decade, first with Fox, then with Warner Bros, he was far from being a top Hollywood actor. As he himself said, moviegoers knew him mainly as the 'second banana gangster': the heavy who generally cops a bullet for the star of the show. When it came to *High Sierra*, he wasn't first choice for the role. Only after the role had been turned down by the studio's top gangster stars, George Raft, James Cagney and Edward G. Robinson did Bogart get the chance to play Roy Earle. And he took it.

Raoul Walsh's film gave Humphrey Bogart his first opportunity to play a more complex and sympathetic character. It also allowed him, finally, to bring his unique personal qualities to a role: the ability to dominate a scene with a minimum of effort, using only a glance, a laconic gesture, or a few well-placed lines. Walsh directs the film efficiently, but it's largely Bogart's powerfully understated performance that makes *High Sierra* more than a piece of melodramatic kitsch. He dominates the film with his portrayal of a hardbitten professional, playing the rest of the cast off the screen. And he radiates a peculiar integrity: Roy Earle is undoubtedly a crook, but he's as unswervingly loyal to his boss as he is to the little dog he adopts, though he knows it's brought its previous owners nothing but bad luck. He also plays it straight with Marie, who is played by Ida Lupino – prob-

ably Bogart's strongest film partner – as a kind of female equivalent to Roy Earle.

Behind the mask of cynicism, the gangster is revealed to be an aging moralist. The role of Roy Earle was a kind of template for Bogart's later performances. What distinguishes this particular character is that we also sympathize with him because he is so clearly a victim of a corrupt society. The figure of Earle is said to have been based on the legendary bandit John Dillinger, who achieved a semi-heroic status amongst the impoverished rural population of the U.S. Indeed, the film does explain Earle's criminal career as a result of a childhood trauma following his family's eviction from their farm. Walsh's film is thus in the tradition of socially-critical gangster movies produced by Warner Bros. in the 1930s. Yet *High Sierra* is also an epilog to this

---

IDA LUPINO
(1914–1995)

In the opening titles to *High Sierra* (1940), she got top billing, with her name above Humphrey Bogart's. Yet Ida Lupino was never one of Hollywood's really big stars, which may have had something to do with the fact that she also took an interest in directing. Ida Lupino was born into a family of vaudeville artistes in London, and she made her first stage appearances as a young girl. In 1931, she made her film debut, and two years later went to Hollywood with a contract from Paramount.

Despite some promising starts, her career only really took off when she signed for Warner Bros. in 1940. Under Raoul Walsh's direction, she gave convincing performances in *They Drive by Night* (1940) and *High Sierra*, in both cases playing an energetic and hardboiled gangster's moll. She also played feisty women in other genres, appearing in Michael Curtiz's adventure movie *The Sea Wolf* (1941) and Vincent Sherman's showbiz drama *The Hard Way* (1943). In real life too, Lupino showed toughness and determination: she left Warner, formed her own production company in 1949, and became one of the first female directors in Hollywood. By 1953, she had directed five full-length features for the cinema. The critic David Thompson has said they were "as tough and as quick as those of Sam Fuller". Then she spent many years working in TV, with credits including episodes of *The Virginian / The Men from Shiloh* (1962–1971) and *The Rifleman* (1958–1963). She also made numerous guest appearances as an actress in *Bonanza* (1959–1973). In 1966, she directed her last movie, a comedy called *The Trouble with Angels*.

Ida Lupino remained present on the screen over the years, appearing, for example, in Nicholas Ray's *On Dangerous Ground* (1951/52), Robert Aldrich's *The Big Knife* (1955) and Fritz Lang's *While the City Sleeps* (1956). In *Junior Bonner* (1972), Sam Peckinpah gave her a wonderful role as the wife and mother of two washed-up rodeo riders.

1 Sticking to their guns: Escaped convict Roy 'Mad Dog' Earle (Humphrey Bogart) and his sweetheart Marie (Ida Lupino) prepare to go out with a bang in High Sierra.

2 Turn the other cheek: It'll take more than a closed fist to break Marie Garson's will. Off screen, Ida Lupino, proved herself every bit as assertive as the characters she played and went on to become one of Hollywood's first female directors.

3 Quarter pounder with cheese: Whether you're the type to indulge in a Big Mac (Donald MacBride) or just need to lighten the load with a pit stop, it's hard to ignore the call of the golden arches.

4 Pleasure domes: Marie uses her feminine charms to appeal to Mad Dog's captors.

5 Life's a bitch: Roy Earle's enemies feed him to the dogs and give him an ending worthy of his name.

"Remember what Johnny Dillinger said about guys like you and him; he said you're just rushing toward death – that's it, you're rushing toward death."

Film quote: Doc Banton (Henry Hull)

> "As gangster pictures go, this one has everything — speed, excitement, suspense and that ennobling suggestion of futility which makes for irony and pity. Mr. Bogart plays the leading role with a perfection of hard-boiled vitality ... Especially Ida Lupino is impressive as the adoring moll." *The New York Times*

6

6 You scratch my back, I'll scratch my belly: High Sierra gave Humphrey Bogart a chance to show his vulnerable side. Prior to the picture, Hollywood often typecast him as a cold-blooded killer.

7 Wheelers and dealers: Ida Lupino bids Humphrey Bogart a fond farewell as he boards the 'Star Bus' and joins the ranks of Hollywood A-listers. Next stop, Casablanca!

8 Blood money: Mad Dog returns to a life of crime to fund Velma's (Joan Leslie) foot operation.

9 Check out time: Patrons of the "Gangsters' Lodge" often complain about the joint's stiff rates.

classical phase of the genre, and its fatalistic mood already anticipates the existential pessimism of film noir. That Earle is heading towards an inexorable fate is indicated in the early scenes, when he drives into the archaic wilderness of the Californian highlands to meet with his accomplices. Walsh stretches out this sequence for a surprising length of time, while both the camerawork and the music conjure an atmosphere of indefinable unease. Very quietly, a spirit of irrationality enters into the film – a tale of romance that culminates in a somber finale.

Only when he's on the run does Earle realize what he feels for Marie, but by that time it's far too late. This is a couple without a future. As matters come to a head, Earle leaves his lover behind and tries to escape through the mountains alone. In vain. Earle is encircled by the cops and seeks a hiding place in the rock face. Marie, who has heard through the press that he's on the verge of being captured, hurries to join him, and thereby hastens his end: when the little dog breaks free from her leash and scampers into the line of fire, Roy Earle rushes out to save it – and dies in a hail of bullets.   JH

THE THIEF OF BAGDAD

1940 - GREAT BRITAIN - 108 MIN. - COLOR - ADVENTURE MOVIE, FANTASY MOVIE

DIRECTORS LUDWIG BERGER (1892–1969), MICHAEL POWELL (1905–1990), TIM WHELAN (1893–1957), ZOLTAN KORDA (1895–1961), WILLIAM CAMERON MENZIES (1896–1957), ALEXANDER KORDA (1893–1956)
SCREENPLAY LAJOS BIRÓ, MILES MALLESON **DIRECTOR OF PHOTOGRAPHY** GEORGES PÉRINAL **EDITING** WILLIAM HORNBECK, CHARLES CRICHTON **MUSIC** MIKLÓS RÓZSA **PRODUCTION** ALEXANDER KORDA for LONDON FILM PRODUCTIONS.

STARRING CONRAD VEIDT (Jaffar), SABU (Abu), JUNE DUPREZ (Princess), JOHN JUSTIN (Ahmad), REX INGRAM (Genie), MILES MALLESON (Sultan), MORTON SELTEN (Old King), MARY MORRIS (Halima), BRUCE WINSTON (Merchant), HAY PETRIE (Astrologer).

ACADEMY AWARDS 1940 OSCARS for BEST CINEMATOGRAPHY (Georges Périnal), BEST ART DIRECTION / SET DECORATION (Vincent Korda), and BEST SPECIAL EFFECTS (visual effects: Lawrence W. Butler, sound effects: Jack Whitney).

"Violence, terror and contempt are the keys to ruling the earth."

"Build it four times as high and paint the damn thing red." According to legend, such were the demands Alexander Korda made on his brother, *The Thief of Bagdad's* production designer, while the movie was in the midst of its excruciatingly lengthy shoot. Whether or not he followed these instructions to the letter we'll never know; but Vincent Korda did, in fact, come up with dazzling sets that won him the Oscar.

To this day, *The Thief of Bagdad* remains one of the loveliest cinematic fairy tales of the desert sands, veiling the screen in an aura of fantasy, adventure and romance. While some of the magic is certainly the result of Alexander Korda's naively impossible guidelines, the impeccably stylish work of cinematographer Georges Périnal not to mention that of the aforementioned Vincent was just as influential.

Movie producer Alexander Korda's knack for showmanship and spectacle is undeniable. And he invested accordingly, intending the audience to get its money's worth of rich costumes, decorations, special effects and brilliant colors. Korda, who also directed numerous pictures during his impressive career, was thus partial to wide angle and panoramic shots that displayed the opulent and costly sets to best effect.

Unfortunately, the man originally commissioned to direct *The Thief of Bagdad*, Ludwig Berger, had a vision for the film that was altogether different from the producer's. Korda had hoped that the German-born Berger's vast knowledge of fairy tales, including those of Hans Christian Andersen and E. T. A. Hoffmann, would be an invaluable asset to the project. Berger had, after all, filmed a highly regarded 1923 silent-screen version of Cinderella, known as *Der verlorene Schuh (Cinderella)*. Nevertheless, his skills as a director betrayed a theatrical background that gave priority to working with the actors. Consequently, Berger was unable to relate to Korda's love for production values and special effects, and refused to comply with the producer's wishes where these were concerned.

Korda responded by making the shoot as unpleasant as possible for his director. Two additional filmmakers, Michael Powell and Tim Whelan, were brought in to supervise the action and fantasy sequences. Beyond being persistently present for all the remaining bits under Berger's command – principally the love scenes between the Princess of Basra (June Duprez) and Ahmad (John Justin), the rightful Prince of Bagdad cast out by his Grand Vizier Jaffar (Conrad Veidt) – Korda brazenly gave his own in-

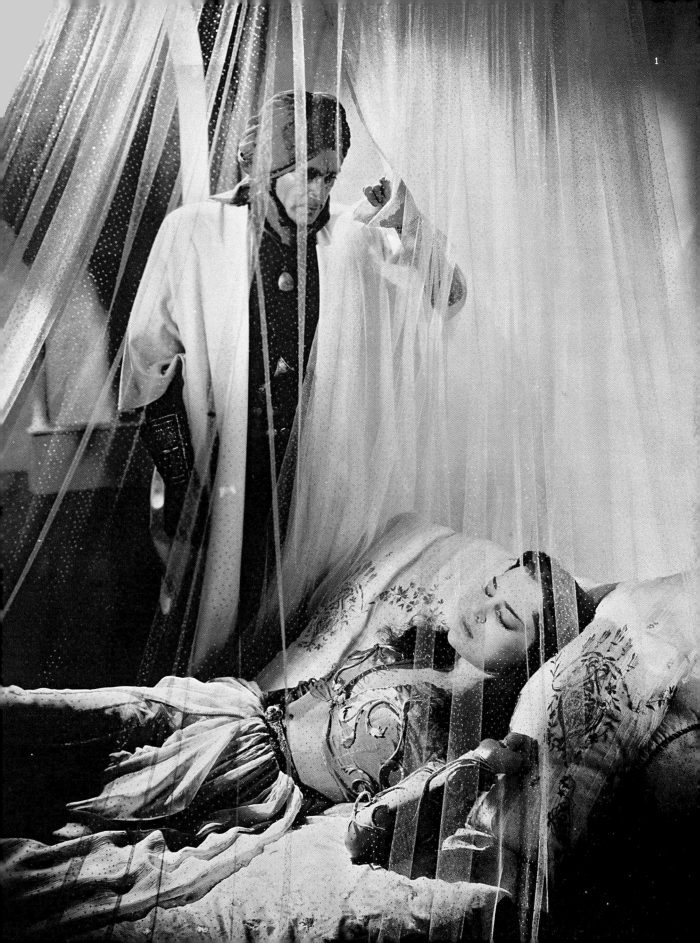

structions to the cast to undermine those of the director. After a while, the atmosphere grew so intolerable that Berger had no choice but to throw in the towel. Korda's problems, however, were far from over; for the rising winds of World War II soon brought the project to a standstill. *The Thief of Bagdad* would have to wait until 1940 before Korda's brother Zoltan and set designer Cameron Menzies could resume the shoot and finally complete the picture in Hollywood.

Given the production's turbulent background story, it's no wonder that Prince Ahmad and Abu, the so-called Thief of Bagdad (Sabu), embark on a quest far less sophisticated than Berger had in mind. Carrying out their episodic adventures one by one, the duo combats Jaffar, rescues the princess

ture's timelessness is its childlike naivety, making it only natural for the young Abu to act as its narrator. He endows the tale with all the wonder worthy of it as he comes face to face with an almighty genie (Rex Ingram), a gigantic spider and the fairytale land's friendly king, from whom he steals a flying carpet.

The movie's other unforgettable character is the Grand Vizier Jaffar, a villain beyond compare. Portrayed by Conrad Veidt, Jaffar's flashing eyes, red turban, black clothing and white cape make him the very personification of evil. Yet as imposing and devious as he may be, the vizier is rendered powerless by his all-consuming love for the princess. And thus, at the end of the day, he too has human vulnerabilities that even his magic powers can-

1   Magic carpet ride: Grand Vizier Jaffar (Conrad Veidt) intends to give the beautiful princess (June Duprez) a rude awakening.

2   Arabian nights: Prince Ahmad (John Justin, left) befriends the Thief of Bagdad, Abu (Sabu), when Jaffar locks him out of the palace one fateful evening.

3   A whole new world: Jaffar introduces Bagdad to the darker side of life with the help of a magic lamp.

"*The Thief of Bagdad* is one of the most colorful, lavish and eye-appealing spectacles ever screened. It's an expensive production accenting visual appeal, combining sweeping panoramas and huge sets, amazing special effects and process photography, and the most vividly magnificent Technicolor yet." *Variety*

CONRAD VEIDT (1893–1943)

Conrad Veidt was one of the most celebrated stars of the German silent screen. Born in Berlin, he studied acting with Max Reinhardt and performed at his renowned Deutsches Theater. In 1917, Veidt made his first motion picture and quickly became a leading screen actor. His highly expressive facial features often led to his being cast as a torn and tragic figure or villain. In the role of the homosexual violinist, Veidt caused quite a stir in Richard Oswald's *Different from the Others* (*Anders als die Anderen*, 1918/19), a cinematic protest against Paragraph 175 of German law, which banned sexual relations among men. That same year, he also slipped into the shoes of the sleepwalking Cesare in Robert Wienes' Expressionist masterpiece *The Cabinet of Dr. Caligari* (*Das Cabinet des Dr. Caligari*, 1919), a piece in which Wienes underlined his characters' spiral into insanity with a maze of jarringly angular set pieces, painted shadows and esoteric symbols.

In the years that followed, Veidt would continue to prove the extent of his range as the maharajah in Joe May's epic *The Indian Tomb* (*Das indische Grabmal*, 1921). This calculating character is determined to take vengeance upon his unfaithful wife and her lover. Veidt need but raise an eyebrow or purse his lips to let the audience know exactly what the maharajah is up to – whether he's bored, arrogant, up to no good or just caught in a moment of desperation.

Although Veidt found work in several Hollywood productions between 1927–1929, his reception in the United States wasn't what it had been in Germany. With the advent of sound, he thus returned to his homeland and went on to play entertaining characters such as Prince Metternich in Erik Charell's film operetta *Congress Dances* (*Der Kongress tanzt*, 1931). When the Nazis gained control of Germany in 1933, Veidt and his Jewish wife emigrated to England, where he landed parts in Powell/Pressburger productions like *The Spy in Black* (1939) and *Contraband* (1940). These roles, as well as that of the Grand Vizier in *The Thief of Bagdad* (1940), brought him renewed cinematic acclaim. Shortly thereafter, Veidt was Hollywood-bound once again. The greatest role he landed there would also be one of the last he'd ever play – that of the Nazi, Major Strasser, in Michael Curtiz's *Casablanca* (1942). At the age of 50, Conrad Veidt died of a heart attack.

Perhaps the most spellbinding aspect of the picture is its brilliant colors, which add texture to every scene and piece of stage decoration. From the opening shot, in which a ship comes sailing towards the camera under an immaculate sky, *The Thief of Bagdad* captures the screen, a glittering fantasy in red and blue, the colors with the greatest color saturation in the Technicolor spectrum.

Still, with all respect to the grandeur of Korda's spectacle, one can't help but wonder how the *The Thief of Bagdad* might have turned out had Ludwig Berger been permitted to shoot the film his way. Michael Powell, who was familiar with the screen-tests Berger had shot with his actors, said they were the most impressive he had ever seen.

LP

4 Let your heart decide: One look at Ahmad and the princess drops Jaffar like a hot potato.

5 Memento mori: Abu has a brush with death during his escape from the dungeon.

6 Bait and switch: The princess wonders whether she can avoid marrying Jaffar by disguising herself as one of the royal attendants.

"You must be prepared to accept with an open and childlike faith a fabulous run of miracles performed amid oriental splendor. In short, you must take to heart the wise words of the white-bearded elder in the Land of Legend, to which the little thief goes. 'Everything is possible,' says he, 'when seen through the eyes of youth.'" *The New York Times*

THE GREAT DICTATOR

1940 - USA - 124 MIN. - B & W - SATIRE, COMEDY

DIRECTOR CHARLES CHAPLIN (1889–1977)
SCREENPLAY CHARLES CHAPLIN DIRECTORS OF PHOTOGRAPHY KARL STRUSS, ROLAND H. TOTHEROH EDITING WILLARD NICO
MUSIC MEREDITH WILLSON, CHARLES CHAPLIN PRODUCTION CHARLES CHAPLIN for CHARLES CHAPLIN PRODUCTIONS,
UNITED ARTISTS.

STARRING CHARLES CHAPLIN (Adenoid Hynkel / A Jewish Barber), PAULETTE GODDARD (Hannah),
JACK OAKIE (Benzini Napaloni), REGINALD GARDINER (Commander Schultz), BILLY GILBERT (Filed Marshal Herring),
MAURICE MOSCOVITCH (Mr. Jaeckel), EMMA DUNN (Mrs. Jaeckel), BERNARD GORCEY (Mr. Mann),
PAUL WEIGEL (Mr. Agar), GRACE HAYLE (Madame Napaloni).

"Democracy? Schtonk! Liberty? Schtonk!"

On a battlefield in World War I, a soldier (Charles Chaplin) suffers a total loss of memory. Only after years of medical treatment, long after the war has ended, is he free to return to his home in Tomania, where he reopens his barber's shop in the Jewish ghetto. What he doesn't realize is that the country is now ruled by the dictator Hynkel (Chaplin again), who resembles him so closely they could be twins, and who is also brutally suppressing the Jews.

When Charles Chaplin started work on *The Great Dictator* in 1938, not everyone in the States was delighted at the prospect of a film that satirized Hitler. It wasn't just pro-Fascists and Americans of German descent who took

offense, but that large part of the population that feared seeing the still officially neutral U.S.A drawn into another world war. Chaplin stubbornly stuck to his plan: by depicting Hitler as an essentially ridiculous character, the Little Tramp would take revenge for the 'theft' of his moustache by a loudmouthed upstart born four days after him.

It goes without saying that Chaplin also wanted to draw attention to the victims of Nazi brutality. Thus the childlike hero of the film – embodied for the last time in the persona of the Little Tramp – is confronted soon after returning home with a gang of Hynkel's stormtroopers. He stands up to

"The film itself is filled with sad, pathetic little jokes; this is Chaplin's most serious, most tragic, most human work. He did not find Hitler at all funny, needless to say, and so although he uses his own comic genius to inspire the movie, the comedy is never neutral." *Chicago Sun-Times*

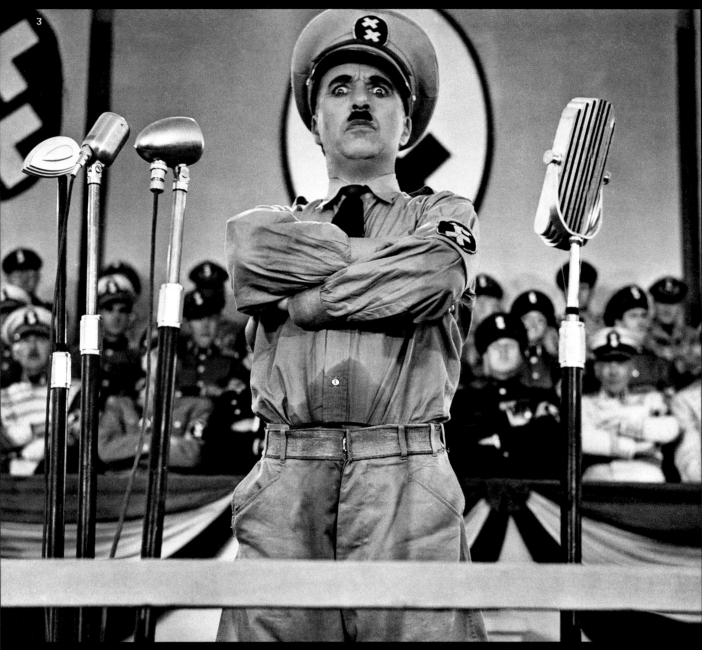

1   You oughta be in pictures: Comedian satirist Charlie Chaplin smiles for the camera as Adenoid Hynkel in *The Great Dictator*, one of the first Hollywood movies to criticize National Socialism.

2   Swallowed up by the room: Chaplin spotlights Nazi architecture and proves that bigger isn't always better.

3   Up to his eyeballs in it: Exaggerated Nazi poses makes Hynkel seem like the King of Corn rather than a serious political force.

them, not realizing that legality is a thing of the past, and so his arrest is a foregone conclusion – but the pretty Hannah (Paulette Goddard) stands up for the Jewish hairdresser, with whom she has fallen in love, and succeeds in setting him free. Nonetheless, it's clear that there's no future for the Jewish citizens of Tomania with Hynkel in charge. The dictator's henchmen destroy and set fire to the hairdressing salon, and before the little barber can flee to the free country of Austerlitz, he is arrested and imprisoned in a concentration camp.

It cannot be denied that Chaplin's vision of the everyday terror of Nazism is no longer as powerful as it was when first released. The images of real horror are too present to us, and Chaplin himself later admitted that he would not have made the film if he had known the true extent of the Nazis' crimes. Nonetheless, *The Great Dictator* does give a convincing impression of the arbitrary violence to which the Jews of Europe were subjected. What's timeless about the movie, though, is Chaplin's brilliant depiction of Hynkel. He studied Hitler's public appearances in detail to reveal the sheer absurdity

"The prospect of little 'Charlot' the most universally loved character in all the world, directing his superlative talent for ridicule against the most dangerously evil man alive has loomed as a titanic jest, a transcendent paradox." *The New York Times*

7

4 Oktoberfest sweetheart: Paulette Goddard, Chaplin's wife at the time of filming, enchants the screen as a chambermaid meets Black Forest beauty.

5 Look out, you're rocking the boat: In Hynkel's world, things are never as peaceful as they seem.

6 Two inches tall: Hynkel is intimidated by Benzini Napaloni's (Jack Oakie, right) overwhelming self-confidence and machismo.

7 Killer kaleidoscopes: It doesn't take long for the Jewish barber (also played by Chaplin) to see that Tomania's technology is as colorful as it is advanced.

8 Friends of uniformity: Hynkel has an outfit for every occasion.

9 Adding insult to injury: A lowly private (Charlie Chaplin) explodes when a bomb he fired proves to be a dud.

of this histrionic tyrant. When addressing his adoring followers, the self-appointed Führer postures and pontificates; and his blaring speech is an absurd gibberish laced with vaguely Teutonic noises. Chaplin shows Hitler's rhetoric for the obscene nonsense that it is. The charismatic Tribune of the People is a cheap phrasemonger, a demagogue who appeals to the basic instincts that drive his own hunger for power.

Yet the highpoint of Chaplin's film is a quiet scene where Hynkel, alone in his palace, broods over his fantasies of world domination. Dreamily, the dictator steps over to the globe in his office, removes it from its frame with surprising ease, and lets it drift softly from one hand to the other. Then Hynkel takes a gravity-defying leap onto his monstrous desk, where he juggles the globe with his boot and his backside. This weird ballet comes to an abrupt

11

10 Tradition! Chaplin has the Jewish barber dress up as his most beloved character to ensure that his political message hits home.

11 I'm having a ball: Hynkel thinks he's got the whole world in his hands.

end when Hynkel presses the planet passionately to his breast … and it bursts like a bubble.

Chaplin's double role in *The Great Dictator* has also been interpreted as a reflection on his own legendary screen persona; a kind of Jekyll-and-Hyde version, in which Hynkel embodies the amoral side of the Tramp, and the barber the sympathetic downtrodden outsider. Whatever the merits of this interpretation, it seems more important that this clear-eyed satire constitutes a further stage in Chaplin's development as a political filmmaker after *City Lights* (1931) and *Modern Times* (1936). Interestingly, this increasing politicization accompanied Chaplin's developing interest in language as an ele-

ment in his artistic vocabulary; for he had of course been a passionate defender of the silent film. *The Great Dictator* was in fact the first of Chaplin's films to really use language. Indeed, the famous six-minute monolog that concludes the film is also its most decisive scene. As a result of a curious mix-up, the Jewish barber is obliged to make an important speech instead of the tyrant Hynkel. The little man faces the assembled audience, in terror; but then he seizes the moment and calls upon the people to stand up together for peace and democracy. It's a deeply moving moment.

UB

HOLLYWOOD'S ANTI-NAZI FILMS

Together with *Confessions of a Nazi Spy* (1939), *The Great Dictator* (1940) is regarded as the first American film that openly attacked Nazi Germany. Hollywood had in fact been notably reticent in the 1930s, which no doubt had much to do with the fact that the U.S.A. remained officially neutral until 1941. In addition, there was a broad section of American society that opposed U.S. involvement in the European conflict. And finally, almost all the major studios did lucrative business distributing their films in Germany.

Nonetheless, there were also anti-Nazi initiatives, especially on the part of Warner Bros. Warners did not merely cease doing business with Germany in 1934; they also started producing various short films and cartoons opposing Hitler – and with *Black Legion* (1936/37), they even pointed a finger at fascist tendencies within the U.S. itself. Other movies, such as *The Adventures of Robin Hood* (1938) made indirect reference to the Nazi threat. This tendency gained in strength from 1939 onwards.

When the U.S. joined the war in December 1941, Hollywood went into full-scale mobilizing mode, and the Dream Factory became the main pillar of U.S. propaganda. Movies such as *Casablanca* (1942) convinced the population that America had been right to join the fray. Others, such as *Mrs. Miniver* (1942), promoted solidarity with the Allies. Many people from the film industry joined the armed forces, while others went to work entertaining the troops or advertising war bonds. Hollywood directors such as John Ford and John Huston made war documentaries; Frank Capra worked for the film section of the War Department. Not least, however, Hollywood also comforted the domestic population with escapist entertainment, and reaped handsome rewards: 1945 and 1946 were the most profitable years in the history of the U.S. film industry.

547

ACADEMY AWARDS *1931–1940*

1931 OSCARS

1 A tribute to Old Hollywood: Actor Lionel Barrymore appeared in circa 300 films between 1909 and 1953. His sole Oscar win came for his portrayal of an alcoholic in Clarence Brown's melodrama *A Free Soul*.

2 Motion picture peanuts: Norman Taurog was honored with an Oscar for his direction of *Skippy*, the cinematic adaptation of a popular comic strip. The film starred Taurog's nephew Jackie Cooper in the title role.

BEST PICTURE	CIMARRON
BEST DIRECTOR	NORMAN TAUROG for *Skippy*
BEST LEADING ACTRESS	MARIE DRESSLER in *Min and Bill*
BEST LEADING ACTOR	LIONEL BARRYMORE in *A Free Soul*
BEST SUPPORTING ACTRESS	NOT AWARDED
BEST SUPPORTING ACTOR	NOT AWARDED
BEST ORIGINAL SCREENPLAY, BEST STORY	JOHN MONK SAUNDERS for *The Dawn Patrol*
BEST ADAPTED SCREENPLAY	HOWARD ESTABROOK for *Cimarron*
BEST CINEMATOGRAPHY	FLOYD CROSBY for *Tabu*
BEST ART DIRECTION	MAX RÉE for *Cimarron*
BEST FILM EDITING	NOT AWARDED
BEST MUSIC	NOT AWARDED
BEST ADAPTED MUSIC	NOT AWARDED
BEST SONG	NOT AWARDED
BEST VISUAL EFFECTS	NOT AWARDED
BEST SOUND	PARAMOUNT PUBLIX STUDIO SOUND DEPARTMENT
BEST SOUND EFFECTS EDITING	NOT AWARDED

1932 OSCARS

3 A heavyweight at the hotel: Wallace Beery (left of John Barrymore) was one of the many MGM stars to appear in *Grand Hotel*, the Best Picture recipient of 1931/32. That same year, Beery was also honored for his performance as a former prizefighter in *The Champ*.

4 Bad girls and sinners don't mix: After receiving an Academy Award for *The Sin of Madelon Claudet*, actress Helen Hayes teamed up with the 1931/32 season's Oscar-winning director Frank Borzage *(Bad Girl)* for *A Farewell to Arms* – and failed to be nominated the following year.

BEST PICTURE	GRAND HOTEL
BEST DIRECTOR	FRANK BORZAGE for *Bad Girl*
BEST LEADING ACTRESS	HELEN HAYES in *The Sin of Madelon Claudet*
BEST LEADING ACTOR	WALLACE BEERY in *The Champ* and FREDRIC MARCH in *Dr. Jekyll and Mr. Hyde*
BEST SUPPORTING ACTRESS	NOT AWARDED
BEST SUPPORTING ACTOR	NOT AWARDED
BEST ORIGINAL SCREENPLAY, BEST STORY	FRANCES MARION for *The Champ*
BEST ADAPTED SCREENPLAY	EDWIN J. BURKE for *Bad Girl*
BEST CINEMATOGRAPHY	LEE GARMES for *Shanghai Express*
BEST ART DIRECTION	GORDON WILES for *Transatlantic*
BEST FILM EDITING	NOT AWARDED
BEST MUSIC	NOT AWARDED
BEST ADAPTED MUSIC	NOT AWARDED
BEST SONG	NOT AWARDED
BEST VISUAL EFFECTS	NOT AWARDED
BEST SOUND	PARAMOUNT PUBLIX STUDIO SOUND DEPARTMENT
BEST SOUND EFFECTS EDITING	NOT AWARDED

1933 OSCARS

1 A new day has dawned: Katherine Hepburn was one of the cinema's brightest young faces in the 1930s. She was honored with her first of four Best Actress accolades for *Morning Glory*.

2 Fool's gold: Anyone who thinks winning an Academy Award is tantamount to immortality could take a lesson from *Cavalcade* director Frank Lloyd. Although he was a two-time Oscar winner and one of the most highly regarded filmmakers of the 20s and 30s, only a handful of audiences still know who he is today.

BEST PICTURE	CAVALCADE
BEST DIRECTOR	FRANK LLOYD for *Cavalcade*
BEST LEADING ACTRESS	KATHARINE HEPBURN in *Morning Glory*
BEST LEADING ACTOR	CHARLES LAUGHTON in *The Private Life of Henry VIII*
BEST SUPPORTING ACTRESS	NOT AWARDED
BEST SUPPORTING ACTOR	NOT AWARDED
BEST ORIGINAL SCREENPLAY, BEST STORY	ROBERT LORD for *One Way Passage*
BEST ADAPTED SCREENPLAY	VICTOR HEERMAN, SARAH Y. MASON for *Little Women*
BEST CINEMATOGRAPHY	CHARLES LANG for *A Farewell to Arms*
BEST ART DIRECTION	WILLIAM S. DARLING for *Cavalcade*
BEST FILM EDITING	NOT AWARDED
BEST MUSIC	NOT AWARDED
BEST ADAPTED MUSIC	NOT AWARDED
BEST SONG	NOT AWARDED
BEST VISUAL EFFECTS	NOT AWARDED
BEST SOUND	FRANKLIN HANSEN (PARAMOUNT STUDIO SOUND DEPARTMENT) for *A Farewell to Arms*
BEST SOUND EFFECTS EDITING	NOT AWARDED

1934 OSCARS

3 High five: Sleeper comedy *It Happened One Night* takes the five top honors at the 1934 Oscars. Director Frank Capra couldn't have asked for a happier ending.

4 Skidrow-superstars: Clark Gable and Claudette Colbert looked down upon upstart studio Columbia Pictures and its second-rate productions. Good thing for them that the Academy of Motion Picture Arts and Sciences thought otherwise.

BEST PICTURE	IT HAPPENED ONE NIGHT
BEST DIRECTOR	FRANK CAPRA for *It Happened One Night*
BEST LEADING ACTRESS	CLAUDETTE COLBERT in *It Happened One Night*
BEST LEADING ACTOR	CLARK GABLE in *It Happened One Night*
BEST SUPPORTING ACTRESS	NOT AWARDED
BEST SUPPORTING ACTOR	NOT AWARDED
BEST ORIGINAL SCREENPLAY, BEST STORY	ARTHUR CAESAR for *Manhattan Melodrama*
BEST ADAPTED SCREENPLAY	ROBERT RISKIN for *It Happened One Night*
BEST CINEMATOGRAPHY	VICTOR MILNER for *Cleopatra*
BEST ART DIRECTION	CEDRIC GIBBONS, FREDRIC HOPE for *The Merry Widow*
BEST FILM EDITING	CONRAD A. NERVIG for *Eskimo*
BEST MUSIC	LOUIS SILVERS for *One Night of Love*
BEST ADAPTED MUSIC	NOT AWARDED
BEST SONG	CON CONRAD (Music), HERB MAGIDSON (Lyrics) for "THE CONTINENTAL" in *The Gay Divorcee*
BEST VISUAL EFFECTS	NOT AWARDED
BEST SOUND	JOHN P. LIVADARY for *One Night of Love*
BEST SOUND EFFECTS EDITING	NOT AWARDED

1935 OSCARS

1   Assuming command: Last year's Oscar laureates Frank Capra and Clark Gable congratulate MGM producer Irving Thalberg (left) on his win for *Mutiny on the Bounty*, the Best Picture of 1935.

2   Luck of the Irish: British leading man Victor McLaglen is named Best Actor for his portrayal of an IRA snitch in John Ford's *The Informer*. Nonetheless, many people attribute his Oscar win to the fact that the three other men in his category were all nominated for their work in *Mutiny on the Bounty*.

BEST PICTURE	MUTINY ON THE BOUNTY
BEST DIRECTOR	JOHN FORD for *The Informer*
BEST LEADING ACTRESS	BETTE DAVIS in *Dangerous*
BEST LEADING ACTOR	VICTOR MCLAGLEN in *The Informer*
BEST SUPPORTING ACTRESS	NOT AWARDED
BEST SUPPORTING ACTOR	NOT AWARDED
BEST ORIGINAL SCREENPLAY, BEST STORY	BEN HECHT, CHARLES MACARTHUR for *The Scoundrel*
BEST ADAPTED SCREENPLAY	DUDLEY NICHOLS for *The Informer*
BEST CINEMATOGRAPHY	HAL MOHR for *A Midsummer Night's Dream*
BEST ART DIRECTION	RICHARD DAY for *The Dark Angel*
BEST FILM EDITING	RALPH DAWSON for *A Midsummer Night's Dream*
BEST MUSIC	MAX STEINER for *The Informer*
BEST ADAPTED MUSIC	NOT AWARDED
BEST SONG	HARRY WARREN (Music), AL DUBIN (Lyrics) for "LULLABY OF BROADWAY" in *Gold Diggers of 1935*
BEST VISUAL EFFECTS	NOT AWARDED
BEST SOUND	DOUGLAS SHEARER for *Naughty Marietta*
BEST SOUND EFFECTS EDITING	NOT AWARDED

1936 OSCARS

3 The crème de la crème: Actor Paul Muni sterilizes the competition as man of science Louis Pasteur.

4 New Deal idealism: Mr. Deeds (Gary Cooper, left) provides America's farmers with as many plots of land as he can afford and helps director Frank Capra (left) win an Oscar – lock, stock and barrel.

BEST PICTURE	THE GREAT ZIEGFELD
BEST DIRECTOR	FRANK CAPRA for *Mr. Deeds Goes to Town*
BEST LEADING ACTRESS	LUISE RAINER in *The Great Ziegfeld*
BEST LEADING ACTOR	PAUL MUNI in *The Story of Louis Pasteur*
BEST SUPPORTING ACTRESS	GALE SONDERGAARD in *Anthony Adverse*
BEST SUPPORTING ACTOR	WALTER BRENNAN in *Come and Get It*
BEST ORIGINAL SCREENPLAY, BEST STORY	PIERRE COLLINGS, SHERIDAN GIBNEY for *The Story of Louis Pasteur*
BEST ADAPTED SCREENPLAY	PIERRE COLLINGS, SHERIDAN GIBNEY for *The Story of Louis Pasteur*
BEST CINEMATOGRAPHY	TONY GAUDIO for *Anthony Adverse* (black & white)
BEST CINEMATOGRAPHY (HONORARY AWARD)	W. HOWARD GREENE, HAROLD ROSSON for *The Garden of Allah* (color)
BEST ART DIRECTION	RICHARD DAY for *Dodsworth*
BEST FILM EDITING	RALPH DAWSON for *Anthony Adverse*
BEST MUSIC	LEO F. FORBSTEIN for *Anthony Adverse*
BEST ADAPTED MUSIC	NOT AWARDED
BEST SONG	JEROME KERN (Music), DOROTHY FIELDS (Lyrics) for "THE WAY YOU LOOK TONIGHT" in *Swing Time*
BEST VISUAL EFFECTS	NOT AWARDED
BEST SOUND	DOUGLAS SHEARER for *San Francisco*
BEST SOUND EFFECTS EDITING	NOT AWARDED

1937 OSCARS

1 Go fish: As Portuguese seaman Manuel Fidello, Spencer Tracy sheds his all-American image to deliver an Oscar-winning performance in *Captains Courageous*.

2 Double whammy: Luise Rainer became the first actress to ever win a set of back-to-back Oscars thanks to her outstanding characterizations in *The Great Ziegfeld* (1936) and *The Good Earth* (1937).

BEST PICTURE	THE LIFE OF EMILE ZOLA (HENRY BLAKE)
BEST DIRECTOR	LEO MCCAREY for *The Awful Truth*
BESTE DARSTELLERIN	LUISE RAINER in *The Good Earth*
BEST LEADING ACTOR	SPENCER TRACY in *Captains Courageous*
BEST SUPPORTING ACTRESS	ALICE BRADY in *In Old Chicago*
BEST SUPPORTING ACTOR	JOSEPH SCHILDKRAUT in *The Life of Emile Zola*
BEST ORIGINAL SCREENPLAY, BEST STORY	WILLIAM A. WELLMAN, ROBERT CARSON for *A Star Is Born*
BEST ADAPTED SCREENPLAY	HEINZ HERALD, GEZA HERCZEG, NORMAN REILLY RAINE for *The Life of Emile Zola*
BEST CINEMATOGRAPHY	KARL FREUND for *The Good Earth* (black & white)
BEST CINEMATOGRAPHY (HONORARY AWARD)	W. HOWARD GREENE for *A Star Is Born* (color)
BEST ART DIRECTION	STEPHEN GOOSSON for *Lost Horizon*
BEST FILM EDITING	GENE HAVLICK, GENE MILFORD for *Lost Horizon*
BEST MUSIC	CHARLES PREVIN for *One Hundred Men and a Girl*
BEST ADAPTED MUSIC	NOT AWARDED
BEST SONG	HARRY OWENS for "SWEET LEILANI" in *Waikiki Wedding*
BEST VISUAL EFFECTS	NOT AWARDED
BEST SOUND	THOMAS T. MOULTON for *The Hurricane*
BEST SOUND EFFECTS EDITING	NOT AWARDED

1938 OSCARS

3 Where the boys are: Spencer Tracy retains his title as the reigning Best Actor in the business for his work in *Boys Town*. That same year, co-star Mickey Rooney (right) received an honorary acting Oscar.

4 Three for three: Within the course of four years, Frank Capra was thrice nominated and named Best Director. The third time he received the award, he was also honored for his work as producer on *You Can't Take It With You*. This rare portrait of Capra (left) was taken during the shooting of *American Madness* (1932).

BEST PICTURE	YOU CAN'T TAKE IT WITH YOU (FRANK CAPRA)
BEST DIRECTOR	FRANK CAPRA for *You Can't Take It With You*
BEST LEADING ACTRESS	BETTE DAVIS in *Jezebel*
BEST LEADING ACTOR	SPENCER TRACY in *Boys Town*
BEST SUPPORTING ACTRESS	WALTER BRENNAN in *Kentucky*
BEST SUPPORTING ACTOR	FAY BAINTER in *Jezebel*
BEST ORIGINAL SCREENPLAY, BEST STORY	ELEANORE GRIFFIN, DORE SCHARY for *Boys Town*
BEST ADAPTED SCREENPLAY	GEORGE BERNARD SHAW, IAN DALRYMPLE, CECIL LEWIS, W. P. LIPSCOMB for *Pygmalion*
BEST CINEMATOGRAPHY	JOSEPH RUTTENBERG for *The Great Waltz* (black & white)
BEST CINEMATOGRAPHY (HONORARY AWARD)	OLIVER T. MARSH, ALLEN M. DAVEY for *Sweethearts* (color)
BEST ART DIRECTION	CARL JULES WEYL for *The Adventures of Robin Hood*
BEST FILM EDITING	RALPH DAWSON for *The Adventures of Robin Hood*
BEST MUSIC	ERICH WOLFGANG KORNGOLD for *The Adventures of Robin Hood*
BEST ADAPTED MUSIC	ALFRED NEWMAN for *Alexander's Ragtime Band*
BEST SONG	RALPH RAINGER (Music), LEO ROBIN (Lyrics) for "THANKS FOR THE MONEY" in *The Big Broadcast of 1938*
BEST VISUAL EFFECTS (HONORARY AWARD)	GORDON JENNINGS, JAN DOMELA, DEVEREAUX JENNINGS, IRMIN ROBERTS, ART SMITH, FRANCIOT EDOUART, LOYAL GRIGGS for *Spawn of the North*
BEST SOUND	THOMAS T. MOULTON for *The Cowboy and the Lady*
BEST SOUND EFFECTS EDITING (HONORARY AWARD)	LOREN L. RYDER, HARRY D. MILLS, LOUIS MESENKOP, WALTER OBERST for *Spawn of the North*

1939 OSCARS

1 It was a very good year: *Gone With The Wind* is proclaimed Hollywood's Best Picture, making producer David O. Selznick a giant among men in what was arguably the greatest year in American filmmaking.

2 Many hands make light work: No fewer than three directors contributed to the creation of *Gone With The Wind*, the first being George Cukor, the last Sam Wood. However, it was Victor Fleming who was awarded an Oscar for Best Director.

BEST PICTURE	GONE WITH THE WIND (DAVID O. SELZNICK)
BEST DIRECTOR	VICTOR FLEMING for *Gone with the Wind*
BEST LEADING ACTRESS	VIVIEN LEIGH in *Gone with the Wind*
BEST LEADING ACTOR	ROBERT DONAT in *Goodbye, Mr. Chips*
BEST SUPPORTING ACTRESS	HATTIE MCDANIEL in *Gone with the Wind*
BEST SUPPORTING ACTOR	THOMAS MITCHELL in *Stagecoach*
BEST ORIGINAL SCREENPLAY, BEST STORY	LEWIS R. FOSTER for *Mr. Smith Goes to Washington*
BEST ADAPTED SCREENPLAY	SIDNEY HOWARD for *Gone with the Wind*
BEST CINEMATOGRAPHY	GREGG TOLAND for *Wuthering Heights* (black & white)
BEST CINEMATOGRAPHY	ERNEST HALLER, RAY RENNAHAN for *Gone with the Wind* (color)
BEST ART DIRECTION	LYLE R. WHEELER for *Gone with the Wind*
BEST FILM EDITING	HAL C. KERN, JAMES E. NEWCOM for *Gone with the Wind*
BEST MUSIC	HERBERT STOTHART for *The Wizard of Oz*
BEST ADAPTED MUSIC	RICHARD HAGEMAN, W. FRANKE HARLING, LEO SHUKEN, JOHN LEIPOLD for *Stagecoach*
BEST SONG	HAROLD ARLEN (Music), E. Y. HARBURG (Lyrics) for "OVER THE RAINBOW" in *The Wizard of Oz*
BEST VISUAL EFFECTS	FRED SERSEN for *The Rains Came*
BEST SOUND	BERNARD B. BROWN for *When Tomorrow Comes*
BEST SOUND EFFECTS EDITING	EDMUND H. HANSEN for *The Rains Came*

1940 OSCARS

3 When cowboys strike gold: Walter Brennan garners his third Best Supporting Actor of the decade for *The Westerner*.

4 Turning best sellers into Best Pictures: David O. Selznick sets Hollywood ablaze for the second year in a row with his screen adaptation of Daphne du Maurier's novel *Rebecca*, the first American film to be directed by Alfred Hitchcock.

BEST PICTURE	REBECCA (DAVID O. SELZNICK)
BEST DIRECTOR	JOHN FORD for *The Grapes of Wrath*
BEST LEADING ACTRESS	GINGER ROGERS in *Kitty Foyle*
BEST LEADING ACTOR	JAMES STEWART in *The Philadelphia Story*
BEST SUPPORTING ACTRESS	JANE DARWELL in *The Grapes of Wrath*
BEST SUPPORTING ACTOR	WALTER BRENNAN in *The Westerner*
BEST ORIGINAL SCREENPLAY	PRESTON STURGES for *The Great McGinty*
BEST ADAPTED SCREENPLAY	DONLAD ODGEN STEWART for *The Philadelphia Story*
BEST STORY	BENJAMIN GLAZER, HANS SZÉKELY for *Arise, My Love*
BEST CINEMATOGRAPHY	GEORGE BARNES for *Rebecca* (black & white)
BEST CINEMATOGRAPHY	GEORGES PÉRINAL for *The Thief of Baghdad* (color)
BEST ART DIRECTION	CEDRIC GIBBONS, PAUL GROESSE for *Pride and Predjudice* (black & white)
BEST ART DIRECTION	VINCENT KORDA for *The Thief of Baghdad* (color)
BEST FILM EDITING	ANNE BAUCHENS for *Northwest Mounted Police*
BEST MUSIC	LEIGH HARLINE, PAUL J. SMITH, NED WASHINGTON for *Pinocchio*
BEST ADAPTED MUSIC	ALFRED NEWMAN for *Tin Pan Alley*
BEST SONG	LEIGH HARLINE (Music), NED WASHINGTON (Lyrics) for "WHEN YOU WISH UPON A STAR" in *Pinocchio*
BEST VISUAL EFFECTS	LAWRENCE W. BUTLER for *The Thief of Baghdad*
BEST SOUND	DOUGLAS SHEARER for *Strike Up The Band*
BEST SOUND EFFECTS EDITING	JACK WHITNEY for *The Thief of Baghdad*

INDEX OF FILMS

INDEX OF FILMS

GENERAL INDEX

Production companies are listed in italics; film categories are preceded by a dash; numbers in bold refer to a glossary text.

GENERAL INDEX

GENERAL INDEX

GENERAL INDEX

GENERAL INDEX

ABOUT THE AUTHORS

Ulrike Bergfeld (UB), *1969, studied Art. Numerous publications on art-related subjects. Lives in Berlin.

Philipp Bühler (PB), *1971, studied Political Science, History and British Studies. Film journalist. Writes for various regional German publications. Lives in Berlin.

David Gaertner (DG), *1978, studied Film and Art History. Freelances for the German film archives division of the Berlin Film Museum. Lives in Berlin.

Steffen Haubner (SH), *1965, studied Art History and Sociology. Author of many academic and press articles. Runs a press office in Hamburg, the city he lives in.

Jörn Hetebrügge (JH), *1971, studied German Literature. Author and journalist; many articles on film. Lives in Berlin.

Heinz-Jürgen Köhler (HJK), *1963, film and TV reporter; author of many academic and press articles. Lives in Hamburg.

Oliver Küch (OK), *1972, studied English Literature and British History. Media and computer journalist; author of articles on film and television. Lives in Zwingenberg.

Petra Lange-Berndt (PLB), *1973, studied Art History and German Literature, doctoral candidate at the Department of Art History, University of Hamburg. Academic assistant at the Trier University Institute of Art History since summer 2004. Author of numerous academic articles. Lives in Trier.

Nils Meyer (NM), *1971, studied German Literature and Politics. Internship at the Ev. School of Journalism, Berlin. Academic assistant at the German Hygiene Museum, Dresden, and freelance journalist for newspapers and magazines, radio and TV. Lives in Dresden.

Eckhard Pabst (EP), *1965, studied German Literature and Art History. Works at the Kiel Institute for Contemporary German Literature and Media, and the Kommunalen Kino in Kiel. Film theorist. Publications on film and TV.

Lars Penning (LP), *1962, film journalist, works for numerous national newspapers. Author of various articles and books on the history of film. Lives in Berlin.

Stephan Reisner (SR), *1969, studied Literature and Philosophy in Hanover. Freelance journalist and author in Berlin, writing for *Edit*, *BELLAtriste*, *Glasklar* and the *Tagesspiegel*.

Burkhard Röwekamp (BR), *1965, academic assistant at the Institute for Contemporary German Literature and Media at the Philipps University in Marburg. Has taught numerous courses and published many articles on the aesthetics and theory of contemporary film. Lives in Marburg.

Jörg Schweinitz (JS), *1953, PD Dr., film theorist, Professor of Film Studies at the Ruhr University in Bochum. Visiting professorships at the Free University of Berlin, the universities of Marburg and Klagenfurt, and the University of Chicago. Numerous publications on the history and theory of film. Lives in Berlin.

CREDITS

The publishers would like to thank the distributors, without whom many of these films would never have reached the big screen.

ALAMODE, BONNER KINEMATHEK, BUENA VISTA, DELPHI, FOX, JUGENDFILM, KINOWELT, LUPE, MFA, MGM, MIEKUS, NEUE VISIONEN, PALLAS, PRANKE, PROGRESS, RING, TRANSIT, UIP, VOLLMANN, WARNER.

Academy Award® and Oscar® are the registered trademark and service mark of the Academy of Motion Picture Arts and Sciences.

If, despite our concerted efforts, a distributor has been unintentionally omitted, we apologise and will amend any such errors brought to the attention of the publishers in the next edition.

ACKNOWLEDGEMENTS

As the editor of this volume, I would like to thank all those who invested so much of their time, knowledge and energy into the making of this book. My special thanks to Martin Holz from TASCHEN for his coordination work and truly amazing ability to keep track of everything. Thanks also to Birgit Reber and Andy Disl for their ingenious design concept that gives pride of place to the pictures, the true capital of any film book. My thanks to Philipp Berens and Thomas Dupont and Rainer Gootz from defd and *Cinema* and Wolfgang Theis from the Deutsche Kinemathek for their help in accessing the original stills. Then, of course, I am hugely indebted to the authors, whose keen analyses form the backbone of this volume. I would also like to thank David Gaertner for his meticulous technical editing, and Petra Lamers-Schütze, whose commitment and initiative got the project going. And last but not least, Benedikt Taschen, who not only agreed to produce and publish the series, but enthusiastically followed each volume's progress from start to finish. My personal thanks to him and everyone else mentioned here.

ABOUT THIS BOOK

The 88 films selected for this book represent a decade of cinema. It goes without saying this involved making a number of difficult choices, some of which may be contested. A note also on the stills from some of the earlier films: it is a regrettable but inevitable fact that the older the film, the more difficult it is to obtain images of the required technical quality.
Each film is presented by an essay, and accompanied by a glossary text devoted to a person or a cinematographic term.
An index of films and a general index are provided at the back of the book to ensure optimal access.
As in the preceding volumes, the films are dated according to the year of production, not the year of release.

IMPRINT

ENDPAPERS / PAGES 1–31
AND PAGES 548–549

M / Fritz Lang / DEUTSCHE KINEMATHEK, Berlin

PAGE 32

EDWARD SCISSORHANDS / Tim Burton / 20TH CENTURY FOX

PAGES 359–365, 507–511

© DISNEY

To stay informed about upcoming TASCHEN titles, please request our magazine at www.taschen.com or write to TASCHEN America, 6671 Sunset Boulevard, Suite 1508, USA-Los Angeles, CA 90028, Fax: +1-323-463.4442. We will be happy to send you a free copy of our magazine which is filled with information about all of our books.

© 2006 TASCHEN GMBH
Hohenzollernring 53, D-50672 Köln
WWW.TASCHEN.COM

PHOTOGRAPHS

defd and CINEMA, Hamburg
DEUTSCHE KINEMATHEK, Berlin (pp. 143–145, 199–201, 268, 321–325, 459–463, 535–539)

PROJECT MANAGEMENT

PETRA LAMERS-SCHÜTZE, Cologne

EDITORIAL COORDINATION

STILISTICO and MARTIN HOLZ, Cologne

DESIGN

SENSE/NET, ANDY DISL and BIRGIT REBER, Cologne

TEXTS

ULRIKE BERGFELD (UB), PHILIPP BÜHLER (PB), DAVID GAERTNER (DG), MALTE HAGENER (MH), STEFFEN HAUBNER (SH), JÖRN HETEBRÜGGE (JH), KATJA KIRSTE (KK), HEINZ-JÜRGEN KÖHLER (HJK), OLIVER KÜCH (OK), PETRA LANGE-BERNDT (PLB), NILS MEYER (NM), ECKHARD PABST (EP), LARS PENNING (LP), STEPHAN REISNER (SR), BURKHARD RÖWEKAMP (BR), JÖRG SCHWEINITZ (JS).

TECHNICAL EDITING

DAVID GAERTNER, Berlin

ENGLISH TRANSLATION

PATRICK LANAGAN (introduction and texts), SHAUN SAMSON (texts and captions) for ENGLISH EXPRESS, Berlin

EDITING

DANIELA KLEIN for ENGLISH EXPRESS, Berlin

PRODUCTION

TINA CIBOROWIUS, Cologne

PRINTED IN SPAIN
ISBN-13: 978-3-8228-4010-8
ISBN-10: 3-8228-4010-6